Y0-EFZ-207
POPE PIUS XII LIB., ST. JOSEPH COLLEGE
3 2528 01270 6562

THE BEST PLAYS OF 1961–1962

THE BURNS MANTLE YEARBOOK

Illustrated with photographs, and with drawings by HIRSCHFELI

from "How to Succeed in Business Without Really Trying"

THE BEST PLAYS OF 1961–1962

EDITED BY HENRY HEWES

DODD, MEAD & COMPANY

NEW YORK · TORONTO

Library of Congress Catalog Card Number: 20-21432

PRINTED IN THE UNITED STATES OF AMERICA

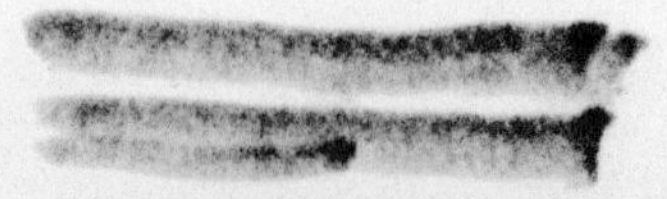

FOREWORD

MY pleasure at being chosen for the honor of editing this book is inextricable from the pleasure of knowing that I have been recommended for the post by John Mason Brown and Louis Kronenberger. Any worries I may have about letting down the quality of America's most important and distinguished theatre annual will run second to my anxieties about disappointing two of the finest drama critics who ever practiced in the American theatre, not to mention probable "tut-tuts" from my former teachers, Joseph Wood Krutch and John Gassner, and from Brooks Atkinson, who gave me my first chance to review a play for the *New York Times,* while I was still a copy boy there.

I knew that when Mr. Kronenberger had taken over the book in 1952 he had immediately effected three vital improvements. These were the addition of a section of performance photographs and costume and scene design sketches; the reprinting of *Variety's* seasonal tabulation of Financial Hits and Flops; and last but most important, the inclusion of Al Hirschfeld's drawings which through this unique artist's economy of line, proportional judgment and sense of humor caught the essence of live theatrical performance better than could any critical words or any literal camera. Happily and gratefully these features will be continued in this and future volumes of the *Best Plays* series.

It was Mr. Kronenberger, too, who recognized that some of the best theatre was happening in Off Broadway playhouses, and who instituted the listing of some of the better Off Broadway programs, and even the reprinting of excerpts from *The Connection* at the end of the 1959-60 season.

The changes we have instituted in this volume are partly the result of carrying this trend even further. Of the Ten Best Plays, two are from the Off Broadway Theatre, and the section on Off Broadway listings has been expanded to include a more nearly complete record of Off Broadway activity. In order to keep the cost and the bulk of the book down, some of these listings are presented in abbreviated form, for which we will probably be sorry when some beginning actor we have left out of a cast list turns out to be tomorrow's star.

Two new features that deal with the New York season are being introduced. The first is a section which lists in chart form most of the prizes and awards in the New York Theatre. And the second is a reprinting of the voting in the Drama Critics Circle by each critic. The theory behind the latter is to supply the reader with some indication of the taste of various critics, which may help them to find a drama critic whose opinions tend to coincide with their own, or better still a drama critic whose opinions tend to challenge their own.

There are several critics who are of the opinion that some of the best theatre is taking place outside New York, particularly in the Shakespeare festivals and in several professional theatre operations in other American cities. Therefore we have included sections on the Shakespeare festivals, and the theatre originating in Washington, Boston, Texas and San Francisco. Not that these are the only areas that deserve to be included, but until there is some reader response that suggests a great demand for more such sections, these and a listing compiled for us by George Freedley will have to constitute a cautious beginning.

In order to include all of the above, we have reluctantly had either to dispense with the reprinting of other material, or to find a way of boiling it down so that the readers might be given the same or more information in a smaller space. By adding a brief summary of each play's content in the listings, we have made possible a shorter introductory article. And by categorizing and by condensing the obituaries to only the most essential information we have shortened that section considerably. The London and Paris Theatre seasons are presented in the form of charts which give more factual information than before, although they must inevitably lack the color and readability of longer critical essays. And for the first time there is an attempt to cover the most important events in other European theatres.

Because the publishers and the new editor feel that readers may want to have some of the omitted features, plus some of the new ones extended back through the last decade, we are preparing a supplemental volume covering the years 1949-1961, which will include among other features, Off Broadway listings, shows that closed out of town, Shakespeare Festivals, theatre books and original cast recordings, prize listings, an expanded and categorized list of where and when prominent theatre personalities were born, and condensed coverage of the European theatre. Finally, there will be an alphabetical list of plays that were produced in New York which will give the author, the opening date, and number of performances of plays registering 200 or more consecutive New York performances, and of those previously selected as one of the Ten Best by editors of the *Best Plays* series. Furthermore, any British production of these plays will not only be listed, but will also include the opening date abroad and number of performances there.

Finally, a note of personal thanks to Dodd, Mead for calmly accepting the "state of chassis" that attended all this revision and expansion, and particularly to Jonathan Dodd for his patient help, without which the book would have sunk several times. My thanks also to Al Hirschfeld, for his drawings, to Mr. Abel Green and *Variety,* for the use of the tabulation of Hits and Flops, to Mr. Coe, Mr. Norton, Mr. Quill, Mr. Knickerbocker, Mr. Freedley, and Mr. Trilling for their reports, and to the following designers for allowing us to reprint their work: Oliver Smith, Rouben Ter-Arutunian, Motley, Ben Edwards, David Hays, Franco Zeffirelli, Tanya Moisiewitsch, Theoni V. Aldredge, Donald Brooks and Lucinda Ballard.

HENRY HEWES

CONTENTS

THE SEASON IN PICTURES

(Photographs follow page 82)

Art Carney and Elizabeth Ashley in "Take Her, She's Mine"

Barbra Streisand in "I Can Get It for You Wholesale"

Phyllis Newman and Orson Bean in "Subways Are for Sleeping"

James Earl Jones and Vinnette Carroll in "Moon on a Rainbow Shawl"

Peggy Burke and Colleen Dewhurst in "Great Day in the Morning"

David Burns and Zero Mostel in "A Funny Thing Happened on the Way to the Forum"

Dancers in "Kwamina"

SUMMARIES OF THE SEASONS

THE SEASON IN NEW YORK

THE 1961-62 season might be described as "deceptively good." There were fewer Broadway evenings in which one knew one was in for it the moment the curtain went up, and several new American playwrights made their debuts.

However, a closer examination of matters proves somewhat less cheering. Fully fifty per cent of the top fourteen Broadway plays—those running ninety-three or more performances—were imported from abroad. And although six of the Ten Best Plays reprinted in this book are by American writers, even half of these had already been given their first professional productions in Europe before being seen in New York. All of this suggested that the New York climate for theatrical production was continuing to deteriorate, and perhaps that American playwrights were going fallow in a too well-plowed field of naturalism.

That the public was tired of the conventional Broadway play would seem to be borne out by the overwhelming popularity of *A Man for All Seasons*. Robert Bolt's chronicle of Sir Thomas More's attempt to live within the English laws of his time, and yet to hold a private opinion about King Henry VIII's right to divorce Queen Catherine in favor of Anne Boleyn, would hardly appear to be smash hit material. For one thing its hero is executed to no purpose at the end of the play. For another, the personal beliefs he so cherishes involve the blind acceptance of a ruling by a Pope whom More himself acknowledges to be corrupt. Furthermore, there is nothing romantic about More's behavior. He wishes to be neither a revolutionist nor a martyr. He merely accepts the reality of life after death, and refuses to jeopardize his chances for eternal paradise to gain a few years' extra earthly existence. He is equally realistic in his opinion of the function of the law, and his description of it as "a causeway" would be heartily endorsed by today's most conservative big business tycoons who feel perfectly justified in avoiding millions of dollars in taxes by ingenious exploitation of tax-law loopholes.

The same realism is used in presenting the other characters. For instance, Alice More is written as a nagging and stupid old cow who needs her husband desperately while he needs her not at all.

With such an unromantic gallery and unromantic theme, one must look elsewhere for the secret of this play's popularity. Is it perhaps the fascinating struggle of a brilliant man to defeat or at least stalemate the overwhelming forces against him? If so it is rather a letdown for More to be so easily defeated by the simple perjury of one weak character.

No. We suspect that *A Man for All Seasons* is the ideal play for an audience in transition, an audience which has come to recognize the romantic theatrical conventions as false and which at the same time yearns to escape into something a little larger and a little more splendid than naturalistic behavior. Mr. Bolt offers just these commodities. Historical figures swirling down a gracefully curved stairway in stylish capes and gowns please the eye. Machiavellian court intrigue spiced with wit tickles the ear. And the curse of falsity is removed not only by Mr. Bolt's steadfastly nonromantic approach, but also by Paul Scofield's delivery of More's speeches as if he were too preoccupied with the next idea to waste much time or emphasis on the present one. But perhaps most valuable of all is the device of using one scrubby little actor to talk directly to the audience as The Common Man. A sort of undeluded Falstaff, he intermittently reminds everyone that the proletarian and vulgar world we recognize as real still surrounds the upper-class figures of the play.

The comparative lack of success enjoyed by the season's best play, *The Caretaker,* would seem to demonstrate that although audiences are thirsty for the nonromantic, they are not yet quite prepared to accept a masterpiece of realism minus visual splendor and the illusion of larger purpose. For sociology, psychology, and conventional dramaturgy seemed light years away from the play's junk-filled garret where we watch a tattered and vicious bum in his tragicomic struggle to stave off recognition of his low estate.

This man, whose name may be Mac—it is Harold Pinter's method to let us know no more about concrete fact in his plays than we do about those dramatic real-life situations we imaginatively fill in after seeing a number of blurred surface manifestations—is universal. He stands for all of us who in moments of humiliation have felt the suddenly increased necessity of holding onto some nonsensical identity or status. In this case, Mac keeps his dubious personality from complete disintegration by feeling superior to "foreigners," "blacks," and "nuts," or by fostering the illusion that if he could only "go down to Sidcup and pick up his papers" he would be able to sort himself out, or by being more critical than he can afford to be about the handouts he is offered.

We watch Mac, who in utter selfishness pursues his best chances between his initial benefactor, Aston, an introverted non-violent man with an obsession for acquiring junk and tools for future building and repair projects he never seems to be able to carry through, and Aston's extroverted brother Mick, who cruelly pushes Mac into behaving so obnoxiously that his brother will be forced to defend himself, and thereby emerge from his passivity. There is no artificial building up of urgency, and little apparent consciousness on the part of the three characters of the intent and probable effect of their moves. Each moment is played in the limbo of the Chekhovian present, with each speaker more absorbed in the sound and wonder of his own fancies than he is in their logic. This can make both for hilarity, as it does in Mac's speech about needing a clock, or for sadness, as in Aston's long description of his shock treatment made to an unhearing and insensitive roommate.

Because everything must occur right there in front of us, and because we have no more knowledge of the characters' histories and motives than they choose to reveal, *The Caretaker* proved to be an actors' delight, and director Donald McWhinnie encouraged his performers to explore and exploit the dramatic possibilities of each situation, provoking each other into surges of comedy or grief to rediscover the wonder and glory of the human condition. Donald Pleasence's characterization of Mac was the season's best performance. While his shabby costume, his unkempt hair and whiskers, and his gaping toothless mouth defined him as a tramp, there was something else in him, something we sensed from his sudden anguished pounding of his fist into his other hand as he searched for lost shreds of security. And Mr. Pleasence made Mac's final wretched humiliation almost beatific in its feeling of release from security seeking pretense.

While some attempted to give *The Caretaker* an added dimension by making it into an allegory about mankind torn between an Old Testament God and a New Testament Christ, or by viewing Aston's state as an indictment against a society that approves shock therapy, Mr. Pinter disavowed any such intentions, and indeed they would have detracted from the play's greatness as a simple and universal human document.

Graham Greene made an almost successful attempt to write a lament for our age's lost romanticism and disguise it as drawing-room farce. A great deal of the time *The Complaisant Lover* did manage to demonstrate the absurdities faced by a modern lover with a deep passion for a married woman who although she is thoroughly in love with him doesn't want to make her seedy but kindly dentist husband unhappy. However, the play's theme was a difficult one for American audiences, particularly when the cuckolded husband was played by the handsome and virile Sir Michael Redgrave.

Three other imports from England written in conventional style seemed worthy but slightly dated. In *Ross* Terence Rattigan accepted the challenge of treating an instance of homosexual masochism in the life of Lawrence of Arabia with such skill that "Aunt Edna" would not be offended, but in the long run it was Lawrence's picaresque swagger and the irony of a hero fallen into oblivion that gave the play the bursts of theatrical effectiveness it had. It will be interesting to compare Mr. Rattigan's treatment with that of the forthcoming film on Lawrence, written in what we presume will be a more historically realistic style by *A Man for All Seasons'* Mr. Bolt.

Santha Rama Rau's adaptation of E. M. Forster's novel, *A Passage to India,* achieved a few genuinely compelling moments, but in general reduced a great novel to a minor colonial incident in the now ancient history of British Rule in India. And in its Broadway production Michael Redgrave's adaptation of Henry James's *The Aspern Papers* seemed to turn a rather subtle and complex story into a boring melodrama whose only distinction was a superb final scene. In the latter Wendy Hiller follows her anguished attempt to buy herself a husband by pulling herself up from the depths of humiliation to a pride in herself more durable and honest than fashionable but false relationships.

American playwrights faced the shifting theatrical convention here in a number of ways. Tennessee Williams, who has already found his own formula for treating the dirty truths of our lives with elegance, and exaggerating natural pain into operatic manifestations to arrive at the required magic combination of convincing realism and splendor, offered us his *The Night of the Iguana.* In it he conjured up a run-down Mexican hotel called the Costa Verde, as a place of reckoning for those "who live on the fantastic level, but who have got to operate on the realistic level."

The play's protagonist, the Reverend T. Lawrence Shannon, a defrocked minister leading a bus tour of ladies through Mexico, must fight two battles at the Costa Verde. The first is a realistic and essentially humorous one in which he loses his independence as leader of the tour, and falls into the clutches of a coarse middle-aged Gorgon. The other is a fantastic one which with courage and the assistance of a highly spiritual woman he may win against bedevilment by "the spook in the rain forest." Margaret Leighton won much praise for her sensitive performance as the spiritual woman and Patrick O'Neal captured an El Greco quality as Shannon. The play was voted the Best American Play of the Season, and a couple of critics even went so far as to call it Tennessee Williams' best play.

Paddy Chayefsky tackled the problem in what was perhaps the toughest way of all by setting out to make a biblical miracle and a

Zia Mohyeddin, Anne Meacham, Eric Portman and Gladys Cooper in "A Passage to India."

capricious God credible to a modern audience. In *Gideon* his hero became The Common Man and his God became an irritable patriarch who, considering his omnipotence, seemed to cherish his earthly status to an amusingly absurd degree. Unfortunately modern audiences didn't seem to equate biblical spectacle with splendor, and except for one sensational belly-dance, the crowd and battle scenes tended at best to be only moderately effective. However, the dialogues between Gideon and the Lord were profound, provocative and humorous, and *Gideon* placed a respectable second in the critics' voting.

In October a book called *The Theatre of the Absurd* was published, in which Martin Esslin attempted to group certain modern playwrights by the fact that they used exaggeration of people's logical reactions to illogical premises as a principal tool. Overnight the phrase became a hot conversation topic and one convenient for those who wished to merchandise plays that might be rejected by the public unless they were made to seem something new that the theatregoer could not afford to miss. While the book itself contained valuable and stimulating analyses of some fascinating plays, the phrase, though it may have extended slightly the run of a few plays, failed to turn any of these into hits. Samuel Beckett's *Happy Days,* which could only succeed with a great actress, seemed clever but depressing with a good one, and led Walter Kerr to begin his review with: "Well, happy days are gone again." The Living Theatre's presentation of Jack Gelber's *The Apple* seemed a wild and weird nightmare. How much of its apparent meaninglessness was due to its production remains to be seen, but Jimmie Davis of *The Daily News* became so annoyed that he departed early and wrote: "The Living Theatre should drop dead." N. F. Simpson's *One Way Pendulum* also created a madhouse on stage, but here we *could* see the point. Yet the antics, sparked as they were by British institutions and restrictions, struck American audiences as less funny because they did not apply directly to them.

While playwright Arthur Kopit was still too young, too unscowling and unknown to qualify as a member of "the absurd," his first New York play used the technique of absurdity even in its marathon title, *Oh Dad, Poor Dad, Mamma's Hung You in the Closet and I'm Feelin' So Sad.* Not only did he borrow the techniques of the absurdists, but also those of Thornton Wilder, Tennessee Williams, Giraudoux, Duerrenmatt and Anouilh. However, the subject matter was his own, as he hilariously and outrageously painted the whole disgusting top-heavy spectacle of a society whose fantastically unreal myths and traditions lead either to their perpetuation and the resultant further widening of the gap between them and reality, or to a pathological and destructive way of life.

While the farce concerned an over-protected child and his cruelly realistic mother, whose life has become an obsessive crusade against the sentimental and romantic notions that turn our lives into deluded falsehoods, a major part of the show's popularity may have come from Barbara Harris's hilarious but nonetheless erotic performance as the nineteen-year-old girl who sets out to seduce the sheltered young man with a selfishness and determination equal to that of his mother who opposes her. But although the frosting may have sold the cake, the cake was worth eating, and the Phoenix Theatre, which this season took the wise step of moving into a smaller playhouse, not only had a solid hit, but a piece of truly exciting theatre to make us forget the recent uninspired years that this high-purposed theatre's dutiful followers had so gamely endured.

Mr. Kopit's claim to the title of "most promising new playwright of the year" received its severest challenge from Herb Gardner, whose *A Thousand Clowns* eschewed the technique of the absurd in favor of the more naturalistic describing of a comic non-conform-

First reading of "Happy Days": with Alan Schneider (director), John C. Becher and Ruth White (the sole performers) and Richard Barr (co-producer).

ist's coming to terms with a real-life situation. While the play's Murray Burns sees the absurdities of a phony world around him and barks brilliantly at it, he is realistic enough to acknowledge his own vulnerability to its human if sentimental appeals. And as did Jean Kerr's still-running hit of last season, Mr. Gardner's "Murray, Murray" abounded with original funny lines and accurate observations of daily life.

Then there was poet Arnold Weinstein, who blithely concocted a free-swinging vaudeville called *Red Eye of Love*. This comical chronicle parodized the progress of the naïve American spirit as it quixotically opposes the stronger representatives of our growing materialism who still end up both with all the marbles and the delusion that they are part of the American dream. While the play's plot owed something to Paul Green's *Johnny Johnson,* its devices and dialogue were highly original, and it ran Off Broadway for several months.

Three other new American playwrights who also must be regarded as promising were Alice Cannon (*Great Day in the Morning*), Frank D. Gilroy (*Who'll Save the Plowboy?*), and Val Coleman (*Jackhammer*). Mrs. Cannon's drama of backyard St. Louis of the Prohibition Era was unabashedly maudlin, but it erupted into one marvelous drunken party scene with José Quintero's direction and Colleen Dewhurst's performance glowing hot through the whole life-rich business. Mr. Gilroy invented a load of misery for an unfortunate married couple suddenly called upon to play "happy home" for the husband's wartime buddy who is dying of wounds incurred in saving him, and who seeks to reassure himself that his heroic act had some value. And although Mr. Coleman's ambitious play about a group of post-World War II veterans testing their guilty consciences, while locked in a building that is being demolished, was mercilessly panned for its overwritten dialogue, it was clear that its author possessed the reach, the passion and the intellect with which he might write important plays in the future.

Finally there was Ossie Davis with his first Broadway offering, *Purlie Victorious*. Whatever one thought of the play, which wavered between parody of the Negro-White relationship in backwoods Georgia and simple folk-comedy, it represented a new departure in the stage treatment of this problem. For while the thin plot borders on fantasy, in that the illiterate cotton-pickers outwit their white boss, it does express its author's belief that there is a comic side to the racial problem and maybe even a happy ending. Perhaps because they are making fun of the situation, the Negro actors are perfectly willing to play the exaggerated stereotypes that correspond with the worst that has been said of them, and they even take cracks at themselves with such biting remarks as: "You're a disgrace to the Negro profession." Rather astonishingly it chalked up more performances than had any other play through May 31st of this year, and was rumored to have been the second strongest contender for the Pulitzer Prize.

That Broadway audiences were still willing to support not-very-effective comedy provided it was spiced with a little harmless sex, featured a familiar star, and did not require them to think, was shown by the long run of Marcel Achard's *A Shot in the Dark,* as adapted by Harry Kurnitz. While most of the real fun of the original French play came out of its saucy mocking of a pompous French society, the tone of the Broadway version was strangely subdued, as if it were a gentle comedy about an innocent young girl and the nice young man who saved her from being tried for murder. Are Americans still unwilling to accept the fact that some good people

June Harding, Phyllis Thaxter, Art Carney and Elizabeth Ashley in "Take Her, She's Mine."

happily live lives that are frequently sordid and immoral? Julie Harris, in an amazingly wanton performance for an actress who this year won an Emmy for her *Victoria Regina,* did her best to make this point, as did Walter Matthau in one entertaining second act scene, but the rest of the comedy seemed disappointingly mundane.

Compare this with another French comedy, *The Egg*. Félicien Marceau's highly original farce *was* sordid and immoral and *did* require its audience to think. With a different cast and performed relaxedly in the round last season at Washington, D. C.'s Arena Stage, it had proven the most popular play of the Washington season with audiences and critics alike. Why had the Broadway production pleased neither? Was it just the starring of a highly extroverted night club performer in the role of the happy-go-lucky and extremely ordinary "Common Frenchman"? Or did the producer rightly sense a hostility to the play by Broadway audiences and futilely attempt to overcome that rejection by hitting them over the head with it? Whatever the reason, the naïve and sunny charm of the play had evaporated to leave us with something calculated and cold. However, mainly from the memory of its Washington production, the editor has included it as one of the Best Plays of 1961-1962.

Two vastly inferior comedies and one very modest murder mystery chalked up much longer runs than they deserved. In *Take Her, She's Mine* Henry and Phoebe Ephron strung together a series of episodes that presented some of the amusing things that happen when adoring fathers send their daughters away to college. Nothing in the comedy was any better than one might expect in a "Fathers Are Funny" TV serial, but Art Carney, who plays exasperation well, seems Broadway's No. 1 draw to out-of-towners who feel that they know him—and perhaps what is more important, that their neighbors know him—because of his many TV appearances. And newcomer Elizabeth Ashley looked an attractive and wholesome daughter in her New York debut.

Norman Krasna's *Sunday in New York* began promisingly as if it were really going to explore the paradox of a young man who believes in exploiting a single standard philosophy with his girl friends, but who cannot face his kid sister's embracement of the same code. However, the comedy soon subsided into a routine romantic plot in which both undressed sex, and wholesome characters were reconciled.

In his first play since *Dial M for Murder* Frederick Knott again devised an ingenious murder method, and a victim who well deserves his fate. To extend this one-act idea to full length Mr. Knott merely surprised us by making the first murder unnecessary, and thereby gave *Write Me a Murder* a second act in which to start afresh on another victim.

Of the remaining Broadway plays, at least three deserved more than they got. Hugh Wheeler, who had been selected as last season's most promising new playwright, came through with a second play *Look: We've Come Through,* which unfortunately did not. For while Mr. Wheeler's honest and accurate description of characters was again in evidence, he this time made the mistake of presenting too explicitly and objectively the sordid deflowering of his heroine, and the detailing of the homosexual past of the young man with whom she goes on to establish a truer relationship. It is interesting to compare the reception of this play which actually faced the facts of homosexual experience with that of the earlier *Tea and Sympathy,* in which we saw a young man persecuted for homosexuality, although he had in fact had no such experience.

Gore Vidal's adaptation of Friedrich Duerrenmatt's *Romulus* offered us two puzzling heterogeneous types of entertainment. The first was gay trivia stylishly delivered by Cyril Ritchard who, as the last Roman Emperor, seemed interested in nothing but his next

Kevin McCarthy, Sal Mineo, Gretchen Walther and Ralph Meeker in "Something About a Soldier."

bon mot. The second was a biting and comically challenging view of history that came belatedly and partially to life in the play's final scene between the wise and ultra-civilized Romulus, who understands the futility of Rome's all-conquering past, and the Goth chief, Ottiker, who foresees the futility of future conquests by barbarous powers of more civilized countries. Amusingly, but not necessarily untruthfully, they both agree that the world will ultimately be ruled by big business, represented in the play by a nouveau riche pants manufacturer named Otto Rupf. The production of a more faithful translation of what now stands as a sporadically effective play might easily place *Romulus* among the Best Plays of a future season.

Do You Know the Milky Way?, a post-World War II fantasy about a legally dead soldier who tries to return to the opportunistic, faithless and cruelly competitive world of post-war Germany, appeared to be a lovely and simple play suffering under the weight and pretensions of its production. Or perhaps Americans found such overpowering post-war disillusionment of one passive individual a peculiarly European situation.

Two plays about American soldiers in World War II failed to run very long. *Something About a Soldier* was an honest effort to draw the character of a bright and non-conformist draftee and a sensitive officer's unethical rescue of him from having to go into combat. The other, *A Cook for Mr. General,* by new playwright Steven Gethers, achieved the funniest single moment of the season when a group of rehabilitation camp soldiers are thrown into such chaos that a sergeant's "Atten-hut"—automatically barked at the sight of an entering general—causes two stretcher bearers to drop an unconscious lieutenant on the ground, and salute. With a slightly better cast, this comedy might have been a hit. Shenanigans in a peacetime Army supply depot proved only moderately amusing in *Blood, Sweat and Stanley Poole,* but young Peter Fonda made an impressive debut as a frightened and awkward private whose superior I.Q. allows him to save the day for his rugged but dumb lieutenant.

Certainly the spectacle of a man dying of cancer is universal and tragic, but *A Gift of Time* found itself repeating two responses to the situation for most of the evening. One of these was to make light of it with small talk, and the other was to make "last speeches" for an entire act. However, Boris Aronson's French seacoast setting, painted on a transparent drop, came to life under Jean Rosenthal's dramatic lighting to make memorable the final scene.

In addition to the aforementioned *Oh Dad, Poor Dad,* three other new Off Broadway dramatic presentations registered one hundred or more performances. Despite the fact that none of Brecht's plays have ever had any success in New York, the public went mad for an evening of recitations titled *Brecht on Brecht.* While one hopes that this response heralds a new readiness for the works of a great artist previously unappreciated here, the performances were not very Brechtian, and the best part of the evening was supplied by Lotte Lenya's zestful singing.

At Circle-in-the-Square, Thornton Wilder returned to the American theatre with three new one-act plays. The first two were from a projected cycle of seven based upon the seven ages of man. *Infancy* used the ingenious theatrical device of putting two adult actors dressed as babies in perambulators and letting us hear what Mr. Wilder thinks babies would be entitled to say to adults if they could talk. *Childhood* turned out to have much of the same flavor as *Our Town* when it showed us a fantasy bus ride by three newly made "orphans," during which their sought-after adventures become more and more frightening, increasing their need to return to their parents. The third play in *Plays for Bleecker Street* was one of another projected cycle based upon the seven deadly sins. Subtitled *Lust,* it

Three of the players in "Infancy": Mary Doyle, Jack Dodson and George Furth, in the baby carriage. (Mr. Furth replaced Richard Libertini.)

presented St. Francis of Assisi eagerly facing the result of a past sin and experiencing from this the beatific ecstasy carnal pleasure can only temporarily imitate. Mr. Wilder's assorted package was respectfully treated, but he did not seem to have broken any new ground nor made any great addition to the body of his work. Perhaps when the whole cycle of seven is presented in one piece these fragments will turn out to be a more significant entity.

Kermit Bloomgarden became the first major Broadway producer to mount a play Off Broadway. He chose *Moon on a Rainbow Shawl* by Trinidad's Errol John, and director George Roy Hill so beautifully caught the bubbling rhythm of West Indian life that three of the performances won awards.

Three of the season's best plays had undeservedly short Off Broadway runs. One of these, Robert Ardrey's *Stone and Star,* produced under the title *Shadow of Heroes,* is included in this book for several reasons. For one thing its method of presenting a highly complex story out of historical fact makes an interesting comparison with *A Man for All Seasons.* Both plays seek to avoid blurring the truth by oversimplification. But Mr. Ardrey's figures lack the costumed splendor and the wry jokes of The Common Man. Instead of relieving the tension of the situation, Mr. Ardrey's interlocutor intensifies it. Nevertheless, this play about the Hungarian Rebellion represents the season's only full-scale attempt to deal with a large international contemporary event.

Just as contemporary, but strictly American, was William Archibald's *The Cantilevered Terrace,* which managed to remain provocative and interesting through two hours of pure talk. It dealt, within the confines of one wealthy family, with the decline of the American aristocrat, who is being destroyed both by inbred ineffectual offsprings with the aid of an opportunistic middle class, and by its own double code of hardness towards others and softness about itself. If the book had room for an eleventh play this would have been it. The audaciousness of its impossibly artificial dialogue, which makes this play so challenging and unique, is perhaps suggested in the following exchange between Mrs. Perpetua and her Negro maid, Angela.

* Mrs. P.—The musical comedy stage has allowed your race too much encouragement.

Angela—Has it, ma'am?

Mrs. P.—Yes. There was, for instance, that silliness—it had an oceanic title. It went on and on—as though one's color were a problem. Did it not make you feel your color was a problem?

Angela—It made me see how difficult it is to become an American. But the problem of being an American has little to do with color, ma'am. It's more a matter of losing one's identity. I intend to become like you.

Mrs. P.—Me?

Angela—I intend to embrace your vulgarity of principle.

* From "The Cantilevered Terrace" by William Archibald. Copyright © 1962 by William Archibald. Used by permission.

MRS. P.—My dear, colored friend, I have nothing in common with other Americans. Do you suppose another mistress would allow this sort of conversation!

ANGELA—If she were an American, yes. It's part of the democratic ideal. Or have I been misinformed?

While it is hardly a new play, Claudel's *Noontide* received its first New York presentation Off Broadway, where it proved obscure but fascinatingly mystical and complex. This play, written fifty years ago, is a less realistic but in some ways more hardboiled version of *The Night of the Iguana,* in which we watch a sensitive man's voyage to Heaven by way of Hell. But, as all dramatists have discovered, Hell is easier to dramatize than Heaven, and the third act was not as successful as the first two. Yet the shipboard moment, when at the climax of a conversation an awning is suddenly pulled back to flood the white deck with blinding light, remains one of the season's most unforgettable and truly theatrical consummations.

Other memorable moments in new Off Broadway plays include the quiet singing of "Say After Me" between the violently dramatic scenes of *Bring Me a Warm Body;* a short satire on voyeurism by the previously unproduced in this country, Jean Tardieu; the crucifixion on bicycle handlebars of the hepcat hero in Arrabal's *The Automobile Graveyard;* the beginning of Elaine May's first short play, *Not Enough Rope;* and Langston Hughes's *Black Nativity,* a more genuinely joyous celebration of Christmas than was to be had in austere churches or Radio City Music Hall. In the latter, one of the singers suddenly spontaneously lamented Bethlehem's inhospitality to Mary with the exclamation, "No room at the *Ho*-tel!," and the story suddenly seemed brand new.

Paul Roebling's performance fully caught the flavor of life among the wildly romantic inconsolables of the twenties in an inventive and imaginative dramatization of Scott Fitzgerald's *This Side of Paradise.* And although the project had been intended more as an experimental series of exercises than as a full-scale attempt to make a play out of the book, it achieved an astonishing three months' run on the intimate open stage at the Sheridan Square Playhouse.

Broadway has apparently abandoned the idea of reviving plays, since there is no subsidiary profit available from producing works whose movie, television, and stock rights have already been sold. This function is therefore left to City Center and to Off Broadway. Most successful of the revived dramas at City Center was Franco Zeffirelli's Old Vic production of *Romeo and Juliet,* which though it neglected the verse, made up for it with violently realistic action, and a freshly humorous treatment of the balcony scene.

And Off Broadway's best revival turned out to be a production of *The Hostage* which, because it was staged in an intimate theatre with the audience virtual guests in the same bar with the play's characters, was more effective than the Broadway version of the season before. David Ross's production of *Ghosts* and *Rosmersholm* registered long runs, as did a production of Sean O'Casey's *Red Roses for Me,* which had failed on Broadway a few seasons ago. Shaw's *Misalliance,* featuring Donald Moffat, not only set a new record for number of performances of that play, but also proved again that this 1910 comedy about parents and children was still as miraculously modern as *Look Back in Anger.* Similarly Arthur Storch's production of *Two by Saroyan* reminded us that the great one—the paragraph about dentists in his new autobiographical *Here Comes/There Goes/You Know Who* made the funniest single piece of writing by a playwright this season—had been concerned with total annihilation before the invention of atom bombs.

Oddly enough the two most perfect and entertaining play revivals had only limited runs. *The Ticket-of-Leave Man* was, of course, ridiculously dated. But under Robert Moore's disciplined direction, a fine cast headed by Philip Bosco, Joseph Plummer, and Mary Harrigan played each scene as if their lives depended upon it and were ten times funnier than a cute or camping presentation would have been. In much the same way the APA (Associated Producing Artists) Repertory's revival of *The Tavern* gave us a hilarious but fantastically disciplined and warm version of George M. Cohan's philosophical melodrama. While this and its productions of *The School for Scandal* and *The Seagull* received rave notices, the inaccessible location of their theatre worked against them. What this company needs in the future is a smaller City Center uptown.

Foreign language companies performing here during the season included the Greek National Theatre, with its strong but youthfully beautiful star Aspassia Papathanassiou; the Dusseldorf Schauspielhaus, led by Ernst Deutsch and Eva Boettcher; and the Swedish Royal Dramatic Theatre of Stockholm. The latter offered Sweden's greatest actor, 75-year-old Lars Hanson, in a tremendous performance of Strindberg's *The Father,* but regretfully excused him from playing the role he created in *Long Day's Journey Into Night,* and thereby considerably lessened the force of what in Stockholm had seemed a terrifying production. However, Inga Tidblad was impressive with the repetition of her incredible portrayal of Mary Tyrone, and Jarl Kulle and Ulf Palme were again fine as the two brothers.

John Stride (Romeo) and Joanna Dunham (Juliet) in the Old Vic revival of "Romeo and Juliet."

The Broadway musical theatre seemed as yet exempt from the effects of any shift in public taste. However it was interesting to note the season's biggest hit, *How to Succeed in Business Without Really Trying,* was essentially a non-romantic musical. Indeed its premise was rather Brechtian, in that it suggested that all that was necessary for success was blindly to follow empirical rules drawn from a coldly objective investigation of the way big businesses operated, and a willingness to use deceit to ride roughshod over the backs of one's less ruthless fellow employees. And its heroine's attraction to the young opportunist, Finch, was based purely on the fact that she sensed in him a future successful executive. It was, if you like, a belated but merry funeral service for Horatio Alger. And as the producers of *The Threepenny Opera* had discovered, the way to make such cynical comment popular with American audiences was to make its basically ignoble protagonist as charming as possible.

Even then *How to Succeed* pulled its punches a bit, surrounding pertinent caustic observation with more innocuous material, including several numbers which represented restful diversionary interludes. And its final song about "giving one's brother everything one can" appeared deliberately ambiguous.

On the positive side, Broadway veterans Abe Burrows and Frank Loesser courageously stuck to their guns in insisting that the musical avoid many of the romantic cliches musical comedy tradition dictates. The giving of the show's best ballad, "I Believe in You," not to young people in love with each other, but to Finch who, in love with himself, sings the song into a mirror while shaving, is a case in point. Mr. Loesser's lyrics were the best of the year, and the book and the performances were about the funniest in any musical within recent memory.

The second biggest musical hit also concentrated on fun, rather than on romance. Putting together a pastiche of several Roman comedies, *A Funny Thing Happened on the Way to the Forum* presented the absurdly intricate plot in the earthy manner of present-day burlesque. Zero Mostel, Jack Gilford and David Burns reduced society's pretensions to the lowest common denominator, and used subtlety and artistry, but never with condescension, to reproduce vulgarity and carry out the intricate complex of barely averted near meetings. And Mr. Mostel stopped the show when suddenly he illustrated by means of a mercurial burst of pantomimed poses and gestures all the drawings on one of those highly improper Roman friezes.

For some reason the romantic plot never involved the audience very much, and Stephen Sondheim's generally pleasant words and music seldom asserted themselves to achieve the quality of his best love lyric—"I pine, I blush, I squeak, I squawk/Today I woke too weak to walk." Yet it didn't matter too much in a jamboree that made Roman comedy work so merrily and well.

No Strings drew no great critical praise, but that fact seldom bothers a Richard Rodgers musical. In this case, Mr. Rodgers' writing of both music and lyrics—the latter alternately reminiscent of both Hammerstein and Hart, but well above average in quality—Samuel Taylor's selection of a sophisticated romance between a "Europe bum" of a novelist and a chic Negro fashion model in Paris as the challenging core of his book, scene designer David Hays's concept of providing manually changeable screen backgrounds that would tell the whole story as if it were being shot in a fashion photographer's studio, and the notion of putting instrumental groups on-stage to be part of the action, rather than just the hired help in the orchestra pit, all promised much in the early part of the show. In addition, Diahann Carroll looked adorable in gorgeous Donald Brooks gowns, and in songs like "Loads of Love" demonstrated a distinctive and thrilling delivery. But at the beginning of Act II

Barbra Streisand, Lillian Roth and Elliott Gould in "I Can Get It for You Wholesale."

the charming formal love duet, "Look No Further," unwittingly turned out to be excellent advice, as the show's plot disintegrated in the more general sense of the word. This fact failed to daunt audiences who found the fine score and the unusualness and sophistication of the show sufficient attractions.

That the conventionally romantic Broadway musical can still survive was proved by *Milk and Honey,* which featured richly melodic music, a nominal love story set in present-day Israel between an older man and a pretty widow, some vigorous Hebrew folk dancing, and the special comic touch of Molly Picon as an American widow who likes marriage simply because with a husband there's always "someone if you wake up in the middle of the night and you want a glass of water, he should get it for you."

On the other hand, a hard-boiled musical about an unattractive cloak-and-suiter and the lives he wrecks was also popular. *I Can Get It for You Wholesale* somewhat softened the ending of the novel by implying that a highly competitive society needs unscrupulous and aggressive hatchet men and will therefore breed this type.

Nevertheless the most entertaining things in the show were the comic contrast between the backstage frantic costume-changing and the casual poised fashion parade out front, and 19-year-old Barbra Streisand's amusing portrait of Miss Marmelstein, the over-worked and under-loved secretary.

Newsday's critic George Oppenheimer titled his review of *Subways Are for Sleeping* "Sick Transit," and just about everyone agreed. One suspects that so did its producer David Merrick, but, as in the past, this did not stop him from merchandising the show into a partially successful run. One of his stunts was an amusing hoax in which he located seven men who had the same names as the critics of the seven leading New York newspapers. He then took a full page ad in which he published seven glowing opinions of his musical, attached to the names of Howard Taubman, Walter Kerr, John Chapman, Robert Coleman, Richard Watts, Jr., John McClain and Norman Nadel. To keep it legal he printed a small photograph of *his* seven men, and of course avoided identifying them with any publication. The *New York Herald-Tribune* unwittingly ran the advertisement in its early edition, before discovering that it was a hoax and yanking it. The next day the *Herald-Tribune* ran a story in which it reprinted in smaller size the Merrick ad, and beside it ran pictures of the real critics and some of the unfavorable opinions they had written about the show.

The critics themselves were amused by the hoax and did not feel that anyone would have been taken in by it. However, many in the publishing profession were incensed by what they considered to be a fraud on the public, and there was cause for lively debate.

The remaining Broadway musicals were not terribly distinguished. Only one Noel Coward song, "Something Very Strange," and an occasional witticism kept the proceedings on a cruise ship from seeming as unpleasant, boring and inept as the worst vacation most of us had ever spent. *The Gay Life* had a hilarious comic scene in a Viennese night club, and a nice song or two, but we never quite believed its thesis that Anatol had really renounced the gay life in favor of a more genuine love. *Kean* appeared to be a combination of bright excerpts from a witty and cynical play, decorative romantic music, and Alfred Drake's special musical comedy panache, with no one of these ingredients doing any of the others very much good. Neither did Ray Bolger's unique relaxed charm fit the character of a tense little refugee professor in *All American.* And George Gobel's soft-spoken timidity demanded that *Let It Ride* either find another star more appropriate to the story of *Three Men on a Horse,* or rewrite the book to suit Mr. Gobel. They did neither, but the show

Larry Kert, Eileen Heckart, Bibi Osterwald, Shelley Berman and Rita Gardner in "A Family Affair."

did achieve one very funny patter song called "Just an Honest Mistake." Its best stanza went as follows:

* Mr. Gallup said that Truman
  was the losing candidate.
Mr. Bonaparte marched to Moscow
  and got clobbered at the gate.
Mr. Ford put out the Edsel;
  Mr. Nixon said "Let's Debate!"

Shelley Berman, Eileen Heckart, and Morris Carnovsky almost succeeded in making the hopelessly ordinary *A Family Affair* into something memorable, and Agnes de Mille's choreography and Sally Ann Howes's voice and beauty shone through the disaster of *Kwamina,* which attempted to wed musical comedy and the large subject of the coming struggle between tribal superstitions and mod-

* From "Let It Ride," music and lyrics by Jay Livingston and Ray Evans. © 1961 by Livingston & Evans, Inc.

ern African government, and which evasively presented a miscegenatory romance between a young African doctor and a white girl. Both weddings failed to come off.

Off Broadway attempted the all time high of twenty-three musicals, of which only two had much distinction. *Fly Blackbird* made fun of the widely expressed attitude that racial integration should be a slow and gradual process handed out as a favor. And *King of the Whole Damn World* amusingly and pleasantly celebrated the LaGuardia era in New York. Of the others, *All in Love,* a musical version of *The Rivals,* had the most success.

On the other hand, two revivals of old musicals found audiences. Robert Turoff's imaginative staging of *The Golden Apple* gave a much-needed spontaneity to an admirable and ingenious work that, because it is all sung in formal couplets, can seem studied. And *Anything Goes,* reinforced with a few songs from other Cole Porter musicals, amused by becoming a parody of itself.

Aficionados of that wonderfully vulgar and pretension-shattering genre of theatre called burlesque were delighted when its shabby comics and its uninhibited strippers returned to New York in the form of a revue titled *This Was Burlesque.*

The real musical revue seems to be a vanishing species, now giving way to evenings of improvised sketches with little or no music included. From the Compass Theatre in Chicago came a show called *From the Second City,* featuring a talented group of young comedians in a relatively unshaped series of sketches that had grown out of improvisation. Its best moments tended to come in scenes that were really portions of whole unwritten plays. A hilarious lesson in beatnik art appreciation, administered by a real gone guy (Alan Arkin) to a timid culture-conscious girl (Barbara Harris), would make a fine opening scene. A male and female centaur left behind by Noah, because she was late and he waited for her, would provide a touching second act curtain. And the conversation between a disturbed father and his fifteen-year-old daughter, who has bravely carried out an impersonal love-making excursion with a boy for whom she pretends not to care, was a profoundly emotional denouement.

After a modest Broadway engagement this company shifted to an Off Broadway cabaret and continued to perform second and third editions of the same sort of material. In one of these, Barbara Harris sang "The Question Song," and demonstrated that besides possessing a distinctive comic personality, she could also deliver a song with beauty and pathos.

Already a going concern Off Broadway was *The Premise,* which was also a descendant of the original Compass Theatre. It too performed a program of political sketches, short revue numbers, and spontaneous improvisations. *The Premise* performers seemed slightly more anxious to entertain, worked in a smaller and more intimate club, and concentrated a little more on shaping their sketches. One effective piece of new material there, in which a nervous and not very bright private is stationed in a Pentagon sub-basement room containing nothing but a button, which if pushed would set off our entire system of nuclear missile retaliation, may have hit so close to the truth of the matter that Washington was stimulated to revise our defense set-up.

Whatever the difference between these two companies, they both were attempting to create drama out of our own lives and times to a greater extent than were most of our playwrights, whose works often seemed more closely related to other plays than to anything else.

In passing one must mention a charming Off Broadway revue titled *Signs Along the Cynic Route;* John Fearnley's beautifully staged *Oscar Hammerstein II Festival,* with a host of stars ranging from the irrepressible Mary Martin to the quietly effective though less familiar Leon Bibb; and two offerings at City Center. One, Robert Ward's opera based on Arthur Miller's *The Crucible,* won its composer a 1962 Pulitzer Prize, and the other, a revival of *Brigadoon* starring Sally Ann Howes and the dynamic dancer, Edward Villella, was, if memory serves, better than the original.

The season will also be remembered as the one during which the city finally removed its five percent admissions tax to give producers a bit more leeway in their struggle with ever-rising production costs. Unfortunately the savings could not be used to bring down the high cost of tickets, which seemed to be keeping a great many people from going to the theatre at all. However, the second balcony seats, which were low-priced, continued to be the hardest to sell, which suggests that Americans are becoming more and more status conscious and less and less interested in the most genuine part of the theatre-going experience.

This problem was brought up at the Greater New York Chapter's Board of Standards and Planning for the Living Theatre annual symposium on the future design of new theatres, attended by an elite of theatre professionals, architects, and engineers, and it became apparent that the theatre of the future would have to take into account the American compulsion always to have the illusion of going "first-class." Democracy, to the theatre-goer at least, was not classlessness, but the right of every citizen to be at the top.

Another interesting argument came out of this symposium when director Tyrone Guthrie challenged the country's foremost consultant-theatrical inventor, George Izenour. Sir Tyrone took Mr. Izenour to task for promulgating multiform theatres like Harvard University's Loeb Drama Center, which attempted to make available within one auditorium a great number of different audience-stage relationships. He voiced the opinion that the theatre artist works best with a highly restricted number of choices. Mr. Izenour's view was that twentieth century man and twentieth century theatre could not ignore technical progress, and that the capacity of future artists would be infinitely greater and infinitely more able to create with the wealth of possibilities now made easily available to them by the machine.

The Ford Foundation also provoked interest in theatre design by a showing at New York City's Museum of Contemporary Crafts of eight new design concepts for theatres developed by designer-architect teams working under Ford grants.

And the plans for the new drama repertory theatre at Lincoln Center designed by scene designer Jo Mielziner, in equal collaboration with the late architect, Eero Saarinen, were revealed to the public. The building will contain two theatres. The first will be an 1100-seat playhouse whose stage can be altered within a couple of hours from a proscenium arch form to an open stage. And the other will be a 299-seat rehearsal studio, which will be used for rehearsal and for experimental productions of limited appeal. When the latter is not being used by the regular company it will be made available to other groups.

Elia Kazan and Robert Whitehead, who will guide the destinies of the Lincoln Center Repertory Company, plan to inaugurate its first thirty-five-week season of three plays in the fall of 1963, and move into Lincoln Center's Vivian Beaumont Theatre in May, 1964.

Mr. Kazan also announced his resignation from Actors Studio, and Lee Strasberg, the director-teacher who has been its active guiding light for the last decade, announced that the Studio had formed its own producing company which planned to present its first play in January, 1963. Will the resultant competition for actors hurt both companies? European example suggests that it will not, for in many European cities non-subsidized theatres like the Actors Studio one, flourish side by side with subsidized organizations like the Lincoln Center Repertory Company.

The question of subsidy, which Europe takes for granted but which our lawmakers resist, seems to be on its way to eventual resolution. Secretary of Labor Arthur J. Goldberg, who had stepped in to avert the cancellation of the Metropolitan Opera Season by mediating the labor-management quarrel there, made a long statement which appeared in *The New York Times* of December 15, 1961, urging more government support of the arts including the theatre. He augmented this with an article in *The New York Times* Magazine of March 11, 1962, in which he said that if art was essential to a free society, it must be helped to flourish by relieving it of "total dependence upon the market place, and upon majority opinion and taste."

He suggested a six-point partnership of the public, private patrons and benefactors, corporations, labor organizations, local and state governments, and the Federal Government. And he urged a Federal Advisory Council on the Arts to stand between the artist and the direct political process that might affect his work.

The White House also seemed interested in the problem and risked the charge of pretentiousness by entertaining many of the country's finest artists there. The President also appointed August Heckscher as White House cultural coordinator, which meant that there could be more continuity in working out a rational long-range arts program for the government's consideration.

Indeed, a good case could be made for the proposition that while the 1961-62 season revealed a continuing downward spiral in the conditions faced by New York theatre artists and theatre audiences, it also gave evidence of a growing awareness of the realities to be faced and a taking of first steps towards improvement and change.

THE SEASON IN LONDON AND PARIS

THE theatre in London this season might be described as all undressed with no place to go. The revolution that had been started almost a decade ago by Joan Littlewood, the Arts Theatre Club, and the Royal Court Theatre had succeeded in changing the taste of the London Theatre away from the overly formal and artificial play toward something more shapeless but more closely resembling life experience. While this was a fine first step, where did the English Theatre go from here? Miss Littlewood had taken a sabbatical saying that she was tired of training actors to be immediately whisked away to the West End, instead of being allowed to grow from play to play in one company. The Royal Court simply continued to produce plays by new writers, and by those it had previously introduced, but it could hardly hope to equal the impact it had achieved when its plays made such a violent contrast with those in the West End. And the Arts Theatre Club, which this season had aroused a certain excitement with a stage adaptation of *Lady Chatterly's Lover,* found it harder and harder to locate good scripts that were not also eagerly sought either by West End managers, whose eyes had been opened to the commerciality of the supposedly uncommercial play, by the Royal Court, or by Bernard Miles's Mermaid Theatre, although the latter seemed to fare best with large productions like *The Wakefield Mystery Play Cycle* or Mayakovsky's *The Bed Bug.*

The most hopeful solution to this problem seemed to be the Royal Shakespeare Theatre Company which because it could offer performers annual employment in a balanced repertory of modern and classic plays had been able to assemble a first-rate acting company. Furthermore with its three outlets, The Shakespeare Memorial Theatre at Stratford, and the Aldwych and the Arts Theatre Club, which it took over in London, it could juggle productions around without disrupting its ensemble. And when it produced a commercial success, it could transfer it to a regular West End theatre, and gradually retrieve from it most of its regular actors by replacing them with others. It was most flexible using guest artists like Christopher Plummer, whose performance as King Henry in *Becket* was the hit of the London season, or like Sir John Gielgud and Dame Peggy Ashcroft, who added lustre to Michel Saint-Denis's production of *The Cherry Orchard.* However, some of the greatest praise has gone to such younger actors in its company as Vanessa Redgrave, Judi Dench, Patsy Byrne, who played Grusche in *The Caucasian Chalk Circle,* and Ian Holm. Admittedly its director, Peter Hall, seemed to be making the best of a practical eclecticism, while London awaited the development of a director of the caliber of Brecht, Strehler, Planchon or Kazan. (Peter Coe, Franco Zeffirelli and William Gaskill had shown sputtering signs of possessing such a potential, but perhaps needed more opportunity for continuous work with a company they controlled.) However, the unavailability of future Arts Council support for the company's London operations threatened Mr. Hall's admirable project.

The season in Paris was disappointing. The Algerian crisis seemed to have made everyone nervous and irritable, and its greatest successes were either imported from other countries, or revivals of plays originally produced in previous seasons. Renée Jeanmaire and Juliette Greco each flourished in personal appearance concoctions made up of their own special brands of entertainment. American actress Betsy Blair scored with a performance in French of Mrs. Puffy-Picq in the revived *Tchin-Tchin.* But Françoise Sagan's *Les Violons Parfois* was poorly received, and Jean Anouilh was represented with three plays, none of which were up to the high standard he had set for himself. And there were no new plays by Genet, Ionesco, Beckett, or Sartre produced in Paris to raise even a mild breeze of controversy.

One of the most popular productions in Paris was, oddly enough, the Madeleine Renaud–Jean-Louis Barrault Company's production of *The Hostage,* with Pierre Blanchar as Monsewer, Arletty as Meg, and Mme. Renaud as Miss Gilchrist. Parisian audiences, fed up with the Algerian hostilities, seemed to relish this play's blaspheming about causes and faith and obviously found some resemblances between Behan's IRA and their own OAS. And perhaps the most delightful blasphemy of all was achieved when in the staid historic Odeon, the entire cast at one point suddenly broke out into "the twist."

On the following pages we have attempted to present highlights and brief factual information about the London and Paris Seasons. The outstanding performances and the outstanding plays are *not* listed in order of merit, nor do they include all that are deserving of mention. They represent a collaboration between the editor, who can see only a portion of the London and Paris Theatre, and London's most peripatetic drama critic, Ossia Trilling. For the theatre elsewhere in Europe and at the annual Festival des Nations, Mr. Trilling has obliged us with a short report of his own.

OUTSTANDING NEW ENGLISH PLAYS

Chips With Everything by Arnold Wesker. Set in a peacetime R.A.F. camp, it portrays the futile attempt of a General's conscripted son to identify himself with the morons and the underprivileged enlisted men against the superior pull of the Establishment as symbolized by the officers. With Frank Finlay, John Kelland.

The Private Ear and The Public Eye by Peter Shaffer. Two amusing one-act variations on the eternal triangle: (a) shy music-loving clerk loses dim-witted pick-up to superior technique of his pal (b) suspicious philandering husband almost loses his dim-witted wife to the eccentric private detective he has sent to spy on her. With Maggie Smith, Kenneth Williams.

Two Stars for Comfort by John Mortimer. A pessimistic picture of present-day youth and middle age as an aging country publican disburses illusions around him until his own come crashing down when his wife leaves him. With Trevor Howard, Isabel Dean.

Everything in the Garden by Giles Cooper (D). A middle-class suburban English husband is taught the hard way that life can be easier if his wife augments the family income with fees earned as a high-class call-girl. With Geraldine McEwan, Derek Godfrey.

Luther by John Osborne. A Brechtian treatment, with psychoanalytical overtones, that explores the motives for Luther's rift with the Vatican, the founding of the Protestant Church, and his betrayal of the Peasant Revolt. With Albert Finney.

August for the People by Nigel Dennis. A satire about the Establishment's relatively feeble though witty attempt to put the lower orders in their place. With Rex Harrison, Rachel Roberts.

The Keep by Gwyn Thomas (D). A mother-dominated Welsh family changes directions in midstream when they learn the truth about Mom and about each other, amid an effusion of Welsh humor. With Mervyn Johns.

The Knack by Ann Jellicoe. How to seduce a girl without really trying, as interpreted by an over-sexed, lower middle-class Midlands layabout, his willing but ineffectual pupil, their arty roommate, and the eager victim. With Rita Tushingham.

Play With a Tiger by Doris Lessing (D). A bohemian middle-aged lady novelist faces a hopeless situation with her younger American boy friend who has carelessly acquired the responsibilities of a pregnant American middle-class girl his own age. With Siobhan McKenna, Alex Viespi.

The Affair by Ronald Millar. Based on C. P. Snow's novel about the efforts of some of the faculty at Cambridge University to correct an injustice to a colleague they all dislike. With John Clements.

Nil Carborundum by Henry Livings. A comedy about an imaginary nuclear attack. With Nicol Williamson, James Booth.

(D)—Author's London debut as a playwright.

OUTSTANDING LONDON PERFORMANCES

John Gielgud as *Gayev* in THE CHERRY ORCHARD	Robert Stephens as *Peter* in THE KITCHEN	Christopher Plummer as *King Henry II* in BECKET
Wilfrid Lawson as *Luka* in THE LOWER DEPTHS	Vanessa Redgrave as *Rosalind* in AS YOU LIKE IT	Ralph Richardson as *Sir Peter Teazle* in THE SCHOOL FOR SCANDAL
John Clements as *Sir Lewis Eliot* in THE AFFAIR	Ruth Meyers as *Cassandra* in THE AGAMEMNON	Irene Handl as *Mrs. Puffin* in GOODNIGHT, MRS. PUFFIN
Siobhan McKenna as *Anna Freeman* in PLAY WITH A TIGER	Peter Ustinov as *Sam Old* in PHOTO FINISH	Margaret Rutherford as *Mrs. Candour* in THE SCHOOL FOR SCANDAL
Colin Blakely as *Schmitz* in THE FIRE RAISERS	Albert Finney as *Luther* in LUTHER	Hugh Griffith as *Azdak* in THE CAUCASIAN CHALK CIRCLE

OUTSTANDING DIRECTORS

John Dexter CHIPS WITH EVERY-THING	Peter Hall BECKET	William Gaskill THE CAUCASIAN CHALK CIRCLE

OUTSTANDING SCENE DESIGNERS

Jocelyn Herbert LUTHER	Sean Kenny BLITZ	Leslie Hurry BECKET

POPULAR ATTRACTIONS

BECKET by Jean Anouilh (translated by Lucienne Hill). With Christopher Plummer, Eric Porter, Ian Holm, Gwyn Ffrangcon-Davies. (264)
BLITZ by Lionel Bart. With Amelia Bayntun. (26+)
BOEING-BOEING by Marc Camoletti (adapted by Beverly Cross). (109+)
BONNE SOUPE by Felicien Marceau (translated by Kitty Black). With Coral Browne. (251+)
GOODNIGHT, MRS. PUFFIN by Arthur Lovegrove. With Irene Handl. (362+)
GUILTY PARTY by George Ross and Campbell Singer. (329+)
ONE FOR THE POT by Ray Cooney and Tony Hilton. With Brian Rix. (348+)
PHOTO FINISH by Peter Ustinov. With Peter Ustinov, Diana Wynyard, Paul Rogers. (42+)
STOP THE WORLD—I WANT TO GET OFF by Anthony Newley and Leslie Bricusse. With Anthony Newley, Anna Quayle. (315+)
Also THE AFFAIR; THE PRIVATE EAR and THE PUBLIC EYE; LUTHER.

INTERESTING LIMITED RUNS OF NEW BRITISH PLAYS

A WHISTLE IN THE DARK by Thomas Murphy (D). With Patrick Magee. (91)
BIG SOFT NELLIE by Henry Livings. With Roy Kinnear. (28)
MY PLACE by Elaine Dundy (D). With Diane Cilento, Barry Foster. (38)

OUTSTANDING NEW FRENCH PLAYS

La Fourmi dans le Corps (Ant in the Flesh) by Jacques Audiberti. A love story set in 1670 against the fantasticated background of squabbling nuns, proving that love will find a way through a chink to even the most obdurate heart. With Therese Marney.

Les Maxibules by Marcel Aymé. A middle-class-satire-cum-love story in which a man travels the world over in search of customers who will buy his "Maxibules" (invented word). With Jacques Dufilho.

Boulevard Durand by Armand Salacrou. A true documentary tragedy of a labor organizer framed for murder at the height of a strike. With Maurice Sarfati.

Mon Faust by Paul Valéry. Is the devil outmoded? Faust and Mephistopheles carry on their discussions in our scientific age. With Pierre Fresnay, Pierre Dux, Daniele Delorme.

Va Donc Chez Törpe (Go to Törpe's) by François Billetdoux. The guests in Ursula Törpe's inn have taken to committing suicide mysteriously. Is she to blame? A Police Inspector finds no final answer. With M. Billetdoux, Katherine Renn.

Les Pupitres (Music Stands) by Raymond Devos (D). A dream play about an orchestra conductor who fires his musicians for their indiscipline. The consequences of this act become immediately apparent in a series of scenes incorporating music, cross-talk, and surprise punch lines. With Raymond Devos, Michael Roux, Denise Benoit.

La Révélation by René-Jean Clot (D). A girl delinquent in a remand home claims to have seen a vision of the Virgin. The Mother Superior's incredulity provokes the girl's suicide, and the Mother's qualms of conscience. With Madeleine Renaud.

Naïves Hirondelles by Roland Dubillard (D). Four characters try in vain to leave one another. With Tania Balachova.

La Contessa by Maurice Druon (D). An aging Contessa relives her unusual life of easy virtue. With Elvire Popesco.

La Foire d'Empoigne (Animal Grab) by Jean Anouilh. A historical fantasy in which the French propensity for rapid change of governments satirizes both Napoleon and the current events. With Paul Meurisse. (Given on the same bill with L'Orchestre by Jean Anouilh. The latter deals with adultery and jealousy during a concert by a fifth-rate restaurant band, at once comic and bitter. With Adile Mallet.)

Les Cailloux (Pebbles) by Félicien Marceau. Several destinies cross in the sophisticated international society of Capri. With Michel Piccoli.

Un Certain Monsieur Blot by Robert Rocca, taken from the story by Pierre Daninos. Monsieur Blot becomes a celebrity and then returns to his modest life. With Michael Serrault, Francine Olivier.

(D)—Author's Paris debut as a playwright.

OUTSTANDING PARIS PERFORMANCES

Claudine Maugey as *Helen Keller* in THE MIRACLE WORKER

Loleh Bellon as *Judith* in JUDITH

Daniel Sorano as *Shylock* in THE MERCHANT OF VENICE

Katherine Renn as *Ursula Törpe* in GO TO TÖRPE'S

Laurent Terzieff as *Anton* in THE THOUGHT

Robert Hirsch as *Bouzin* in A THREAD IN THE PAW

Elvire Popesco as *La Sanziani* in THE CONTESSA

Georges Wilson as *Pat* in THE HOSTAGE

Jacques Dufilho as thirty characters in MAXIBULES

Pierre Dux as *Mephistophélès* in MY FAUST

Pierre Fresnay as *Faust* in MY FAUST

Michel Galabru as *Lunardo* in THE BORES

Jean Bouise as *Schweik* in SCHWEIK IN WORLD WAR II

Paul Meurisse as *Napoléon* and *Louis XVIII* in ANIMAL GRAB

Jacques Fabbri as *Sir John Falstaff* in THE MERRY WIVES OF WINDSOR

OUTSTANDING DIRECTORS

Edmond Tamiz THE SERVANT OF TWO MASTERS

Roger Planchon GEORGE DANDIN

Guy Lauzun THE MERRY WIVES OF WINDSOR

OUTSTANDING SCENE DESIGNERS

Jacques Le Marquet THE HOSTAGE

Jacques Noel SIMPLE-MINDED SWALLOWS

René Allio SCHWEIK IN WORLD WAR II

POPULAR ATTRACTIONS

UN ÔTAGE by Brendan Behan. With Georges Wilson, Arletty, Pierre Blanchar, Jean-Pierre Moulin, Madeleine Renaud.
UN FIL A LA PATTE by Georges Feydeau. With Jacques Charon, Robert Hirsch.
L'AVARE (THE MISER) by Molière. With Jean Vilar.
MARIE-OCTOBRE by Jacques Robert, Julien Duvivier, and Henri Jeanson. With Jandeline.
LA COQUINE (THE FIBBER) by André Roussin, adapted from a play by Diego Fabbri. With Jacqueline Gauthier, Jean Meyer, Jean Poiret.
HUIT FEMMES (EIGHT WOMEN) by Robert Thomas. With Claude Génia.
LA POLKA DES LAMPIONS (CHINESE LANTERN POLKA) by Marcel Achard. With Georges Guétary.
Also LES MAXIBULES; LES PUPITRES; LA FOIRE D'EMPOIGNE.

INTERESTING LIMITED RUNS OF NEW FRENCH PLAYS

CLAUDE DE LYON by Albert Husson. With Julien Berthau.
WILLIAM CONRAD by Pierre Boulle (D). With Marc Cassot.
LA CLOISON (THE PARTITION) by Jean Savy (D). With René Dupuy.

AMERICAN PLAYS PRODUCED IN LONDON

The American Dream with Mavis Villiers. (29)
The Andersonville Trial with Maurice Denham, William Sylvester. (67)
Bye Bye Birdie with Chita Rivera, Marty Wilde. (268)
Come Blow Your Horn with David Kossoff, Bob Monkhouse. (120+)
Critic's Choice with Ian Carmichael, Muriel Pavlow. (195)
The Death of Bessie Smith with Gene Anderson. (29)
Do Re Mi with Max Bygraves. (170)
The Fantasticks with Timothy Bateson, Stephanie Voss. (44)
Little Mary Sunshine with Patricia Routledge, Bernard Cribbins. (25+)
Look Homeward, Angel with Andrew Cruikshank, Mary Ellis. (46)
A Loss of Roses with Joan Miller. (14)
Oh Dad, Poor Dad, Mamma's Hung You in the Closet and I'm Feelin' So Sad with Stella Adler, Susan Burnet, Andrew Ray. (13)
Write Me a Murder with Fabia Drake, Kenneth Warren, Judith Stott. (75+)
A Thurber Carnival with Tom Ewell. (18)

Number of performances given in parentheses. + indicates that the play was still running as of May 31, 1962.

AMERICAN PLAYS PRODUCED IN PARIS

Miracle en Alabama (The Miracle Worker) with Françoise Spira, Claudine Maugey. (S)
Adieu Prudence (The Marriage-Go-Round) with Sophie Desmarets, Jean Chevrier. (S)
Spéciale Derniere (The Front Page) with Pierre Mondy, Philippe Nicaud. (S)
Moe et le Colonel (Jacobowsky and the Colonel) with Maurice Teynac.

THE SEASON ELSEWHERE ABROAD

By Ossia Trilling

IN a year's travel covering theatre on the Continent, the three plays that stick longest in the memory turn out all to have been performed in German-speaking theatres. The first was Samuel Beckett's *Happy Days* at the Studio Theatre of Berlin's Schiller Theatre. In the Schiller's Werkstatt, which was the first to introduce Edward Albee's early plays to the world, avant-gardism is taken for granted. It seemed the natural home for this study of the declining years in the personal and sexual relations of a couple. Bertha Drews's performance as Winnie was among the most penetrating in this actress's magnificent career, and the production by director Walter Henn was taut, meaningful, and full of humor.

The other two most memorable plays came not in Germany but in neighboring Switzerland, at Zurich's Schauspielhaus. Here is where the banner of the progressive and democratic German-speaking theatre was upheld through the dark Nazi years by the late Oskar Wälterlin and a team of brilliant theatrical artists including the present manager, Kurt Hirschfeld, the director, Leopold Lindberg, and the designer, Teo Otto. Here is where Thornton Wilder and Bertolt Brecht made their first impact on the European scene. And here is where two young and wholly unknown Swiss dramatists, Max Frisch and Friedrich Duerrenmatt, suddenly emerged to attract world attention, and this year sustained their already-established reputations with a new play apiece.

Mr. Frisch's latest drama is *Andorra* and it burst upon the European scene like a nuclear explosion. The play is the tragic study of antisemitism based on the proposition that for good or ill the Jews tend to see themselves as the Gentiles will have them see themselves. Andri, foster-child of a schoolteacher in the thinly disguised mythical mountain state of Andorra, a country threatened with invasion by its blackshirted neighbors, is presumed to be of Jewish parentage. When it turns out that Andri is not, the revelation is ironically unacceptable either to the good-natured Andorrans or to their vicious invaders. Frisch's most acute and technically devastating drama to date, it broke records in Zurich and was immediately taken up by a score of theatres in Germany and even in Israel. Among these Fritz Kortner's production in Berlin rated highest.

Mr. Duerrenmatt's newest work, *Die Physiker* (*The Nuclear Scientists*) was also compellingly staged with striking Teo Otto settings. It featured the incomparable Therese Giehse as the psychiatrist in charge of a private mental home, where three crazy eponymous physicists are interned. Their relation to one another provides a farcical tragedy that puts the author's earlier plays in the shade by its dramatic sobriety and incisiveness and symbolizes the universal dilemma threatening today's world.

This being Pirandello anniversary year, Italy came out in a rash of plays by the late Italian dramatist. Among the more important of these productions—which included Vittorio Gassman's *Tonight We Improvise,* acted by his recently formed Italian Popular Theatre company, and the Milan Piccolo Teatro's *Enrico IV,* directed by Italy's No. 1 director, Giorgio Strehler—Luigi Squarzina's handling of *Each in His Own Way* at the Turin City Theatre was the most fascinating. Only a shade less effective than *Six Characters in Search of an Author,* this ironical backstage drama in which illusion and reality become inextricably mixed, provides an oblique critique of the incipient fascist society and in many ways anticipates *La Dolce Vita.*

In his Theatre de la Cité in Villeurbanne, Roger Planchon, who has already made his mark as France's most vital young director, turned dramatist with his first original play, *La Remise* (*The Outhouse*). The play deals with the pauperization of the peasants of the Ardèche country after the first World War. Driven off the land and into the factories, and then when the crash comes denied work, they are forced into a life of violence and destruction. This new work, which is a landmark of writing, acting and production in the French theatre, presents a cruel and often extremely brutal picture of human wastage caused both by social conditions and the stubborn pride and narrow-mindedness of a dehumanized population.

Other memorable productions included the Royal Dramatic Theatre of Stockholm's revival of Strindberg's *The Ghost Sonata,* masterfully directed by Olof Molander; the Teatro Maria Guerrero of Madrid's presentation of Lope de Vega's little-known *La Bella Malmaridada,* for which the clever reconstitution by youthful director José Luis Alonso of a 16th Century Spanish inn courtyard won his production much kudos. Both of these went on to the annual festival at the Theatre des Nations in Paris, which opened with a distinguished production of Euripides' *The Phoenician Women* by the National Theatre of Greece, headed by Alexis Minotis and Katina Paxinou. Also arousing much interest at the festival was Moscow's Maly Theatre production of Axenov and Stabava's *The Colleagues* (or perhaps *The Buddies* would be a more appropriate translation), which appeared to be the first contemporary Soviet play to talk frankly about present-day dissidents of the younger generation.

Finally mention should be made of Gustav Gründgens' world premiere production of Lawrence Durrell's *Actis* at the Hamburg Schauspielhaus, verbose and halting, but finely staged; the Budapest Madach Theatre's modern-style *Hamlet* which finally parted company with the crippling naturalism of the "socialist-realist" trend; and Harry Buckwitz's monumental production at Frankfurt of Brecht's *Galileo* at a time when politicians were trying with partial success to have Brecht banned throughout Western Germany.

THEATRE DES NATIONS 1962 AWARDS *

ALL-ROUND PERFORMANCE	The National Dahomey Ensemble for SONG AND DANCE FROM DAHOMEY
ACTOR	Raoul Montenegro of Chile in EL PRESTAMISTA (THE MONEY-LENDER)
ACTRESS	Peggy Ashcroft of the United Kingdom in THE HOLLOW CROWN
DIRECTOR	Giorgio Strehler of Italy (Milan) for EL NOST MILAN (OUR MILAN)
SCENE DESIGNER	Kurt Halleger of Germany (Munich) for THE WALL
MUSICAL DIRECTOR	Lovro von Matacic of Germany (Frankfurt) for SALOME
MALE SINGER	Hans Wilbrink of Germany (Frankfurt) in THE PRINCE OF HOMBOURG
FEMALE SINGER	Maria Kouba of Germany (Frankfurt) in SALOME
CHOREOGRAPHER	Paul Taylor of the United States for THE PAUL TAYLOR DANCE COMPANY
FEMALE DANCER	Rosa Duran of Spain of the ZAMBRA BALLET
SPECIAL PRIZE	Greece for the National Theatre and the Art Theatre (Athens)
RESEARCH PRIZE	The Polish Pantomime Theatre (Wroclaw)

* Made by the Young Critics' and Theatrical Research Workers' Circle.

THE SEASON AROUND THE UNITED STATES

WASHINGTON

By Richard L. Coe
Drama Critic, Washington *Post*

Culture made loud noises along the Potomac, but actualities were unchanged. Bills were touted, but were ultimately ignored on Capitol Hill. The White House, of necessity, limited invitations to novel, widely-remarked East Room appearances by the American Shakespeare Festival Company and Fredric March. The State Department's theatrical exchange program found it had no money for more after sending Helen Hayes and company to Europe in three plays, though the department did relish the accompanying cheers. At last an experienced arm, Roger Stevens', guides the projected National Culture Center.

In its annual series, Catholic University's speech and drama department, now owning its own summer theatre at Olney, Md., achieved a notable original revue, *All Systems Are Go*. The Washington Theatre Club managed Equity performances with Anne Revere. Howard University presented a premiere, James Forsyth's *Defiant Island,* and Off Broadway's *The Premise* settled into the Shoreham Hotel.

Arena Stage continued as our major home-grown theatre, its new building the season's Event. Lounges and administration quarters are linked to the open acting space surrounded by 750 seats, the design of Harry Weese. Not the least thrilling aspect were the throngs of patrons, suggesting Arena's growing, sensibly-priced, pioneer status.

Artistically, this acting area reflects the freedom gained by breaking strictures of expensive proscenium staging—"stripping the onion," in Richard Southern's fitting phrase. Many seasons may be needed to realize its potentials, but the major fact is that *many* are assured. Producer Zelda Fichandler's choice of plays was individually creative if, in aggregate, it lacked the ideal philosophical variety. This was the first of three seasons under the Ford Foundation's acting grant.

Of the resident players, Melinda Dillon impressed everyone with an electric personality that varied little with her roles, and Stephen

Joyce displayed a gratifying clarity of speech and crispness of performance in a wide range of parts. Indeed the company included many outstanding actors who delighted the audience with their versatility in presenting such a remarkable number of different portraits.

Resident Arena Stage Acting Company: Harry Bergman, Marie Carroll, Kendall Clark, J. Robert Dietz, Melinda Dillon, David Hurst, Craig Jackson, Stephen Joyce, Jean LeBouvier, Alan Oppenheimer, Robert Prosky, Robert Quarry, Ray Reinhardt. The Arena Stage presented the following plays for 28 performances each during the 1961-62 season.

THE CAUCASIAN CHALK CIRCLE by John Holmstrom, based on Bertolt Brecht's drama. Oct. 31, 1961. Director Alan Schneider; new music by Teiji Ito; with David Hurst, Melinda Dillon.

THE AMERICAN DREAM by Edward Albee. With Stephen Joyce, Anne Chodoff. WHAT SHALL WE TELL CAROLINE? by John Mortimer. With Melinda Dillon, Robert Quarry. Nov. 28, 1961. Two one-act plays directed by Mr. Schneider.

THE MADWOMAN OF CHAILLOT by Jean Giraudoux, adapted by Maurice Valency. Dec. 26, 1961. Director F. Cowles Strickland; with Aline MacMahon, David Hurst.

THE MOON IN THE YELLOW RIVER by Denis Johnston. Jan. 23, 1962. Director Mr. Strickland; with Marie Carroll, Stephen Joyce.

MISALLIANCE by Bernard Shaw. Feb. 20, 1962. Director Warren Enters; with Robert Prosky, Shirley Cox.

THE BURNING OF THE LEPERS by Wallace Hamilton. Mar. 20, 1962. Director Mr. Schneider; with Stephen Joyce, Ray Reinhardt.

UNCLE VANYA by Anton Chekhov, trans. by Stark Young. Apr. 17, 1962. Director Mr. Schneider; with Nan Martin, David Hurst.

THE TIME OF YOUR LIFE by William Saroyan. May 15, 1962. (31 perfs.) Director Mr. Schneider; with Alan Oppenheimer, Melinda Dillon.

BOSTON

BY ELLIOT NORTON

Drama Critic, Boston *Record American* and *Sunday Advertiser*

Although Boston gets most of its theatre either in the form of Broadway tryouts or road productions, there is a fair amount of original creative work done here each year on a reasonably professional basis. During the 1961-62 season, the best of this work was done by the company at the Charles Playhouse, a 500-seat, three-quarters-round theatre made from a nightclub, at 76 Warrenton

Street. The Charles company, which began to operate six years ago in an upstairs room over a fish market on Charles Street, has passed through an initial phase of earnest amateurism to assume its place as the solidest and most satisfactory of our Off Broadway troupes. The quality of its productions is, however, still variable, ranging from good to not nearly good enough. While its most interesting production was Genet's *The Maids,* its finest performances were registered in Shaw's *You Never Can Tell.* In the latter, Jane Quigley made the new woman of 1896 seem comically haughty and at the appropriate moments outrageously romantic. And Norman Bowler's young dentist was easy, assured and entertaining in the Shavian spirit.

Earlier, at the Metropolitan Boston Arts Center, an organization called the American Festival had presented, during the summer, two new productions. Of these, *Anatol* was less enthusiastically received than was *Elizabeth the Queen,* a new production of the Maxwell Anderson drama.

The Poets' Theatre of Cambridge, an amateur group dedicated to the production of new scripts, carried on through this their twelfth season with reasonable success, ending with an ingenious production of three "plays" derived from the works of Robert Frost.

Also two new little theatre groups bid for recognition in Boston. The Image Theatre began its first semester in a coffee house on Huntington Avenue, and progressed from there to a basement coffee shop in the Copley Square Hotel, where its production of Anouilh's *Medea* caught some of the fire of this fascinating play.

The other little group, the Winter Theatre, began operating in South Boston and moved in May to a playhouse seating 48 people in an upstairs room at 68 Hudson Street, on the fringe of Chinatown. There it presented attractively a curious one-act play called *The Bespoke Overcoat,* by the Englishman Wolf Mankowitz.

Also of interest were two productions by the student actors of Boston University's Division of Theatre Arts. One, the American premiere of Christopher Fry's version of *The Lark,* proved more interesting but less theatrically effective than Lillian Hellman's American adaptation. The other, guest-director Lloyd Richards' production of the previously unplayed and longer first draft of Arthur Miller's *The Crucible,* seemed less political in its implications and in its final scene more dramatically forceful than did the Broadway version.

At Harvard, the Loeb Drama Center was used during the regular academic season for productions of the Dramatic Club and of various other student groups. During the summer of 1961, it served as the home of the Harvard Summer Players, composed of actors and actresses recruited from students and faculty enrolled in a special seasonal program of ancient and modern classics. This proved quite popular, and the group's production of Brecht's *Man Is Man* excited much attention.

CHARLES PLAYHOUSE

THE GREAT GOD BROWN (56)—By Eugene O'Neill. Oct. 11, 1961. Director Michael Murray.

THE CHAIRS by Eugene Ionesco and THE MAIDS by Jean Genet (32)—Nov. 29, 1961. Director Mr. Murray.

THE FANTASTICKS (63)—Musical with book and lyrics by Tom Jones; music by Harvey Schmidt. Dec. 27, 1961. Director William Francisco.

YOU NEVER CAN TELL (39)—By Bernard Shaw. Feb. 22, 1962. Director Mr. Murray.

UNCLE VANYA (31)—By Anton Chekhov. Mar. 28, 1962. Director Mr. Murray.

THE AUTUMN GARDEN (31)—By Lillian Hellman. Apr. 25, 1962. Director Mr. Murray.

BOSTON ARTS CENTER

ANATOL (24)—Musical based on Schnitzler's "The Affairs of Anatol"; with book and lyrics by Tom Jones; music based on melodies of Jacques Offenbach. July 31, 1961. Director Warren Enters; with Jean Pierre Aumont, Marisa Pavan, Jacques Aubuchon.

ELIZABETH THE QUEEN (20)—By Maxwell Anderson. Aug. 22, 1961. With Eva La Gallienne, Scott Forbes.

THE IMAGE THEATER

DEATH WATCH (35)—By Jean Genet; ESCURIAL (53)—By Michel de Ghelderode; THE LESSON (42)—By Eugene Ionesco; THE SANDBOX by Edward Albee and DEVIL'S DISCOURSE by Paul Jean Austin (33); MEDEA (34)—By Jean Anouilh.

THE POETS' THEATRE

THE TREE WITCH (4)—By Peter Viereck. Loeb Drama Center, June 1, 1961. Director Christine Denning; with Deborah R. Steinberg.

THE YELLOW LOVES (6)—By Howard Sackler. Loeb Drama Center, Feb. 1, 1962. Director George Serries.

THE JULES FEIFFER SHOW (1)—Revue, which included "Crawling Around." Sanders Theatre, Feb. 25, 1962. Director W. W. Hillier. There were two additional performances in March.

THE THEATRE OF ROBERT FROST (4)—Dramatic synthesis of the poet's "The Masque of Mercy" and "The Masque of Reason," plus several New England dialogue poems adapted to the stage. Kresge Little Theatre, May 30, 1962. Director Mr. Hillier.

POETS' WORKSHOP PRODUCTIONS

THE PORTABLE TIGER (3)—By Firman Houghton. Nov. 10, 1961.

THE CALM (3)—By Ted Hughes. Nov. 24, 1961. Director Laurence Channing.

FROM SWERVE OF SHORE TO BEND OF BAY (3)—By John Wolfson. Director June Judson.

THE JAR (3)—By Donald Finkel. Dec. 8, 1961. Director John Beck.

The Florestan Dimension (2)—By Gabriel Marcel. Dec. 13, 1961. Director Mr. Beck.

Devils and Angels (3)—By Richard Eberhart. Director Mr. Channing. The Mad Musician by Mr. Eberhart. Director Robert Stewart. Double bill which opened Mar. 30, 1962.

Lorna (2)—By W. W. Hillier. May 18, 1962. Director Ann Chittenden.

TEXAS

By Gynter Quill

Drama Critic, Waco *Herald-Tribune*

The season in Texas was characterized by even more than the usual amount of hammering, via production of new plays, which produced some sparks but few fires.

Houston's Alley Theatre, where Nina Vance has recently relied more upon sure contemporary fare, had its best season in years with a repertoire featuring three classics, which were well received—one of them spectacularly so—and a new script which was not. Its finest portrayal was Jeanette Clift's Ophelia, all the more tragic in her madness for her obedience to her father.

Dallas Theatre Center, whose director Paul Baker became best known for his unconventional staging of Shakespeare, had its most successful season with a program that included none of the classics but four new plays. Of the latter, Charles W. Ferguson's *Naked to Mine Enemies* was the most distinguished. The Texas season's most memorable performance, however, was given by Burl Ives in *Joshua Beene and God*. Mr. Ives was no stereotyped folk hero, but a man towering above his townspeople more because of his dedication and forceful personality than by his bulk and bombast. And Miriam Gulager was a delight as Little Mary Sunshine.

The University of Texas, whose distinguished Shakespearean director B. Iden Payne won the 1962 Rodgers and Hammerstein award for his many years of Shakespeare producing at Texas, uncovered a remarkable new actor in Robert Palmer, who played Falstaff in Mr. Payne's *The Merry Wives of Windsor*. But the University created more theatrical excitement with Francis Hodge's staging of *The Good Woman of Setzuan* and with the new *No Time for Heaven*, by its playwrighting instructor, E. P. Conkle. The latter was a folksy comedy set in 1835 Boston, and concerned a young girl determined to go to medical school and her grandmother's God-inspired efforts to make her marry a reforming preacher.

Continuing the new-found Brecht acceptance in Texas, Baylor

Theatre had its best fortune since Baker's *Hamlet* with *The Caucasian Chalk Circle,* but found more merriment than weight in the new *Dike 13, You're Leaking,* a wildly inventive modern satire on Madison Avenue by graduate Ronald Wilcox.

State Fair Musicals' fourth losing season was almost terminal. The Fair board absorbed part of the loss, touched underwriters for the balance (for the first time), and said that unless Dallasites pledged $100,000 for 1962, Musicals would fold. They didn't, but the board supplied the short $15,000 to give Tom Hughes a second term as managing director.

ALLEY THEATRE

THE WINSLOW BOY (35)—By Terence Rattigan. June 6, 1961. Director Joyce Randall; with George Anderson, Tom Toner.

PERIOD OF ADJUSTMENT (34)—By Tennessee Williams. July 12, 1961. Director John Wylie; with Jim Jeter, Bettye Fitzpatrick.

JOHN BROWN'S BODY (25)—By Stephen Vincent Benét. Aug. 15, 1961. Director Angela Wood; with Robert Donley, Angela Wood.

MISALLIANCE (28)—By Bernard Shaw. Oct. 17, 1961. Director Nina Vance; with Chris Wiggins, Jeanette Clift.

COME BACK, LITTLE SHEBA (27)—By William Inge. Nov. 15, 1961. Director Mr. Wylie; with Russell Gold, Virginia Payne.

VOLPONE (51)—By Ben Jonson. Dec. 13, 1961. Director Miss Vance; with Ronald Bishop.

A MAJORITY OF ONE (43)—By Leonard Spigelgass. Jan. 24, 1962. Director Miss Randall; with Russell Gold, Virginia Payne.

HAMLET (27)—By William Shakespeare. Mar. 7, 1962. Director Mr. Wylie; with Chris Wiggins, Jeanette Clift.

GARDEN SPOT, USA (13)—By George Garrett. World premiere Apr. 25, 1962. Director Miss Vance; with John Wylie, Jeanette Clift, William Trotman. The manifestations of evil which crop up when townspeople try to free their village from an invasion by vultures.

THE MIRACLE WORKER (27)—By William Gibson. May 16, 1962. Director Miss Vance; with Bella Jarrett, Joann Rose.

DALLAS THEATRE CENTER

LITTLE MARY SUNSHINE (43)—Musical with book, lyrics and music by Rick Besoyan. Oct. 19, 1961. Director Ivan Rider; with Miriam Gulager.

LET THE DOGS BARK (9)—By Sergio Vodanovic, trans. by Lysander Kemp. North American premiere Nov. 10, 1961. Director Pedro Mortheiru; with Ronald Wilcox, Mary Bozeman Raines. A Chilean drama about a minor politician caught up in graft.

JOSHUA BEENE AND GOD (22)—By Hal Lewis and Clifford Sage. Dec. 12, 1961. Director Paul Baker; with Burl Ives.

THE MADWOMAN OF CHAILLOT (26)—By Jean Giraudoux, adapted by Maurice Valency. Jan. 16, 1962. Director Angna Enters; with Mary Sue Fridge.

THE CROSSING (15)—By Howard Fast. World premiere Feb. 16, 1962. Director Mr. Baker; with Edmon Ryan, Randy Moore. Drama about Washington crossing the Delaware.

THE MOUSETRAP (10)—By Agatha Christie. Mar. 14, 1962. Director Kenneth Latimer; with David Martin, Robin Baker.

Naked to Mine Enemies (16)—By Charles W. Ferguson. World premiere May 17, 1962. Director Warren Hammack; with David Pursley. Series of episodes in the final years of the life of Cardinal Wolsey.

SAN FRANCISCO

By Paine Knickerbocker
Drama Critic, San Francisco *Chronicle*

One of San Francisco's three commercial theatres was demolished this year, but—like an understudy running in from the wings as a replacement—a bright and popular series of musicals was presented in-the-round in the elegant Garden Court of the Sheraton-Palace Hotel.

To provide another parking place, the Alcazar was also torn down, despite determined efforts by a citizens' committee to save it. Russell Lewis and Howard Young, who have been producing musicals in a tent for eleven summers in Sacramento, opened in January at the Sheraton-Palace with *Guys and Dolls,* starring Lloyd Bridges, and then followed up with *Take Me Along* (Dan Dailey); *Damn Yankees* (Joe E. Brown played the Devil); and *Can-Can* (Lilo). All were directed by Oliver Cliff, who also performed in the casts. The innovation was an immediate success, with the price of the dinner including the show, and no food service once the musical had started. These were not condensed versions, but full-length productions with an intermission.

The Actor's Workshop gave *Serjeant Musgrave's Dance* its American unveiling, but the local production was not quite ready and was not well received, playing at least forty minutes longer than it should opening night. The company also presented the world premiere of Mark Harris's *Friedman & Son,* a thin play that was only moderately successful. However, its revivals of established plays were all warmly acclaimed. Robert Symonds' performance as Falstaff in *King Henry IV, Part I* strengthened an excellent and vigorous production, and although most of the Workshop's presentations were this season dominated by males, Beatrice Manley contributed a brooding and effective portrayal as the smoldering wife in *Dance of Death,* which Mr. Symonds directed.

A. E. Hotchner's *A Short Happy Life,* fashioned from material by Ernest Hemingway and starring Rod Steiger, lasted only a few nights. In spite of the general excellence of the cast, which included Salome Jens, Kier Dullea, and Nan Martin, the trickiness of the staging splintered the mood of the piece, set within the framework of *The Snows of Kilimanjaro,* and emasculated the Hemingway man by placing him awkwardly in recollected situations.

Paul Gregory opened *The Captains and the Kings* and *Prescription for Murder,* the latter by William Link and Richard Levinson, and starring Thomas Mitchell, Agnes Moorehead, and Joseph Cotten. When the reviews were not ecstatic, Mr. Gregory vowed he would never again open in San Francisco.

In November, the Interplayers, a resident company, presented Wallace Hamilton's *The Burning of the Lepers,* an unusual melodrama about the conditions of lepers in 14th Century France. They later opened a small new theatre when the company was forced out of the Bella Union, the oldest theatre in the city which is now being prepared to show films. Irma Kay's Opera Ring continued with a busy repertory of musicals—three a week: *The Threepenny Opera, West Side Story,* and *Once Upon a Mattress.* The Playhouse presented *San Francisco's Burning,* an original musical by Helen and Pat Adam and Warner Jepson, and it was obviously the liveliest and most distinctive production of the season. It was obvious that musicals again proved durable fare, including a cabaret show of saucy wit by David Davenport, entitled *The Macaroni Show,* which was presented at the Old Spaghetti Cafe.

The following productions were presented by the Actor's Workshop during their 1961-1962 season.

SERJEANT MUSGRAVE'S DANCE (9)—By John Arden. Director Herbert Blau; with Tom Rosqui, Ray Fry, Norma Jean Wanvig, Robert Haswell. Anti-war parable set in 1860 England, in which some deserting soldiers try to impress some townspeople of the futility and cruelty of war by publicly unveiling the skeleton of a fellow-soldier from the town.

BECKET (22)—By Jean Anouilh. Director Robert W. Goldsby; with Mal Throne, Tom Rosqui, Jack Aranson, Robert Symonds, Elizabeth Keller.

FRIEDMAN & SON (9)—By Mark Harris. Director Jules Irving; with Donald Buka, Roger DeKoven, Wolfe Barzell, Mary Brauer, Edward O'Brien, Alan Mandell. Comedy about a stubborn father and his long-standing quarrel with his successful novelist son.

THE THREE SISTERS (25)—By Anton Chekhov. Director Robert Symonds; with Hal Burdick, Priscilla Pointer, Winifred Mann, Susan Darby.

DANCE OF DEATH (29)—By August Strindberg. Director Mr. Symonds; with Michael Granger, Beatrice Manley, Dean Goodman, Katie Porter.

HENRY IV, PART I (27)—By William Shakespeare. Director Mr. Irving; with Jack Aranson, Robert Phalen, Robert Symonds, Roger DeKoven.

WAITING FOR GODOT (?)—By Samuel Beckett. Director Mr. Blau; with Jules Irving, Edward Winter, Robert Symonds, Ray Fry, David Irving.

Note: For other plays produced around the United States, see page 346.

THE TEN BEST PLAYS

THE CARETAKER

A Play in Three Acts

BY HAROLD PINTER

[HAROLD PINTER *was born in London, October 10, 1930. He began his theatrical career as an actor in British and Irish repertory companies, and it was not until 1957 that he wrote his first short play "The Room." A longer play, "The Birthday Party," which deals in a Kafkaesque manner with a young concert pianist who finds a ruthlessly apathetic society crushing whatever originality and talent he may have had, was performed in London in 1958, and is scheduled for Broadway next season. He has also written a number of short plays for the theatre and television.*]

THE curtain rises on a junk-filled attic somewhere in London. In the center of the stage stands Mick, a young man in a leather jacket. He is looking up at a bucket suspended from the eaves to catch the occasional drop of water that leaks through the roof. Suddenly he hears the downstairs door open, followed by the sound of voices. Without panic he quietly slips out of the room. After a moment two men enter. The first, a slow-moving and neatly dressed young man named Aston, appears to be the inhabitant of this attic room. He is followed by Davies, an older man who is unshaven and dressed in tattered and ill-fitting clothes. He enters unsurely and is invited to sit down in a chair which Aston fishes out of the pile of newspapers, valises, bric-a-brac and secondhand furnishings that clog the room. Davies accepts, tipping his forehead with his forefingers in a routine gesture of thanks carrying no personal warmth in it. Aston offers him the makings of a cigarette which he disdainfully declines, but he condescends to accepting just enough cigarette tobacco to fill his pipe. With more bitterness towards his persecutors than gratitude to his rescuer, he recounts the incidents of the fracas from which Aston has saved him.

DAVIES—When he came at me tonight I told him. Didn't I? You heard me tell him, didn't you?

ASTON—I saw him have a go at you.

DAVIES—All them toe-rags, mate, got the manners of pigs. I might have been on the road a few years, but you can take it from me I'm clean. I keep myself up. That's why I left my wife. No more than a week after I married her, I took the lid off the saucepan, you know what was in it? A pile of her underclothing, unwashed. The pan for vegetables, it was. The vegetable pan! That's when I left her and I haven't seen her since. (*He pauses.*) This git comes up to me, parks a bucket of rubbish at me, tells me to take it out the back. It's not my job to take out the bucket! My job's cleaning the floor, clearing up the tables, doing a bit of washing-up, nothing to do with taking out buckets!

ASTON—Uh. (*He starts to fix an electric toaster.*)

DAVIES—I told him what to do with his bucket. Didn't I? (*Pause.*) If you hadn't come out and stopped that Scotch git I'd be inside the hospital by now. I'll get him. One night I'll get him. When I find myself around that direction.

Davies inquires about the house and discovers that the rest of it is closed up for renovation and repair, and that Aston, though not the owner of the house, is "in charge." When informed that there is a family of Indians next door, Davies is visibly upset and pounds his fist into the palm of his hand and exclaims spitefully, "Blacks!" A moment later he asks if Aston might have a spare pair of shoes he could let him have. Bitterly he tells of his futile quest for a free pair at a monastery down at Luton, as he tries on a pair of shoes Aston has managed to locate for him.

DAVIES—Not a bad pair of shoes. They're strong, all right. Yes. Not a bad shape of shoe. This leather's hardy, en't? You can't beat leather. Yes. Good shoe this.

ASTON—Good.

DAVIES (*waggles his feet*)—Don't fit though.

ASTON—Oh?

DAVIES—No. I got a very broad foot. These are too pointed, you see. They'd cripple me in a week. I mean, these one's I got on, they're no good but at least they're comfortable. (*He takes them off and gives them back.*) Thanks anyway, mister.

Aston promises to look out for another pair for him and suggests that Davies can share the room with him till he is able to get himself fixed up. Davies hesitatingly accepts but "just till he gets himself sorted out," and helps Aston remove the junk off the room's other bed. Aston informs him that there's a lavatory down the hall, and Davies wants to know if he has to share it with "them Blacks." Aston repeats that they live next door, but Davies seems skeptical: "They don't come in? Because, you know . . . I mean . . . fair's fair. . . ."

After Aston has made the bed he gives Davies a few shillings, which Davies takes to tide him over until he can get down to Sidcup and get his papers.

ASTON—What are they doing at Sidcup?

DAVIES—A man I know has got them. I left them with him . . . in the war. They prove who I am! I can't move without them papers. They tell you who I am. You see! I'm stuck without them.

ASTON—Why's that?

DAVIES—You see, what it is, you see. I changed my name! Years ago. I been going around under an assumed name! That's not my real name!

ASTON—What name you been going under?

DAVIES—Jenkins. Bernard Jenkins. That's my name. That's the name I'm known, anyway. But it's no good to me going on with that name. I got no rights. I got an insurance card here. Under the name of Jenkins. It's got four stamps on it. Four of them. But I can't go along with these. That's not my real name, they'd find out, they'd have me in the nick.

ASTON—What's your real name, then?

DAVIES—Davies. Mac Davies. That was before I changed my name.

ASTON—It looks as though you need to sort all that out.

DAVIES—I've been waiting for the weather to break.

Aston goes over to his own bed where he sits down and starts working with a screwdriver on an electric light plug. Meanwhile Davies takes off his coat and trousers to reveal his tattered long underwear. He gets into his bed and starts to go to sleep as the lights fade out.

SCENE II

It is the next morning. Davies is still asleep in his bed by the window, but Aston is up. When he coughs, Davies wakes up and Aston tells him that he was making noises in his sleep during the night. Davies seems insulted by this and says: "Maybe it were them Blacks next door making noises, coming up through the walls." When Davies discovers that Aston is about to go out to purchase a secondhand jig saw, which he "quite liked the look of" and which might come in handy, Davies offers to go out, too. Aston, however, astonishes him with his trustfulness when he tells him he doesn't have to and even gives him a set of keys to the house. Davies is still bothered about Aston's statement that he made noises in his sleep and suggests that maybe Aston dreamed it, or even made the noises himself and didn't know it. Aston says he doesn't dream and tells a little story.

ASTON—I was sitting in a café the other day. I happened to be sitting at the same table as this woman. Well, we started to . . . we started to pick up a bit of conversation. I don't know . . . about her holiday, it was, where she'd been. She'd been down to the south coast. I can't remember where though. Anyway, we were just sitting there, having this bit of a conversation . . . then suddenly she put her hand over mine . . . and she said, how would you like me to have a look at your body?

DAVIES—Get out of it.

ASTON (*slowly*)—Yes. To come out with it just like that, in the middle of this conversation. Struck me as a bit odd.

DAVIES—They've said the same thing to me.

ASTON—Have they?

DAVIES—Women? There's many a time they've come up to me . . . and asked me . . . more or less the same question. (ASTON *starts to leave.*) Eh, I was going to ask you, mister, what about this stove? I mean, do you think it's going to be letting out any . . . what do you think?

ASTON—It's not connected.

DAVIES—You see, the trouble is, it's right on top of my bed, you see? What I got to watch is nudging . . . one of them gas taps with my elbow when I get up, you get my meaning? (*He starts examining the stove.*)

ASTON—There's nothing to worry about.

DAVIES—Now look here, don't you worry about it. All I'll do, I'll keep an eye on these taps every now and again, like, you see. See, they're switched off. You leave it to me.

Aston goes out and Davies begins to rummage through everything in the apartment in what seems a compulsive effort to appease his insecurity and satisfy his curiosity about his illogically benevolent host. While he is doing this the door opens and Mick slips in unnoticed. Suddenly Mick grabs Davies from behind and forces him to the floor. Davies cries out. Mick puts a finger to his lips, and Davies watches him in a frightened silence as Mick tantalizes him by slowly examining the room and going scornfully through Davies' raggedy trousers. Finally Mick sits in the chair and, looking expressionlessly at Davies on the floor, asks: "What's the game?"

ACT II

The action begins exactly where it left off at the end of the first act. Mick cruelly interrogates Davies, alternately employing mock respect and brutal scorn. Suddenly he asks Davies: "How do you like my room?"

DAVIES—Your room?

MICK—Yes.

DAVIES (*slowly*)—This ain't your room. I don't know who you are. I ain't never seen you before.

MICK—You know, believe it or not, you've got a funny kind of resemblance to a bloke I once knew in Shoreditch. Actually he lived in Aldgate. I was staying with a cousin in Camden Town. This chap, he used to have a pitch in Finsbury Park, just by the bus depot. When I got to know him I found out he was brought up in Putney. That didn't make any difference to me. I know quite a few people who were born in Putney. Even if they weren't born in Putney they were born in Fulham. The only trouble was, he wasn't born in Putney, he was only brought up in Putney. It turned out he was born in the Caledonian Road, just before you get to the Nag's Head. His old mum was still living at the Angel. All the buses passed right by the door. She could get a 38, 581, 30 or 38A, take her down the Essex Road to Dalston Junction in next to no time. Well, of course, if she got the 30 he'd take her up Upper Street way, round by Highbury Corner and down to St. Paul's Church, but she'd get to Dalston Junction just the same in the end. I used to leave my bike in her garden on my way to work. Yes. It was a curious affair. Dead spit of you he was. Bit bigger round the nose but there was nothing in it. (*Pause.*) Did you sleep here last night?

DAVIES—I was brought here!

MICK—I'm afraid you're a born fibber. You're speaking to the owner. This is my room. You're standing in my house.

DAVIES—Now wait—

MICK—You're stinking the place out. You don't belong in a nice place like this. You got no business wandering about in an unfurnished flat. I could charge seven quid a week for this if I wanted. Get a taker tomorrow. Three hundred and fifty a year exclusive. No argument. I mean, if that sort of money's in your range don't be afraid to say so. Say the word and I'll have my solicitors draft you out a contract. Otherwise I've got the van outside, I can run you to the police station in five minutes, have you in for trespassing, loitering with intent, daylight robbery, filching, thieving and stinking the place out. What do you say? Unless you're really keen on a straightforward purchase. Of course, I'll get my brother to decorate it up for you first. I've got a brother who's a number one decorator. He'll decorate it up for you. If you want more space, there's four more rooms along the landing ready to go. Bathroom, living room, bedroom and nursery. You can have this as your study.

So what do you say? Eight hundred odd for this room or three thousand down for the whole upper storey. On the other hand, if you prefer to approach it in the long-term way I know an insurance firm in West Ham'll be pleased to handle the deal for you. No strings attached, open and above board, untarnished record: twenty per cent interest, fifty per cent deposit; down payments, back payments, family allowances, bonus schemes, remission of term for good behaviour, six months lease, yearly examination of the relevant archives, tea laid on, disposal of shares, benefit extension, compensation on cessation, comprehensive indemnity against Riot, Civil Commotion, Labour Disturbances, Storm, Tempest, Thunderbolt, Larceny or Cattle all subject to a daily check and double check. Of course we'd need a signed declaration from your personal medical attendant as assurance that you possess the requisite fitness to carry the can, won't we? Who do you bank with?

Davies can't answer, but is saved when Aston enters carrying a bag. Mick abruptly breaks off his persecution of Davies and sits down. Mick and Aston converse about the leak in the roof. Then Aston tells Davies: "I got your bag." As Davies takes the bag, Mick snatches it from him. Quickly Aston takes it from Mick and hands it back to Davies. Mick intercepts. Patiently Aston takes it from Mick again and is about to hand it to Davies when an idea occurs to him. Abruptly he hands the bag to Mick who is so surprised he hands it on with equal abruptness to Davies, and then leaves.

Davies—Who was that feller?
Aston—He's my brother.
Davies—He's a bit of a joker, en' he.
Aston—He's got a sense of humor.

DAVIES—Yes, you could tell that. (*Pause.*) I could tell the first time I saw him he had his own way of looking at things.

ASTON—I'm supposed to be doing the upper part of the house for him.

DAVIES—What . . . you mean . . . you mean it's his house?

ASTON—Yes. I'm supposed to be decorating this landing for him.

Aston tells Davies of the plans he has for decorating the flat and that he's always been good at doing things with his hands.

Davies discovers that the bag Aston brought him is not the one he left behind where he worked, and Aston tells him that someone had gone off with his bag so he had "picked up cheap" another bag with some clothes in it. Davies takes out some checked shirts which he rejects because what he needs is a "good solid shirt with stripes going up and down." However after he's tried on a velvet smoking jacket, which looks absurdly grand next to his worn out trousers, he decides he "wouldn't say no to this." Aston then offers him the job of being caretaker of the house and Davies keeps finding reasons for hesitating to accept it. He's never been a caretaker before. He'd need implements. It would be dangerous for him to answer the doorbell because it might be the Scotch git persuing him, or the government after him to explain the assumed name on his unemployment card. As he fumbles pathetically with these phobias, the lights fade out.

SCENE II

The room is only dimly lit by a little moonlight coming through the window. The door bangs and there is the sound of a key turning. Davies enters and tries the light switch. Nothing happens. He takes a box of matches out of his pocket and lights one. The match goes out and he drops the box. He stoops for it, but someone kicks it away from him. Davies takes out his knife, crying out: "Who's in here!" There is silence, and suddenly the electrolux begins to roar and whine, filling the room with an eery sound. Davies moans in terror. Suddenly the noise stops, and the lights go on to reveal Mick standing on the bed holding the electrolux plug near the light socket. He apologizes with mock sincerity.

MICK—I was just doing some spring cleaning. I'm sorry if I gave you a start. But I had you in mind too, you know. I mean, my brother's guest. We got to think of your comfort, en't we? Don't want the dust to get up your nose. How long you thinking of staying here, by the way? As a matter of fact, I was going to suggest that we'd lower your rent . . . until you get fixed up. (*Looks at* DAVIES' *knife.*) Still, if you're going to get spiky, I'll have to reconsider the whole proposition.

Davies gradually puts away the knife, saying that he doesn't mind a bit of a joke now and then, but that no one starts anything with him. Mick says he is very impressed with what Davies has said and offers him a sandwich. Then as Davies eats, Mick asks his advice about his brother.

MICK—His trouble is, he doesn't like to work.

DAVIES—Go on!

MICK—He's just shy of it. Very shy of it.

DAVIES—I know that sort.

MICK—You know that type?

DAVIES—I've met them.

MICK—Look! I got a proposition to make to you. I'm thinking of taking over the running of this place. I think it could be run a bit more efficiently. I got a lot of ideas, a lot of plans. How would you like to stay on here, as caretaker.

DAVIES—Well, I don't mind doing a bit of caretaking.

MICK—Of course, we'd come to a small financial agreement, mutually beneficial. There's only one thing. Can you give me any references? Just to satisfy my solicitor.

DAVIES—I got plenty of references. All I got to do is go down to Sidcup tomorrow. I got all the references I want down there. I was going down today, but I'm . . . I'm waiting for the weather to break. (*The lights fade out.*)

SCENE III

It is the next morning, and Aston, who is already dressed, wakes up Davies.

ASTON—You said you wanted me to get you up.

DAVIES—What for?

ASTON—You said you were thinking of going to Sidcup.

DAVIES—Ay, that'd be a good thing, if I got there.

ASTON—Doesn't look like much of a day.

DAVIES—Ay, well, that's shot it, en't it?

Davies complains that the draught from the window has been blowing in on his head, and asks if Aston couldn't keep it shut at nights. Aston refuses, saying that he's "got to have a bit of air."

Davies replies indignantly: "Don't tell me about air, boy! I've lived all my life in the air!"

Aston suggests that Davies might sleep the other way round in his bed. Davies considers the notion and decides he couldn't do that because he's gotten used to sleeping this way. "It isn't me that has to change," he says, "it's that window." Aston finally agrees to close the window for the time being. Davies, discouraged by the weather, crawls back into bed as Aston, who thinks he is still listening, tells him about a café nearby where he can get a cup of tea.

Aston—I used to go there quite a bit. Some of these men, from the café, we used to knock about together sometimes. And they used to listen, whenever I . . . had anything to say. The trouble was, I used to have kind of hallucinations . . . I used to get this feeling I could see things . . . very clearly . . . but maybe I was wrong. Anyway, someone must have said something. And . . . some kind of lie must have got around. Then one day they took me to a hospital, right outside of London. They . . . got me there. I didn't want to go. They asked me questions in there, all sorts of questions. Well, I told them . . . anyone who asked . . . what my thoughts were. Then one day . . . this man . . . doctor, I suppose . . . the head one . . . he was quite a man of . . . distinction . . . although I wasn't so sure about that. He called me in. He said . . . I had something, some complaint. He just said, "You've got . . . this thing. And we've decided . . . we're going to do something to your brain." He said, "If we don't, you'll be in here for the rest of your life, but if we do, you stand a chance. You can go out and live like the others." About a week later they started to come round and do this thing to the brain. In this ward I could see quite clearly what they did to the others.

They used to come round with these . . . big pincers, with wires on, attached to a little machine. They used to hold the man down, and this chief doctor used to fit the pincers on either side of the mans' skull. There was a man holding the machine, you see, and he'd . . . he'd do something . . . and the chief would just press these pincers on the skull and keep them there. Then he'd take them off. They'd cover the man up . . . and they wouldn't touch him till later on. Some used to put up a fight, but most of them just lay there. Well, they were coming round to me. I knew they had to get me on the bed because if they did it while I was standing up they might break my spine. So I stood up against the wall and then one or two of them came for me, well, I was much stronger than I am now, and I laid one of them out and I had the other one round the throat, and then suddenly this chief had these pincers on my skull and I knew he wasn't supposed to do it while I was standing up, that's why I . . .

Anyway, he did it. So I did get out of the place, but I couldn't walk very well. My thoughts . . . had become very slow . . . I couldn't think at all. I couldn't hear what people were saying. I couldn't look to the right or left, because if I turned my head around . . . I couldn't keep . . . upright. And I had these headaches. But I didn't die. I never had those hallucinations any more. And I never spoke to anyone anymore. The thing is, I should have been dead. I should have died. After a time I got a bit better, and I started to do things with my hands, and . . . I came here because my brother had got this house, and so I decided to have a go at decorating it . . . I started to collect wood, for my shed, and all these bits and pieces, that I thought might come in handy for the flat, or around the house, sometime. I feel much better now. But I don't talk to people now. I steer clear of places like that café. I don't talk to anyone . . . like that. I've often thought of going back and trying to find the man who did that to me. But I want to do something first. I want to build that shed out in the garden.

ACT III

Two weeks have elapsed. It is afternoon and Mick is lying on the floor, his head against a rolled-up carpet, looking up at the bucket hanging from the ceiling. Davies, dressed in his smoking jacket and smoking his pipe, is sitting in a chair. He is complaining about Aston, who is not present. First there is the bucket which might come down on his head. Then there is his uncommunicativeness. And finally there is the fact that Aston gives him no knife with which to cut his bread. When Mick reminds him that he has a knife, Davies explains that it's not a bread knife, and besides, since he picked it up somewhere, he doesn't know where it's been. Davies goes on to express his anxiety about the gas stove. "How do I know it's not connected?" he complains. "It's right next to my face, it might blow up." When this gets no sympathy from Mick, Davies switches to his other illogical phobia, the Blacks from next door. He claims that he's found that the bannisters and the lavatory were all dirty and black, from being used by the Blacks, but that Aston doesn't do anything about it. Davies suggests that he and Mick got "ideas for this place, we could get this place going."

Mick—Yes, you're quite right. I could turn this place into a penthouse. For instance . . . this room. This room you could have as the kitchen. I'd have . . . I'd have teal-blue, copper and parchment linoleum squares. I'd have those colors re-echoed in the walls. I'd offset the kitchen units with charcoal-grey worktops. We'd have a small wall cupboard, a large wall cupboard, a corner wall cupboard with revolving shelves. You wouldn't be short of cupboards. You could put the dining room across the landing, see? Yes. Venetian blinds, venetian blinds on the window, cork floor, cork tiles. You could have an off-white pile linen rug, a table in . . . in afromosia teak veneer, sideboard with matt black drawers, curved chairs with cushioned seats, armchairs in oatmeal tweed, beech frame settee with woven sea-grass seat, white-topped heat-resistant coffee table, white-tile surround. Yes . . . it wouldn't be a flat, it'd be a palace.

DAVIES—I'd say it would, man.

MICK—A palace.

DAVIES—Who would live there?

MICK—I would. My brother and me.

DAVIES—What about me?

MICK (*ignoring the question*)—All this junk here. You couldn't make a home out of this. There's no way you could arrange it.

Mick suggests to Davies that he have a talk with his brother about it, since they are friends. Davies denies this friendship and tells Mick he prefers a straightforward chap like him to a bloke with whom "you never know where you are." To prove this he registers another complaint about Aston.

DAVIES—I said to him, I said, look here, what about getting in a clock, so's I can tell what time it is. I mean, if you can't tell what time you're at you don't know where you are, you understand my meaning? What I got to do now, if I'm walking about outside, I got to get my eye on a clock, and keep the time in my head for when I come in. But that's no good, I mean, I'm not in here five minutes and I've forgotten it. I've forgotten what time it *was!* Look at it this way. If I don't feel well I have a bit of a lay down, then when I wake up, I don't know what time it is to go and have a cup of tea! It's not so bad when I'm coming in. I can see the clock on the corner, the moment I'm stepping into the house, but when I'm *in!* It's when I'm *in* . . . that I haven't the foggiest idea what time it is! No, what I need is a clock in here, in this room, and then I stand a bit of a chance. But he don't give me one.

Since Mick pretends to be sympathetic, Davies continues to attack Aston for waking him up in the middle of the night on the grounds that he is making noises. Sleep is essential, says Davies, but when he wakes up in the morning he's so worn out that he cannot see to his business, or get himself sorted out as he had planned. Furthermore, Aston goes without telling him where he is going or when he's coming back. Davies bends close to Mick and tells him: "What you want to do is to tell him . . . that *we* got ideas for this place, *we* could build it up, *we* could get it started. You see, I could decorate it for you, I could give you a hand in doing it . . . between us." Mick replies that maybe he will, but at this moment the downstairs door bangs. Mick rises quickly and slips out as Davies shouts helplessly after him: "Where are you going? This is him!"

Aston comes in carrying a pair of shoes he has picked up somewhere and offers them to Davies. Davies tries them on, but complains that they don't fit. However he says he is willing to wear them until he can get another pair of shoes. He asks Aston for the laces, and Aston says there aren't any.

DAVIES—Well now, look, that puts the tin lid on it, don't it? I mean, you couldn't keep these shoes on right without a pair of laces. The only way to keep a pair of shoes on, if you have got no laces, is to tighten the foot, see? (*He illustrates by holding the curled up fingers of his hands in a tense position and making a strained expression with his face.*) Walk about with a tight foot, see? Well, that's no good for the foot.

Aston goes to a small box by his bed and fishes out a pair of laces and hands them to Davies. Davies complains that they are brown and do not go with the shoes, which are black, but finally accepts them until he can get another pair, as he wants badly to get down to Sidcup tomorrow.

DAVIES—I've been offered a good job. Man't's offered it to me, he's . . . he's got plenty of ideas. He's got a bit of a future. But they want my papers, you see, they want my references. I'd have to get down to Sidcup before I could get hold of them. Trouble is, getting down there. The weather's dead against it. (ASTON *goes out quietly unnoticed by* DAVIES.) It's a hard road, I been down there before. Coming the other way, like. Last time I was there, it was . . . getting on a while back . . . the road was bad, the rain was coming down, luckily I didn't die there on the road, but I got here . . . I kept going all along . . . But all the same, I can't go on like this, what I got to do, I got to get back there, find this man. (*He turns and looks about the room.*) Christ! That bastard, he ain't even listening to me!

Scene II

The same night. Davies and Aston are in bed. Davies starts to groan. Aston sits up, gets out of bed and goes over to Davies and shakes him to wake him up.

Aston—You're making noises.

Davies—What do you expect me to do, stop breathing? I tell you, mate, I'm not surprised they took you in. Waking an old man up in the middle of the night, you must be off your nut! I've had just about enough with you mucking me about. I've seen better days than you have, man. Nobody ever got me inside one of them places, anyway. So don't you start mucking me about. Just you keep your place, that's all. Because I can tell you, your brother's got his eye on you. He knows all about you. I got a friend there, don't you worry about that. Treating me like dirt! Why'd you invite me in here in the first place if you was going to treat me like this? You got another think coming. They had you inside one of them places before, they can have you inside again. They can put them pincers on your head again, man! They can have them on again! Any time. All they got to do is get the word. They'd come here and pick you up and carry you in! They'd take one look at all this junk I got to sleep with, they'd know you were a creamer. You're half off! You can tell it by looking at you. Your brother's got his sights on you, man. He's got ideas for this place, he's going to set it up. And one thing you want to understand is I got as much rights as you have. (Aston *takes a step towards him and* Davies *takes his knife from his pocket.*) Don't come nothing with me, mate. I got this here. Don't come it with me. (*Pause as they stare at each other.*)

Aston (*quietly, controlling his anger*)—I . . . I think it's about time you found somewhere else. I dont' think we're hitting it off.

Davies suggests that it is not him but Aston who should go, that Mick has offered him the job of caretaker here. Aston is surprised and insecure at this news, and offers Davies a few shillings to help him get down to Sidcup. Davies scorns it and challenges Aston to "build your stinking shed first!" Aston is hurt and tells Davies: "You have no right to call that shed stinking. You stink." Davies becomes angrier and points his knife at Aston. Aston does not move and after a pause tells Davies to get his stuff and leave. Aston shoves Davies' belongings into his bag and hands it to him as Davies protests. Reluctantly he takes the bag and leaves saying: "You ain't heard the last of this. Now I know who I can trust."

Scene III

It is early evening. Mick is seated in the chair listening to Davies who is moving about as he talks to him. Mick pretends to be sympathetic when Davies tells him that Aston said he stank, and he becomes bolder and starts to flatter Mick by telling him that he told Aston: "Your brother'll be along, he's got sense, not like you." When Mick challenges this slur to his brother, Davies backtracks and says he doesn't take orders from Aston, but from Mick. Mick points out that Aston does live here, that he's "the sitting tenant," and that giving his brother notice is "a technical matter, depending upon whether you regard the room as furnished or unfurnished." Mick thinks a moment and decides that he's going ahead and give Davies the job of decorating the place, but adds that Davies had better be as good an interior decorator as he says he is.

Davies—What do you mean? I never been an interior decorator. I been too busy. Too many other things to do, you see. But I could always turn my hand to most things . . . give me a bit of time to pick it up.

Mick—I don't want you to pick it up. I want a first-class experienced interior decorator. I thought you were one.

Davies—Me? Now wait a minute—wait a minute—

Mick—You mean you wouldn't know how to fit teal-blue, copper and parchment linoleum and have those colors reflected in the walls?

Davies—I never said that! It was your brother who must have told you. He's nutty, he's half way gone, it was him that told you.

Mick—Did you call my brother nutty? That's a bit of an impertinent thing to say, isn't it? What a strange man you are. Ever since you came into this house there's been nothing but trouble. Every word you speak is open to any number of interpretations. Most of what you say is lies. You're violent, you're erratic, you're just completely unpredictable. You're nothing else but a wild animal, when you come down to it. You're a barbarian. And to put the old tin lid on it, you stink from arse-hole to breakfast time. It's all most regrettable but it looks as though I'm compelled to pay you off for your caretaking work. Here's half a dollar. (*He tosses a half-crown at* Davies' *feet.*)

Davies (*crushed*)—All right then . . . you do that . . . if that's what you want.

Mick (*picks up a china figure of Buddha and hurls it against the stove*)—THAT'S WHAT I WANT! Anyone would think this house was all I got to worry about. I've got my own business to build up. I've got to think about expanding . . . in all directions. My brother can worry about this house. He can do it up, he can decorate it, he can do what he likes with it. I'm not bothered.

DAVIES (*wretchedly*)—What about me?

Aston comes in. He and Mick exchange a faint smile and Mick goes out. Davies makes a fumbling excuse that he has just come back for his pipe. Aston starts to work with a screwdriver on the same electric light plug. Davies makes conversation with him about it and then asks him about the remarks he made earlier.

DAVIES—You didn't mean that did you, about me stinking, did you? (*Pause.*) Did you? Listen. I been thinking, why I made all them noises, it was the draught on me, so I been thinking, if you was to give me your bed, and you have my bed, I'll be out of the draught, see, I mean you don't mind a bit of wind, you need a bit of air, I can understand that, you being in that place that time with all them doctors and all they done, closed up. So I reckon that'd be the best way out of it, we swap beds, and then we could get down to what we was saying, I'd look after the place for you, not for your brother, I'll be your man, you just say the word. . . .

Aston refuses, explaining that his brother occasionally uses the other bed when he comes to visit. Davies frantically points out that he could also help Aston put up his shed. Aston again turns him down. Davies modifies his previous demands and asks to stay on sleeping in the same bed. Again Aston says no, and turns away from him. Davies begs: "Listen . . . if I . . . got down . . . if I was to . . . get my papers . . . would you . . . would you let . . . would you . . . if I got down . . . and got my . . . (*Long silence.*)

HOW TO SUCCEED IN BUSINESS WITHOUT REALLY TRYING

A Musical in Two Acts

BASED ON THE BOOK BY SHEPHERD MEAD

BOOK BY ABE BURROWS, JACK WEINSTOCK AND WILLIE GILBERT

MUSIC AND LYRICS BY FRANK LOESSER

[ABE BURROWS *was born in New York City on December 18, 1910. He is the co-author and director of four other musicals including "Guys and Dolls," and the author-director of two musicals and of one play with music.*

WILLIE GILBERT *was born in Cleveland, Ohio, on February 24, 1916 and* JACK WEINSTOCK, M.D., *in New York City on May 15, 1909. They had written "How to Succeed" as a straight comedy and were then persuaded to change it into a musical with Mr. Burrows as a collaborator. Previously Messrs. Gilbert and Weinstock had written comedy material for television and for one Broadway revue. They are presently at work on a new musical called "Hot Spot" with music by Mary Rodgers, which is scheduled for Broadway in the spring of 1963.*

SHEPHERD MEAD, *whose 1952 best-seller inspired a second success without really trying, was born April 26, 1914, in University City, Missouri, and he is currently writing an as yet untitled novel.*

FRANK LOESSER *was born in New York City on June 29, 1910. He has written the words and music of many popular songs including "Two Sleepy People," "Praise the Lord and Pass the Ammunition," and "I Don't Want to Walk Without You." Of the songs he has written for Broadway, perhaps his "Once in Love With Amy" from "Where's Charlie?" and his "Fugue for Tin Horns" and "Adelaide's Lament" from "Guys and Dolls" are the best remembered.*]

IN front of the World Wide Wicket Company office building, a scaffold descends. On it is a young man named J. Pierrepont Finch, who is working at a window with a squeegee in one hand, while in the other he holds a paperback edition of "How to Succeed in Business Without Really Trying." Over a loudspeaker we hear a voice speaking what Finch is reading.

BOOK VOICE—Dear Reader: Let us assume that you are young, healthy, clear-eyed and eager, anxious to rise quickly and easily to the top of the business world. You can!

FINCH—I can!

BOOK VOICE—If you have education and intelligence and ability, so much the better. But remember that thousands have reached the top without any of these qualities. Just have courage and memorize the simple rules in the chapters that follow.

FINCH (*stepping off scaffold onto side walk and singing as he reads from the book*)—

> *" 'How to apply for a job
> How to advance from the mail room
> How to dictate memorandums
> How to commute—in a three button suit
> With that weary executive smile.'
> This book is all that I need
> How to—How to—Succeed!"

SCENE II

The exterior of the building disappears to reveal a corridor inside, and Finch finds himself among various company employees. The Book Voice continues in its instructions: "Before applying for a job, make sure you have chosen the right company. It is essential that the company be big enough so that nobody knows exactly what anyone else is doing." Finch listens to the confused talk in the corridor and quickly reassures himself that this is "the right company." He removes his coveralls and turns to look for the personnel office. As he does he accidentally bumps into a preoccupied

*"How To": © Copyright 1961 by FRANK LOESSER. All Rights Throughout the Entire World Controlled by Frank Music Corp., 119 West 57th Street, New York 19, New York. Used by Permission.

well-dressed executive who turns out to be J. B. Biggley, president of the company. J.B. bawls him out and leaves Finch still looking for the personnel office. Rosemary Pilkington, a pretty secretary, is impressed with the fact that Finch is undaunted by his embarrassing encounter with J.B. and offers to help him through her friend Miss Smith, who works for the personnel manager, Mr. Bratt. Despite Finch's protests that the book doesn't say such help is necessary she goes off to find Smitty, and Finch starts to enter the personnel office. As he does, Mr. Bratt comes out.

BRATT—We're not hiring anyone today.
FINCH—Well, I was just speaking to Mr. Biggley. . . .
BRATT—J. B. Biggley himself? You were speaking to him?
FINCH—Yes, sir. I just bumped into him.
BRATT—Ah, is he a friend of yours?
FINCH (*hesitating in order to seem more modest*)—Sir, I don't think a man should trade on friendship to get a job.
BRATT—Very well put, young man. Well, if you step into my office, I think we can work something out.

Meanwhile Rosemary has found Smitty and is pleading with her to help Finch. While they are talking Bratt comes out patting Finch on the shoulder and telling him that it is nice to have him aboard. When Finch fumbles for a match to light the cigar Bratt has given him, Bratt lights it for him. He introduces Finch to Rosemary and Smitty.

BRATT—Mr. Finch will be starting out in the mail room. Glad you don't mind that, Finch.
FINCH—Sir, in a big pond like this, everyone must begin as a little fish.
SMITTY (*to* ROSEMARY)—Even a barracuda.

Bud Frump, who works in the mail room, but constantly uses the fact that he is the boss's nephew in the most obnoxious way, enters and is also introduced to Finch. Frump immediately warns him not to be ambitious and to remember who Frump is, because if he doesn't—

ROSEMARY—You'll go crying to your uncle.
BUD—I beg your pardon. I do *not* go crying to my uncle. If I feel that anything is wrong, I phone my mother. She phones Mrs. Biggley and Mrs. Biggley phones Mr. Biggley. That's the democratic way. (*He leaves haughtily.*)

Rosemary asks Finch if he has a girl, and Finch tells her that when a man wants to rise in the world of business he cannot afford an emotional involvement. She thinks that a very intelligent attitude. He leaves to fill out his personnel forms, as Rosemary dreams of a future in New Rochelle as the wife of her "darling tycoon." Smitty points out that Rosemary will be in New Rochelle alone while Finch will be staying late nights at the office in New York. Rosemary says that this is exactly how she has dreamed it and sings:

*"I'll be so happy to keep his dinner warm
While he goes onward and upward.
Happy to keep his dinner warm
'Til he comes wearily home from downtown.

"Oh, to be loved
By a man I respect,
To bask in the glow
Of his perfectly understandable neglect.

"Wearing the wifely uniform
While he goes onward and upward. . . ."

Scene III

It is morning a week later, and the secretaries are arriving in the outer office of the World Wide Wicket Company. Just as they are all seated to begin work, a man enters with a coffee machine and announces "Coffee break!" Everyone rushes to get in line for a cup of coffee. Bud Frump enters, goes to the head of the line, holds his cup under the spigot and discovers that there is no coffee. Everyone groans and Bud leads them in an hysterical lament.

Bud—

†If I can't take my coffee break,
My coffee break, my coffee break,
If I can't take my coffee break
Something within me dies.

SMITTY—

If I can't make three daily trips,
Where shining shrine benignly drips,
And taste cardboard between my lips
Something within me dies.

SMITTY *and* BUD—

Gone is the sense of enterprise.

SMITTY (*collapsing*)—

Somehow the soul no longer tries.

ALL—

Coffee or otherwise, coffee or otherwise,
Something inside of me . . . dies.

A girl enters carrying a fresh pot of coffee and almost everyone follows her off. Finch stumbles in carrying a basket of mail and reading his book. The Book Voice tells him that the mail room is a place out of which he must get as quickly as possible, and that he has an advantage over his rivals, not all of whom realize this important precept. At this moment Frump sees him carrying the executive mail and takes it from him in order to deliver it himself. Rosemary sympathizes with Finch and gives him the flower off her desk for his buttonhole. Just then Mr. Biggley's stern-looking secretary, Miss Jones, comes by. Tipped off by Rosemary as to her identity, Finch offers her his flower.

MISS JONES—You just want me to have this flower? You don't know who I am?

FINCH—That doesn't matter. What matters is that the flower seemed to cry out to be worn by you.

MISS JONES—Young man, I'm Miss Jones, Mr. Biggley's secretary.

FINCH—No, you can't be. I mean . . . that is . . . you just can't be.

MISS JONES—Why not?

FINCH—Well, from Bud Frump's description of you, I'd never have . . . I mean . . . you're not a frightening person. If it's not out of place for me to say so, Miss Jones, I think you're a very attractive person. No matter what Bud Frump says.

MISS JONES—What did you say your name was?

FINCH—Finch, ma'am. F-I-N-C-H.

MISS JONES—How is it I haven't seen you before?

FINCH—Oh, I'm not supposed to deliver the executive mail.

That's his job. Bud Frump. F-R-U-M-P. (MR. GATCH *comes by and* MISS JONES *introduces* FINCH *to him.*)

MISS JONES—Mr. Gatch would be a good man for you to know. His department is very important.

FINCH—Oh, I know all about Mr. Gatch. He's in charge of (*Rattling it off.*) Plans and Systems and Interdepartmental Evaluation. Also Pre-Promotional Promotion, Post-Administrative Research, and Multiple Development on a multi-level level.

Gatch is impressed, and there is mention of an unfilled opening in his department. After they've gone, Rosemary is upset about Finch giving her flower to Miss Jones, but reconciles herself with the thought that it was more important for Finch's future that he be nice to Miss Jones. In response to Smitty's query as to how she is doing, Rosemary says: "Oh, I don't know. He's . . . he's . . . Smitty what's the opposite of a sex maniac?" Smitty responds: "A business man."

SCENE IV

It is a little while later in the mail room. Bud Frump is seated at the counter telephoning his mother to get her to intercede for him about being appointed the new head of the mail room. He tells her he is next in line, but that he is worried about this new fellow, Finch. "He works hard," he tells his mother, "comes in on time, never goofs off, he's polite . . . you know, a real rat." The light goes out on Frump and picks up Biggley who is telling his wife that the head of the mail room must pick his own successor: "If I interfered that would be nepotism. Nepotism? That's when your nephew is a goddam fool." Mr. Biggley is so upset by his wife he is forced to calm his nerves by knitting.

Back in the mail room its present head, Mr. Twimble, is complimenting Finch on his "inborn sense of mailroomery," while Bud is looking daggers. The phone rings and it is Mr. Bratt who tells Twimble that he has been promoted to the shipping department and that "we want you to choose your successor on merit. On merit, alone." "That's not fair," yelps Bud, who senses defeat, and goes out to call his mother. Meanwhile Twimble shows Finch his quarter-of-a-century medal.

TWIMBLE—Yep, it's not easy to get a medal like this. It takes a combination of skill, diplomacy and bold caution.

FINCH—You play it safe?

TWIMBLE (*singing*)—

* I play it the company way
Wherever the company puts me
There I stay.

FINCH (*joins him*)—

But what is your point of—?

TWIMBLE—

I have no point of view.

FINCH—

Supposing the company thinks—?

TWIMBLE—

I think so too.

FINCH—

Your face is a company face,

TWIMBLE—

It smiles at executives,
Then goes back in place.

FINCH—

Your brain is a company brain,

TWIMBLE—

The company washed it
And now I can't complain.

FINCH—

The company magazine?

TWIMBLE—

Boy, what style! What punch!

FINCH—

The company restaurant?

TWIMBLE—

Every day, same lunch.

Twimble adds that the haddock sandwich is delicious—"early in the week." Bud returns followed by Bratt, who asks Twimble to name his successor. Twimble appoints Finch, but to the disgruntled Frump's astonishment, Finch turns it down in favor of Bud, who "is better qualified." Bratt telephones J.B. to explain to him the unexpected turn of events. When the newly promoted Frump goes off to phone his mother, Bratt thanks Finch for getting him off the spot with his boss. Timing it just right, Finch asks Twimble if he shouldn't take the mail to Mr. Gatch, and Bratt remembers the opening in Gatch's department for a junior executive.

BRATT—Your generosity and thoughtfulness may prove to have been a very good thing for you.

FINCH—By George, ethical behavior always pays.

Bud returns overjoyed with his new post and, standing with his hands at his sides in abject solemnity, he is joined by the office staff in singing a reprise of "The Company Way."

BUD—Come on everybody. It's a celebration. I want to invite all of you to have lunch on me. (*They applaud and start off.*)

BRATT—Boys and girls. (*They all stop.*) I have another announcement to make. Mr. Gatch is taking young Finch into his department as a junior executive. (*Everyone applauds and starts again to follow* BUD *off to lunch.*)

BUD (*shouting futilely to be heard*)—Wait a minute! Just a minute! That lunch is Dutch. In fact, it's cancelled. (*They all go off.*)

Rosemary congratulates Finch and sort of invites herself to lunch with him, but while she's getting her things Mr. Gatch comes in and invites Finch to lunch, because he can put him on his expense account. Naturally Finch accepts, standing up Rosemary who again sings of her love for Finch and that she'll still be "Happy to Keep His Dinner Warm."

SCENE V

While Mr. Biggley takes a firm stand about Bud Frump's circuitous complaints, a sudden crack of vulnerability appears in his character when he arranges to have Mr. Bratt hire a young lady whose father was . . . er . . . a classmate of J.B.'s at Old Ivy. Her name is Hedy La Rue. Miss La Rue turns up in the corridor of World Wide Wickets, where her bountiful figure and brassy poise excite all the male members of the office. Every executive asks Bratt to assign her to them, but he insists upon following procedure. He reminds them with a song.

BRATT—

* A secretary is not a toy,
No, my boy, not a toy,
To fondle and dandle
And playfully handle

* "A Secretary Is Not a Toy": © Copyright 1961 by FRANK LOESSER. All Rights Throughout the Entire World Controlled by Frank Music Corp., 119 West 57th Street, New York 19, New York. Used by Permission.

In search of some puerile joy.
No, a secretary is not
Definitely not, a toy.

All—

The secretary you've got
Is definitely not
Employed to do a gavotte,
. . . or you know what
Before you jump for joy,
Remember this, my boy,
A secretary is not
A Tinker Toy.

Scene VI

At the elevator landing Finch is standing inconspicuously on one side as Mr. Biggley and Miss Jones emerge. J.B. is giving her last minute instructions. He is planning to stay in town tonight as he has a golf date in the morning with Mr. Womper, the chairman of the board, and he will pick up his golf clubs at the office early next morning. J.B. is called back into the office to answer a phone call from his wife, which gives Finch a chance to pump Miss Jones about J.B.'s college affiliations. Rosemary and Smitty come along and Rosemary gives Finch an opening to ask her out for dinner. But he just stands waiting for the elevator. Smitty, Rosemary and Finch sing their separate thoughts:

Smitty—

*Now she's thinking—:

Rosemary—

I wonder if we take the same bus?

Smitty—

And he's thinking—:

Finch—

There could be quite a thing between us.

Smitty—

Now she's thinking—:

Rosemary—

He really is a dear.

Smitty—

And he's thinking—:

FINCH—

But what of my career?

SMITTY—

Then she says—:

ROSEMARY (*yawns*)—

SMITTY—

And he says—:

FINCH (*to make conversation*)—

Well it's been a long day.

ALL (*in accord*)—

Well it's been a long,
Been a long,
Been a long,
Been a long day.

By the end of the song Rosemary has persuaded Finch to take her to dinner and they go down in one elevator, and Smitty goes down in another. Biggley emerges again and this time encounters Bud Frump. Hedy La Rue enters and Bud overhears her exchanging intimacies with J.B. as he goes off to the mail room. In a moment he returns and Biggley notices that Bud is dressed exactly the same as he is. This infuriates J.B.

BIGGLEY (*going over to* BUD)—Why don't you go home?

BUD—I'm waiting for the elevator.

BIGGLEY—Why don't you walk down?

BUD—It's thirty floors. (*Puts on gloves.*) Very attractive girl, Miss La Rue.

BIGGLEY (*nervously*)—I was just, uh, trying to make her feel at home.

BUD—Yes. Well you go right ahead, J.B. *I'm meeting Mother for dinner.* (BUD, BIGGLEY *and* HEDY *sing their version of "Been a Long Day."*)

BUD—

* Now he's thinking—:

BIGGLEY—

The kid could really put me through Hell.

BUD—

And she's thinking—:

HEDY—

The kid could even name the hotel.

BUD—

And he says—:

BIGGLEY—

It's a holdup!

BUD—

And she says—:

HEDY (*to elevator operator*)—

Down?

BIGGLEY (*spoken; to* BUD)—

Wait a minute! Okay, you're promoted.

ALL (*each for his own reason*)—

Well, it's been a long,
Been a long,
Been a long,
Been a long day.

SCENE VII

It is Saturday morning. Two scrubwomen have just finished cleaning the outer office. They disappear into the executive suite as Finch rushes in from outside with an attaché case. He opens it and takes out papers which he strews around on top of the desk and on the floor around it. He takes out four empty coffee containers and puts them on the desk. He empties a paper bag full of cigarette butts into the ashtray. He loosens his tie, rumples his hair and collapses on the desk as if sound asleep. Biggley enters dressed for golf, and is impressed to find that Finch has been working all night. He is about to go into his office to get his clubs when he hears Finch humming. He stops and asks "What's that you're humming?"

FINCH—I didn't realize I was humming, sir.

BIGGLEY—You were humming the Old Ivy fight song.

FINCH—I guess it was unconscious on my part.

BIGGLEY—Did you go there? Were you a Groundhog?

FINCH (*hesitantly*)—Well, sir . . .

BIGGLEY—Say it, boy! Come out with it. You're not ashamed of Old Ivy, are you?

FINCH—No, sir, not a bit.

BIGGLEY—That's the Groundhog spirit. I should have known you were Old Ivy. What year? (FINCH, *lost in thought, makes a football forward pass motion.*) Finch, when did you graduate?

FINCH—Oh, I'm sorry, sir. I was thinking of the big game today. We're playing the Chipmunks.

Virginia Martin, Rudy Vallee, Robert Morse and Bonnie Scott in "How to Succeed in Business Without Really Trying."

BIGGLEY—That's right. I hope those damned Chipmunks don't give us too much trouble.

FINCH—Well, even though we're not there in person, we'll be rooting for 'em. Right?

BIGGLEY—Right. (*He begins to march and sing:*)

*"Stand Old Ivy,
Stand firm and strong.
Grand Old Ivy
Hear the cheering throng.

(FINCH *joins him.*)

"Stand Old Ivy,
And never yield
Rrrrip! Rip! Rip the chipmunk
Off the field!"

Mr. Biggley goes in to get his golf clubs, and when he comes back out he finds Finch *knitting*. He is pleasantly surprised and they compare notes. He then asks Finch what his ambition is in this company. Finch replies: "Something solid . . . the advertising department." Mr. Biggley says he wouldn't want that for an old schoolmate, that it is too insecure, that he has fired fifteen advertising managers in the past year alone.

FINCH—But if you got a man with ideas, he could swing it.

BIGGLEY—Ideas! That's what I look for. I keep hiring men who are supposed to have brilliant ideas, and not one of them will ever do what I tell him.

With the advice to stay in his present department and J.B.'s promise to keep an eye on him, Finch marches off beside J.B. singing "Grand Old Ivy." The two scrubwomen overhear the song. One asks: "What college song was that?" The other looks at the knitting that Finch has left behind and replies: "I'd say Vassar."

SCENE VIII

Finch's strategy is working. Mr. Biggley has telephoned Mr. Bratt about Finch. J.B. tells him: "The poor devil worked here all week-end. The lad needs help. First of all, I want him to have an office of his own." The next day Finch shows Rosemary his new office, and they discuss their date the other night. Finch answers Rosemary's complaint that he didn't do anything romantic on their date with the simple, untroubled, logical "I had to get up early." Hedy La Rue comes in and explains that a secretary was ordered to be assigned to Finch, and that she is his "assignation." Rosemary leaves and Finch consults his book for advice on this new complication.

Book Voice—Choosing a secretary can be fraught with peril. Take a good look at the young lady who has been assigned to you. If she is so attractive that you feel things are too good to be true, be very careful. It may be that one of the big men in the company is *Interested-In-Her-Career.* There is a simple test for this. Check on her secretarial skill. The smaller her abilities, the bigger her protector.

Finch tries Hedy on dictation and finds she can only take it slowly in longhand and that her typing speed is twelve words a minute. Hedy then reveals that Mr. Biggley got her her job. Finch comes to an immediate decision. Handing Hedy a folder he tells her to take it to Mr. Gatch. "He's my boss," says Finch. "Make sure you give it to Mr. Gatch himself. (*She starts to go.*) Hedy (*She stops.*) . . . *personally.*"

Hedy follows instructions and Mr. Gatch immediately obliges by dating her. "You're in the big time now. Don't fool around with small fry," says Mr. Gatch, unaware that her boy friend is J.B. After a blackout to indicate the passage of a few days, the lights come up on Gatch's office, but now sitting at the Department Head's desk is J. Pierrepont Finch. On the telephone Finch is explaining: "I'm running Plans and Systems now. Huh? Mr. Gatch? Oh, he's been transferred to one of our out-of-town offices . . . Venezuela.

Scene IX

A few days later the company announces the appointment of a new advertising manager named Benjamin Burton Daniel Ovington, and are having a reception for B.B.D.O. to which all the executive secretaries are invited. This includes Rosemary, who has been made secretary to B.B.D.O. himself, and for the occasion she has bought a new dress with which she hopes to dazzle her Ponty. She hugs the box containing it and sings to Smitty.

* "I slipped out this afternoon
And bought some love insurance,

A most exclusive dress from gay Paree,
It's sleek and chic and magnifique
With sex beyond endurance.
It's me!
It's me!
It's absolutely me!

"Suddenly he will see me,
And suddenly he'll go dreamy
And blame it all
On his own masculine whim.
Never knowing that
This irresistible Paris original,
So temptingly tight
I'm wearing tonight
Specially for him,
For him.
For him."

Smitty, who is considering boosting her popularity by spreading a rumor that she is a nymphomaniac, decides that maybe she'll get a new dress, too. A few hours later, as the party is about to begin, Rosemary enters still singing about and wearing her cherished "Paris Original." Another girl appears wearing exactly the same dress.

ROSEMARY (*notices her double and sings:*)—
* Some irresponsible dress manufacturer
Just didn't play fair
I'm one of a pair.

SMITTY (*enters in same dress and sings her version*)—
This irresistible Paris original
Tres sexy—n'est-ce pas?

(*Suddenly she spots the other girls in the same dresses.*)
Goddamit—voila!

(*More girls enter in identical dresses.*)

ALL—
Oh! Thirty-nine bucks I hand out,
For something to make me stand out
And suddenly I've gone
Into mimeograph.

MISS JONES (*ruefully*)—
Some laugh!

Mr. Biggley introduces Ovington who tells everyone that his theory of advertising is to "shove it down their throats with a soft sell." Meanwhile Hedy has had one too many Martinis and J.B. has commissioned Bud to take her down to his office and sober her up. Hedy insists upon taking a shower in J.B.'s private shower, and tells Bud that he is cute, but not as cute as Finch. Suddenly Bud gets an idea. He sends someone to tell Finch that he wants to see him down in J.B.'s office. Bud begins to hum and dance in glee at his evil machinations.

BUD—De da da dum, la da de de . . . Old sexy Hedy is in there, taking a shower (*Dances.*) . . . And I've got a little something up my sleeve . . . Ole! (*Dances some more.*) That's going to put old Finchy right out on his . . . (*Kicks floor with heel Spanish-style.*)

He stops dancing when he sees Finch coming. He tells Finch to wait in J.B.'s office, that J.B. will be down in a minute to talk to him about something important. Finch waits dreamily in the sumptuous surroundings. Soon Hedy emerges from her shower, and Ponty tries to excuse himself and go back to the party. Hedy, however, orders him to kiss her with the threat that if he doesn't she will tell J.B. he did. Finch complies and collapses under the effect of the kiss. He rises with the sudden realization that he is in love, not with Hedy, but with Rosemary, and sings of his feelings.

* "Suddenly there is music
In the sound of your name.
Rosemary!
(*He dances around in search of her face.*)
'Rosemary' was the melody locked inside me
'Til at last out it came.
Rosemary!
Rosemary!

"Just imagine if we kissed.
What a crescendo!
Not to be missed."

Rosemary, suspicious that Ponty and Hedy are up to something, enters to find Ponty in a trancelike ecstasy. "Can't you hear it?"

he asks her. She says she can't and wants to know if Ponty's lost his mind. Finch responds by asking Rosemary to marry him, and Rosemary says she hears the music now. Finch joins her in singing "Rosemary" and they kiss. Their bliss is interrupted by Hedy, who appears in a bath towel, and by Rosemary's new awareness that Ponty is wearing two shades of lipstick. Rosemary is furious and walks out, but changes her mind when she sees J.B. approaching. She rushes back and orders Hedy to return to the shower.

HEDY—I have nothing to hide.

ROSEMARY—Yes you have, and keep it hidden. (HEDY *leaves and* ROSEMARY *rushes over and grabs* FINCH.) You snake. Kiss me. (*They kiss as* BUD *and* J.B. *enter.* J.B. *is surprised to find* FINCH *kissing* ROSEMARY *instead of* HEDY.)

BIGGLEY—I'm sorry, Finch. I owe you an apology. However, I want you to know I still do not approve of what you were doing when I walked in. I do not care for anything like that between executives and their secretaries.

FINCH—But Miss Pilkington is not my secretary.

BIGGLEY—Oh, yes. Good point. (OVINGTON *comes in and* J.B. *introduces him to* FINCH.)

FINCH—Mr. Ovington, I've read a lot about you in *Fortune* magazine. Some wonderful stuff.

OVINGTON—Thank you.

FINCH—By the way, Mr. Biggley, did you know that Mr. Ovington was an All-American halfback at college?

BIGGLEY—Is that so? Where did you play, Ovington?

OVINGTON—The greatest little college in the world—Northern State.

BIGGLEY (*exchanging a shocked glance with* FINCH)—A Chipmunk!

OVINGTON—I sure am a Chipmunk. Did you see the way we murdered the Groundhogs last Saturday?

BIGGLEY—Ovington, I'm not a bigot. I've hired men from all colleges—Tigers, Bulldogs, Trojans, Gophers, Badgers—but never a Chipmunk! (*Hands* OVINGTON *a pen and a resignation form.*) Your resignation is accepted. (OVINGTON *signs as* J.B. *and* FINCH *sing "Rip! Rip! Rip the Chipmunk off the field."*)

Bratt asks what J.B. is going to do for a new advertising manager, and Biggley decides on Finch as the new vice president in charge of advertising. Bratt hesitantly questions J.B.'s decision, but J.B.'s answer of "I like him" settles the matter. J.B. tells Bratt that

Finch is loaded with great ideas. Bratt asks Finch to tell them some, and Finch is embarrassed, but finally explains he'd like to give them a clear-cut campaign. Bratt suggests that the Plans Board Meeting the day after tomorrow would be an appropriate time and place.

BIGGLEY—Better get going, Finch. You're vice president in full charge of advertising and, frankly, up to now I'm pretty dissatisfied with your work. (J.B. *and* BRATT *leave.*)

FINCH (*going to desk and picking up phone*)—Hello, get me the stationery shop downstairs. Hello, this is Mr. Finch. Remember those cards I spoke to you about last week? Go ahead and print them right away.

Rosemary and Hedy come out of the shower room and Hedy offers to be his new secretary. Finch says he'd love that but that Rosemary is going to be his secretary. Rosemary refuses, but Finch convinces her that he needs her and she gives in.

FINCH—Wonderful. Now let's get to work.

ROSEMARY—Just like that? Haven't you forgotten something?

FINCH—Oh, yeah. (*Goes to phone.*) Hello, operator. Who paints names on office doors?

ROSEMARY—Finch, aren't you going to kiss me?

FINCH—Kiss you? I can't.

ROSEMARY—Why not?

FINCH—You're my secretary. Wait a minute, Rosemary. (*Into phone.*) Hello, name painter? (BUD *enters just in time to overhear the conversation.*) This is Mr. Finch. I want my name on my door in gold leaf. (BUD *collapses holding onto door, as the three of them sing, simultaneously.*)

FINCH (*spoken into phone*)—	ROSEMARY (*singing*)—
* J. Pierrepont Finch	Suddenly there is music
J. Pierrepont	
All capitals!	In the sound of my name
Yes, block letters	
(*Sings.*)	
Jay Pierrepont	Rosemary
(*All sing.*)	

FINCH (*proudly*)—	ROSEMARY (*dismayed*)—	BUD (*shattered*)—
Vice president	Rosemary	
In charge of	All of my lifetime	Vice president
advertising	Program will be more	There must be a
F-I-N-C-H	Of the same	Way to stop him
The usual spelling	Remember me	There must be
There is	There is	
Wonderful music	Wonderful music	
In the very sound	In the very sound	I will return!
Of your name	Of your name	I will return!

ACT II

The office is buzzing with gossip about today's big meeting at which the new vice president in charge of advertising is scheduled to present his plans and ideas. To make matters worse Rosemary, who cannot stand being treated impersonally by Ponty, has resigned. Smitty pleads with her to reconsider and points out that Ponty did say he wanted to marry Rosemary. Smitty and the girls are upset and remonstrate with her, saying that it is her duty to be loyal, not to Ponty, but to them. She is their Cinderella and she should behave accordingly.

SMITTY (*singing*)—

* How often does a Cinderella
Get a crack at the prince?
You're a real live fairy tale,
A symbol divine,
So if not for your own sake
Please, darling, for mine,
Don't turn down the prince.

ALL—

We were raised on you, darling
And we've loved you ever since.
Don't louse up our favorite fairy tale
Don't, Cinderella,
Don't! Don't turn down the prince.

ROSEMARY (*spoken*)—

All right, I'll give him one more chance.

Photo by LIFE photographer Leonard McCombe, ©. 1962. TIME, Inc.

Margaret Leighton and Alan Webb in "The Night of the Iguana"

CHARLES NELSON REILLY
as Bud Frump

ROBERT MORSE
as Finch
in "How to Succeed"

COLLEEN DEWHURST
as Phoebe Flaherty in
"Great Day in the Morning"

FREDRIC MARCH
as The Angel in
"Gideon"

MARGARET LEIGHTON
as Hannah Jelkes in
"The Night of the Iguana"

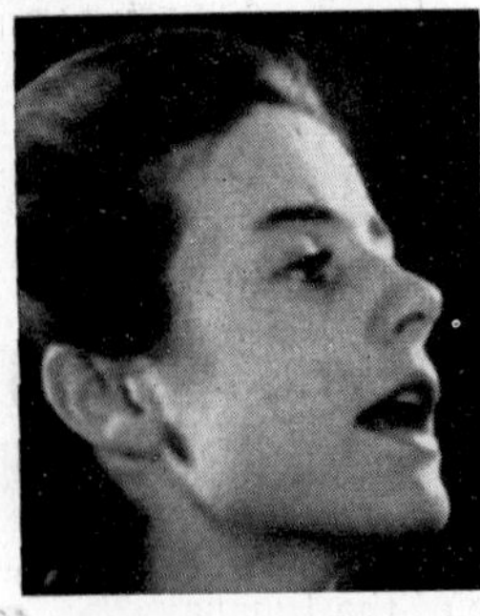

PATTY DUKE
as Deirdre Striden in
"Isle of Children"

RALPH WILLIAMS
as Bobby Kraweig in
"Look: We've Come Through"

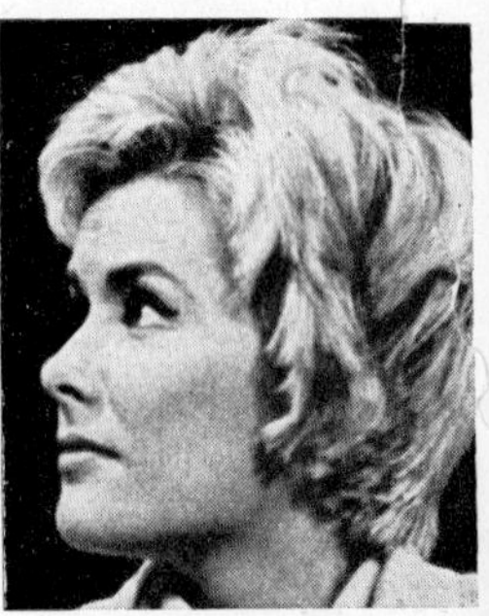

SALLY ANN HOWES
as Eve in
"Kwamina"

PERFORMANCES 1961-1962

DONALD PLEASENCE
as Davies in
"The Caretaker"

PAUL SCOFIELD
as Sir Thomas More

GEORGE ROSE
as The Common Man

in "A Man for All Seasons"

BARBARA HARRIS
as Rosalie in
"Oh Dad, Poor Dad"

PHILIP BOSCO
as Hawkshaw in
"The Ticket-of-Leave Man"

ZERO MOSTEL
as Pseudolus in
"A Funny Thing Happened
on the Way to the Forum"

DIAHANN CARROLL
as Barbara Woodruff

NOELLE ADAM
as Jeanette Valmy

in "No Strings"

Photo by Werner J. Kuhn

Molly Picon and chorus in the "Independence Day Hora" number from "Milk and Honey"

Roger C. Carmel, Ci Herzog, Beah Richards, Ruby Dee, Ossie Davis, Alan Alda, Sorrell Booke and Godfrey M. Cambridge in "Purlie Victorious"

Photo by Friedman-Abeles

Photo by Friedman-Abeles

Charles Nelson Reilly (second from left), Robert Morse (center) and executives in "How to Succeed in Business Without Really Trying"

Photo by Sheldon Secunda

Jason Robards, Jr. and Sandy Dennis in "A Thousand Clowns"

Photo by Friedman-Abeles

Julie Harris and Walter Matthau in "A Shot in the Dark"

By permission of Barry Hyams

Two views of Motley's stage setting for "A Man for All Seasons"

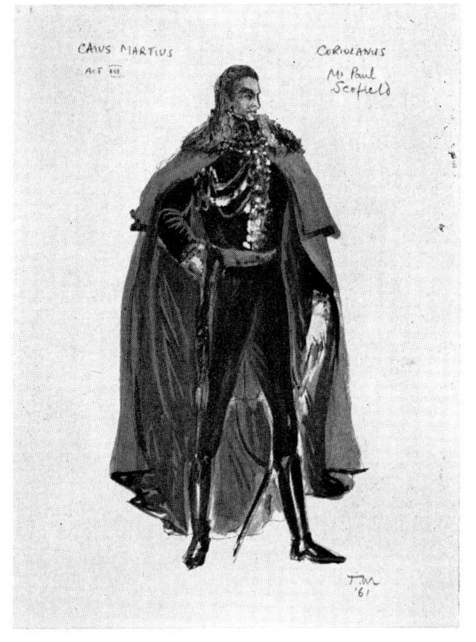

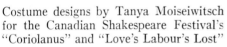

Costume designs by Tanya Moiseiwitsch for the Canadian Shakespeare Festival's "Coriolanus" and "Love's Labour's Lost"

Costume designs by Theoni V. Aldredge for the New York Shakespeare Festival's "Much Ado About Nothing"

Set design by Rouben Ter-Arutunian for "A Passage to India"

Oliver Smith's set design for "The Night of the Iguana"

Set design by Ben Edwards for "The Aspern Papers"

By permission of Houston Rogers

Franco Zeffirelli's set for the Old Vic's "Romeo and Juliet"

Photo by Friedman-Abeles

One of David Hays's stage settings for "No Strings"

Costume design by Lucinda Ballard for "The Gay Life"

Costume design by Donald Brooks for "No Strings"

Photo by Graphic House, Inc.

Art Carney and Elizabeth Ashley
in "Take Her, She's Mine"

Photo by Friedman-Abeles

Barbra Streisand in "I Can Get It for You Wholesale"

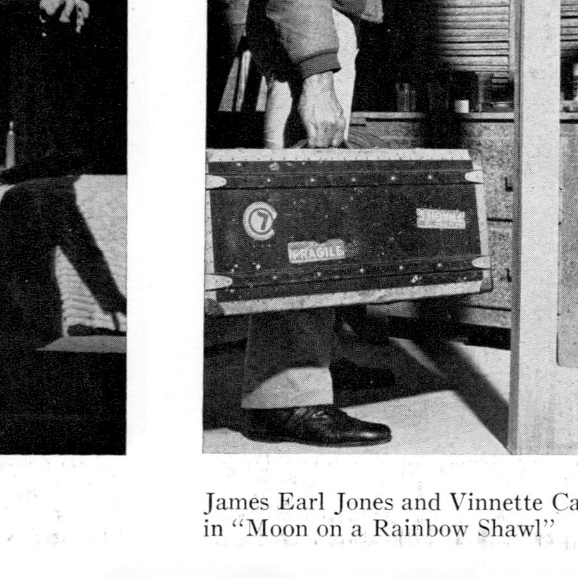

Photo by Friedman-Abeles

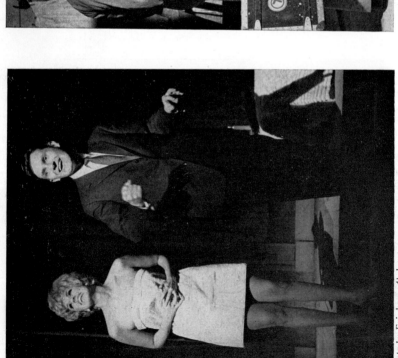

Phyllis Newman and Orson Bean
in "Subways Are for Sleeping"

Photo by Friedman-Abeles

James Earl Jones and Vinnette Carroll
in "Moon on a Rainbow Shawl"

Photo by Friedman-Abeles

Peggy Burke and Colleen Dewhurst
in "Great Day in the Morning"

Photo by Friedman-Abeles

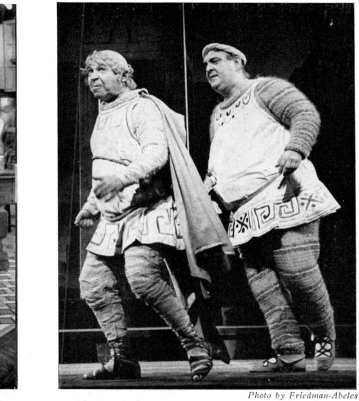

David Burns and Zero Mostel in
"A Funny Thing Happened on the Way to the Forum"

Photo by Friedman-Abeles

Dancers in "Kwamina"

SCENE II

Back in Finch's office, Ponty is at his desk reading his faithful paperback.

BOOK VOICE—So you are now a vice president. You have climbed the ladder of success, rung by painful rung, until you have almost reached the top. You have done beautifully. (PONTY *smiles.*) Unless, that is, you are vice president in charge of advertising. In that case you are in terrible trouble. There is only one thing that can save you. You must get a brilliant idea. The quickest ways to get ideas is to develop them. That is, you must examine the undeveloped, worthless notions of others and add to them that little extra something that makes the idea your own. An undeveloped notion may come from the least likely source. Be alert. You never know who will bring it to you.

Bud Frump enters and says he wants to "smokum peacepipe" with Ponty, and to prove his good faith he has brought him an idea for a TV giveaway show called the "World Wide Wicket Treasure Hunt." Ponty is suspicious, but Bud maintains he has never shown it to J.B. Ponty says he'll give it "a bit of a think-think," and Bud leaves telling him he is free to use it. Once outside Bud elatedly sings "I have returned."

Ponty and Rosemary make up, and he then asks her what she thinks of the new giveaway show idea.

FINCH—The prize would be a thousand dollar bond. Do you think that's enough? (ROSEMARY *looks at him raptly but doesn't answer.*) Maybe we ought to make that twenty-five thousand dollars. Or what would you say if we gave away a hundred thousand dollars? Two hundred thousand?

ROSEMARY—I don't care if you give away the whole company. I love you.

FINCH—Say that again.

ROSEMARY—I love you.

FINCH—No, before that.

ROSEMARY (*puzzled*)—I said I don't care if you give away the whole company.

FINCH—That's it. We'll give away the company. I mean stock in the company. Nobody could resist that these days. (*He rushes off to see* J.B. *about postponing today's meeting.*)

ROSEMARY (*sings*)—

* "Oh, to be loved by a man with a goal
To watch as he climbs
With a purpose in life and purity of soul.
Happy to keep his dinner warm
'Til he comes wearily home from downtown."

SCENE III

J.B. is in his office knitting when Hedy comes in. She is surprised at his secret hobby and asks: "Are you pregnant or something?" Bud Frump intrudes and inquires of J.B. whether he remembers the television treasure hunt idea he once told him about. J.B. tells him what he thought of that idea, and Bud leaves saying: "I just wanted to remind you that you didn't like it." Hedy then informs J.B. that she is leaving World Wide Wickets to become a department store demonstrator of a new skin cream made from sharkbelly jelly.

BIGGLEY—How will I spend those lonely nights?
HEDY—You could stay home.
BIGGLEY—I can't stay home. I'm a married man.
HEDY—Oh, you'll do all right.
BIGGLEY—Hedy, nothing means anything without you. (*Taking her hand, he sings with unabashed sentimentality.*)—

† "Where will I find a treasure
Like the love from a heart of gold.
Ever trusting and sweet and awaiting
my pleasure,
Rain or shine,
Hot or cold.

(HEDY *sings.*)

"Wealth far beyond all measure
Maybe soon in my hands I'll hold.
Ah, but where will I find that one
treasure of treasures,

(*Both sing.*)

"The love from a heart of gold."

* "Happy to Keep His Dinner Warm": © Copyright 1961 by FRANK LOESSER. All Rights Throughout the Entire World Controlled by Frank Music Corp., 119 West 57th Street, New York 19, New York. Used by Permission.

† "Love from a Heart of Gold": © Copyright 1961 by FRANK LOESSER. All Rights Throughout the Entire World Controlled by Frank Music Corp., 119 West 57th Street, New York 19, New York. Used by Permission.

Hedy agrees to stay, but gives him twenty-four hours to find a suitable job for her at World Wide Wickets. As she leaves she bumps into Finch. When he hears that she is thinking of quitting he suggests that maybe they can help each other, and they go off to discuss it.

Scene IV

A few hours later, the executives are in the washroom talking about the upcoming meeting. They are all beginning to get a little scared of Finch, who they see as a threat to their jobs. Bud tells them not to worry, that he knows something and Finch is "dead-dead-dead." Finch comes in and looks into the mirror. The executives sing their thoughts ("Gotta stop that man, or he'll stop me.") while Finch sings his own reaction to his mirror image.

* "You have the cool clear eyes of a
Seeker of wisdom and truth,
Yet there's the upturned chin and the
Grin of impetuous youth.
Oh, I believe in you, I believe in you.

"I hear the sound of good solid
Judgment whenever you talk,
Yet there's the bold brave spring of the
Tiger that quickens your walk.
Oh, I believe in you. I believe in you.

"And when my faith in my fellow man
All but falls apart, (*Clenches hands to lather soap.*)
I've but to feel your hand grasping mine
And I take heart,
I take heart
To see the cool clear eyes of a
Seeker of wisdom and truth,
Yet with the slam bang tang
Reminiscent of gin and vermouth.
Oh, I believe in you. I believe in you."

There is a second chorus of the song played by the orchestra on kazoos, which sound like the electric razor Finch is using, interspersed with the nervously whispered "Gotta stop that man" by the worried executives. At the end Finch goes out reassured with himself and singing "I believe in you."

Scene V

The big meeting in the boardroom is starting. After everyone is seated, Finch enters followed by two office boys carrying an easel on which are a series of painted cards. The top card reads modestly "A Finch Presentation." Finch clicks a cricket and the boys remove the top card revealing a painting of a volcano.

Biggley—What the hell is that?

Finch—A picture of Mt. Vesuvius in eruption. That gives you an idea of the impact our new television show is going to have. Now, J.B., an example (*He clicks cricket for the next card.*) of the kind of national publicity you can look forward to.

Bud (*seeing cover of* Time *with* J.B.'s *picture on it*)—Oh, God!

Finch—The cover of *Time.* (*Clicks cricket and next chart appears showing the cover of* Newsweek *carrying* J.B.'s *portrait.*) The cover of *Newsweek.* (*Clicks cricket to reveal his master stroke: the cover of* Sports Illustrated *on which there is the figure of a golfer.*) And finally, J.B., the Golfer of the Year.

Biggley—Very interesting.

Finch—Now . . . (*A large map of the world is disclosed.*) This is a map of the potential wicket market. It shows how we will make deep penetration and overwhelming saturation in those areas where resistance has long been peakiest.

Biggley—I like this thinking.

Finch—Thank you. (*Shows the sales chart for the past year on which the sales line curves downward, and then dramatically turns the chart upside down so the sales line curves upward. At the same time he releases a toy rocket.*) And this is what's going to happen to our sales when we finally get going, as we will. Up, up, up.

Biggley—Finch, I think you've done it. Very good.

Bud—But what is his idea?

Biggley—You heard. A television show that will give us penetration and peak reaction.

Bud—But what's the idea for the show?

Biggley—I don't know why you have to be so damned negative. The only things you ever come up with are lousy ideas like treasure hunts. All right, Finch, what *is* the idea for the show?

Finch (*recovering*)—You know, J.B., there are treasure hunts and treasure hunts. When Bud brought it to me, I thought it was a rotten idea, too. But then I remembered something. J.B., you know an idea in itself is nothing. It's the development that counts. Leonardo da Vinci drew some sketches for a flying machine, but it took American know-how to develop them into the Boeing 707. When I thought of that, Bud's silly little idea became a challenge to me, and I said, "I'm going to take this idea of Bud Frump's and de-frump it." First of all, my treasure is not a bond, and it's not money. It's stock. Fifty thousand shares of stock in our company.

BRATT—How can we issue fifty thousand shares of extra stock?

FINCH—It's a simple matter of taking the convertible debentures from the sinking fund, issuing stock options which are exchangeable for rights, which we then convert into non-voting common and replace with warrants.

BRATT—Tell me that again.

FINCH—I can't.

BIGGLEY—It can't be done.

FINCH—We give away stock dividends, don't we? Please let me go on with my demonstration.

BIGGLEY—Finch, I hate give-away shows.

FINCH—So do I, J.B. But the public loves them. And I have a new twist. Gentlemen, the World Wide Wicket Treasure Girl. (HEDY *enters in a very abbreviated pirate costume.*)

BIGGLEY—What is this?

FINCH—This, J.B., is the thing that will take the country by storm. I'm combining greed and sex. Can't miss. Go ahead, Hedy.

HEDY (*reciting*)—Hello there. I'm the World Wide Wicket Treasure Girl. Each week I'm going to bring you a clue to where the World Wide treasure has been stashed.

BIGGLEY—Very nice, Miss La Rue, very nice.

FINCH—Of course, Miss La Rue is just helping me demonstrate the idea. She won't be our regular Treasure Girl. When we actually go on the air we need a big name personality.

There is a storm of protest about the unfeasibility of the idea, and J.B. asks the others to leave him alone with Finch. They take a recess, and J.B. voices his objections. These have nothing to do with the idea for the show, but with the fact that Finch wants to use a big name personality as the Treasure Girl. J.B. suggests using Miss La Rue, and Finch tells him that it's a brilliant idea: "Instead of an artificial actress, we have plain simple Hedy La Rue —the girl next door." When J.B. asks Finch where he is going to hide the treasure, Finch explains that the show must be completely unrigged and that not even the Treasure Girl will know where the treasure is hidden. At J.B.'s insistence, however, Finch shares the secret with him and tells him that he is going to hide five thousand shares of stock in each of the ten World Wide Wicket buildings. Biggley calls the others back in.

BIGGLEY—Gentlemen, I'm thinking of going ahead with the World Wide Wicket Treasure Hunt. Of course, I want your approval.

BRATT—Well, J.B., I think it's an absolutely crazy notion and . . .

BIGGLEY (*sharply*)—I like it.

BRATT (*in a booming voice*)—I like it.

MEN (*in unison*)—We like it.

SCENE VI

The moment of the first World Wide Wicket Treasure Hunt Television show has arrived. At a TV set Biggley, Finch and the other executives watch a routine pirate production number, which is followed by the introduction of Hedy La Rue, the World Wide Wicket Treasure Girl. As Miss La Rue is about to read her first clue, the announcer stops her and asks her to swear on a Bible that the show is honest and unrigged. Miss La Rue does so. Then she is asked to swear that she herself doesn't know where the treasure is hidden. Hedy hesitates.

BIGGLEY—This can be very dangerous.

FINCH—Why? You and I are the only ones who know where the treasure is hidden. She doesn't know. (*All the executives look at* J.B.) *Does she?*

BIGGLEY (*nervously*)—Watch the program.

HEDY (*on the screen*)—Look, I do not wish to take a bum rap. I will not swear false witness to perjury. I do know where the treasure is. I found out last night. There is treasure hidden in all the World Wide Wicket Buildings right now. (J.B. *collapses in his chair.*)

SCENE VII

It is the next day in the completely ransacked and wrecked outer office where the executives are sadly viewing the wreckage. The Book Voice is explaining how to handle a disaster, provided it is only a little problem: "However, should you be the cause of a disaster that's really disastrous, we suggest that your best bet is to review the first chapter of this book, 'How to Apply for a Job.' "

Everyone is looking for Finch. He finally shows up and Rosemary tries to cheer him up with a half-chorus of "I Believe in You." She promises to stick with him even if he has to go back to being an "exterior decorator" (window washer) again. Meanwhile Bud is taking his triumph very seriously and solemnly summons Ponty to J.B.'s office. Enroute Bud says he'll help Ponty escape, but Finch says he is willing to take what's coming to him. "I should think you'd be happy," says Finch, "if they *killed* me." Bud says in an aside: "If I could only be sure."

Scene VIII

Inside J.B.'s office Biggley introduces the waiting executives to Mr. Wally Womper, the chairman of the board. J.B. explains that though he is president of the company and responsible for what goes on, he is in no way to blame for the present state of affairs. "There's one bright thing, Wally," says J.B. "You'll be happy to know we've somebody to pin it on." He asks Bratt if they have found Finch yet, and Bratt says they're bringing him in now. Finch arrives and J.B. asks him to sign a letter of resignation in which Finch accepts all the blame for what happened. To his surprise, Finch cheerfully agrees, explaining that he is going back to his old job of window washer.

Womper—No kiddin'. I started as a window washer, myself.

Finch—You did, Mr. Womper?

Womper—Call me Wally.

Finch—Call me Ponty.

Womper—Ponty, how did this happen? I could understand a college man pulling a boner like this, but not no window washer. Now this idea of yours . . .

Finch—Hold it, Wally. If there's one thing I won't do, it's take credit for another man's idea. Especially when he's the boss's nephew.

Womper (*looks at* Bud *and then turns to* J.B.)—You never told me you hired your nephew.

Biggley—Nephew? Oh, nephew. He's not really my nephew—he's my wife's nephew. I've never shown him any favoritism. In fact, I hate him.

Womper—But you love his ideas.

Biggley—No! When he first told me the idea I thought it was a lousy idea. Then when Finch brought it to me I still said it was a lousy idea. And I told Finch it was a lousy idea.

Womper—Why did you buy it?

BIGGLEY—It seemed like a good idea.

WOMPER—But who the hell picked the bubble-headed tomato? (*Everyone moves away from* BIGGLEY, *who looks sheepish.*) Well, I think I've got the whole picture. Now the question is what to do and who to do it to.

FINCH—Now wait a minute, Wally. Before you make any hasty decision I'd like to say a few words.

WOMPER—About what?

FINCH—Humanity. You see, Wally, even though we're all part of the cold corporate set-up . . . deep down under our skins there is flesh and blood. We're all brothers.

BIGGLEY (*sighs*)—Some of us are uncles.

FINCH (*singing*)—

*"Now you may join the Elks, my friend,
And I may join the Shriners,
And other men may carry cards
As members of the Diners.
Still others wear a golden key
Or small Greek letter pin,
But I have learned there's one great club
That all of us are in.

"There is a brotherhood of man,
A benevolent brotherhood of man.
A noble tie that binds
All human hearts and minds
Into one brotherhood of man."

Womper, Finch, Biggley and the executives join in a hand-clapping rivivalist dance as they continue to sing the song, all except Bud, whom Biggley has excluded from the festivities.

SCENE IX

In the hallway there is the sound of rolling drums as Bud Frump appears with his head down in disgrace and guarded by an escort of four employees. He pleads with the men, each of whom greets him with stony silence. He asks the first man to give him a break, tells the second that he thought they were friends, and reminds the third of the fun and good times they used to have. To the fourth man he says: "You I never liked." They usher him off as he protests vainly.

SCENE X

In the outer office some days later, the secretaries are awaiting developments. Bratt emerges and tells the employees that all the vice presidents have been shifted around. He then introduces J.B., who is still president.

BIGGLEY—I can truly state that World Wide Wickets is now stronger than ever. And I feel a lot of the credit should go to a certain bright and very loyal young man. Come out here, Finch.

FINCH—I would like to say that if any credit is due, it should go to a great man and a great humanitarian, the chairman of the board, Mr. Wally Womper, who has his charming wife with him today. (WOMPER *and* HEDY *appear, arm in arm.*) Mr. Womper told me he didn't feel like making any speeches. He's still a newlywed. But I have a surprise announcement to make about him. Wally Womper has decided he's going to retire as chairman of the board and he and his wife are going to take a long honeymoon trip around the world. (*Everyone applauds.*)

BIGGLEY—Wally, who's going to be the new chairman of the board, as if I didn't know.

FINCH—Just a moment, I don't know if I can accept. I'll have to consult Mrs. Finch. Rosemary, what do you think?

ROSEMARY—Darling, I don't care if you work in the mail room, or you're chairman of the board, or you're President of the United States, I love you.

FINCH—Say that again.

ROSEMARY—I love you.

FINCH—No, before that.

Everyone sings "We'll play it the company way," as outside the office window a scaffolding appears. On it is Bud Frump washing the windows with one hand and reading "How to Succeed" with the other.

THE COMPLAISANT LOVER

A Play in Two Acts

BY GRAHAM GREENE

[GRAHAM GREENE *was born in Berkhamstead, England, October 2, 1904. Although he is a converted Roman Catholic, his many novels often involve suicide, which he once unsuccessfully attempted himself. His first play, "The Living Room," deals with the difficulty an adulterous husband has in breaking up his marriage. He doesn't like to think of himself as a pessimist, and the quality he despises most in people is cultivated innocence. "The Complaisant Lover" is his fourth play, and he is reported to be working on a fifth that takes place in a South American brothel.*]

VICTOR Rhodes, dentist, practical joker, and reteller of boring anecdotes, is giving a small dinner party in his North London home. As the curtain rises he has just finished telling a funny story to his guests, who include William Howard, the local bank manager, Mrs. Howard, their nineteen-year-old daughter Ann, and Clive Root, a romantic looking middle-aged man who deals in rare books.

VICTOR (*smugly*)—Mr. Root, you are looking tonight at a very rare phenomenon—two men who are happily married. And why are we happily married?

HOWARD—Because we happen to like our wives.

VICTOR—That's not enough. It's because we've got a sense of humor. A sense of humor means a happy marriage.

CLIVE—Is it as simple as that, Mr. Rhodes?

VICTOR—I can assure you there are very few situations in life that a joke won't ease.

The port is passed and Victor cannot restrain himself from making a professional observation.

VICTOR—Too much wine causes acidity. Acidity causes tartar. Tartar . . .

CLIVE—I'll have another glass. There are worse things than tartar.

VICTOR—Such as . . . ?

CLIVE—The worms that eat my stock. They're like some people, Mr. Rhodes. You can only tell where they have been by the holes they leave behind.

VICTOR (*excitedly*)—For goodness' sake, Root! Your cigar! It's burning the tablecloth. (CLIVE *snatches up a cigar butt and finds it to be only a trick one, with the glowing end made of red paper.* VICTOR *and* HOWARD *laugh at* CLIVE'S *consternation.*)

CLIVE—I used to be very fond of these tricks—when I was a child.

VICTOR—You aren't offended, old chap, are you?

CLIVE—No. Interested, that's all. Jokes like this must be a compensation for something.

VICTOR—I just think jokes like that are funny. I don't see why you have to analyze everything.

CLIVE—You should read Freud on the nature of a joke.

VICTOR—Oh, I suppose he sees sex in it. (*He holds up the cigar butt vertically.*) Can you see sex in that, William?

HOWARD—Well, frankly, Victor, yes, I can. (VICTOR *looks at the cigar butt and drops it hastily.*)

A moment later Victor attempts another practical joke when he invites Clive to sit down, but before he can, Mary Rhodes steps in and removes an apparatus from under the seat cushion explaining to Clive that it would have played "Auld Lang Syne" had he sat on it. The conversation then turns to Robin, the Rhodes' twelve-year-old son who is going through a phase of being passionately in love with Ann Howard.

HOWARD—Has he proposed yet, Ann?

ANN—No. Unless you count giving me a stuffed mouse. He's stuffed it himself—very badly.

MARY—Give him a smile, Ann, when he comes in. The mouse meant a lot. I can never understand why people laugh at children's love. Love's painful at any age.

VICTOR—Oh, come, Mary. I don't find it painful.

The guests go off to the next room to watch a popular TV show leaving Clive and Ann behind. Ann reveals that she is fed up with still being considered a child at nineteen, and with living in a small community where everyone knows what everyone else is doing.

ANN—Sometimes I think I'd marry anyone who wanted to get away. Not necessarily *marry* either. Clive, let's go away together.

CLIVE—Go away?

ANN—For a time. It needn't be for always if you don't like me. It could be a trial week.

CLIVE—Ann, dear, you aren't in love with me.

ANN—How do you know? You mean *you* are not in love with *me.* I know that. It doesn't matter so much, does it? There's always lust. And I've got a body under this puppy-fat.

CLIVE—You aren't fat, Ann. You're very pretty.

ANN—As pretty as the girls in Curzon Street?

CLIVE—I don't go to bed with the girls in Curzon Street.

ANN—Never?

CLIVE—I've done it. Two or three times, I suppose. When I've been fed up and alone.

ANN—You aren't alone now?

CLIVE—Yes. I'm very alone.

ANN—Well, then, why go to Curzon Street when there's me?

CLIVE—Lust isn't very strong, Ann, unless there's love, too. Curzon Street takes only half an hour. And there are twenty-four hours in a day.

ANN—We have things in common. Books.

CLIVE—*Riders of the Purple Sage* is a subject we might exhaust.

ANN (*chagrined*)—You'll be able to boast now, won't you, that you've had an immoral proposal from a girl of nineteen.

CLIVE—I'm not the boasting kind. I've been trained in a different school, Ann. You see, the first woman I loved was happily married.

ANN—Have you loved a lot of people?

CLIVE—Only four. It's not a high score at thirty-eight.

ANN—What happened to them, Clive?

CLIVE—In the end the husbands won.

ANN—Were they all married?

CLIVE—Yes.

ANN—Why do you choose married women?

CLIVE—I don't know. Perhaps I fell in love with experience.

ANN—One has to begin.

CLIVE—Perhaps I don't care for innocence. Perhaps I'm trying to repeat the first time. Perhaps it's envy of other men, and I want to prove myself better than they are. I don't know, Ann. But it's the school I've been brought up in.

ANN—You don't sound so happy in your school.

CLIVE—I hate the lessons, but I'm very good at them.

ANN—What lessons?

CLIVE—Oh, how to make a husband like you. How to stay in the same house as the two of them and not to mind that, when night comes, she'll pay you a short visit if the coast is clear and he'll sleep away the whole night beside her. Then, of course, there are all kinds of elementary lessons. On passports, hotel registers, and on times when it's necessary to take adjoining rooms. And how to postpone discovery in spite of those kind mutual friends whom you always meet at unlikely little hotels in the Midlands.

ANN—Does the husband always discover?

CLIVE—They always have. And then the worst lessons begin.

ANN—You mean—about divorce?

CLIVE—No. I've heard about divorce. I've never encountered it. In my case the husbands have always been complaisant. You see, they love their wives too much to leave them, so they say. I seem to have always had an eye for very lovable women. (*Sympathetically to* ANN.) Don't marry an Englishman, Ann. Englishmen prefer their friends and their clubs to their wives, but they have great staying power and a great sense of duty. The lover relieves them of their duty. And then you see without that—trouble, a beautiful brother-and-sister relationship can develop. It's very touching. And so damned boring for the lover.

ANN—Are you in love now?

CLIVE—Yes.

Ann sees that her position is even worse than she had expected, and asks Clive to promise not to tell this unknown woman about her. Clive says he'll try, but reminds her that "when you're in love, you don't have secrets." Ann goes off to join the others watching the tele, as Mary enters to talk to Clive.

MARY—It was sweet of you to come.

CLIVE—I didn't want to.

MARY—It was necessary, Clive. If we are to see more of each other. Now he knows you, he won't worry.

CLIVE—When are we going to get some time together, Mary?

MARY—I only missed one day with you this week.

CLIVE—You know what I mean by time.

MARY—Dear, I promise. Sometime, somehow. But it's difficult. It wouldn't be safe in England.

CLIVE—We can go abroad . . . next week . . .

MARY—Sally comes back next week for half-term. I have to be here. Then there's a Dental Association dinner, and Victor would think it odd if I was away. I always go with him.

CLIVE—After that . . .

MARY—Robin's got to have three teeth out. Don't look angry. You shouldn't have chosen a woman with a family, Clive. My job is full time just as yours is. You can't pack up and go away whenever you like either.

CLIVE—All the same, I'd do it if you asked me to.

MARY (*sharply*)—Perhaps children are more important than second-hand books.

Clive is hurt nevertheless, and he blurts out Ann's proposal to Mary and presents her with the gift of his refusal. To his surprise Mary sympathizes with Ann.

MARY—You should have said yes. There wouldn't be any complications with Ann. She wouldn't have to write postcards home and buy presents for the children. She wouldn't remember suddenly in the middle of dinner that she'd forgotten to buy a pair of football boots. She's free. Don't you think I envy her? I even envy her virginity.

CLIVE—That's not important.

MARY—Oh yes it is. Men are jealous of a past if there's nothing else to be jealous of. You need your bloody sign.

CLIVE—I need a few weeks' peace of mind. If you're with me, I can sleep because you're not with him.

MARY—I've told you over and over again—I've promised you—we haven't slept together for five years. But I have no sign to prove it.

CLIVE—After a dental dinner and a drink or two, things happen . . .

MARY—When *that* dies out, Clive, it doesn't come back. And sooner or later it always dies. Even for us it would die in time. It dies quicker in a marriage, that's all. It's killed by the children, by the chars who give notice, by the price of meat. With Victor I talk about Sally's room which needs re-painting. Can we postpone it till the autumn? Her school report says she has a talent for music. Ought she to have extra lessons in the holidays? And then there's the dinner which went wrong. Too much garlic in the salad and the potatoes were undercooked. Clive, that's the sort of talk that kills desire. Only kindness grows in that soil.

The television show in the next room is over, and everyone returns to the living room. Robin is sent upstairs to finish his homework. Clive attempts to make Mary jealous by arranging to have Ann come down and help him with his cataloguing the next morning. Victor tries to play another practical joke on Clive by offering him whiskey in a dribbling glass, but Clive takes the wrong glass leaving Victor "hoist with his own petard."

After Clive and the Howards have left, Victor tells Mary that he thinks Ann and Clive would make a good couple. He then proceeds to see that all the windows are locked, because his father practiced this ritual on account of a piece in the Church of England service about a strong man keeping his house. Victor starts to talk about dentistry and stops when Mary seems bored.

VICTOR—There was a time, Mary, when you were interested in what I did.

MARY—Of course I'm interested.

VICTOR—Admit you aren't. There's nothing wrong in that. If those two young ones marry, you can be sure Ann won't be so interested in the bookshop after a few years. It's human nature, Mary. I used to enjoy shopping with you. I don't now. I get impatient when you can't decide about the new curtains. I feel out of place among the shop assistants—as you would feel in my surgery in town. I'm not a mother and you aren't a dentist. That's not enough to break a marriage.

MARY—Of course not. Who said it was?

VICTOR—I've felt for the last month that you were unhappy.

MARY—I've been a little tired, that's all.

VICTOR—We are both working too hard. We ought to go off somewhere—by ourselves. Suppose after Sally goes back—

MARY (*quickly*)—There's the Dental Association dinner.

VICTOR—Oh, yes. I'd forgotten.

MARY—Suppose I went off for a few days on my own. Somewhere abroad—somewhere quiet. I could go with Jane.

VICTOR—Have I ever met Jane.

MARY (*lying hard*)—I think once.

VICTOR—I have an idea. You could go away with what's-her-name—Jane—and then four days later I'd join you—after the dinner. Perhaps we could even get rid of Jane.

MARY (*desperately seeking a solution*)—It doesn't seem fair to Jane. To come all that way—

VICTOR—What way?

MARY—From Northumberland.

VICTOR—Well then, why not take our holiday in Northumberland?

MARY—But I want sun. We have enough rain here.

VICTOR—When did I meet Jane?

MARY—When we were married, I think. She never comes to London.

VICTOR—Just stays there in the rain? What's her other name?

MARY (*the first word that comes*)—Crane.

VICTOR—Jane Crane stays in the rain. (*Laughs at his own rhyme.*) I've always wanted to see the Dutch dental hospitals. So you and Jane could go to Amsterdam and I could join you on the seventeenth.

MARY—Leave one day, Victor, for a hangover. You won't be in bed till two.

VICTOR—Right.

With this settled, Victor goes upstairs to use the bathroom first, leaving Mary free to make a telephone call.

MARY—Clive? . . . I'm coming away with you, Clive . . . I only mean a holiday. I can only manage four days. I'm sorry, but that's how things are. And Clive, it's got to be Amsterdam. . . . Oh, he's quite happy about it. He thinks I'm going with someone called Jane Crane. . . . What do you mean, "Jane, Jane, tall as a crane?" Why do you all have to make up verses about her? . . . I don't care if Edith Sitwell wrote them. I can't alter Jane's name now. . . . (*The curtain falls as she continues talking.*)

SCENE II

Amsterdam, two weeks later. In the hotel bedroom where Mary and Clive have been staying, we see the two single beds have been moved together to make one large bed, which is unmade. Clive is packing his bag. Mary, in her dressing gown, emerges from the bathroom.

MARY—I've been happy, Clive. Haven't you?

CLIVE—Yes, in a way. The first day I was happy. Even the second. Yesterday was not so good.

MARY—I loved yesterday.

CLIVE—The shadow of today was over it. But I didn't know then what a shadow. Mary, why didn't you tell me about Victor before we came away?

MARY—I was afraid you wouldn't come.

CLIVE—You could have told me yesterday.

Mary—And spoilt it all. All the lying late in bed, the wine we drank at lunch, even that silly film we saw . . . .

Clive—Yes, you were happy, and all the time you were deceiving me.

Mary—I've been happy deceiving Victor, too, haven't I? You didn't mind me being happy doing that.

Clive—I understood our relationship was rather different.

Mary—Do you think I like packing up and going off to the Amstel to meet Victor?

Clive—He gets a whole week of you.

Mary—I've booked two single rooms, Clive.

Clive—And tonight I suppose you'll take him to that little restaurant by the canal . . . and that bar . . .

Mary—I won't take him anywhere we've been together.

Clive—There aren't so many good restaurants in Amsterdam.

Mary asks Clive to help her lock her suitcase. He tries, but the lock is broken. The valet arrives and Clive sends him downstairs with his suitcase and then volunteers to go out and buy a strap to wrap around Mary's case.

Clive—When do you have to report at the Amstel?

Mary—He's on the midday plane.

Clive—We may pass each other at the airport. I'll hide my face behind a newspaper.

Mary—You needn't. He wouldn't think there was anything wrong.

Clive—Is he as dumb as that?

Mary—It's not dumbness. When a man doesn't want a woman any more, he can't imagine anyone else desiring her—that's all.

Clive goes out to buy a strap. Mary goes to the phone to tell the desk that they are checking out. The doorbell rings and she shouts "Entrez" over her shoulder as she goes on with her phone conversation. Meanwhile the valet has entered followed by Victor and another man. The valet leaves and Mary finally sees Victor, who has come by the night boat to surprise her. He had gone to the Amstel, but since she wasn't there he decided to come over and join Mary here. He inquires about Jane, and is sorry to hear that she has gone home. However, he likes the hotel and suggests they stay on here instead of moving to the Amstel. He introduces his companion, Dr. Van Droog, a Dutch manufacturer of dental instruments he met at the Dental dinner. Unfortunately, Dr. Van Droog speaks no English, and they ring for the valet to translate.

VALET (*translating*)—He says it is a great pleasure, sir, to him to have met your wife. (*To* VAN DROOG.) Waar ontmoeete U de vrouw van deze heer?

VICTOR—What are you saying?

VALET—I am asking him, sir, where he had the pleasure of meeting your wife.

VICTOR—Here, of course. This is my wife.

VALET (*looking reproachfully at* MARY)—I see. I did not understand. I am sorry.

Mary tries to get Victor to take Dr. Van Droog out before Clive returns. However, Dr. Van Droog is persistent in his cordial efforts to invite Mary and Victor to visit his dental instrument factory, and because everything has to be translated it takes a lot of time, and Mary becomes more and more frantic. Suddenly, as she had feared, Clive returns. The valet is disconcerted as he anticipates a violent scene. Instead Victor greets Clive cordially.

VICTOR—How are you, Root? Nice to see you.

CLIVE (*awkwardly*)—I didn't know you were here.

VICTOR—Just moved in.

CLIVE—I thought you were going to the Amstel.

VICTOR—It's better here. What are you doing in Amsterdam?

CLIVE—I was getting a strap. For this suitcase.

MARY (*coming to the rescue*)—Clive's been buying books. It was such a surprise when Jane and I ran into him.

Dr. Van Droog is introduced with the perplexed valet continuing reluctantly his translation of formalities that completely ignore the true situation. Victor even suggests that Clive stay on in Amsterdam and keep Mary company while he is visiting the dental clinics. He leaves Clive behind with Mary as he goes off with Dr. Van Droog.

CLIVE—He likes to give the final turn of the screw, doesn't he? He's not satisfied with moving into our room and our bed. He has to make it a cheap farce with his Dutch manufacturer of dental instruments. We aren't allowed a tragedy nowadays without a banana skin to slip on and make it funny. But it hurts just the same.

Mary and Clive begin to argue about her attachment to Victor, as she goes back and forth into the bathroom getting dressed as she talks. Suddenly, while she is in the bathroom, Clive takes a small package from his pocket, leaves it on the dressing table, and starts for the door.

MARY (*calling from the bathroom*)—What are you doing, Clive?
CLIVE—Catching my plane.
MARY (*coming out into the room*)—Why don't you stay, as Victor asked?
CLIVE—Good God, do you really expect me to take the next-door room . . . ?
MARY—Victor's going to be busy all day.
CLIVE—Mary, you're either the most immoral woman I've ever known—or the most innocent.

Mary spots the package and on opening it discovers that it contains a pair of diamond ear-rings. Clive tells her they are a present for her bought with some black market currency obtained from a man he was sent to by a film magnate, who had bought some erotica from him. Clive says he would rather have given her a plain gold ring. Mary says she wants that too, but that she just can't up and leave a good man she has known for sixteen years and who is the father of her children.

CLIVE—It can't go on like this, Mary. Odd days arranged by Victor. You have to choose.
MARY—And if I won't choose?
CLIVE—I'll leave you.
MARY—You're so free, aren't you? You don't have to choose. You don't have to go to someone you love and say, "I'm leaving you. After sixteen years I'm leaving you for a man I've slept with for a month. You'll have to see to things for yourself—the dentist for Robin and writing to Matron about Sally, booking rooms for the seaside in August and getting all those damned little objects for the stockings in time for Christmas." I'm married, Clive. You aren't. You are a foreigner. Even when I sleep with you you are a foreigner.
CLIVE—If we were married—
MARY—You don't want that sort of marriage and I don't. You only marry that way once, and you've never tried.
CLIVE—Oh, yes, I've tried.
MARY—You want to be a lover with a license, that's all. All right. You win. I'll leave Victor, but not just yet, Clive. Not before Christmas. Please not before Christmas. Be patient until January, Clive.
CLIVE—I'd wait for longer than that if you'd promise—

MARY—Couldn't we wait until he finds out?

CLIVE—He has a wonderful capacity for not noticing.

MARY—If he found out, there wouldn't be a struggle, or a choice. He'd throw me out. Say you'll wait till then, Clive.

CLIVE (*an idea has been born*)—Till he finds out. It's possible.

MARY—I must go down, Clive. It's all right, isn't it, now?

CLIVE—Yes, it's all right.

They say goodbye with Clive staying behind to write a letter. As soon as he is alone he rings for the valet, who arrives after a moment. Clive offers the valet a hundred guilder to write a letter for him, and Clive dictates as the valet writes: "Dear Sir: I am the valet who looked after you in room 121. I am sorry to see a gentleman like you so sadly deceived. A beautiful woman your wife—" The door opens and Victor enters. He asks for Mary and Clive explains that she has gone downstairs to meet him. Clive adds that he is using the room to write a short bread-and-butter letter in Dutch. Victor tells him to go right ahead and goes into the bathroom to wash. Clive is forced to continue his dictation in Victor's hearing, and he does so to the hopelessly confused valet: "I have so much enjoyed my stay with you (*The* VALET *hesitates, but* CLIVE *tells him to go on.*) The windmills were just as I'd always imagined them." Victor emerges, drying his hands, says goodbye to Clive and departs.

CLIVE (*to the* VALET)—Go on now with the letter. (*Dictates.*) "I feel that it is my duty to tell you . . . that before your arrival . . . your wife was sharing room 121 . . . with the gentleman who went out to buy a strap. They behaved very intimately together." Now sign it and post it a week from today to Victor Rhodes, Esq., 18 South Heath Lane, London, N.W., England.

DR. VAN DROOG (*poking his head inside the door*)—Het spyt my ik ben Mr. en Mrs. Rhodes kwytgeraakt?

VALET (*getting to his feet and translating for* CLIVE)—He wishes to know where is Mr. and Mrs. Rhodes. I do not know who he is. I do not know who you are. I do not understand this. (*Indicates letter.*) I do not understand one damned thing.

ACT II

It is eight days later and in the living room of the Rhodes' house. Mary and Robin are discussing his homework. Robin asks if he can take a new Dutch stamp off a letter that has arrived, and they then go on to talk about the cocktail party the Rhodes' are giving that afternoon in the garden. Robin asks if Jane Crane is coming. When Mary tells him that she went straight home from Holland by train, Robin replies: "Jane Crane went home by train. She'll never be seen here ever again." Victor comes home weary and talking about his day of "four fillings, three scalings, and one extraction." He sits down and opens his mail as Mary takes some cocktail glasses out to the garden. Victor opens the letter from Holland, reads it and after a moment tears it in two. Mary keeps talking to him from the garden about the party preparations, and Victor continues to answer woodenly. Mary comes back into the room.

MARY—Did I tell you I got a letter from Jane this morning? She's so sorry she missed you in Amsterdam, but perhaps she'll come to London after Christmas and then you'll meet her.

VICTOR (*who can bear no more*)—It seems unlikely.

MARY—Unlikely?

VICTOR—Mary, was Root sleeping with you in Amsterdam?

MARY (*after a long pause*)—Yes. How did you find out?

VICTOR—This letter. From the valet in the hotel.

Victor reads her the letter, including some confusing lines in the middle about "windmills."

VICTOR—Are those his ear-rings you are wearing?

MARY—Yes.

VICTOR—An expensive present. I couldn't buy you much on my ten-pounds-a-day allowance.

MARY—He went to a black marketeer in Knightsbridge.

VICTOR—It's the only romantic thing a man can do in these days, risk prison for a woman. I can't even do that. I'm a father.

MARY—You talk as though he bought me.

VICTOR—He did buy you. He bought you with novelty, anecdotes you hadn't heard before, books instead of teeth. Does Root want to marry you?

MARY—Yes.

VICTOR—Do you want to marry him?

MARY—I want to be with him, when I can, as much as I can.

VICTOR—Marriage isn't the answer. First editions can be just as boring in time as dentist's drills. He'll have his hobbies, too, and you won't care for them in a year or two. The trouble about marriage is, it's a damned boring condition even with a lover.

MARY—I didn't know you'd been bored too.

VICTOR—I can put up with any amount of boredom because I

love you. It's the way of life that's boring, not you. Do you think I'm never bored with people's teeth? One has to put up with it. Boredom is not a good reason for changing a profession or a marriage.

MARY—We haven't been married properly for years.

VICTOR—Oh, yes, we have. Marriage is living in the same house with someone you love. I never stopped loving you—I only stopped giving you pleasure. And when *that* happened I didn't want you any more. I wasn't going to use you like a pick-up in the park.

MARY—How did you know *that?*

VICTOR—You were always very quiet when we made love, but you had one habit you didn't know yourself. In the old days just before going to sleep, if you had been satisfied, you would touch my face and say, "Thank you." And then a time came when I realized that for months you had said nothing. You had only touched my face. (*In sudden anguish.*) Do you say thank you to Root?

MARY—I don't know. Perhaps. (*Looking at him.*) You are talking to me now as though I was a woman, and not just your wife Do I have to sleep with another man before you do that?

The mood is suddenly broken by Robin calling his mother to ask her help with his homework. Victor begs Mary to stay with him. Mary doesn't want to choose. Victor is suddenly panic-stricken at the necessity of having to meet Clive. As Mary goes off to help Robin, Victor stands helplessly alone in the room. Unwittingly he collapses on to the musical chair, burying his face in his hands. The chair starts playing "Auld Lang Syne" but Victor doesn't hear. He is weeping.

SCENE II

Two hours have elapsed and the cocktail party is approaching its end. Victor is sitting alone at the table with an empty glass in front of him. Robin comes in from the garden with a glass of orange squash. Robin complains that there is a sort of mood around, "like the last act of Macbeth." Victor asks Robin to sit down and begins to question him about one of his schoolmates, whose father ran away with a girl who works in the zoo.

VICTOR—Does he mind much?

ROBIN—Not very much. He said it was more fun in the old days.

VICTOR—Weren't there quarrels?

ROBIN—Oh, that was part of the fun. He said you never knew what was going to happen next. It's very quiet now, he says.

Mary enters with the Howards. Robin is sent off to fetch Ann, who is in the garden talking to Clive.

MRS. HOWARD—What lovely ear-rings, Mary. Did Victor give them to you?

MARY (*hesitating slightly*)—Yes.

HOWARD (*to* MRS. HOWARD)—That's what comes of being a dentist. If I gave you diamonds I'd be suspected of embezzlement.

MRS. HOWARD—If you gave me diamonds nobody would believe it. They'd think I had a lover.

HOWARD—Now we know why you chose Amsterdam, Victor. How did you work the currency, old fox?

VICTOR (*unable to take any more*)—I worked no currency. I'm not a black marketeer, William.

He walks out of the room into the garden, and the Howards apologize to Mary, who in turn explains that Victor is just overtired. They decide not to wait for Ann and leave. As soon as they are gone, Mary goes to the living room door and calls Victor. Clive and Ann enter from the garden, and inform Mary that Victor has gone to the garage. Mary tells Clive that Victor has had some bad news in a letter from Holland, and Clive confesses that he dictated that letter. Mary is furious with him, but Ann defends him and tells Mary that she loves Clive, and that she is jealous of Mary's *experience.*

MARY—Go and find it with someone of your own age. Clive's too used for you.

CLIVE—Mary!

MARY (*to* CLIVE)—Aren't you? Even I didn't expect this last clever stroke of yours. An anonymous letter to a husband. He's lived with wives too long, Ann. He's learned too many tricks.

ANN—You drove him to it.

MARY—If you took Clive on, you'd have to learn to love where you don't trust. Better wait a while. You'll be riper for him in a few years, after you've been married, too.

ANN—She calls you too used. Look at her. Can't you see what she's like now?

CLIVE—I see someone I love and want, that's all.

Ann starts to cry and Mary offers her a handkerchief, as Robin appears unnoticed from the garage.

ANN—Not one of yours. (*She takes a handkerchief from her bag and accidentally drops a glass object that breaks. It is an electronic eye that* ROBIN *has made for her.* CLIVE *stoops to pick it up for her but she stops him.*) Don't bother. It's only some nonsense her child gave me. (ROBIN *comes forward and picks up the pieces in silence.*) I'm sorry, Robin. I didn't mean . . .

ROBIN—It doesn't matter. It didn't work anyway.

Mary is growing anxious about Victor, and when Robin reports that he heard him start the car but that he didn't come out, the thought of suicide occurs to everyone. Mary starts off to see, just as Victor enters. Clive says that he will see Ann down the street and come back in a few minutes. He and Ann leave Mary and Victor alone.

MARY—You scared us. We half thought . . . Robin heard the engine running.

VICTOR—Yes?

MARY—Of course, I knew you wouldn't do anything silly, really.

VICTOR—Silly is the operative word. I only wanted to be alone so I sat in the car. Then I remembered something I had read in the papers. I turned the engine on. I shut the garage doors. But the word "silly" came to my mind too, and the headline in the newspaper: "Love Tragedy in West Drayton." This isn't West Drayton, but the district is wrong for tragedy too. We're only dressed for domestic comedy.

Mary and Victor discuss their situation. Mary says she won't give Clive up, and Victor says he doesn't know how to give Mary up either.

VICTOR—Does anybody have to leave? I can forget the letter, Mary. Just give me time. You needn't promise me anything.

MARY—It wouldn't work.

VICTOR—It can. Just don't make things too obvious locally, that's all. If you go away for a holiday now and then, I won't ask you where.

MARY—Clive would never agree. He told me that he couldn't go on much longer like this.

VICTOR—If he loves you, he can go on. If I can.

Clive returns and Mary abruptly goes out into the garden in order to leave Victor and Clive together.

VICTOR—Sit down. (CLIVE *is about to sit in the musical chair when* VICTOR *stops him.*) Not that one. Oh, it doesn't matter. The tune's run out. (*He hands* CLIVE *a glass.*) This is good stuff. Black Label. I can get only two bottles a month. I keep it for special friends.

CLIVE—I wouldn't have called myself a special friend.

VICTOR—I think perhaps it would be better if you did. We shall see a great deal of each other from now on, and that is the best explanation, isn't it?

Victor reveals to Clive that Mary has told him about the earrings and the black marketeer in Knightsbridge. Clive is upset because this gives Victor the power to turn him over to the police and have him sent to jail. However, Victor assures him that he would not do this, that his only concern is to help Mary, who needs to have the illusion that she'll love someone for the rest of her life.

CLIVE—I can give you all the evidence for a divorce you want.

VICTOR—I don't want a divorce. The only thing I ask you is to carry on your affair at a distance. You see, there are the children to be considered. May I make a suggestion?

CLIVE—Of course.

VICTOR—Mary's mother is dead. Nobody around here knows that. She can be critically ill three or four times a year. If you require it. She lived in Pontefract.

CLIVE—Do you really expect us to live like that, not seeing each other except three or four times a year? In Pontefract?

VICTOR—My dear Clive—I'd better get accustomed to calling you Clive—I hope you'll dine with us almost every week.

CLIVE—No. I'm damned if I will. You can be a complaisant husband if you like, I'm not going to be a complaisant lover.

VICTOR—The two are inseparable.

CLIVE—Then I'm walking out. You won't be bothered with me any more.

VICTOR—If you walk out, I think she'll walk out with you.

CLIVE—But that's the best solution for all of us. Can't you see that?

VICTOR—For you and me perhaps. But we've only one object, you and I, to make it a degree less hard for her. I'll make the effort. Can't you do the same?

CLIVE—What makes you think she'd be happier—with the two of us?

VICTOR—The four of us. There's Robin and Sally. She told me herself she doesn't want to choose.

CLIVE—She wants to have her cake and eat it.

VICTOR—That's exactly what she said. Don't you love her enough to try to give her that kind of cake? A child's cake with silver balls and mauve icing and a layer of marzipan.

CLIVE—You do really love her, don't you?

VICTOR—Yes, I do.

CLIVE (*after a moment*)—Is Pontefract a bracing climate? (ROBIN'S *voice begins to call, "Mother, Mother."*) I suppose you can supply me with the dates of the childrens' holidays and your dental dinners.

Victor excuses himself to go up and see what Robin wants. Mary enters and Clive tells her of the new arrangement. She is very pleased at keeping both her sixteen-year-old past and an "even longer future" with Clive. Clive is not so sure.

CLIVE—I know that one day I shall get tired of going away at night and leaving you two together. I shall get tired of arranging our holidays to suit his convenience. I shall get tired of all the times we have to cancel things at the last moment. And I shall get tired of waiting outside the shops in Paris or Brussels while you buy the children's shoes.

MARY—And then you'll leave me?

CLIVE—No. Then, when you see how tired I am, you will leave me. That's what I dread.

MARY—I don't believe it's true. It needn't be true.

Victor comes in and invites Clive to stay for dinner, but Clive says he cannot. Victor invites him then for Thursday dinner, just the three of them. Mary is so proud of Victor she puts her arm around him. Together they both urge Clive to come. He looks at the contented married pair and sadly accepts his fate.

CLIVE—Oh, yes, I'll come. (*Pause.*) I expect I'll come. (*He turns to leave as the curtain falls.*)

GIDEON

A Play in Two Acts

BY PADDY CHAYEFSKY

[PADDY CHAYEFSKY *was born in New York City on January 29, 1923. He attended the DeWitt Clinton High School, City College and Fordham University. Son of a Bronx dairy manager, he grew up as an Orthodox Jew learning to speak Hebrew. As a private in the infantry he was wounded at Aachen when he stepped on a land mine, and acquired the name "Paddy" when he tried to get out of KP duty to attend a Catholic Holy Day mass. His earliest produced work was an army musical, "No T.O. (Table of Organization) for Love," which ran in London and Paris, and his first two plays, which were optioned but never produced, were "Put Them All Together" and "The Man Who Made the Mountains Shake," later called "Fifth from Garibaldi." Although he had written many scripts for television, it was his original TV play "Marty" which established him as the poet of the non-heroic little man. He properly resents, however, the notion that he is a good "little playwright," which was the tenor of the reviews of his very successful first play, "Middle of the Night." It was in his second play, "The Tenth Man," originally called "The Dybbuk of Woodhaven," that he first worked with Tyrone Guthrie, whom he calls "the finest director I have ever known." Mr. Guthrie also directed "Gideon." The playwright's decision to call Yahweh "The Angel" is partly to avoid complaints about anthropomorphism and partly because he is so described in the Bible. Mr. Chayefsky, who doesn't believe that the basic human problems are solved appreciably better under one system than another, has projected the Russian Revolution and the years between it and Lenin's death in 1924 as the subject of his next play.*]

IT is 1100 B.C. and the scene is impoverished Palestine. We see the tent of Joash and near it a crude, stone sacrificial altar. At one side of the stage stands a white-bearded figure in black robes. Joash and the other Hebrew elders enter, approach the altar, and address their deity, Baal, begging him to save them from the Midianites, one hundred thousand of whom are encamped on the other side of the Jordan River, about to rob the Hebrews of their harvest. If their predicament is serious their ritual is comic as they squabble about which part of the animal is supposed to be offered Baal as a sacrifice, and they obviously don't believe that the nonsense they are going through will do any good. Being a practical elder, Joash instructs his son, Gideon, to thresh the wheat harvest by hand, secretly in the wine press in front of the tent. Gideon, whom the elders regard as a "witless ass," resignedly begins this arduous task as the elders go off and Joash disappears into the tent. The black-robed figure comes forward and watches Gideon whacking away at the wheat. After a moment he says to him: "The Lord is with you, O mighty man of valor." Gideon, who has no way of knowing that he is in the presence of The Angel of the Lord, looks up startled, sizes up the speaker as a crackpot, smiles sheepishly at him, and goes over to the tent.

GIDEON—Father, there is a strange fellow by our terebinth tree.

JOASH (*handing* GIDEON *a pan of little cakes*)—Well, give him a cake and show him the road to Schechem. (GIDEON *does so and then starts to resume his threshing.* THE ANGEL *eats a cake, but sits down on the edge of the wine press.*)

GIDEON (*patient but annoyed*)—Sir, it is hard for me to do my work if you sit there like that.

THE ANGEL—I am the Lord your God, Gideon, who delivered you from bondage.

GIDEON (*unimpressed*)—Well, as you say, sir. Now, let me be about my work.

THE ANGEL—I have heard your groans under the Midianite yoke. My wrath was hot against you, for you have bowed down and served the Amorite gods and the Baals of the Canaanites. I am a jealous God; and I have delivered you into the hands of the Midianites. But I have remembered the bargain I struck with Moses, and I will redeem you from the Midianite oppression.

This is all too much for Gideon, who excuses himself and tries to get Joash to come out and deal with the stranger. Joash can't be bothered, and Gideon starts back towards the wine press.

THE ANGEL (*shouting majestically in booming tones*)—Ten plagues I hurled at Pharaoh to awe you with my might. I drove back the sea with a strong east wind, and Israel walked through the waters! Would that not be sign enough? But you are a stubborn people! From that day to this have you rebelled against the Lord! I shattered the walls of Jericho with trumpets. But this mighty God was not enough for you! A cult of whores did you require! You have reveled before eyeless gods! You have done evil in mine eyes!

GIDEON (*unnerved*)—Sir, I don't know why you are so enraged.

THE ANGEL—Gideon, do you not know me? I am your Lord Yahweh, the Kinsman of Jacob, who was the father of all the houses of Israel.

GIDEON—I shall not say you are not.

THE ANGEL (*shouting*)—I tell you I, even I, am he!

GIDEON (*thoroughly distressed*)—What would you have me say? I find all this an unusual business. I do not hold everyday traffic with gods. I said: "Very well." What else should I have said?

THE ANGEL—I did not mean to discomfit you.

GIDEON—And now that I am put to it, I will tell you plainly—I do not believe in gods. You say that you are the god, Yahweh. The fact is, sir, in these parts, you are but a minor divinity. We Abiezrites are poor farmers, and we must pray for fertility, so we adopted a goddess with breasts and a womb, Ishtar—a sportive lady, I must say; her festivals are lively times. And now we have added the rain Baal of Beth-shean! To these gods I give my awe. For I am a child in many ways and truly thought the air was cluttered with fierce powers. But lately I have come to wondering. (*Indicating the sacrificial goat on the altar.*) What god will eat this sacrifice? Only that black bird. A carrion crow is not much of a god really; I can chase him away with a stick.

THE ANGEL—I like you, Gideon; you are a straightforward man.

GIDEON—Well, you are quick to temper, I see, but there is a sweetness in you.

THE ANGEL—Come, we will talk. I promised Jacob I would make of him a great people, and I did. Jacob was but a wandering Aramaean with a household of seventy people when I sent him down into Egypt. And when I led them out of the land of Egypt, the house of Jacob had become six hundred families, rich with flocks and servants. And I gathered the whole twelve tribes of them by the Jordan River. "Look here," spoke I, "I shall give this land across the Jordan to you, and you shall prosper there. Your part of the bargain is simple enough. You shall not bow down to any other god." Could it have been more plainly stated? (THE ANGEL *goes on to review the history of the Hebrews who foolishly turned to Amorite gods. As he talks he gets more and more worked up at the comparative insignificance of these other gods, and the stupidity of people who worship them.*) Your god is no cat. Nor can his likeness be chipped from stone. Not by gold nor red carbuncle can your god be wrought. Your god is beyond dimension. (*He is beginning to shout and prance at the thought of his own omnipotence.*) Your god is all! I am what is! I am the Lord! (*Stops and sees* GIDEON *watching open-mouthed.*) What was it we were talking of?

GIDEON—You were saying our fathers bowed down to other gods.

THE ANGEL—Your fathers indeed! Have *you* not bowed down to Ishtar and Baal? And so I have given you into the hands of the Midianites. (*Rising to godlike majesty.*) This one last time shall I redeem you! But if you break faith with me one more time, then cursed shall you be. You shall serve your enemies in nakedness! Among all nations, you shall find no rest! For *I* am the Lord! I *am* the Lord! I am the *Lord!*

The Angel tells Gideon that he is raising him up as the redeemer who will deliver the Hebrews from the Midianites. Gideon points out that he is "the donkey of the clan," knows nothing about warfare, and is therefore incapable of inspiring the confidence of anyone. "Who will join Gideon's army?" he asks. At this point one of the elders rushes in to announce that the Midianites are crossing the river, and everyone starts rushing about, preparing to run and hide in the caves. Gideon calls attention to the presence of the stranger, but no one else is able to see him.

THE ANGEL (*to* GIDEON)—The spirit of the Lord is upon you, Gideon, and the people shall do as you tell them.

GIDEON (*chanting in a state of possession*)—Rise up, ye elders! The Lord of Jacob will redeem you. And the Midianites will flee before you seven ways!

HELEK—On my head, is this *Gideon* who prophesies?

GIDEON—Sound the trumpet, Father! Gather the Abiezrites upon this hill. We shall make war with Midian. (*He seizes the sacrificial knife from the altar and with a quick stroke slashes off a section of* HELEK's *robe.*) Send messengers to the chiefs of Manasseh, who shall say: "Whosoever does not come out after Gideon, thus shall my sword be brought down on him." The battle shall be met in three days' time. It is the word of the Lord! The trumpet, Father! Go fetch the horn and sound it! (JOASH *shuffles dumbly into his tent to get the horn, as* GIDEON *continues his instructions. The other elders obey him and the women sing "We have raised up a savior!"* JOASH *comes out with a large trumpet and lets loose a mighty blast which causes* GIDEON *to wince.*)

JOASH—Shall we sound the horn again, my lord Gideon? (GIDEON *is startled but pleased with his new appellation. He looks at* THE ANGEL, *who nods approvingly.*)

GIDEON (*smiling with delight and disbelief*)—Yes, I suppose we had better.

SCENE II

It is late afternoon three days later, and on the hill at Harod a pessimistic group of thirty-two thousand Hebrew "warriors" have assembled. Shillem, a grizzled old campaigner who rather fancies himself, is criticizing Gideon for his lack of forcefulness in a situation where their army is outnumbered by one hundred and twenty thousand Midianites in the valley below.

SHILLEM—I took our general, Gideon, up to the crest of this hill this morning and we looked down upon this awesome multitude. I said to Gideon, "My General, what plan of battle have you for this?" "I haven't the beginnings of an idea," he said, "have you?" And that was this morning.

HEZEKIAH—You mean we have no plan of battle?

SHILLEM—Absolutely none. So I have been conceiving a clever shift or two. Still, we are badly favored in this battle. (*He takes a stick and starts to outline his battle plan to the others.* GIDEON, *dressed in a leather corselet, has been sitting gloomily on one side of the stage. Suddenly* THE ANGEL *enters in excellent spirits.*)

GIDEON (*irritatedly*)—Where have you been?

THE ANGEL—Why are you suddenly so cross? When I left you this morning, you kissed the hem of my robe and vowed eternal love to me.

GIDEON—This corselet chafes.

THE ANGEL—Oh, take it off. It is much too hot for leather. But you will posture as a general and swagger among the troops.

GIDEON—That old man Shillem is driving me out of my wits.

THE ANGEL—A vain old man, why do you listen to him?

GIDEON—The captains sit in my tent now. "What is the plan of battle?" they shall say. "The Lord of Moses is with you," I shall answer, "and you shall not fear." Well, I shall have to have something cleverer to say than that.

The Angel tells Gideon that he has a plan, but that Gideon has been so busy showing off as a general, he hasn't thought to ask him for it. The Angel instructs Gideon to gather together three hundred oil lamps and three hundred horns, and also to send messengers to the chiefs of Ephraim to set men to slaughter the fleeing Midianites at the place they will try to cross the Jordan. With much misgiving Gideon hands Yahweh's strange instructions on to his captains, and on being questioned by them admits that he is as curious about how Yahweh's plan will work as they are. However, they resignedly obey. Gideon returns to talk with The Angel, who has now decided that if Midian is to be defeated by thirty-two thousand Hebrews, it will not be clear that Israel won by the hand of God alone. He therefore commands Gideon to send home all who are fearful and trembling. Gideon argues with him. The Angel gets angry and starts to threaten him.

GIDEON—All right, pray, do not shout, sir. It shall be done. (*Petulantly* GIDEON *assembles his captains.*) Well, harken to this. You are each to go to your separate camps and proclaim: "Whoever is fearful and trembling, let him return home."

SHILLEM—Are you insane?

GIDEON—Well, what am I to do? It is the word of the Lord! He spoke it to me; I speak it to you! I too am ill-disposed to this idea. If we are to talk of those who tremble and fear, well, sir, I am surely the captain of *that* army!

SHILLEM—Peace, peace, Gideon.

GIDEON—Go and parley with him yourself if you think you can reap a better crop from him than I!

JAHLEEL—But the Lord keeps himself invisible to all but you.

GIDEON—Well, perhaps I am insane. Have you ever considered that? Not every man who sees a vision is a prophet! You may all be gathered here at the fancy of a maniac! At any moment, I may drop down to all fours and howl.

The chiefs look questioningly at one another, shrug, and go off to follow Yahweh's order. The Angel congratulates Gideon on his handling of the situation. But he has now decided that he wants the troops even further reduced so that there can be no question of the miraculousness of the impending victory. He wants Gideon to keep only the three hundred most frightened soldiers. Then he is to give each a lamp and a horn, and he is to place one hundred men at Shunem, one hundred men at Endor and keep one hundred at Harod. On a signal all three companies will light their lanterns, wave them in the air and simultaneously blow loud blasts on their trumpets, which Yahweh believes will send the Midianites fleeing down the valley to Beth-barah, where they will be slaughtered. Gideon regards The Angel quizzically.

GIDEON—This is the plan for which you had me assemble four tribes of Israel?

THE ANGEL—Well, it *is* intended to be a miracle, Gideon.

GIDEON—Oh, *that* is clear enough. (*He is deeply annoyed and can scarcely conceal his disappointment.*) It is a silly plan, sir! Three hundred tootling cowards will not send a hundred thousand men of Midian ranting down the Jordan Valley. The Midianites will simply look up and say: "What is all that tootling?" Then they will unsheathe their scimitars, root us out and slash us up. And see how clear this night! A full moon, not a cloud! No night for hidden warfare, this!

The Angel cannot understand why Gideon no longer believes in the Lord's ability to accomplish this miracle, and points out that he has given him proofs of his godhood, such as making a fleece be wet in the morning on an otherwise dry hill.

THE ANGEL—I am plainly confused. I have loved you, and you have turned your back.

GIDEON—I do find you personable, sir.

THE ANGEL—Personable! Gideon, one does not merely fancy God. I demand a splendid love from you, abandoned adoration.

GIDEON—I'm afraid I'm not the splendid sort, my Lord!

THE ANGEL—I shall make you love me. I'll do another miracle for you. The moon is too manifest for you, is it? Shall I eclipse it?

GIDEON—I have no faith in miracles; they are too easily denied. If you could send me a dream, my Lord . . .

THE ANGEL—You will not honor my miracles performed openhandedly before your eyes, but you put great stock in dreams?

GIDEON—Oh, sir, it is a well-known fact that dreams portend the future.

THE ANGEL—What a devious mind man has developed. Well, then, what would you say to the dream dreamed last night by the kings of Midian?

GIDEON—Oh, sir, such a dream would be most portentous.

The Angel causes to appear before Gideon two kings of Midian, who are discussing a dream one of them had in which a cake of barley bread tumbled into the Midianite camp and upset his tent. The other king interprets this as Gideon victorious. Suddenly we see them both sent into further fright by an eclipse of the moon. Gideon is most impressed with this, and embraces the knees of The Angel. Then he lifts his face and sings out a psalm of love to the Lord.

Scene III

It is several hours later and of course Yahweh's plan has worked out. We see Gideon and his captains rushing about shouting: "For the Lord and Gideon!" as they tend to the final details of the massacre. Gideon is full of the victory.

GIDEON (*to* THE ANGEL)—Oh, my Lord, it came to pass, as you said. One hundred and twenty thousand Midianites lie slain this night. How great you are, my Lord, and how impermanent is man. (*He begins to laugh.*) You will not believe this. One hundred and twenty thousand of them slain, and I, captain of the hosts of Israel, did not so much as unsheathe my dagger! I never got within a mile of a Midianite! I watched the whole night from the hills! (THE ANGEL *encourages* GIDEON *to rest beside him.*) Have I found favor in your eyes tonight, my Lord?

THE ANGEL—Indeed you have.

GIDEON (*after a moment*)—Have you loved many men, my Lord?

THE ANGEL—I love all men. It is my essence.

GIDEON—I love you more than I have ever loved anyone.

THE ANGEL (*recounting the other mortals with whom he has talked*)—I have loved five men, or six if I add in Phinehas, but I could not say I truly loved Phinehas. A nice man, Phinehas, good family, son of Eleazar the son of Aaron; but, still, not my sort. Too pinchpenny with his passions. Abraham . . . Isaac . . . Jacob of course . . . Joshua. But the man I loved most was Moses. And he was scarcely Hebrew. He was bred as an Egyptian and married a gentile woman. A hulking, harelipped, solitary man, quite unattractive really, stammered, sullen, lacking wit, one of those ever-earnest fellows. Yet I fancied Moses from the first. Gaunt he stood against the crags of Horeb, a monumentally impassioned man. It is passion, Gideon, that carries a man to God. It inspirits man's sessile soul above his own inadequate world and makes real such things as beauty, fancy, love, and God. Passion is the very fact of God in man that makes him other than a brute.

The Angel tells Gideon that he didn't have much passion in him until he went to work on him, and that Gideon's special attraction to him is that he is a plain man. "I would have plain men love me, not just saints," says The Angel. Gideon is hurt momentarily, but admits that "like all modest men" he is impossibly vain. He tells The Angel he has had very little esteem in life, and that even his only child uses him lightly. The Angel promises him seventy sons and "the ardor of many wives." Furthermore, he promises to bless him and make him prosper, so that all Israel shall regard him as the most blessed of men because he is beloved of God.

GIDEON—Yes, but all this good fortune which you will make mine, will not really be mine. There is no honor that reflects to me in it at all, merely that I am beloved of God.

THE ANGEL—Well, that is a somewhat less than gracious thing to say.

GIDEON (*ashamed*)—Forgive me.

THE ANGEL—I wonder if this vanity of yours is as ingenuous as it seems, and if it is not a sinister thing rather. What is vanity in man really, but the illusion that he has a purpose? Do not presume to matter, Gideon. You are a meaningless thing and live only in my eye. I shall make you great, Gideon, because I love you; but it is merely my caprice. To love me, you must abandon all your vanities. They are presumptuous and will come between us.

Gideon is truly penitent and assures The Angel that he will never betray him. Some troops come by with their captain, Shillem, who is worried that the whole army will find out that during the battle he swooned at the sight of blood and hid all night in a cave. Hezekiah and Malchiel enter and tell exaggerated stories of Gideon's deeds in the battle. Malchiel goes into a trance and divines from configurations on the ground that Gideon is the dazzling son of Yahweh, and cries out praise for him. Hezekiah explains that unlike his brother, he prefers to find more reasonable explanations for things than gods, and that when all the facts of the battle are known Gideon's stratagem with the horns and lamps will prove simply a clever move to stampede the cattle. "Taken piece by piece," he says, "the events of the night become less mystical."

They are interrupted by the arrival of the prince of Ephraim, who appears in a litter carried by exhausted slaves. He is furious that Gideon went ahead in his battle without asking his counsel, and without appointing an Ephraimite to lead the other tribes in war. Hezekiah warns him that he had better be more humble when Gideon comes, and tells of Gideon's powerful battle deeds such as the smiting of one hundred Midianites with an ox-goad. At this point Gideon enters and the prince bows down to him. However, when Gideon tells him that the truth of the matter is that he killed no Midianites at all, the prince is enraged at being gulled and demands to take over the army.

GIDEON—Hear, O Ephraimite! Do not contend with me for glory, for it is neither yours nor is it mine! This glory is the Lord's!

Give praise to the Lord for he has triumphed gloriously. Bow down! (*All bow down, and while they are supplicating* GIDEON *turns to* THE ANGEL *and prostrates himself.*) Did you truly fear my vanity?

THE ANGEL—Rise up, good Gideon, and pursue after the kings of the enemy.

GIDEON (*standing up*)—Rise up! These are my charges to you all. Let the Ephraimites count the dead and bury them. Captains of Asher and Naphtali, come with me. We shall pursue the kings of Midian. (GIDEON *raises his hand with a flourish.*) For Gideon and for the Lord!

THE OTHERS—For Gideon and the Lord! (*They rush off after* GIDEON.)

THE ANGEL (*muttering to himself*)—"For Gideon and for the Lord," indeed. It used to be: "For the Lord and for Gideon."

ACT II

The scene is a threshing floor on a hill by the city of Succoth. At one side we see three of the elders of Succoth bound and guarded by soldiers. Shillem enters and gives orders to prepare a feast for Gideon, who has just won the battle of Karkor and smote the last of the Midianites. He also has orders that the Hebrew elders of Succoth who have jeered at the word of the Lord must die. When Gideon arrives, and is offered grapes and obeisance, he warns the people to make no god of him, as it was the Lord that redeemed them from Midian. Then he smites down the two captured kings of Midian. He is about to start on the elders but seeing their tears, decides to wait until after he has eaten. He commands everyone to bow down to the Lord, and while they are in this position he goes over to where The Angel is standing. After an embrace, which The Angel notices is rather perfunctory, Gideon suggests that The Angel wait for him at his tent at Ophrah. The Angel agrees to do so and starts to leave when Gideon calls to him. The Angel stops, and Gideon asks him if he cannot commute the sentences of the elders of Succoth from death to being scourged with whips. The Angel is adamant that Gideon smite them down for their homosexuality, their incest, and their other Godless acts, "so that all Israel may hear and fear." Gideon sorrowfully submits.

THE ANGEL—Oh, Gideon, you make so much of death. You must not be so temporal. It is all right for the bulk of men to fear death, for in death they fear me. But, in truth, there isn't anything to it at all. Nothing happens, nothing changes; the essence of things goes on. You see, you measure things in time, but there is no time in truth. You live now ten million years ago and are at this moment ten million years hence, for there are no years. The slaying of seventy-seven elders happens but it does not happen, for they live even so and have died before, and all is now, which was and is forever. (*Sees* GIDEON's *puzzled expression.*) Oh dear, I see this is heavy going for you. Well, you shouldn't bother your head with all these speculations anyway. I am the final truth, so you need only love me, and live your life as I will it for you.

GIDEON—My point, you see, is that I pity these old men.

THE ANGEL—Of course you do. But you are being vain again, for to pity a man's death is to say his life was significant, which it isn't. Now go and smite the elders. I am the Lord.

There is another matter troubling Gideon, and nervously he approaches The Angel about it. He has found that he enjoys having the people make a fuss about him and calling him king. He knows it is vanity, but he wonders if perhaps the Lord will let him be nominal king of Israel, and promises that he will have altars built to God and make his name greater. The Angel is furious at this new demand and calls Gideon a presumptuous man. Gideon, who is in a temper, replies that he doesn't find it an easy thing "to love you, God." The Angel points out that he has struck down many men for less than what Gideon is doing now, and refuses to make him king over these people.

THE ANGEL (*explaining*)—They shall see a king and forget about the Lord. They will seek blessings from this king who cannot bless them and fear this king who cannot frighten. Oh, Gideon, let us not quarrel. I said I shall exalt you above your fellows, and I shall. I vowed seventy sons to you; well, then, (*Snaps fingers in air, twice.*) know that both your wives at home are now with child. (GIDEON *incredulously snaps his own fingers twice in the air, and looks questioningly at* THE ANGEL, *who nods affirmatively.*) Indeed, from this moment all women shall plead to be your wives. Now lay and rest; then go and smite the elders.

The Angel departs, leaving a half-satisfied Gideon muttering to himself. He tries to forget about his quarrel and begins to eat and drink with the rest. Meanwhile Orpah, the voluptuous fourteen-year-old daughter of one of the condemned elders, proceeds to turn her seductive charms loose on Gideon by doing a savagely passionate belly dance for him. It is not clear whether this is the first manifestation of the prediction The Angel has just made, or the girl's attempt to save her father. However, at the end of the dance,

Orpah's father does offer her to Gideon as a sacrifice of atonement, and begs that he spare the lives of the elders. Gideon, who is now fairly drunk with wine, admits that he is tempted, but that it can't be done because it is the word of the Lord that they must die. But since he has a sympathethic audience he begins to complain that although he has faithfully carried out every order of the Lord, and praised him with every breath, the Lord has denied him the little things he wants. He points out that Israel needs a king, in order to become a nation among nations, and to unite tribes that otherwise might fight with each other. Gideon's captains urge him to be the king and all press Gideon to accept this honor.

Gideon—Nay, I will not rule over you, and my son will not rule over you; the Lord will rule over you, for he is in truth our king, and we need no other. Come, let us give offering up to God. Give me all the golden rings Midian wore in his ears and all the golden crescents Midian hung about the necks of his camels. I shall melt these golden things and make a sacred golden garment as a gift to the Lord. I shall set it on a high place by my tent, and in the sun it shall be seen for many miles. All who see it shall think of the Lord and his great victory. (*To* Malchiel.) Give me my spear! The spirit of the Lord is upon me and I shall kill these elders! (*He raises the spear above his head to smite the first elder, but a look of horror crosses his face and he lowers the spear, letting it dangle from his hand. He is trembling.*) I cannot do it. Let them live, Shillem, scourge them with whips, with briars and thorns. For surely man must have more meaning than this. (*He shuffles disconsolately, even guiltily, a few steps away as* Shillem *carries out his orders and the elders sing in praise of* Gideon *and his mercy.*)

Scene II

It is two days later back at Gideon's tent. Gideon is bringing the golden ephod he has made and his new wife, Orpah, to Ophrah. The Angel is there waiting to let him feel his wrath. He greets Gideon coldly and is unimpressed by the ephod Gideon puts on the altar in his honor. Gideon excuses himself for a moment to introduce Orpah to his father and to his other wives. Joash tells him that both his wives are with child again and Gideon gives The Angel a look. The Angel nods and snaps his fingers twice. Joash praises Gideon's feats, but Gideon fights down the temptation to take credit for them. Finally Joash tells everyone of Hezekiah's scientific analysis of what happened.

JOASH—"We are all men of reason here," he said, "and need not explain all things in supernatural ways. The savage will say God gave us into the hands of the Midianites, but was it not in fact the economic conditions of drought in the desert that drove the Midianites upon us? Was it the spirit of God that aroused the tribes of Israel, or was it not rather the need to protect our increase in caravan trade? Is the panic of one hundred and twenty thousand Midianites so hard to understand when one realizes that these were a primitive people with a crumbling social fabric? All that was needed was a bold and ingenious general who could exploit these weaknesses of Midian." And, indeed, Gideon, that was you.

GIDEON—Well, it is not altogether illogical, is it?

JOASH—"Indeed," said this Hezekiah, "who is this Yahweh of Gideon's? Has anyone seen him or heard his words? Only Gideon." It was Hezekiah's contention that Yahweh was a masterful fiction you created to inspirit the troops.

GIDEON (*eagerly*)—Now, how did his reasoning go again? It was the economic conditions prevailing in . . .

THE ANGEL (*roaring*)—Gideon! (*The smile disappears from* GIDEON'S *face.*)

GIDEON (*sighing*)—Ah. It is none of it true. There is no honor due me at all, but that I am the device of God.

Gideon's son is embarrassed at his father's humility and shuffles away. Seeing the sacred golden ephod on the altar he goes to examine it, and is prevented from touching it and being instantly struck down by a quick warning from The Angel, transmitted to him by his father. Gideon then asks everyone to go prepare the festival on the hill and leave him alone to talk with the Lord. When they have left, The Angel tells Gideon that the Lord's wrath is not to be turned aside by the golden undercoat. He charges him with attempting to usurp the Lord's function and power by giving life to the elders of Succoth, after the Lord had instructed it to be taken away. And he is furious that Gideon wants to believe all of Hezekiah's claptrap about socio-economic conditions. Gideon points out that Hezekiah is a scholar who knows all about the ecliptic of the sun as it revolves around the earth. The Angel snorts and tells Gideon that it is the earth that revolves around the sun, which Gideon refutes as "patent nonsense." He points at the sky and tells The Angel: "The sun obviously revolves around the earth."

THE ANGEL—Oh! I don't know how I bear with you!

GIDEON (*crying out*)—Oh, my Lord, let me go!

THE ANGEL (*not believing his ears*)—Are you suggesting some kind of divorce between your God and you?

GIDEON—It is too much for me, this loving God. I tried but you are too vast a concept for me. To love you, God, one must be a god himself. I did not kill the elders of Succoth, and I shall tell you why. I raised my spear above their heads, but in that moment I felt a shaft of terror. It was as if the nakedness of all things was exposed to me, and I saw myself and all men for what we truly are, suspensions of matter, flailing about for footholds in the void, all the while slipping back screaming into endless suffocations. That is the truth of things, I know, but I cannot call it truth. It is too hideous, an intolerable state of affairs. I cannot love you, God, for it makes me a meaningless thing.

THE ANGEL (*exasperated*)—Oh!

GIDEON—This is your own doing, for you gave me passion that I might raise myself to you. How shall I think myself an aimless brute now?

THE ANGEL—I meant you to love me, but you are merely curious. You have no feeling for me then at all?

GIDEON—I fear you, God. Perhaps, that's the only love a man can give his god.

THE ANGEL (*hurt*)—What shall we do then, Gideon?

GIDEON—Let me go, God. Go from my sight. Make not your presence known to me again that I might say: "God is a dream, a name, a thought, but not a real thing."

THE ANGEL—You would pretend that God is not, although you know that he is, so that you might be a significant creature which you know you are not. Oh! This is beyond even God's understanding! If fear is all the love you have for me, then you shall fear me, Gideon! As I blessed you for your love, so shall I punish you for your infidelity. You did not slay the seven and seventy elders of Succoth. Then, the seventy sons I promised you shall die in their stead. They shall die in bitterness by each other's hands.

GIDEON—Oh, God, this is most cruel! (*He falls on his knees.*) Behold mine own small world of people there. (*Points to his family who have returned from the hill.*) Could I not pretend there is some reason for their being here? *Pretend,* my Lord, no more than that. Let me have at least some bogus value.

THE ANGEL (*gently*)—I am truth, Gideon. I cannot vary.

GIDEON (*looking around for* THE ANGEL)—You seem blurred, my Lord. I asked you that I might delude myself with some spurious grandeur.

THE ANGEL (*who apparently can no longer be seen or heard by* GIDEON)—You want the universe to please your eye, Gideon, and not mine. You would be God yourself. Hear me well, I am a jealous God and brook no other gods, not even you. Do not make a cult of man, not even in fancy.

GIDEON—My Lord? Where have you gone? We are not finished.

THE ANGEL (*who cannot believe that* GIDEON *can no longer see him*)—I stand right here! (GIDEON *looks right through him.*) O Gideon, do not forsake me! (*Becoming angry.*) I will not be so cast off. Go then to those painted dialectics and libertine philosophies and logics that wait along the road for gulls like you, and, for a shekel, promise you the secret sensuality of time and space. You will be fleeced, and soon abandoned in some red-threaded hovel of despair. Then do not hope that God awaits at home when with ragged beard the penitent returns.

GIDEON—I must aspire, God.

THE ANGEL—Then I shall do this to you and all of Israel! I will scatter you among the nations! Your land shall be a desolation, and your cities a waste! (GIDEON *has gone to the altar and is about to pick up the golden ephod in order to wear it to the festival.*) Do not touch it! This thing is mine!

GIDEON (*crying out*)—O God! I cannot believe in you! If you love me, let me believe at least in mine own self! If you love me, God!

THE ANGEL (*emotionally torn, lowers the arm with which he would have struck down* GIDEON)—I love you, Gideon! (GIDEON *puts on the ephod with the help of* ABIMELECH, *who has just arrived.*)

ABIMELECH—We all wait to hear you tell the miracle of God's victory over Midian.

GIDEON—A miracle? Why do you call it that? (*He puts his arms about* ABIMELECH *and* HELEK *and leads his family off to the festival.*) Nay, the war with Midian was not mysterious, but only the inevitable outgrowth of historico-economic, socio-psychological forces prevailing in these regions.

THE ANGEL—Oh, it is amusing.

God no more believes it odd
That men cannot believe in God.
Man believes the best he can,
Which means, it seems, belief in man.
Then let him don my gold ephod
And let him be a proper God. (*He pauses.*)
Well, let him try it anyway.

(THE ANGEL *bows, the lights black out, and the curtain falls.*)

A MAN FOR ALL SEASONS

A Play in Two Acts

BY ROBERT BOLT

[ROBERT BOLT *was born at Sale, in Cheshire, England, on August 15, 1924. After his graduation from Manchester University, where he majored in history, he became a school teacher and wrote his first play for the children of his school to act at Christmas. His first adult play, "The Last of the Wine," was about the atomic bomb, and his second, "The Critic and the Heart," was performed at Oxford. In 1957 he made his London debut with "Flowering Cherry," which ran more than a year, but a 1959 Broadway production of the play achieved only five performances. He then wrote "The Tiger and the Horse," and this was followed by "A Man for All Seasons," which although it was a London success, was even better received in New York. His political attitudes—that the individual and his society are of equal importance and cannot be considered apart from each other, and that the philosophy of Communism is grossly inadequate to the present world situation—have caused him to be considered middle-of-the-road by both rightists and leftists, who have been involved in far less radical action than has he. His next play will be about a group of very rich people living outside of England, and will be set in the present.*]

THE curtain rises on a dark stage. One spotlight picks up a pot-bellied man dressed in shabby black tights and a black jersey. He is seated on a huge wicker hamper which contains costumes and other objects he will need for setting the ensuing scene.

MAN—It is perverse! To start a play made up of Kings, Cardinals, and intellectuals, with *me*. If a King or a Cardinal had done the prologue he'd have had the right materials. And an intellectual would have shown enough majestic meanings, coloured propositions, and closely woven liturgical stuff to dress the House of Lords! (*Rising to show off his dreary costume.*) But this! Is this a costume? Does this say anything? A bit of black material to reduce Old Adam to the Common Man. Oh, if they'd let me come on naked, I could have shown you something of my own. (*Going to the hamper and opening it.*) Well, for a proposition of my own, I need a costume. (*Takes out the coat and hat of a steward from the basket and puts them on.*) Matthew! The household Steward of Sir Thomas More!

The lights come on to reveal an architectural setting which, by a few slight changes in backgrounds and foreground symbols lowered from above, will represent many locations. Now it is More's house in Chelsea circa 1526 when he was Speaker of the House of Commons. The swift-moving, lively but pale More enters down the stairs, followed by Sir Richard Rich, an unhappy academic in his early thirties.

Rich and More are discussing the notion that every man has his price and all that is necessary to corrupt anyone is to impose suffering on him and then offer him escape. Rich has learned this from reading Machiavelli at the suggestion of Thomas Cromwell, the secretary of Cardinal Wolsey.

MORE—Richard, you should go back to Cambridge; you're deteriorating.

RICH—Well, I'm not used. D'you know how much I have to show for seven months' work—

MORE—Work?

RICH—Work! Waiting's work when you wait as I wait, hard! For seven months, I have to show: the acquaintance of the Cardinal's outer doorman, the indifference of the Cardinal's inner doorman, and the Cardinal's chamberlain's hand in my chest! Oh—also one half of a "Good morning" delivered at fifty paces by the Duke of Norfolk. Doubtless he mistook me for someone.

MORE—The Dean of St. Paul's offers you a post at the new school.

RICH (*bitterly*)—A teacher!

MORE—A man should go where he won't be tempted. (*He picks up a silver cup and brings it to* RICH.) Do you want it?

RICH—Well—thank you, of course—thank you!

MORE—You'll sell it, won't you?

RICH—Well, I . . . Yes, I will.

MORE—And buy what?

RICH—Some decent clothes . . . a gown like yours.

More—You'll get several gowns for that, I should think. It was sent to me a little while ago by some woman. Now she's put a lawsuit into the Court of Requests. It's a bribe, Richard.

Rich—Oh . . . (*Chagrined.*) So you give it away, of course.

More—Well, I'm not going to keep it, and you need it. Of course, if you feel it is contaminated . . .

Rich—No, no. I'll risk it.

More—But, Richard, in office they offer you all sorts of things. I was once offered a whole village, with a mill, and a manor house, and heaven knows what else—a coat of arms, I shouldn't be surprised. (*Looking sympathetically at* Rich.) Why not be a teacher? You'd be a fine teacher. Perhaps—a great one.

Rich—And if I was, who would know it?

More—You, your pupils, your friends, God. Not a bad public, that . . . Oh, and a *quiet* life.

Rich (*laughing*)—*You* say that!

More—Richard, I was commanded into office; it was inflicted on me. (Rich *seems unconvinced.*) Can't you believe that?

Rich—It's hard.

The Duke of Norfolk, Earl Marshal of England, enters with More's wife, Lady Alice. Born into the merchant class, her overdressing and coarseness make her absurd at a distance, but she is more impressive close to. They are followed by the lovely and intelligent Lady Margaret, Sir Thomas's daughter by a former marriage. They are discussing falconry and the quick rise of the farrier's son, Thomas Cromwell, to the post of Cardinal's secretary. The conversation is interrupted by a letter, summoning More to visit the Cardinal immediately. Everyone says their goodbyes and as soon as they have left the stage Matthew removes the table cloth and utensils and replaces them with Wolsey's ornate deskcover and portfolio.

Matthew (*referring to* Rich *who has given him a grudging small tip*)—That one'll come to nothing. My master Thomas More would give anything to anyone. Some say that's good and some say that's bad, but I say he can't help it—and that's bad . . . because some day someone's going to ask him for something that he wants to keep; and he'll be out of practice. (*He closes the hamper, and reflects.*) There must be something that he wants to keep. That's only Common Sense.

The stage is now set as Wolsey's office, where More has been summoned to discuss the Cardinal's dispatch to Rome. It is a lonely den of self-indulgence and contempt inhabited by the old Cardinal who is a combination of megalomaniac ambition and superior intellect. More has told him that he feels the council should be told about the dispatch before it is sent to Italy, which causes Wolsey to comment: "You're a constant regret to me, Thomas. If you could just see facts flat on, without that horrible moral squint; with just a little common sense, you could have been a statesman." Their conversation is interrupted by the sound and sight of the King going by.

WOLSEY—Where has he been? D'you know?

MORE—I, Your Grace?

WOLSEY—Oh, spare me your discretion. He's been to play in the mud again.

MORE (*coldly*)—Indeed!

WOLSEY—Indeed! Indeed! Are you going to oppose me? (*He sees that his exasperation is futile and relaxes.*) All right, we'll plod. The King wants a son; what are you going to do about it?

MORE (*drily*)—I'm sure the King needs no advice from me on what to do about it.

WOLSEY (*gripping* MORE's *shoulder from behind*)—Thomas, we're alone. I give you my word. There's no one here.

MORE—I didn't suppose there was, Your Grace.

WOLSEY—Do you favor a change of dynasty, Sir Thomas? D'you think two Tudors is sufficient?

MORE (*horrified*)—For God's sake, Your Grace! . . .

WOLSEY—Then the King needs a son; what are you going to do about it?

MORE—I pray for it daily.

WOLSEY (*softly*)—God's death, he means it. (*Referring to* ANNE BOLEYN.) That thing out there's at least fertile, Thomas.

MORE—But she's not his wife.

WOLSEY—No, Catherine's his wife and she's as barren as a brick. Are you going to pray for a miracle?

MORE—There *are* precedents.

WOLSEY—All right. Pray. Pray by all means. But in addition to Prayer, there is Effort. My effort's to secure a divorce. Have I your support or have I not?

MORE—A dispensation was granted so that the King might marry Queen Catherine, for State reasons. Now we are to ask the Pope to —dispense with his dispensation, also for State reasons?

WOLSEY—I don't *like* plodding, Thomas.

MORE—Then clearly all we have to do is approach His Holiness and ask him.

WOLSEY—I think we might influence His Holiness' answer—

MORE (*indicating the dispatch*)—Like this?

WOLSEY—Like that and in other ways—

MORE—I've already expressed my opinion on this—

WOLSEY (*rising*)—Then, good night! (*The two men regard each other.*) Oh, your conscience is your own affair; but you're a statesman! Do you *remember* the Yorkist Wars?

MORE—Very clearly.

WOLSEY—Let him die without an heir and we'll have them back again. Let him die without an heir and this "peace" you think so much of will go out like that! (*Extinguishes* MORE's *candle.*) Very well then . . . England needs an heir; certain measures, perhaps regrettable, perhaps not—there is much in the Church that *needs* reformation, Thomas. (MORE *smiles.*) All right, regrettable! But necessary to get us an heir! As Councilor of England how can you obstruct these measures for the sake of your own, private, conscience?

MORE—Well . . . (*Relighting his candle from the* CARDINAL's.) I believe when statesmen forsake their own private conscience for the sake of their public duties . . . they lead their country by a short route to chaos. And we shall have my prayers to fall back on.

WOLSEY—You'd like that, wouldn't you. To govern the country by prayers?

MORE—Yes, I should. (*Starts up the stairs to leave.*)

WOLSEY—More! You should have been a cleric!

MORE (*amused and looking down at him from the stairs*)—Like yourself, Your Grace?

The stage is suddenly transformed into the bankside of the Thames as the patterns of the moon's reflections in the water appear at the back of the stage. An oar and some boatman's clothes are lowered from above, and the Common Man enters and puts them on. More appears and is about to ride home with the boatman when they are interrupted first by the Cardinal's secretary, Thomas Cromwell, who attempts to find out how the interview went, and then by Chapuys, the Spanish Ambassador who, on behalf of his King, Queen Catherine's brother, learns in the indirect language of diplomacy that More has not supported Wolsey and Henry VIII in their efforts to get rid of Catherine. After they have left More remarks that the river looks black tonight and asks the boatman if it is silting up. The boatman replies: "Not in the middle, sir. There's a channel there getting deeper all the time."

On arriving home More is greeted by his daughter, Margaret, and her suitor William Roper, who has just asked her for her hand in marriage.

MORE—Roper, the answer's "no." And it will be "no" so long as you're a heretic.

ROPER—The Church is heretical! Doctor Luther's proved that to my satisfaction!

MORE—Luther's an excommunicate.

ROPER—From a heretic Church! Church? It's a shop! Forgiveness by the florin! Job lots now in Germany! . . . Mmmm, and divorces.

MORE—Divorces?

ROPER—Oh, half England's buzzing with that.

MORE—The Inns of Court may be buzzing, England doesn't buzz so easily.

ROPER—It will. And is that a Church? Is that a Cardinal? Is that a Pope? Or Antichrist! (MORE *angers and* MARGARET *signals frantically.* ROPER *to* MARGARET.) Look, what I know—I'll say!

MARGARET—You've no sense of *place.*

MORE (*ruefully*)—He's no sense of time. (*To* ROPER.) Two years ago you were a passionate Churchman; now you're a passionate—Lutheran. We must just pray that when your head's finished turning, your face is to the front again. (MORE *and* ROPER *part amicably, and* MORE *turns to his daughter.*) Nice boy . . . Terribly strong principles though. You know I think we've been on the wrong track with Will— It's no good arguing with a Roper. Now let him think he's going *with* the current and he'll turn round and start swimming in the opposite direction. What we want is a really substantial attack on the Church.

MARGARET—We're going to get it, aren't we?

MORE—Margaret, I'll not have you talk treason. . . . And I'll not have you repeat a lawyer's gossip. I'm a lawyer myself and I know what it's worth. (ALICE *comes downstairs to interrupt their conversation.*)

ALICE—Thomas—what did Wolsey want?

MORE—He wanted me to read a dispatch.

ALICE—Was that all?

MORE—A Latin dispatch.

ALICE—You don't want to talk about it?

MORE (*gently*)—No.

ALICE—Norfolk was speaking for you as Chancellor before he left.

MORE—He's a dangerous friend then. Wolsey's Chancellor, God help him. We don't want another.

MARGARET—Would you want to be Chancellor?

MORE—No.

MARGARET—But Norfolk said if Wolsey fell—

MORE—If Wolsey fell, the splash would swamp a few small boats like ours. There will be no new Chancellors while Wolsey lives.

The lights dim as they exit, and then a bright circle of light appears at one side of the stage. Into this circle is thrown from the wings the great red robe and the Cardinal's hat. The Common Man enters from the opposite wing, picks up the robe and hat and stuffs it roughly into the hamper. He then takes a book out of the hamper, puts on a pair of glasses and reads.

COMMON MAN—"Whether we follow tradition in ascribing Wolsey's death to a broken heart, or accept Professor Larcomb's less feeling diagnosis of pulmonary pneumonia, its effective cause was the King's displeasure. He died on 29 November, 1530, while on his way to the Tower under charge of High Treason. England's next Lord Chancellor was Sir Thomas More, a scholar and, by popular repute, a saint. His scholarship is supported by his writings; saintliness is a quality less easy to establish. But from his willful indifference to realities which were obvious to quite ordinary contemporaries, it seems all too probable that he had it."

The Common Man exits and the lights come up to illuminate the stage set now as Hampton Court, where Thomas Cromwell, now the King's special agent, and Richard Rich, now employed as the Duke of Norfolk's librarian, are conversing.

RICH—Master Cromwell—what *is* it that you do for the King? (CHAPUYS *enters.*)

CHAPUYS (*roguishly*)—Yes, *I* should like to know that, Master Cromwell. How should we introduce *you,* if we had the happiness?

CROMWELL—Oh sly! Do you notice how sly he is, Rich? Well, I suppose you would call me "The King's Ear." But it's even simpler than that. When the King wants something done, I do it.

CHAPUYS (*mockingly*)—Ah. But then why the Justices and Chancellors?

CROMWELL—Oh, *they* are the constitution. Our ancient, English constitution. I merely do things.

CHAPUYS—For example, Master Cromwell. . . .

CROMWELL—Oho—beware these professional diplomats. Well now, for example; next week at Deptford we are launching the *Great Harry*—one thousand tons. The King himself will be her pilot, and he will wear in every respect a common pilot's uniform. Except for the material, which will be cloth of gold. These innocent fancies require more preparation than you might suppose and someone has to do it. Meanwhile, I do prepare myself for higher things. I stock my mind.

CHAPUYS—Alas, Master Cromwell, don't we all? After the launching, I understand the King will take his barge to Chelsea to—

CROMWELL—Sir Thomas More's.

CHAPUYS—Will you be there?

CROMWELL—Oh, no—they'll talk about the divorce. (CHAPUYS *is shocked and* RICH *is uneasy.*) The King will ask him for an answer.

CHAPUYS (*ruffled*)—He has given his answer!

CROMWELL—The King will ask him for another.

CHAPUYS—Sir Thomas is a good son of the Church!

CROMWELL—Sir Thomas is a man. (*The* COMMON MAN *dressed as* MATTHEW, MORE's *steward, passes by.*)

MATTHEW (*conspiratorially*)—Sir, Sir Thomas doesn't talk about it to his wife. (*Waits.*)

CROMWELL—This is worth nothing.

MATTHEW (*significantly*)—But he doesn't talk about it to Lady Margaret—that's his daughter, sir.

CROMWELL—So?

MATTHEW—So he's worried, sir. (CROMWELL *is interested.*) Frightened. (CROMWELL *takes out a coin and pauses.*) Sir, he goes *white* when it's mentioned! (CROMWELL *gives him the coin and exits.*)

CHAPUYS (*approaching* MATTHEW)—Well?

MATTHEW—Sir Thomas rises at six, sir, and prays for an hour and a half. (*Pauses.*) During Lent, he lived entirely on bread and water. (*Pauses again.*) He goes to confession twice a week, sir. Parish priest. Dominican.

CHAPUYS—Ah, he is a true son of the Church. What did Master Cromwell want?

MATTHEW—Same as you, sir.

CHAPUYS—No man can serve two masters, Steward.

MATTHEW—No, indeed, sir; I serve *one.* (*He pulls around to the front of his neck an enormous cross until then hanging concealed behind his back.*)

CHAPUYS (*gives* MATTHEW *a coin*)—Our Lord watch you. (*Exits.*)

MATTHEW—You, too, sir. (*To audience.*) That's a very religious man.

RICH (*approaching* MATTHEW)—What did you tell Signor Chapuys? (*Gives him coin.*)

MATTHEW—I told him Sir Thomas says his prayers and goes to confession.

RICH—Why that?

MATTHEW—That's what he wanted to know, sir. I could have told him any number of things about Sir Thomas—that he has rheumatism, prefers red wine to white, is easily seasick, fond of kippers, afraid of drowning. But that's what he wanted to know. (*Looks at* RICH *with a certain contempt.*) Master Cromwell went that way, sir.

RICH (*furious*)—Did I ask you which way Master Cromwell went? (*To save face he goes off in the opposite direction.*)

MATTHEW (*thoughtfully, to audience*)—The great thing's not to get out of your depth . . . What I can tell them's common knowledge! But they've given money for it and everyone wants value for his money. They'll make a secret of it now to prove they've not been bilked . . . They'll make it a secret by making it dangerous . . . Oh, when I can't touch the bottom I'll go deaf, blind and dumb. (*Holds out coins.*) That's more than I *earn* in a fortnight! (*A fanfare of trumpets and the scene is changed back into* MORE's *house in Chelsea.* KING HENRY VIII *has arrived on his royal barge to sup with* MORE *and his family. The King is agreeably surprised by* MARGARET's *scholarship and her ability to speak with him in Latin.*)

HENRY—Ho! Take care, Thomas: "too much learning is a weariness of the flesh." (*To* MARGARET.) Margaret, are you fond of music?

MARGARET—Yes, Your Grace.

HENRY (*holding out his whistle*)—Blow. (*She does so and we hear the King's musicians begin to play. To* MORE.) Thomas. You *are* my friend, are you not?

MORE—Your Majesty.

HENRY—And thank God I have a friend for my Chancellor. (*Laughs.*) Readier to be friends, I trust, than he was to be Chancellor. Thomas . . . Did you know that Wolsey named you for Chancellor?

MORE—Wolsey!

HENRY—Aye; before he died. Wolsey named you and Wolsey was no fool.

MORE—He was a statesman of incomparable ability, Your Grace.

HENRY—Was he so? Then why did he fail me. It was villainy then. I was right to break him; he was all pride. And he failed me in the one thing that matters, then or now. And why? He wanted to be Pope! I'll tell you something, Thomas—it was never merry in England while we had Cardinals amongst us. (MORE *lowers his eyes.* HENRY *pauses and then resumes in a calculatedly offhand manner.*) Touching this matter of my divorce, Thomas; have you thought of it since we last talked?

MORE—Of little else.

HENRY—Then you see your way clear to me?

MORE—That you should put away Queen Catherine, Sire? Oh, alas—as I think of it I see so clearly that I can *not* come with Your Grace, that my endeavor is not to think of it at all.

HENRY—Then you have not thought enough! (*With real appeal.*) Great God, Thomas, why do you hold out against me in the desire of my heart?

MORE (*drawing up sleeve and baring his arm*)—There is my right arm. Take your dagger and saw it from my shoulder, and I will laugh and be thankful, if by that means I can come with Your Grace with a clear conscience.

HENRY (*uncomfortable*)—I know it, Thomas, I know . . .

MORE—When I took the Great Seal Your Majesty promised not to pursue me on this matter.

HENRY—Ha! So I break my word, Master More! (*Reconsiders.*) No, no, I'm joking . . . I joke roughly. (*Wandering away.*) I often think I'm a rough young fellow. (*Becoming more reasonable and pleasant.*) You must consider, Thomas, that I stand in peril of my soul. It was no marriage; she was my brother's widow. Leviticus: Chapter 18: "Thou shalt not uncover the nakedness of thy brother's wife."

MORE—Yes, Your Grace. But Deuteronomy—

HENRY (*triumphant*)—But Deuteronomy's ambiguous!

MORE (*bursting out*)—Your Grace, I'm not fit to meddle in these matters—to me it seems a matter for the Holy See—

HENRY (*reprovingly*)—Thomas, Thomas, does a man need a Pope to tell him when he's sinned? It was a sin. I admit it; I repent. And God has punished me . . . Son after son she's borne me, Thomas, all dead at birth, or within a month; I never saw the hand of God so clear in anything. It is my bounded *duty* to put away the Queen, and all the Popes back to St. Peter shall not come between me and my duty! How is it that you cannot see? Everyone else does.

MORE—Then why does Your Grace need my poor support?

HENRY—Because you are honest. What's more to the purpose, you're known to be honest. . . . There are those like Norfolk who follow me because I wear the crown, and there are those like Master Cromwell who follow me because they are jackals with sharp teeth and I am their lion, and there is a mass that follows me because it follows anything that moves—and there is you.

MORE—I am sick to think how much I must displease Your Grace.

HENRY—No, Thomas, I respect your sincerity. Respect? Oh, man, it's water in the desert. (*Pauses briefly.*) How did you like our music?

MORE—Could it have been Your Grace's own?

HENRY (*smiling*)—Discovered!

MORE—To me it seemed—delightful.

HENRY—Thomas—I chose the right man for Chancellor.

MORE—I must in fairness add that my taste in music is reputedly deplorable.

HENRY—Your taste in music is excellent. It exactly coincides with my own. (*Turns to* MORE, *his face set.*) Touching this other business, mark you, Thomas, I'll have no opposition. Your conscience is your own affair; but you are my Chancellor. There, you have my word—I'll leave you out of it. But I don't take it kindly, Thomas, and I'll have no opposition! Am I to burn in Hell because the Bishop of Rome, with the Spanish King's knife to his throat, mouths me Deuteronomy? Hypocrites! (MORE *rises.*) Lie low if you will, but—no words, no signs, no letters, no pamphlets—mark it, Thomas—no writings against me!

MORE—Your Grace is unjust. I am Your Grace's loyal minister.

HENRY—You are stubborn. (*Attempting to woo* MORE.) If you could come with me, you are the man I would soonest raise—yes, with my own hand.

MORE (*sitting and covering his face*)—Oh, Your Grace overwhelms me!

HENRY (*uneasily eyeing* MORE)—Oh, lift yourself up, man—have I not promised? (MORE *braces.*) Shall we eat? (*The chimes strike eight.*)

MORE—If Your Grace pleases. (*Recovering, as* LADY ALICE *re-enters.*)

HENRY—Eight o'clock? Thomas, the tide will be changing. I was forgetting the tide. I'd better go. Lady Alice, I had forgotten in your haven here how time flows past outside. Affairs call me to court and so I give you my thanks and say good night. (*He leaves.*)

ALICE (*to* MORE)—You crossed him!

MORE—Well, Alice—what would you *want* me to do?

ALICE—Be ruled! If you won't rule him, be ruled!

MORE—I neither could nor would rule my King. But there's a little . . . little, area . . . where I must rule myself. It's very little—less to him than a tennis court.

ALICE—I wish he'd eaten here . . .

MORE—Yes—we shall be living on that "simple supper" of yours for a fortnight. (ALICE *will not laugh.*) Alice, set your mind at rest—this (*Tapping himself.*) is not the stuff of which martyrs are made.

Roper bursts in, and proclaims that while he is still against the money-changers in the temple, he now interprets any attack on the Church itself as an attack on God. Rich enters and attempts to gain More's confidence by exposing More's steward, Matthew, as an informer. More is unstartled and Rich breaks down and pleads with More to employ him and says he will be steadfast. More refuses, telling Rich: "You couldn't answer for yourself even so far as to-night." Rich leaves and Roper, Margaret, and Alice urge More to have Rich arrested for libel.

MARGARET—Father, that man's bad.

MORE—There is no law against that.

ROPER—There is! God's law.

MORE—Then God can arrest him. I know what's legal, not what's right. I'll stick to what's legal. The currents and eddies of right and wrong, which you find such plain sailing, I can't navigate, I'm no voyager. But in the thickets of the law, oh, there I'm a forester. (*To himself.*) I doubt if there's a man alive who could follow me there, thank God.

ALICE (*exasperated*)—While you talk, he's gone!

MORE—And go he should, if he was the Devil himself, until he broke the law!

ROPER—So now you'd give the Devil benefit of law!

MORE (*to* ROPER)—Yes. What would you do? Cut a great road through the law to get after the Devil?

ROPER—I'd cut down every law in England to do that!

MORE—Oh? And when the last law was down, and the Devil turned round on you—where would you hide, Roper, the laws all being flat? Whoever hunts for me, Roper, God or Devil, will find me hiding in the thickets of the law! And I'll hide my daughter with me! Not hoist her up to the mainmast of your seagoing principles! They put about too nimbly! (*He goes off.*)

ALICE (*near tears*)—He said nothing about hiding me, you noticed! I've got too fat to hide, I suppose!

MARGARET—You know he meant us both.

MORE (*returning sheepishly*)—Roper, that was harsh: your principles are—excellent—the very best quality.

MARGARET—Father, can't you be plain with us?

MORE—I stand on the wrong side of no statute. I have not disobeyed my sovereign. I truly believe no man in England is safer than myself. And I want my supper. (*They all start up the stairs.*)

ALICE (*stopping*)—Why does Cromwell collect information about you?

MORE—I'm a prominent figure. Someone somewhere's collecting information about Cromwell. (ALICE *and* MARGARET *exit at the top of the stairs, and* MORE *and* ROPER *follow together.*) Will, I'd trust you with my life. But not your principles. You see, we speak of being anchored to our principles. But if the weather turns nasty you up with an anchor and let it down where there's less wind, and the fishing's better. Then "Look," we say, "I'm anchored!" (*Inviting* ROPER *to laugh with him.*) "To my principles!"

The Common Man shifts the scene to a pub, in which he will act as the barkeeper, or Publican. In one of the pub's private rooms Cromwell, who has just inherited the post of Secretary to the King's Privy Council, makes a joke about the King to Rich, who is nervous at its impropriety, or that he might be seen laughing at it.

CROMWELL—See how I trust you.

RICH—Oh, I would never repeat or report a thing like that.

CROMWELL—What kind of thing *would* you repeat or report?

RICH—Well, nothing said in friendship.

CROMWELL—D'you believe that?

RICH—Yes!

CROMWELL—Rich; seriously.

RICH (*after a pause*)—It would depend what I was offered.

CROMWELL—Don't say it just to please me.

RICH—It's true.

CROMWELL (*patting* RICH's *arm*)—Everyone knows it; not many people can say it.

RICH—There are *some* things one wouldn't do for anything. Surely.

CROMWELL—Mm—that idea's like these lifelines they have on the embankment: comforting, but you don't expect to have to use them. (*Briskly.*) Well, congratulations! I think you'd make a good Collector of Revenues for York Diocese.

RICH (*consciously cynical*)—What do I have to do for it?

CROMWELL—Nothing. It isn't like that, Rich. With so much wickedness purchasing so much worldly prospering. It's much more a matter of convenience, administrative convenience. The normal aim of administration is to keep steady this factor of convenience—and Sir Thomas would agree. Now normally when a man wants to change his woman, you let him if it's convenient and prevent him if it's not—normally indeed it's of so little importance that you leave it to the priests. But the constant factor is this element of convenience.

RICH—Whose convenience?

CROMWELL—Oh, ours. But everybody's too. However, in the present instance the man who wants to change his woman is our Sovereign Lord, Harry, by the Grace of God, the Eighth of that name. Which is a quaint way of saying that if he wants to change his woman he will. So *that* becomes the constant factor. And our job as administrators is to make it as convenient as we can. I say "our" job, on the assumption that you'll take this post at York I've offered you?

RICH—Yes . . . yes, yes.

CROMWELL—Now our present Lord Chancellor—there's an innocent man. The trouble is, his innocence is tangled in this proposition that you can't change your woman unless the Pope says so. And although his present Holiness is a strikingly corrupt old person, yet he still has this word "Pope" attached to him. And from this quite meaningless circumstance I fear some degree of . . .

RICH (*pleased to supply the right answer*)—Administrative inconvenience.

CROMWELL—Just so. (*Pauses.*) Now there *are* these men—you know—"upright" men who want themselves to be the constant factor in any situation; which, of course, they can't be. The situation rolls forward in any case. And if they've any sense they get out of its way.

RICH—What if they haven't any sense?

CROMWELL—Then they're only fit for Heaven. But Sir Thomas has plenty of sense; he could be frightened.

RICH—You've mistaken your man. Sir Thomas doesn't know how to be frightened.

CROMWELL—Why, then he never put his hand in a candle . . . Did he? (*Seizes* RICH's *wrist and holds his hand in the flame.*)

RICH (*shrieks and hugs his hand in his armpit as he regards* CROMWELL *with horror*)—You enjoyed that! You enjoyed it!

ACT II

COMMON MAN (*illuminated by a spotlight on the dark stage*)—The Intermission started early in the year 1530 and it's now the middle of May, 1532. During that time a lot of water's flowed under the bridge, and one of the things that have come floating along on it is: (*Reads from a book.*) "The Church of England, the finest flower of our Island genius for compromise; that system, which deflects the torrents of religious passion down the canals of moderation. This great effect was achieved not by bloodshed but by simple Act of Parliament. Only an unhappy few set themselves against the current of their times, and in so doing courted disaster. For we are dealing with an age less fastidious than our own. (*Gives audience querying look.*) Imprisonment without trial, and even examination under torture, were common practice. (*The lights come up to reveal* MORE *and his son-in-law,* ROPER, *discussing the Convocation at which the Church's bishops are deciding what to do about* HENRY'S *Act of Supremacy.*)

MORE (*referring to the chain of office he wears round his neck*)—If the bishops submitted this morning, I'll take it off.

ROPER—I don't see what difference Convocation can make. The Church is already a wing of the Palace. The King is already its "Supreme Head!"

MORE—"Supreme Head of the Church of England *so far as the law of God allows.*" How far the law of God does allow it remains a matter of opinion, since the Act doesn't state it.

ROPER—In your opinion, how far does the law of God allow this?

MORE—I'll keep my opinion to myself, Will.

ROPER—Yes? I'll tell you mine—

MORE—Don't! If your opinion's what I think it is, it's High Treason. (CHAPUYS *enters and* MORE *gives* ROPER *the sign to leave them alone.*)

CHAPUYS (*to the departing* ROPER)—*Dominus vobiscum!*

ROPER—*Et cum spiritu tuo!*

CHAPUYS (*thrillingly*)—How much longer shall we hear that holy language on these shores?

MORE—'Tisn't "holy," Your Excellency; just old.

CHAPUYS—Sir Thomas, rumour has it that if the Church in Convocation has submitted to the King, you will resign.

MORE—Would you approve of that?

CHAPUYS—Approve, applaud, and admire. It would show one man—and that man known to be temperate—unable to go further with this wickedness. Such a signal would be seen and understood by half your fellow countrymen! Sir Thomas, I have just returned from Yorkshire and Northumberland. Things are very different there. They are ready for resistance!

They are interrupted by the entrance of Norfolk who has come with the news of the Church's submission. Chapuys, embarrassed to be found there, makes his excuses and leaves hastily. More, with Margaret's assistance, removes the Chancellor's Chain from around his neck.

NORFOLK—Thomas, why? From where I stand this looks like cowardice!

MORE (*angry*)—This isn't "Reformation," this is war against the Church! . . . Our King has declared war on the Pope—because the Pope will not declare that our Queen is not his wife.

NORFOLK—And is she?

MORE (*cunningly*)—I'll answer that question for one person only, the King—and that in private too.

NORFOLK—The Pope's a Prince, isn't he? And a bad one?

MORE—Bad enough. But the theory is that he's also the Vicar of God, the descendant of St. Peter, our only link with Christ.

NORFOLK—And you'll forfeit all you've got—which includes the respect of your country—for a theory?

MORE—Yes, it's a theory. But what matters to me is not whether it's true or not but that I believe it to be true, or rather not that I *believe* it, but that *I* believe it. (*Lowering his voice.*) Have I your word that what we say is between us.

NORFOLK (*impatiently*)—Very well.

MORE—And if the King should command you to repeat what I have said?

NORFOLK—I should keep my word to you!

MORE—Then what has become of your oath of obedience to the King?

NORFOLK (*indignant*)—You lay traps for me!

MORE—No, I show you the times. (NORFOLK *starts to go.*) Oh, Howard! Signor Chapuys tells me he thinks we shall have trouble in the North Country. So do I. The Church—the old Church, not the new Church—is very strong up there. Keep an eye on the border this next spring.

NORFOLK—Thanks for the information. (*Ascending the stairs.*) It is good to know you still have . . . some vestige of patriotism. (*Exits.*)

ALICE—So there's an end of you. What will you do now?

MORE—Son Roper, *you're* pleased with me, I hope?

ROPER—Sir, you've made a noble gesture.

MORE—A gesture? I was not *able* to continue. I would have if I could! Alice, you don't think I would do this for a gesture? I'm practical.

ROPER—You belittle yourself, sir, this was not practical; this was moral!

MORE—Oh, now I understand you, Will. Morality's *not* practical. Morality's a gesture.

MARGARET—It *is,* for most of us, Father.

ALICE (*to* ROPER)—You'd dance him to the Tower, scattering

hymn books in his path! (*To* More.) Poor silly man, d'you think they'll *leave* you here to learn to fish?

More—If we govern our tongues they will! On the King's Supremacy, the King's Divorce—have you heard me make a statement?

Alice—No—and if I'm to lose my rank and fall to housekeeping I want to know the reason; so make a statement now.

More—No. In silence is my safety under the law, but it must extend to you.

The Common Man, who will appear no more as More's steward since he refuses to take a wage cut in order to serve More in his drastically reduced circumstances, resets the stage as Cromwell's office. Cromwell and Rich have tried out on Norfolk the charge of bribery against More, substantiated by the cup More gave Rich. Since Norfolk was present and remembers the giving away of the cup as a proof of More's honesty, the charge becomes ineffective. Furthermore, Norfolk asserts that More is no traitor, that the best policy would be not to push him on the matter of endorsing the Divorce, and that he wants no part of any attempt to threaten More with the Tower.

Cromwell—You have no choice. The King particularly wishes you to be active in the matter. Since you are known to have been a friend of More's, your participation will show that there is nothing in the nature of a "persecution," but only the strict processes of law. But if you like I'll tell the King you "want no part of it." (Norfolk *challenges* Cromwell's *threatening tactics, but is unwilling to risk approving such a message to* Henry. *He leaves and* Cromwell *turns to* Rich *for assistance in trapping* More.)

Rich—I'm only anxious to do what is correct, Secretary.

Cromwell (*smiling*)—Yes, you're absolutely right. It must be done by law. It's just a matter of finding the right law. Or making one. (*He exits as* More's *old steward enters, seeking employment by* Rich.)

Rich—Well, I need a steward. But as I remember, Matthew, your attitude to me was sometimes—disrespectful!

Matthew—Oh, I must contradict you there, sir; that's your imagination. In those days, sir, you still had your way to make. And a gentleman in that position often imagines these things. Then when he's risen to his proper level, sir, he stops thinking about it. I don't think you find people "disrespectful" nowadays, do you, sir?

Rich—There may be something in that. (*Indicating his portfolio.*) Bring my papers. (*He exits and* Matthew *picks up the portfolio.*)

MATTHEW (*to audience*)—Oh, I can manage this one! He's just my size! (*The lighting changes to something more drab and chilly.*) Sir Thomas More's again. Gone down a bit. (*He leaves as* CHAPUYS, *who has come from the King of Spain with a letter for* MORE, *is discussing the latter's refusal to accept it.*)

CHAPUYS—But your views are well known—

MORE—My views are much guessed at. Come, sir, could you convince King Harry that this letter is "in no way an affair of State"?

CHAPUYS—My dear Sir Thomas, I have taken extreme precautions. I came here very much incognito.

MORE—You misunderstand me. It is not a matter of precautions, but my duty, which would be to take this letter immediately to the King.

CHAPUYS (*flabbergasted*)—But Sir Thomas, your views—

MORE—Are well known you say. It seems my loyalty to the King is less so!

Chapuys leaves, disappointed in what he terms More's unreliability. Alice and Margaret enter and both plead with More to accept the 4000 pounds sent him by the Bishops of England as a present. He refuses because he feels it could be interpreted as a sign that he was in the pay of the Church. Roper enters to tell More he is summoned to appear before Cromwell to answer certain charges. For his family's sake More makes light of the situation.

MORE—I'll be back for dinner. I'll bring Cromwell to dinner, shall I? It'd serve him right.

MARGARET—Oh, Father, don't be witty.

MORE—Why not? Wit's what's in question. (*He exits as the scene changes to* CROMWELL'S *office where, as the lights come up,* CROMWELL *is questioning* MORE *and* RICH *is recording the examination.*) I understand there are certain charges.

CROMWELL—Some ambiguities of behavior I should like to clarify —hardly "charges."

MORE—Make a note of that, will you, Master Rich. There are no charges.

CROMWELL (*laughing*)—You know it amazes me that you, who were once so effective *in* the world and are now so *much* retired from it, should be opposing yourself to the whole movement of the times. The King is not pleased with you.

MORE—I am grieved.

CROMWELL—Yet if you could bring yourself to agree with the

Universities, the Bishops, and the Parliament of this realm, there is no honour which the King would be likely to deny you.

MORE (*stonily*)—I am well acquainted with His Grace's generosity.

CROMWELL—Very well. In 1526 the King published a book called *A Defence of the Seven Sacraments.*

MORE (*bitterly*)—Yes. For which he was named "Defender of the Faith," by his Holiness the Pope.

CROMWELL—By the Bishop of Rome. Or do you insist on "Pope"?

MORE—No, "Bishop of Rome" if you like. It doesn't alter his authority.

CROMWELL (*cunningly*)—What *is* that authority? As regards the Church in other parts of Europe; for example, the Church in England?

MORE—You will find it very ably set out and defended, Master Secretary, in the King's book.

CROMWELL—The book published under the King's name. You wrote this book.

MORE—I wrote no part of it. I merely answered to the best of my ability certain questions on canon law which His Majesty put to me. As I was bound to do.

CROMWELL—Do you deny that you *instigated* it?

MORE—It was from first to last the King's own project. And, whatever he may have said to you, he will not give evidence to support this accusation.

CROMWELL—Why not?

MORE—Because evidence is given on oath, and he will not perjure himself. If you don't know that, you don't know him.

CROMWELL—Sir Thomas More, is there anything you wish to say to me concerning the King's marriage with Queen Anne?

MORE (*very still*)—I understood I was not to be asked that again.

CROMWELL—Evidently you understood wrongly.

More is released for the present and unsuccessfully attempts to hail a boat to take him home. Norfolk comes along and tries to persuade More to stop behaving like a crank, for the sake of his friends.

NORFOLK—Goddammit, you're dangerous to know!

MORE—Then don't know me—as a friend.

NORFOLK—You *are* my friend.

MORE—I can't relieve you of your obedience to the King, Howard. You must relieve yourself of my friendship.

NORFOLK—You might as well advise a man to change the color of his hair! I'm fond of you and there it is!

MORE—What's to be done then?

NORFOLK—Give in.

MORE—You might as well advise a man to change the color of his eyes. I can't. Our friendship's more mutable than *that.*

NORFOLK—Oh, *that's* immutable, is it? The one fixed point in the world is that Thomas More will not give in!

MORE—To me it *has* to be, for that's myself! Affection goes as deep in me as you think, but only God is love right through, Howard, and *that's* my *self.* (*Seeing he must break with* NORFOLK, MORE *speaks in an insulting tone to him.*) You're a fool. You and your class have given in because the religion of this country means nothing to you one way or the other.

NORFOLK—The nobility of England has always been—

MORE—The nobility of England would have snored right through the Sermon on the Mount. But you'll labor like Thomas Aquinas over a rat-dog's pedigree. Now what's the name of those distorted creatures you're all breeding at the moment?

NORFOLK—Water spaniels.

MORE—And what would you do with a water spaniel that was afraid of water? You'd hang it. Well, as a spaniel is to water, so is a man to his own self. I will not give in because I oppose it—*I* do—not my pride, not my spleen, but I do—*I!* (*Feels* NORFOLK'S *body as if it were an animal.*) Is there no single sinew in the midst of this that serves no appetite of Norfolk's but is just Norfolk? There is. Give *that* some exercise, my lord.

NORFOLK (*breathing hard*)—Thomas . . .

MORE—Because as you stand, you'll go before your maker in a very ill condition!

NORFOLK—Now steady, Thomas . . .

MORE—And he'll have to think that somewhere back along your pedigree—a bitch got over the wall. (NORFOLK *lashes out at* MORE *who ducks and winces.* NORFOLK *leaves as* MARGARET *and* ROPER *enter.*)

ROPER—There's to be a new Act through Parliament, sir, about the marriage! They're going to administer an oath.

MORE—An oath! Now listen, Will. God made the *angels* to show him splendor—as he made animals for innocence and plants for their simplicity. But Man he made to serve him wittily, in the tangle of his mind! If he suffers us to fall to such a case that there is no escaping, then we may stand to our tackle as best we can, and clamor like champions . . . if we have the spittle for it. And no doubt it delights God to see splendor where He only looked for complexity. But it's God's part, not our own, to bring ourselves to that extremity! Our natural business lies in escaping—so let's go home and study this Bill. (*They exit.*)

The Common Man reappears dragging an iron cage with him. In the background a rack is lowered. The Common Man changes into the costume of a jailer.

JAILER—The pay scale being what it is they have to take a rather common type of man into the prison service. But it's a job. (*He admits* MORE *to the cage and locks the door after him.* RICH, CROMWELL, NORFOLK *and* CRANMER *enter and sit as a tribunal.*) I'd let him out if I could, but I can't. Not without taking up residence in there myself. (*An envelope on a string descends swiftly in front of him. He opens it and reads.*) "Thomas Cromwell was found guilty of High Treason and executed on 28 July, 1540. Norfolk was found guilty of High Treason and should have been executed on 27 January, 1547, but on the night of 26 January, the King died of syphilis and wasn't able to sign the warrant. Thomas Cranmer,"—Archbishop of Canterbury (*Jerks his thumb towards* CRANMER.) that's the other one—"was burned alive on 21 March, 1556. Richard Rich became a Knight and Solicitor-General, a Baron and Lord Chancellor, and died in his bed." So did I. And so, I hope, will all of you. (*He rouses* MORE *from his sleep and leads him to the tribunal who question him about his unwillingness to swear to the Act of Succession.*)

CRANMER—The Act states that the King's former marriage, to the Lady Catherine, was unlawful, she being previously his brother's wife and the—er—"Pope" having no authority to sanction it. Is that what you deny? (MORE *is silent.*) Is that what you are not sure of? (MORE *remains silent.*)

NORFOLK—Thomas, you insult the King and his Council.

MORE—I insult no one. I will not take the oath. I will not tell you why I will not. For refusing to swear, my goods are forfeit and I am condemned to life imprisonment. You cannot lawfully harm me further. But if you were right in supposing I had reasons for refusing, and right again in supposing my reasons treasonable, the law would let you cut off my head.

NORFOLK—Oh, confound all this. Frankly I don't know whether the marriage was lawful or not. But damn it, Thomas, look at those names. . . . You know those men. Can't you do what I did, and come with us, for fellowship?

MORE—And when we stand before God, and you are sent to Paradise for doing according to your conscience, and I am damned for not doing according to mine, will you come with me, for fellowship? (MORE *is returned to his cell, and* CROMWELL *takes the* JAILER *aside commanding him to swear to inform against* MORE *if he should say anything against the King or the Council. The* JAILER *swears, and* CROMWELL *adds that there is fifty guineas in it if he comes up with something.*)

CRANMER—That's not to tempt you into perjury, my man.

JAILER—No, sir. (*To audience.*) Fifty guineas isn't tempting; fifty guineas is alarming. If he'd left it at swearing . . . But fifty—That's serious money. If it's worth that much now it's worth my neck presently. I want no part of it. Let them sort it out. I feel my deafness coming on.

Alice, Margaret, and Roper come to visit More in his cell. They all urge him to swear to the Act of Succession.

MARGARET—Say the words of the oath, and in your heart think otherwise.

MORE (*gently*)—When a man takes an oath, Meg, he's holding his own self in his own hands. (*Demonstrates by cupping his hands.*) Like water. And if he opens his fingers *then*—he needn't hope to find himself again.

MARGARET—There's something else I've been thinking. In any State that was half good, you would be raised up high, not here, for what you've done. It's not your fault the State's three-quarters bad. So if you elect to suffer for it, you elect yourself a hero.

MORE—But if we lived in a State where virtue was profitable, common sense would make us good, and greed would make us saintly. And we'd live like animals or angels in the happy land that *needs* no heroes. But since in fact we see that avarice, anger, envy, pride, sloth, lust and stupidity commonly profit far beyond humility, chastity, fortitude, justice and thought, and have to choose, to be human at all . . . why then perhaps we must stand fast a little—even at the risk of being heroes. (*He urges his family to leave England and says goodbye to* ALICE.) I am faint when I think of the worst they may do to me. But worse than that would be to go with you not understanding why I go. (*They clasp each other fiercely.*)

ALICE—I understand you're the best man that I ever met or am likely to; and if you go—well God knows why I suppose—though as God's my witness, God's kept deadly quiet about it! And if anyone wants my opinion of the King and his Council they've only to ask for it!

MORE (*breaking away from her, his face shining*)—Why it's a lion I married! A lion! A lion!

JAILER (*apologetically ushering the family out*)—You understand my position, sir. There's nothing I can do; I'm a plain, simple man and just want to keep out of trouble.

MORE (*crying out*)—Oh, sweet Jesus! These plain, simple men!

A portentous fanfare and the lights change for the trial scene. Five large Royal Coats of Arms are lowered, and the Jailer removes his coat to become the Common Man again. He starts to tiptoe out when Cromwell stops him.

CROMWELL—Where are you going? You're the Foreman of the Jury.

COMMON MAN—Oh, no, sir. (*Gloomily he submits, putting on the Foreman's cap.*)

CROMWELL—Does the cap fit?

COMMON MAN (*uncomfortably*)—Yes, sir. (*The trial begins.*)

MORE—Why have I been called again?

NORFOLK—On a charge of High Treason, Sir Thomas.

CROMWELL—For which the punishment is *not* imprisonment.

MORE—Death . . . comes for all of us, my lords. Yes, even for Kings he comes, to whom amidst all their royalty and brute strength he will neither kneel nor make them any reverence nor pleasantly desire them to come forth, but roughly grasp them by the very breast and rattle them until they be stark dead! So causing their bodies to be buried in a pit and sending *them* to a judgment . . . whereof at their death their success is uncertain.

CROMWELL (*to jury*)—Treason enough here! (*To* MORE.) Now, Sir Thomas, you stand upon your silence?

MORE—I do.

CROMWELL (*to jury*)—But, Gentlemen of the Jury, there are many kinds of silence. Consider first the silence of a man when he is dead. What does it betoken, this silence? Nothing. This is silence pure and simple. But consider another case. Suppose I were to draw a dagger from my sleeve and make to kill the prisoner with it, and suppose their lordships there, instead of crying out for me to stop, maintained their silence. That *would* betoken a willingness that I should do it, and under the law they would be guilty with me. So silence can, according to the circumstances, speak. Consider, now, the circumstances of the prisoner's silence. The oath was put to good and faithful subjects up and down the country and they had declared His Grace's title to be just and good. And when it came to the prisoner he refused. He calls this silence. Yet is there a man in this country who does not *know* Sir Thomas More's opinion of the King's title? Of course not! Because this silence betokened—nay this silence *was* not silence at all, but most eloquent denial.

MORE—Not so, Master Secretary. (*To jury.*) The maxim of the law is "Silence gives consent." If, therefore, you wish to construe what my silence "betokened," you must construe that I consented, not that I denied.

CROMWELL—Is that what the world in fact construes from it? Do you pretend that is what you *wish* the world to construe from it?

MORE—The world must construe according to its wits. This Court must construe according to the law.

CROMWELL (*indignantly*)—The prisoner is perverting the law—making smoky what should be a clear light to discover to the Court his own wrongdoing!

MORE—The law is not a "light"; the law is not an instrument of any kind. (*To jury.*) The law is a causeway upon which, so long as he keeps to it, a citizen may walk safely. In matters of conscience, the loyal subject is more bounden to be loyal *to* his conscience than to any other thing.

CROMWELL—Your own self you mean!

MORE—Yes, a man's soul *is* his self.

CROMWELL—A miserable thing, whatever you call it, that lives like a bat in a Sunday School! A shrill incessant pedagogue about your own salvation—but nothing to say of your place in the State! Under the King! In a great native country!

MORE (*not untouched*)—Is it my place to say "good" to the State's sickness? Can I help my King by giving him lies when he asks for truth? Will you help England by populating her with liars?

(CROMWELL *calls his star witness,* SIR RICHARD RICH, *to the stand and* RICH *reveals a conversation he has had with* MORE.)

RICH—I said to him: "Supposing there was an Act of Parliament to say that I were to be King, would not you take me for King?" "That I would," he said, "for then you would be King." Then the prisoner said to me: "I will put you a higher case: How if there were an Act of Parliament to say that God should not be God?"

MORE—This is true; and then you said—

CROMWELL—Silence! (*To* RICH.) Continue.

RICH—I said: "Ah, but I will put you a middle case. Parliament has made our King Head of the Church. Will you not accept him?" He said that Parliament had no power to do it. Or words to that effect.

MORE—In good faith, Rich, I am sorrier for your perjury than my own peril.

NORFOLK—Do you deny this?

MORE—Yes! My lords, if I were a man who heeded not the taking of an oath, you know well I need not be here. Now I will take an oath! If what Master Rich has said is true, then I pray I may never see God in the face!

CROMWELL (*to jury*)—That is not evidence.

MORE—There were two other men present. Southwell and Palmer!

CROMWELL—I have their deposition here in which the Court will see they state that being busy with removing the prisoner's books they did not hear what was said.

MORE—I am a dead man. (*To* CROMWELL.) You have your desire of me. What you have hunted me for is not my actions, but the thoughts of my heart. It is a long road you have opened. For first men will disclaim their hearts and presently they will have no hearts. God help the people whose Statesmen walk your road.

The case rests and the Foreman of the jury is asked for his verdict which is "Guilty." More is permitted to make a final statement.

MORE—To avoid this I have taken every path my winding wits would find. Now that the Court has determined to condemn me, God knoweth how, I will discharge my mind . . . concerning my indictment and the King's title. The indictment is grounded in an Act of Parliament which is directly repugnant to the Law of God. The King in Parliament cannot bestow the Supremacy of the Church because it is a Spiritual Supremacy! And more to this, the immunity of the Church is promised both in Magna Carta and the King's own Coronation Oath.

CROMWELL—Now we plainly see that you *are* malicious.

MORE—Not so, Master Secretary. (*Quietly.*) I am the King's true subject, and pray for him and all the realm . . . I do none harm, I say none harm, I think none harm. And if this be not enough to keep a man alive, in good faith I long not to live . . . I have, since I came into prison, been several times in such a case that I thought to die within the hour, and I thank Our Lord I was never sorry for it, but rather sorry when it passed. And therefore, my poor body is at the King's pleasure. Would God my death might do him some good . . . (*Scornfully.*) Nevertheless, it is not for the Supremacy that you have sought my blood—but because I would not bend to the marriage!

The scene changes to the Tower and we see through a black arch at the rear of the stage the silhouette of the block and the executioner's ax. The Foreman takes off his cap, Cromwell takes a black mask and puts it on the Common Man, who now becomes the Headsman, and he ascends the stairs to straddle the block, holding the ax in his hands.

MARGARET (*running to* MORE)—Father! (*She flings herself upon him.*) Father! Father, Father, Father, Father!

MORE—Have patience, Margaret, and trouble not thyself. Death comes for us all; even at our birth death does but stand aside a little. And every day he looks towards us and muses somewhat to himself whether that day or the next he will draw nigh. It is the law of nature, and the will of God. (*He disengages himself from her.*) You have long known the secrets of my heart. (MARGARET *leaves.* MORE *walks swiftly to the stairs and then stops as he realizes that* CRANMER, *carrying his Bible, is following. Kindly.*) I beseech Your Grace, go back. (*Offended,* CRANMER *does so, and* MORE *ascends the stairs to the* HEADSMAN.) Friend, be not afraid of your office. You send me to God. (*Takes off his hat.*) He will not refuse one who is so blithe to go to Him. (MORE *kneels, we hear the harsh roar of kettledrums and the lights at the top of the stairs go out. The drums stop and we hear the stroke of the ax.*)

HEADSMAN—Behold—the head—of a traitor! (*The lights come up and we see the* COMMON MAN *who has removed his mask and come to the center of the stage. He speaks.*) I'm breathing. . . . Are you breathing too? . . . It's nice, isn't it? It isn't difficult to keep alive, friends—just don't make any trouble—or if you must make trouble, make the sort of trouble that's expected. Well, I don't need to tell you that. Good night, friends. If we should bump into one another, recognize me. (*He exits as the curtain falls.*)

STONE AND STAR

A Play in Five Acts

By Robert Ardrey

[Robert Ardrey *was born on October 16, 1908, in Chicago. He graduated from the University of Chicago, where he was a Phi Beta Kappa. His many plays include "Star Spangled" (1935), "How to Get Tough About It" (1938), "Casey Jones" (1938), "Thunder Rock" (1939), "Jeb" (1946), and "Sing Me No Lullaby" (1954). While his plays have always dealt with important contemporary themes, none have been commercial hits here. Mr. Ardrey, however, lives comfortably off his income as one of Hollywood's top screen writers. This gives him the security with which to continue writing an occasional play or book, such as his recent "African Genesis." Under the title of "Shadow of Heroes," "Stone and Star" was produced in London in 1958 with Peggy Ashcroft, Mogens Wieth, Alan Webb, and Emlyn Williams. Its Off Broadway production here this season also used the title "Shadow of Heroes."*]

THE curtain rises on an almost dark stage. Visible are a number of huge wooden packing boxes, which will be rearranged to represent a variety of locations in the city of Budapest, from 1944 through 1956. A man appears from among the packing boxes. It is the Author, in appearance a Hungarian intellectual. His clothes are worn, faded, but clean, and he wears a long dark red woolen scarf. He listens. In the distance we hear a muted exchange of shouts and the scatter of running feet. Then silence.

Author—It's the last year of the Second World War. The Russian Army is approaching Budapest, but the Nazis still control the city. (*Two figures emerge and move a few cases to make a bedroom. One sits down on one of the boxes. The other remains standing.*) The man sitting on the bed is Laszlo Rajk. He's the head of a committee of ten that runs the Communist underground. The man looking out the window is Rajk's deputy in the underground. His name is Janos Kadar. They're waiting for Rajk's wife, Julia. While they wait let me say one further word about the play. It's a story of three people. In its own way it's a love story; but it's also a true story. No decisive action in this play is a matter of author's invention. Where there is conflict of evidence, I shall so report. (*Looking at the two men.*) The first scene may not have taken place at all. But we do know the relationship of the Rajks, their relationship to Rajk's deputy, and what happened next.

A third man, Viktor Babits, who is one of the few fictitious characters in the play, enters with two comrades. They are all worried about Julia Rajk, who has gone to make contact in South Buda with someone who they suspect will give her information about a liaison with the Soviet Army some sixty miles away. Viktor is particularly concerned because Julia is a woman and might tell the Nazi police something about them if she were questioned and tortured. Rajk tells Viktor that when the police took Julia into the Gestapo headquarters at 60 Andrassy Street last winter, she spent most of her six weeks of interrogation hanging naked upside down by her feet, and yet she never gave them her name or the names of the committee. Kadar is very nervous and keeps looking out on the street despite Rajk's orders not to.

RAJK—You disturb me, Janos. You're honest, you're brave, you're able, you're loyal. You have a purity about you, because—you're a workingman. But, Janos, you indulge yourself. You waste yourself with sympathy. You have no discipline at all.

KADAR—I'm thinking about Julia.

RAJK—Forget about Julia! *If* something happened to me and you had to take over—could you handle it? Could you say to yourself, I am meaningless. My pains, pleasures, life, loves, they're scraps in the wind. I am a fraction of something larger than myself. I am a cell in the body of mankind. I have no sympathies nor hungers above the needs of the Party. Could you do it, Janos?

KADAR—I don't know! I'm thinking about Julia.

RAJK—For you Julia represents one problem. Have we gained or lost a contact? Do you understand?

KADAR—I understand, but—

Julia arrives. She has instructions for her husband to attempt to get through enemy lines to make a liaison with the Soviet Army. They will put him in touch with Erno Gero, a skillful and experienced commissar, and with Matyas Rakosi, a Hungarian communist jailed for sixteen years in Horthy prisons. Rajk instructs Kadar to follow him on his mission, so that if Rajk is captured Kadar can continue on in his place to set up with Gero and Rakosi a new Workers Party for a free Hungary. Julia volunteers to go into the street ahead of her husband to be sure the Nazi police are not waiting for him. As they are about to leave, Julia asks Laci to promise to give her a baby after the liberation. He is embarrassed, but he promises and they go off into the night.

AUTHOR—60 Andrassy Street had been the headquarters of the Horthy police. When the Gestapo took over, the Germans were wise enough to leave Hungarians in the more unpleasant jobs. Captain Gyula Szabo, a Hungarian, was still one of the men in charge in the basement.

We see that Szabo has captured Julia and Laci, and that he is using every means to get information from them. We are also told that Kadar got through the Russian lines. There he informs Comrades Gero and Rakosi of the Rajks' capture. They seem quite cynical about it all, and ask Kadar about his qualifications to replace Rajk.

KADAR—I was chosen by Rajk. I know his mind. I'll do what he would do. What more can I say. We fought together.

GERO—Comrade, let me explain. My profession is the Communist Party, not Hungary. Now, can't you tell me something in Party terms? Where's your Party strength? Who trusts you besides Laszlo Rajk? He's in prison.

KADAR—I'm not a functionary. I was a workingman. Workers trust me. (GERO *comes to life. He shouts off.*) Matyas! (*To* KADAR.) You were a workingman! Why didn't you say so? (MATYAS RAKOSI *enters and is introduced.*)

KADAR (*a fisted salute*)—Comrade Rakosi! I bring greetings to one who has endured sixteen years of darkness in the prisons of the monster, Horthy—

RAKOSI—Don't make too much of it, comrade. I gained forty pounds, had a marvellous library and a private phone. I never missed a meal, or a guest, or a single copy of the *New York Times* or the *Manchester Guardian.* And in the end they traded me to the Russians for a mess of old flags. (RAKOSI *and* GERO *laugh about this and about* Kadar's *working-class background, which gives them a vote-getting symbol without the liability of opposition from an intellectual and politically sophisticated hero like* Rajk.)

Kadar (*shocked*)—I am not accustomed to bright conversation. Where I come from, you ask a man which side he is on. And that's all. Or you ask, what's a man want, a new world or an old one? Or how is he in charge of high explosives? You ask him sometimes, even—does he believe? I'd like to know how it is, conversation in Moscow. I've been out of touch.

Gero—Comrade, you sound like a fresh-faced boy emerging from a Marxism-Leninism study group; you look like a Spanish assassin; and you have more than a touch in your manner of an American politician preparing to deliver the vote. I am impressed. I'll try to answer you. I get the impression that we command in Hungary the sympathy of perhaps one man in five. Well, conversations in Moscow suggest that in from three to four years we must somehow create here a total and reliable workers' state. Or God help us. What you've got to get through your head is that the war is over. And that this would hardly be the first one to leave behind it a gang of inbred, Chauvinistic veterans, with their own sacred myths and memories.

Kadar—Are you trying to say that any men led by Laszlo Rajk could be disloyal to the Party? Good Christ, we believed! If we hadn't believed in the revolution, how could we have survived?

Gero—We were speaking of the Party. I fail to see what the revolution has to do with it. What was Rajk's discipline? The revolution? Or the Party?

Kadar—The Party. Rajk would say, "I have no sympathies nor hungers beyond the needs of the Party."

Gero—That's better. All you really need, comrade, is a quick trip to Moscow. Taste a little civilization, see the ballet. Meet a few important people, including a tailor. I'll fix you up with a plane. There's nothing wrong with you that can't be cured by a little perspective and a few dozen litres of toilet water.

Author—We believe Kadar went to Moscow, though there's no real evidence. We know of course where the Rajks went. They were moved to an infamous prison in Germany. Belsen. By now the Nazi collapse was far advanced. There was no transport. They walked. It took three weeks. And then one day they were free. The war over. In Budapest Gero gave a party for the new Central Committee. Janos Kadar came. (*We see* Kadar, *now neatly tailored, as he breaks away from the Moscow group to mingle with his shabbier comrades, a move that disturbs* Gero.)

Gero—Comrades! (*He lifts his glass.*) We give you victory

over the fascist beast! To the workers and peasants all over the world! (*The crowd breaks into the "International."* RAKOSI *beams.* GERO *listens as if to an orchestra he were conducting. At the proper instant he raises his arm.*) Comrades! We give you—Laszlo Rajk! (LASZLO RAJK *and* JULIA *enter. They have just arrived from Belsen.* KADAR *embraces them. As* RAJK *starts to speak the crowd lifts him on their shoulders and they are swept off-stage with* KADAR *and* JULIA *following.* GERO *watches after them thoughtfully.*)

ACT II

AUTHOR—From this point on, almost no reconstruction of events has been necessary. Interpretations—particularly that of Janos Kadar's character—may be disputed. Why did men act as they did? (*Pauses as if struggling to be objective about it.*) What we know, is what they did. (*Figures appear and rearrange the packing boxes.*) Four years later the Communist Party had at last suppressed all opposition in Hungary. Rakosi and Gero controlled the Party and the government, but Laszlo Rajk held the important Ministry of the Interior. The new secret police—the Allam-Vedelmi-Osztaly, the AVO—was under Gabor Peter, Rajk's old colleague in the underground. Julia was pregnant.

Rajk has come to see Gero to inquire about the villa the Party wants him to live in instead of his three-room flat, which is overcrowded because Julia's mother is living with them. He is angry and considers it a matter of Party policy not to accept such a villa. Gero treats it lightly and reasons with him to accept it.

GERO—There'll be four of you soon. Would you want your boy to grow up in the streets?

RAJK—When the time comes that no Hungarian children need grow up in the streets—I'll consider the question.

GERO—What disturbs the Central Committee, comrade, is that one member should live in a manner so flagrantly—some even say opportunistically—in contrast to the rest; that one member of the government should be making such an obvious bid for personal popularity among the rank and file of the Party.

RAJK (*angrily*)—Has it occurred to our comrades that any action I might take to acquire popularity in Hungary would be superfluous?

GERO—It has. It's too bad you make it sound like a threat. The struggle for personal popularity is not my problem. I'm just a Party secretary.

RAJK—Save that for somebody else!

GERO—Well, then let's say that any problems of popularity which I may have reside elsewhere than in a provincial capital named Budapest.

It is revealed that the decision about the villa was taken at a Committee meeting, which Rajk's supporters did not attend because of a "slip-up of notification." Rajk asks if Kadar was there, and is told that he was but that he didn't speak in this connection. Rajk demands a hearing before the full committee.

GERO—Be reasonable. You'll use foolish regrettable words. And after all you *do* need the place, you need room for entertainment—

RAJK—If I were the Foreign Minister, a lackey receiving third-rate ambassadors, making speeches written properly in Moscow, I'd need everything you say. But I am not the foreign minister—

GERO (*blankly*)—But you are. Nobody told you? My God, what a blunder. (KADAR *enters.*)

KADAR (*surprised to see* RAJK)—You said he wasn't coming back till night.

GERO—I said? A confusion.

RAJK—Gero said you were coming to meet me.

GERO—Confusion, confusion! Poor Laci didn't know about the change in ministries. I'm mortified—

RAJK—Who takes my ministry?

GERO—Janos. (*Looks at watch.*) I have to see Comrade Rakosi. You explain to Laci, will you, comrade? (*He leaves.*)

RAJK—You lying, cheating, two-faced, opportunistic, bureaucratic whore. I turn my face from you.

KADAR—That's just what he wants you to do. If he can divide us, clean and complete, it's to his interest. Say you're glad that I have Interior, not Farkas.

RAJK—Why should I discriminate between you? You dress like them, live like them. You share their liquor and their parties and, I assume, their plots. Why should I consider you as different? Are you different?

KADAR (*wretchedly*)—I don't know. Laci, if I'd spoken up for you Farkas'd have Interior. And I'm not unhappy to be in a position where I can speak for you later. You won't resign, will you?

RAJK—I am a Party man. I've survived things I could only have survived because there was a Party to survive for. I've committed crimes in its name—joyfully. I am no bourgeois saint. I have persecuted decent Hungarians, driven them into exile, happily, because all values are relative to the Party's triumph. I believe in the Party no matter who leads it, no matter what it may seem to represent in some few passing years. The Party remains not only man's truest, but only hope. I shall not resign. I shall live in a villa. And do what I'm told.

Kadar is pleased and sends his love to Julia. Rajk returns and breaks the news to Julia that he has accepted the villa, and finds himself trying to answer all the arguments he had previously given Gero. He finally reveals to her that he has been made Foreign Minister and argues that the villa is necessary for his new job. She agrees. She suggests that their child will need a godfather, and that Janos would be a good man for it. Laci agrees to ask him when the time comes.

AUTHOR—Julia's child was a boy. They named him Laszlo. Some evening about the tenth of May, 1949, Kadar came out to the villa.

Janos brings a bottle of wine to celebrate his being a godfather. He tells them he is honoured and that since almost everything he does these days is because it's necessary, it is a great pleasure for him to do something because he wants to. While Rajk is out of the room, Janos warns Julia to be careful of the servants. Laci returns and they have a brief ceremony in which he proposes to Janos that he join them in their unyielding purpose that the world as it shapes this child will be a world of justice, of dignity, and of enlightenment. Janos does so. Julia takes young Laszlo off to bed, and Kadar tells Rajk that Viktor Babits was arrested today on charges of conspiracy with Tito. Rajk is shocked at the absurdity of the charge, but Kadar treats it quite cynically as if he had accepted the fact that a fellow Communist need only to be in the way of another Party member to justify his removal, with the charge being only a matter of form. He tells Laci, "You're too big for them," and departs.

AUTHOR—On the thirty-first of May, about three weeks later, Erno Gero and Janos Kadar walked in the rain from Kadar's Ministry of the Interior to Gero's Party Headquarters.

A few hours later we see Rajk, who has returned home to Julia who is ill with a fever. Suddenly Gabor Peter turns up, and his men arrest Laci.

AUTHOR—The AVO had never bothered to find a headquarters other than that used by the Gestapo a few years earlier. Rajk was taken to the basement at 60 Andrassy Street. Julia wasn't arrested until a few days later. The baby was taken away from her.

We see Julia being questioned by a man who looks very much like the man who tortured the Rajks in Act I.

AUTHOR—This is not a coincidence of casting, or a matter of the same actor playing two parts. Captain Gyula Szabo of the Communist Party secret police—formerly Captain Gyula Szabo of the Nazi secret police—was one of those still in charge of the beating-up gangs in the basement of 60 Andrassy Street.

ACT III

While Rajk is being beaten by the sadistic son of Defense Minister Farkas, Kadar and Rakosi discuss the project of getting a confession out of Rajk. Rakosi suggests that they try to kill two birds with one stone by showing that Cardinal Mindszenty and Rajk worked together. Kadar quotes him Gero's reaction to that idea which is: "We're trying to divide the opposition, not combine it." Gero shows up with the news that General Byelkin is flying in from Moscow. Gabor Peter complains that Moscow is interfering with his problem.

GERO—Comrade, listen. If we can't get a confession from Rajk, then we can't put his crowd on trial. If we can't put his crowd on trial, then we can't show what happens to comrades anywhere who get nationalist ideas. And if we can't show what happens to comrades anywhere who get nationalist ideas, then the Kremlin's got trouble. Not just Tito and Yugoslavia. That's already lost. There'll be problems from Poland to China.

KADAR—Rajk never had any nationalist ideas.

GERO—Janos. Tell me precisely. What's that got to do with it?

They discuss various possibilities of obtaining sufficient evidence to support a case of treason against Rajk. They also discuss who is to get the blame if the case against Rajk fails. First Gabor Peter, who is accused of taking it easy on Rajk; then Rakosi, who at one beating session told them to hold off for fear of killing Rajk; and finally Kadar, who disowns any helping of Rajk. Suddenly Rakosi accuses him of having been Rajk's son's godfather. Kadar replies that Gero told him to do it. Gero is silent and Rakosi feels that he is safe and Kadar will be the one to take the blame, when suddenly Gero admits he told him to be the godfather. The others leave to meet Byelkin at the airport, while Gero and Kadar stay behind.

GERO—You'd have no objection, would you, to talking to Rajk yourself? In the Party interest?

KADAR—I'd have—objection. (*He lowers his head.*)

GERO—It seems to me a rare sort of decision, where at the same time one can serve one's Party, and serve oneself—particularly when one has no alternative. (KADAR *lifts his head and looks at* GERO.) Walk with me, Janos. (*They go off slowly.*)

Kadar visits Rajk in prison. Rajk tells him to get out. But Janos tells him that the Committee knows he is innocent, and that Julia is at another jail, and that the baby is fine and being kept in an orphanage, where they have changed his name. Kadar proposes a deal. If Laci will confess that he worked against the Party, he will be tried and found guilty. It will be announced that he has been hanged, but in reality Laci and Julia and their baby will go to the Crimea where Rajk will be given a new Party post in the Soviet Union. Janos gives Laci his word on it.

RAJK—Let me confess that I conspired against Gero, against Rakosi! Somebody might believe me! But against the Party!

KADAR—I don't think anybody cares whether people who knew you believe it. It's for people who didn't know you.

RAJK—Janos, Janos. I lie in that mud with my face against the stones. I vomit on my beaters, I faint before my hearers. I'd decide—without hope for myself, or for Julia, or the boy—I'd decide in darkness, if it's for the health of the Party, and if I knew what I am a symbol of that they are trying to crush? Do you know? (KADAR *is silent.*) Have they created in me a symbol of counter-revolution that must be put down? Then I accept it! Or do they crush us because we believed?

KADAR—I have no reason to think that they'd do it because we believed.

RAJK—You answer precisely as I would have had you answer. As a Party man you've succeeded. As a Party man, I've failed.

KADAR—Then isn't that the answer? Why you should confess? We know you're innocent. But we also know you've failed. You've confused two kinds of truth, like Gero says, the kind that is and the kind that's necessary. And you wouldn't have done it in the old days. Would you? What would you have said of such private judgment in the old days? (Rajk *bends his head.*) You'd have condemned it as arrogant, as indulgent, as anti-Party. Wouldn't you?

Rajk—I'd have condemned it.

Kadar—The very fact that you believe me . . . Would you believe it if Gero were telling you this? Or Rakosi? You wouldn't. Only because I'm your friend—and Julia's—and your child's godfather—you listen to me. Do you see how you've let your personal likes and judgments influence your acceptance of the truth?

Rajk—Yes.

Kadar—To say to a man who is not only my oldest comrade, but who was my hero, who has never drawn a breath except in the interest of the revolution, and the exploited masses—to say what I have to say, my throat sticks.

Rajk—Say it.

Kadar—There is no place in the Communist Party, Laci, for a man like you.

Rajk—I honour you for saying it.

Kadar tells him he can make up for it by confessing. Rajk asks Janos for a few more days to think it over. Janos warns him that the offer may not last that long. Laci asks for more details about his escape to the Crimea. He would like Julia to know about it beforehand. Janos says this is impossible. Suddenly Rajk seems to see through Kadar as he says to him: "What you wonder, Janos, is this. Where does fraud begin, and truth leave off? And we'll never know. We'll die not knowing." But Rajk accepts the offer.

Author—Laszlo Rajk was tried on September 16, 1949, so Julia heard his voice again over the loudspeaker placed in the prison yard. And his sentence of death. A hanging in Hungary is accomplished by strangulation. Death comes, on the average, in twenty minutes. In the months succeeding the trial she listened to the sounds of fifty-nine hangings, believing each was her husband. Kadar himself was arrested a year or so later. He was tortured by the younger Farkas, and received a permanently crippled arm from the loss of fingernails. He was tried on December 11, 1951, for anti-Party activities and sentenced to prison. Julia was still in prison somewhere.

ACT IV

There is a small boy standing alone onstage. He is holding a toy bear in his arms. The Author enters and asks him his name. He replies that it is Stephen Goryk.

AUTHOR (*to audience*)—Julia was released in 1954. Her baby was now five years old. Janos Kadar was released at about the same time along with a good many others. The death of Stalin had brought on a breathing spell, of a sort. Rakosi had to step down. A man named Imre Nagy succeeded him as Premier. Rakosi got back on top in about eighteen months, but in the meanwhile Nagy—how he did it we'll never know—secured the release of some ninety thousand political prisoners. Nobody knew Kadar's whole part in the Rajk case, and with his prison record and his crippled arm—he even seemed one of us. He got a job as a Party secretary in the Budapest thirteenth district. Julia Rajk found a room somewhere in Budapest. She got a job in a co-operative store. She got her boy back. (*Turning back to the boy.*) Stephen, you don't remember your mother. Nobody does, right now. But some day everyone will remember her. Everyone in all the world. (*Calling to* JULIA, *who has entered.*) Julia. (*The* AUTHOR *turns away, as* JULIA *looks at the child.*)

JULIA—Laci. (*The boy backs away from her frightened.*) Laci! (*She picks him up in her arms as he beats her face with his fists, and she runs off with him.*)

LASZLO—I dropped my bear! I dropped my bear!

We see Julia and young Laszlo in their small windowless apartment. Julia is trying to get young Laci to get undressed for bed, but he resists. Finally she is forced to take his shirt off herself, and when she does she finds his little body a mass of bruises.

JULIA—You're all bruises! My God, My God. Tell Mother what happened, Laci.

LASZLO—My name isn't Laci! It's Stephen!

JULIA (*figuring it out*)—Were they big boys? From Gorky School?

LASZLO—Somebody told you.

JULIA—No, I just thought it wouldn't be children from your little school. So I thought it might be boys from Gorky School, where they come every morning in limousines. What did you say, when the big boys asked your name?

LASZLO—I said I was Laszlo Rajk.

JULIA—What did they hit you with, after you told them your name?

LASZLO—Sticks. (*He is crying.*)

JULIA—Laci, Laci.

LASZLO—I don't want to be Laszlo Rajk! I don't want to be a fascist bastard!

JULIA (*taking his hand*)—He loved you, Laci. I believe in his way he loved everybody in all the world. But he loved you most of all, because you were his son. Some day, some day—you'll be so proud to be Laszlo Rajk.

The boy goes to sleep as she watches him. There is a knock at the door. It is Janos Kadar who has come to see her. Julia is baffled that he should come, but finds herself unable to order him out as she should. She tells him that it never had occurred to her that she could sit in the same room with him again without killing him. Janos asks to look at Laci and she lets him.

KADAR—Things get better, Julia.
JULIA—Is the news that you're back in the Party to be my guarantee that things are getting better?
KADAR—I deserve anything you want to say.
JULIA—What do I do about your godson?
KADAR—Things *are* getting better! The changes—
JULIA—Will you tell the boys from Gorky School who beat him with sticks while I'm at work? Will you tell them that Laszlo Rajk was an innocent man, murdered by Stalinist thugs?

Julia asks him whose side he was on, and how he can now work for the Party again. He replies that he is a good Communist.

JULIA—Is there such a thing?
KADAR—Don't say that. Laci was a good Communist. Just because a great thing got spoiled for a while by a few bad men—
JULIA—Or did a bad thing spoil for all eternity more good men than you can mention?
KADAR—You don't believe that. If we stopped believing in the Party, what justification would there be for anything? If we haven't done things for some greater good, Julia, then we're common criminals.

Julia asks Janos why her husband confessed. And Kadar tells her the truth. Julia is horrified, but refuses to give Janos the satisfaction of relieving his guilt by indicting him. Kadar pleads with her that he cannot carry his guilt around all by himself.

JULIA—Then tell it! Tell Hungary! Tell somebody besides the widow!
AUTHOR—Two years later, Nagy was out and Rakosi was back in power. But Kadar still hadn't told it. (*From amplifiers comes the*

sound of whispers. "Twentieth Party Congress . . . Did you hear . . . Khrushchev denounced Stalin . . .")

RAKOSI—Oh that son of a bitch. That jackass peasant son of a bitch.

FARKAS (*entering*)—What's this about the Rajk case?

GERO—We've got to rehabilitate Rajk. There were violations of socialist legality. We are instructed— (SANDOR HORVATH, *another fictitious character created for the purposes of the play, enters.*)

SANDOR—The delegation from the Csepel Island steel workers— They're being difficult— They want Janos Kadar back on the Central Committee.

GERO (*his nerve breaking for once*)—Get rid of them! Get rid of them!

Sandor Horvath goes to visit Julia Rajk. He is disturbed that she is living so meanly, and tells her that he is going to talk with the committeee about finding a better place for her to live. "A villa?" Julia asks the startled Sandor, and tells him to tell the Central Committee to go to hell. Sandor says he doesn't blame her, and that the Party has made mistakes, but he invites her to address the Petöfi Club, and to tell them about her grievances against the state, although of course the Central Committee would prefer that she not discuss her husband's case at this meeting. Julia promises to think about it.

AUTHOR—Julia spoke on the evening of June 19, 1956, about four months before the actual uprising. Most observers have thought that the Hungarian Revolution had its inception at the tenth meeting of the Petöfi Club on June 27, eight days later. On the platform at that ninth meeting was the Stalinist old Guard and several members of the Central Committee.

We hear a sampling of the speeches, in which the new Khrushchev Party line is echoed, including the excuse of encirclement by fascist-imperialist warmongers and the admission that on occasion the Party in Hungary has strayed from tenets of socialist legality. There are a couple of individual minor complaints, which the Committee representatives promise to rectify. Then Julia is introduced.

JULIA—You know and I know what I am doing here. They've got me here like goods in a shop window, when there aren't any goods inside. They want me to talk to you about the way I live. But do any of you live any differently? Or maybe about prisons.

Is there anybody here who hasn't been to prison? (*Feeble laughter from the platform and the audience.*) Well. Such an opportunity. I wish I had more to complain about. I haven't. I find it loathsome to complain to an audience of Hungarians about experiences that have been our common lot. Am I not perhaps better off than many who sit before me? I've had a husband who loved me. I have a son—in his image—who begins, I believe, to trust me, and will someday, love me, I hope. I have had in my youth a cause. A cause and a purpose of decency and justice that enflamed me. What was pain, what was risk, what was death—with such a cause when one was young? I have known such times! In my heart is a storehouse of heroes. And I can no more complain than to look in my mirror and weep— Where has that young girl gone? (*Pauses.*) Still, I may ask—who murdered my husband? (*She turns and points at the Committee members on the platform.*) You murdered my husband! I single out no one. Your guilt is collective. When you murdered my husband, you murdered all decency, all justice, all hope in Hungary! (*The audience breaks into applause that grows as* Julia *leaves the platform. And helplessly those on the platform join in.*)

Author—When the Petöfi Club met again the following week, five thousand people tried to enter the hall. Authors spoke, and poets and journalists. The meeting lasted till three in the morning. Even by ten o'clock there were shouts of "Down with the government!" and "Live, Hungary!"

We see Gero and Rakosi in a panic about what to do. Rakosi suggests hanging every man who spoke, and Gero points out that the one to be hanged is Julia Rajk, who spoke first. He wants to appease the people by finding Rajk's body and giving the masses a public funeral for Rajk. Rakosi is against compromising with people whom he regards as greedy monstruous animals. "Give them everything or give them nothing," is his attitude. Mikoyan is coming from Moscow, and there is pressure from the Central Committee for reinstatement of Kadar. Kadar is willing to help the Party out, and points out that he will be more satisfactory to the Committee than Imre Nagy, for whom the rank-and-file will push, unless the Committee mollifies them by accepting Kadar. Rakosi denounces Janos as the man who betrayed Rajk personally, which Janos denies.

Author—On the table was a tape recorder. Fifty members of the Central Committee were present. There are fifty living witnesses.

We hear on the tape recorder the portion of the conversation between Kadar and Rajk in which Kadar made his false proposal of a deal in exchange for a confession. Apparently Rakosi recorded it over his private wire to the Andrassy Street basement. The committee members are outraged and attack Kadar who futilely explains that he was obeying Party instructions. Rakosi triumphantly and categorically states that there were no such instructions. While they beat up Kadar, Gero calmly rewinds the tape and suggests they play it again. But this time the tape starts a little earlier than the previous playing, and we hear Kadar tell Rajk that he has come "on behalf of Rakosi," and that "every member of the Central Committee knows that Rajk is innocent." Rakosi and the committee members are devastated at hearing this played in front of Mikoyan, and they helplessly disperse.

Author—On the sixteenth of July, Comrade Rakosi was removed from power by Mikoyan and put aboard a plane for Moscow. Mihaly Farkas was expelled from the Party. Janos Kadar was not. He was even allowed to remain on the Central Committee—just why is a question. Some think that Mikoyan showed remarkable forethought.

Gero goes to see Julia. He wants her to identify the corpse of Laszlo Rajk, so that it can be given a state funeral. Not a public one, which would be too dangerous, but a private one. Shrewdly Julia bargains with Gero, raising the number of people who will be invited to forty members of the government and an equal number of Rajk's old friends. She even pushes him to agreeing on a guard of honour that will stand for twenty-four hours before the ceremony. Then Julia suddenly defies Gero and insists that the funeral be public. He replies that the viewing of the remains by her is a legal technicality that they can bypass if she is going to be difficult.

Julia—I suppose you can. But won't it look rather funny if the widow doesn't come to the funeral?

Gero (*in shock*)—There is no absolute necessity for any kind of funeral! I conceived of it as a generous gesture . . .

Julia—You wouldn't be doing it for a minute if you didn't have to.

Gero—What makes you so sure?

Julia—Well, I wasn't sure at all, until you gave in on so many things about the honour guard. Then I knew where I stood.

Gero—You designing old crock. I wish we'd hung you as well as your husband.

JULIA—Now, that's the kind of talk I can understand.

GERO—What kind of fantasy do you have in your head that you can control the character of this funeral? You're gambling with your husband's memory. But what have you got to win?

JULIA—Oh—the maximum honour for a great man, who loved me. And the maximum humiliation for you.

GERO—This revenge doesn't just fall on me. It falls on the Party.

JULIA—Wherever it should fall.

GERO (*reluctantly*)—I will admit it, there has got to be a funeral! But don't treasure the illusion that all you're defying is a weakened Hungarian Party. It's the will of the Soviet Union too.

JULIA—My, but they really have you down the well, haven't they, Erno?

GERO—God damn you!

JULIA (*cheerfully*)—Well God damn you, comrade.

GERO (*pauses*)—Can you name one person, in a Communist State, who has ever opposed the will of the Party and got away with it—permanently?

JULIA—But I'm not opposed. I want a funeral.

ACT V

On October 6, seventeen days before the outbreak of the Hungarian Revolution, a public funeral—though without any public notice being given—was held in Kerepes Cemetery. Julia and her son enter to stand by the coffin. Some of Rajk's old friends join them. The Central Committee is there too, and the Premier, Andras Hegedus. Gero, who is head of the Committee group, proposes to Viktor Babits, the head of the old friends, that they divide up the honour watch. Viktor consults and then tells Gero they have decided that there are those with whom they cannot stand. Kadar is offered the honor of standing with the old friends group. Anguishedly he declines and stands with the murderers.

Twenty-four hours later Julia and her son return for the ceremony. A limping poet mounts the platform and speaks.

POET—

I whispered. And ancient birds took flight
From stricken fields, soaring, renouncing night,
Singing new songs! Sick tigers walked.
A hawk forgotten, old, tore the sky. Thunder stalked
The stars, and told the dead
What I had said.

I whispered. Stone and star replied.
I whispered, and a silent earth cried
Out. I whispered—to a hero—Rise!
No hero dies.

AUTHOR—They came. There had been no public announcement. But they had heard, and they came. On the sixth of October, 1956, two hundred and fifty thousand people came out of Budapest to the funeral of Laszlo Rajk, and watched, and listened, and found each other there.

As the friends of Rajk lift his coffin on their shoulders and leave, followed by Julia, young Laci, and the government officials, men begin to appear on the rooftops and a tumult begins to rise, until we see the Revolution in full force. We see Gero and Mikoyan, who has flown in from Moscow with the Stalinist, Suslov. Gero tries to stop the uprising by blaming it on "fascist provocators." Then he tries making Imre Nagy Premier again. Gero tells the defense minister to issue a request for Soviet troops in Nagy's name. The fighting continues.

AUTHOR—They fought all Wednesday. On Thursday they won. Comrade Kadar was appointed to replace Comrade Gero. What happened to Erno Gero—we have no record.

POET—

Praise the shadow of heroes!
Praise earth, praise sea!
Praise God! Praise Freedom!
Praise Hungary!

There is dancing in the streets and we see Julia enter with some groceries. She sits down and begins to weep. Laszlo doesn't quite know what to do, so he kisses her. She clutches him and continues to cry in rapture. Laszlo, thinking she's unhappy, gives her his bear to console her. The crowd and the shouting gradually disappear and Viktor Babits enters. He is worried and Julia sends Laszlo to play so that they can talk. He advises her to leave Hungary. Julia asks him if *he* is leaving.

VIKTOR—On these particular days, and at this particular stage of my life, all I seem to know is that I'm a Hungarian, that I shall probably die of it, and that I'm unbearably happy.

JULIA—But you expect me to leave.

VIKTOR—Some of us know who started all this. If we know, it's reasonable to suppose that *they* do.

JULIA—Nobody started it! You know as well as I, there weren't any plots, there weren't any plans. Isn't that the glory of it? A whole nation went mad—and madness—it was the one thing they had no answer for.

VIKTOR—You were the one who spoke first, who brought on the funeral.

JULIA—Oh, if I did! Then how could I possibly run away? Viktor, why are you trying to frighten me? It's over. We've won.

VIKTOR—For the moment.

JULIA—They cannot touch us. Not with the whole world watching. Do you know, Viktor, that the foreign journalists who have come into Budapest, the last forty-eight hours, probably outnumber the local population.

VIKTOR—Would it be just too reasonable for you to take a short holiday in Vienna till we see how things come out?

JULIA—Please stop trying to frighten me.

VIKTOR—Small hope of that. The trouble with you, Julia, the world's got nothing left to frighten you with.

JULIA—*Do* you know something.

VIKTOR—Only that they've chosen Janos Kadar for their man. Janos—the one Hungarian for whom no task of betrayal could equal the ones he's already accomplished.

JULIA—Do you know, I find it difficult to believe that what's happened to ten million others, hasn't happened to Janos himself—a little. I can't leave, Viktor. I don't know why I can't. I'm drunk, I suppose, on some wine of autumn. My Budapest.

AUTHOR—The following Tuesday, Janos Kadar spoke on Radio Budapest. On that day the Council of Ministers had abolished the one-party system.

KADAR—Comrades, Friends. I want you to know that all the resolutions passed today by the Council of Ministers have been fully approved by the Hungarian Communist Workers Party. The leadership of the past years has cast our party under a shadow. We must set an example worthy of a Communist and a man. Only by so doing can we earn the respect of our countrymen.

AUTHOR—On Thursday, the first of November, the new council of Ministers, with all parties represented, received the Soviet Ambassador, Yuri Andropov. The scene is fully witnessed.

Premier Nagy asks Andropov what attitude Hungary may expect from the Soviet Union on its proposals for free elections, the multiparty system, the Hungarian withdrawal from the Warsaw pact, and the Hungarian request for withdrawal of all Soviet military formations from all of Hungary. To his surprise, Andropov replies that the Soviet Union is willing to accept these proposals as a basis for negotiation, and that the Soviet military commanders will meet with the Hungarian staff the day after tomorrow to arrange the details of withdrawal.

KADAR (*passionately*)—Andropov, every man in this room understands that the withdrawal of Soviet forces means the end of Communism in Hungary. Because nothing else supports it. I am a Communist. Whatever I have done or has been done to me, I have justified in terms of our ultimate triumph. The death of the Party in Hungary means my own death. But! Andropov! Listen to me! If what you have told us is not in good faith—if there is any breach, any fraud, any deceit, any act of force to circumvent the will of the Hungarian people—then, Andropov, I shall die at their side! I shall meet your tanks in the street with a pistol.

A little while later, after the meeting, Julia waits for Janos outside of the Radio Budapest building where he is scheduled to speak. She has heard what happened at the Council of Ministers. She suggests that he come to visit her in her flat some evening with a few of her old friends and a bottle of wine. Kadar is pleased but ill at ease.

KADAR—You should know not to trust me, just because I say something.

JULIA—I didn't say I trusted you. Let's not be silly. I don't forgive you, and I forget nothing. There's been nothing to touch you in two thousand years. I call you what you are, Janos. And I accept my share. I share your guilt. It's the burden that a good many of us will have to learn to carry. Those of us who considered ourselves good Communists. To share the guilt, even yours. (*She touches his shoulder, and* JANOS *presses his cheek against her hand.*) Will you share another bottle of wine, Janos?

KADAR—I will share another bottle of wine.

JULIA—I won't rush you, Janos. I know how it is.

KADAR (*looking up at the night sky*)—My God, my God, Julia. Is there some way back? Is it possible? (*He goes into the Radio Budapest building.* JULIA *leaves, and two men arrive. They wait outside the building. A little while later* JANOS *emerges. They go up to him and one says "MVD, Comrade. Soviet Embassy." They talk, and he follows them as he has followed before, at the end of an unseen rope.*)

AUTHOR—That was Thursday. There was some nervousness Friday about Kadar's disappearance. But on Saturday morning the two military commands met, and by four in the afternoon had agreed on every detail of the Soviet withdrawal excepting only the final date. Even this would probably be settled at the evening meeting. At ten o'clock, the Soviet command gave a banquet for the Hungarian staff at the Soviet military headquarters on Csepel Island. At midnight, telephone connections were broken but this didn't seem too peculiar, considering Russian banquets. What nobody knew was that at the stroke of midnight General Serov, the chief of the Soviet secret police, had entered the banquet hall with his men and arrested the entire Hungarian Army staff. Nobody even knew that Serov was in town. Oh, Budapest. Nobody knew anything at all until five in the morning. At five-twenty, from Radio Budapest—Imre Nagy.

NAGY—This is Premier Nagy speaking. Today the Soviet forces have attacked our capital. Our troops are in combat. I notify the people of our country—and of the world.

AUTHOR—Later in the morning from somewhere in Hungary—

KADAR—This is Janos Kadar. I speak to you as Premier of the new Hungarian Worker-Peasant government. Help the Soviet soldier. He is your brother. Put down the fascist thugs. Truth is on our side!

AUTHOR—Nagy, Julia, and some thirty or so others took asylum in the Yugoslav Embassy. After two weeks of negotiation, they received from Premier Janos Kadar a written guarantee of safe conduct to go freely to their homes. A bus came for them at six-thirty in the evening on November 22nd. (NAGY, JULIA *and the others come out of the Embassy to board the bus, when they are intercepted by the same two MVD men who met* KADAR *earlier. Armed soldiers herd them across the stage as* JULIA *picks up the frightened* LASZLO.)

LASZLO—I dropped my bear! I dropped my bear! (*They are herded off, leaving the stage empty except for the bear which lies in a bright pool of light.*)

AUTHOR—The bus went to Soviet military headquarters, where two Yugoslav officials were ejected. Then it left Budapest under armed guard, and was never seen again. At the time of the writing of this play, Julia Rajk was still under Russian arrest, we believe somewhere in Roumania. (*He picks up the bear.*) It is the opinion of her friends that the production of this play—unauthorized in any sense by Mrs. Rajk—can scarcely worsen her situation.

THE NIGHT OF THE IGUANA

A Play in Two Acts

By Tennessee Williams

[Tennessee Williams *was born Thomas Lanier Williams in Columbus, Missouri, on March 26, 1912. In 1930, while attending the University of Missouri, he acquired the nickname of Tennessee because of his southern accent, but he didn't formally adopt it until 1938. While he had written poetry, stories and essays, his first play, "Cairo! Shanghai! Bombay!", was written in collaboration with Dorothy Shapiro for a Memphis little theatre in 1935. Since that time he has written more than seventeen long plays and sixteen short ones, and is the only playwright ever to have won the Drama Critics Circle Award three times. "The Night of the Iguana" began as a shorter play at the 1959 Festival of Two Worlds in Spoleto, Italy. This earlier version did not include Miss Jelkes' confession of her love experiences, or the Freudian explanation of Shannon's reaction against God and Mama. His next play, "The Milk Train Doesn't Stop Here Any More," about a seventy-year-old ex-musical comedy star, was also unveiled at Spoleto in July, 1962, and another new work, "The Mutilated," has been offered to the newly formed Actors Studio producing company, which expects to begin operations in January of 1963.*]

IT is the late summer of 1940. Hitler has occupied Western Europe and driven the British back to England, where their situation seems desperate. And here in Puerto Barrio, a primitive Mexican town not on the Camino Real, we find ourselves at a rundown hotel. The hotel is called the Costa Verde because of its lush rain forest surroundings and its magnificent view of the sea below.

The Costa Verde is operated by Maxine Faulk, a rapacious and sloppily dressed Gorgon, who as the play begins is suddenly roused from her siesta by the sound of a bus horn from the road below.

It is a busload of women taking a guided tour through Mexico. Their guide is T. Lawrence Shannon, a handsome but bedeviled man in his thirties, who is sick with fever and the trouble he is having steering his unwilling party to the Costa Verde. When he asks for Fred, Maxine informs him with shocking casualness that her husband died two weeks ago from blood poisoning after cutting his hand on a fish hook.

SHANNON—You don't seem inconsolable about it.

MAXINE—Aw, baby, Fred was an old man. Years older'n me. We hadn't had sex together in ten years.

SHANNON—What's that got to do with it? (*Bus horn sounds below.*)

MAXINE—How about a rum-coco?

SHANNON—No, no. I want some cold water. If I start drinking rum-cocos now, I won't stop drinking rum-cocos.

Shannon shouts down to the driver to bring the party up to the hotel, but the driver shouts back that the women insist upon returning to town. Maxine tells Shannon: "You're not in a nervous condition to cope with that party; let them go and you stay."

A party of Nazis, who are staying at the Costa Verde, enter like a Wagnerian nightmare. They are on their way to the beach and are dressed with the minimal concession to decency. They are obviously enjoying the physical pleasures of life to the hilt, and the news of the Battle of Britain is joyously received by one of them on a short wave portable radio he is carrying. Maxine says she likes the Nazis: "They're lively and healthy."

The bus driver struggles up the hill and attempts to get Shannon to give him back the ignition key so that he can drive the party back to town. He points out that one girl is crying and all the others suspect Shannon is to blame. Shannon reminds him that he doesn't care what they think, and that he is in charge of the tour. He orders the driver to go down the hill and bring them up by force if necessary. Protestingly the driver obeys. After he has left, Maxine coarsely jokes with Shannon about "taking" a seventeen-year-old girl. He tries to explain.

SHANNON—She's traveling under the wing, the military escort, of this—butch vocal teacher who organizes little community sings in the bus. In fact I'm surprised they're not singing now—some morale-boosting number like "She's a Jolly Good Fellow." God! Each night after supper, after the complaints, and the vomiting by several ladies, who have inspected the kitchen—then the kid opens her mouth and out flies Carrie Jacobs Bond or Ethelbert Nevin. Night before last in Chilpancingo she opens her mouth and out flies "I Love You Truly" straight at *me*, with gestures, all right at *me*. That night, when I went to my room, I found that I had a roommate.

MAXINE—The Texas canary had moved in with you?

SHANNON—No, the spook had moved in with me. And he's been on my tail ever since. I haven't slept in three nights.

MAXINE—You'll sleep tonight, baby. I'll keep that spook off your back.

Miss Fellowes, the butch vocal teacher, storms up the hill. She is furious and protests that the brochure stipulates that they stay at the Ambos Mundos. Shannon explains that the Costa Verde is better and points out the view, but Miss Fellowes is more interested in sanitation and goes inside with Maxine to put in a collect phone call to Texas.

After a moment the worried Shannon is greeted by another lady, who has come up the path. She is ethereal and suggests a Gothic cathedral image of a medieval saint, but animated. She introduces herself as Hannah Jelkes who is seeking accommodations at the Costa Verde for herself and her grandfather. Shannon tells her that there is plenty of room, and she goes off to get her grandfather. Maxine returns and Shannon nervously asks her about the phone call Miss Fellowes made.

MAXINE—She called a judge in Blowing Rock, Texas. Collect.

SHANNON—She's trying to get me fired and she is also trying to pin on me a rape charge, a charge of statutory rape.

MAXINE—What's "statutory rape"? I never knew what it meant.

SHANNON—That's when a man's seduced by a girl under twenty.

MAXINE (*chuckles*)—You don't really want the young ones, do you?

SHANNON—I don't want any, any.

MAXINE—Then why do you take 'em? Why?

SHANNON—People need human contact, Maxine honey.

Shannon tells Maxine that this is his last tour and that he is planning to go back to the church and become a minister again. He has written a letter of complete confession and complete capitulation to his old Bishop, which he intends to rewrite and send off in the morning. Maxine promises him some night-swimming revelry in the meantime. She also suggests that Shannon consider filling her husband's shoes, a notion which Shannon so flatly rejects that we wonder if perhaps he does not recognize this as the path of least resistance, and therefore the one to be most avoided. Maxine discusses her dearly departed.

MAXINE—Dear old Fred was always a mystery to me. He was so patient and tolerant with me that it was insulting. A man and a woman have got to challenge each other, y'know what I mean? I mean I hired these diving-boys the Quebrada Hotel kicked out for being over attentive to the lady guests, and did he care? Did he give a damn when I started night-swimming with them? No. He'd go night-*fishing,* all night. But he just caught fish and threw them back into the sea.

SHANNON—The mystery of old Fred was simple. He was just cool and decent, that's all. (*He flops into the hammock.*)

Miss Fellowes re-enters and insists that she is taking the girls back to town. She accuses Shannon of not having stuck to the itinerary advertised in the Blake Tours brochure. Shannon suggests that the real, true cause of her rage is something less trivial. This erupts into a rapid fire dispute fired by shouts from below that the boys are bringing the girls' luggage up the hill, despite Miss Fellowes' orders to the contrary. Miss Fellowes maintains that Shannon has taken them to third-rate hotels and restaurants in order to collect his rake-off, and that all the girls have dysentery (or "Montezuma's revenge," as Maxine calls it), and that Shannon had even made a personal profit on the Enterovioform pills he sold the girls to counteract it. Shannon replies that he is a gentleman and cannot accept such insults. He also reminds her that she is speaking to an ordained minister of the church.

MISS FELLOWES—DE-FROCKED! But still trying to pass himself off as a minister!

SHANNON (*trying to control himself*)—Miss Fellowes, I try to give my tours a personal quality, the Shannon touch.

MISS FELLOWES—The gyp touch, the touch of a defrocked minister.

SHANNON—Miss Fellowes, don't, don't, don't . . . do what . . . you're doing! (*He is on the verge of hysteria.*) *Don't! Break! Human! Pride!*

At this point they are interrupted by shouts from below. The girls want to have a swim before going back to town, and Miss Fellowes rushes down the hill to put down this latest insurrection. Maxine pleads with Shannon to give them back the ignition key and let them go. She wants him to stay on here in Fred's old bedroom and again offers him a rum-coco. Doggedly he refuses as Hannah and her grandfather, Nonno, in a wheelchiar, arrive. Maxine asks Shannon who they are and remarks that "they look like a pair of loonies." Shannon abruptly shuts up Maxine. Hannah introduces herself and her grandfather, the "ninety-seven years young" poet, Jonathan Coffin. She apologizes for having arrived without advance reservations and pleads for accommodations. Maxine is reluctant, but Shannon intercedes for them and Maxine agrees, but asks them for six dollars in advance. Hannah explains that they always pay their way by entertaining the guests. Nonno recites poetry for them, and Hannah, dressed in a picturesque smock, does quick charcoal sketches. This is too much for Maxine, who wants to call a taxi to take them back to town. Hannah begs her not to and confesses that every hotel in town has turned them down. Again Shannon intercedes and Maxine reluctantly consents to let them stay one night. Maxine leaves them on the verandah with Shannon.

HANNAH—I'm dreadfully afraid my grandfather had a slight stroke in those high passes of the Sierras. I think he's had more than one of them, and all in the last few months. He was amazing 'til lately. I had to show his passport to prove that he was the oldest living and practicing poet on earth. We did well. We made expenses and *more!* When I saw he was failing, I tried to persuade him to go back to Nantucket, but he said: "No, Mexico!" I didn't make any sales in Mexico City; I'd expected to clean up there. So here we are on this windy hilltop like a pair of scarecrows . . .

Shannon leaves her to rest while he goes down to the beach for a swim. In the background we hear a marimba band playing from the beach cantina, and from Nonno's cubicle we hear him reciting a stanza of the first new poem he has started in twenty-five years.

SCENE II

It is several hours later, and Maxine has telephoned the Casa de Huéspedes, a centrally-located boarding house that will give Hannah and her grandfather credit. She points out that the Costa Verde caters to a younger crowd who like to rough it. Hannah tries to persuade her to accept a piece of jade as security and let them stay on, but Maxine refuses, explaining that her husband's death left her in a financial hole. She also tells Hannah that she obeyed his burial instructions which were to drop him into the sea, and that now "old

Freddie the fisherman is feeding the fish." Hannah looks at Maxine and remarks that she doubts he regrets his fate. The Nazis and Shannon come up from the beach. The Germans announce joyously that "London is burning, the heart of London's on fire!", and Maxine laughs with them. After they have gone, Shannon sees Charlotte coming up the hill and makes a hurried escape into one of the cubicles. Hannah tries to help Shannon by telling Charlotte that she thinks that he has gone down to the beach, but Charlotte hears Shannon trying to get out of the window. She pursues him and finally he is forced to talk to her, as Hannah excuses herself and goes to her room. Shannon tells Charlotte that she is going to get him kicked out of Blake Tours, but Charlotte insists that she loves him and insists that he marry her. Shannon replies that he is in no condition to marry, but Charlotte steadfastly refuses to believe that Shannon doesn't love her.

SHANNON—Honey, it's almost impossible for anybody to believe they're not loved by someone they believe they love, but, honey, I love nobody. When I brought you home last night, I just kissed you on the cheek like the little girl you are, but the instant I opened my door you rushed into my room and I couldn't get you out of it—

CHARLOTTE—Yes, but after you made love to me—

SHANNON—*Shut up, shut up about that!*

CHARLOTTE—*You turned mean, acted crazy!* (*She starts to sob.*)

SHANNON—Oh, now, Charlotte, honey, I have, we all have, just so much and no more in our emotional bank account, and mine has been all drawn out, *over*-drawn. I can't write another check on it. (MISS FELLOWES' *voice is heard calling, "Charlotte!"*)

CHARLOTTE (*to* SHANNON)—Larry, help me and let me help you!

SHANNON—The helpless can't help the helpless! (*He goes into a cubicle and slams the door, refusing to let* CHARLOTTE *come in with him. She runs into* HANNAH'S *cubicle to escape* MISS FELLOWES.)

Miss Fellowes, however, hears her crying and goes in and grabs her. She tells Charlotte that she has talked on the phone with her father about Shannon, and that if Shannon attempts to come back to the U. S. there will be a warrant for his arrest waiting for him. Forcibly she drags Charlotte off with her.

With the coast clear, Shannon comes out of his cubicle, dressed in clerical garb, in order to impress the ladies of his tour that he is still a *frocked* minister. Hannah helps him with his collar and then starts to sketch him.

HANNAH—How long have you been inactive in the Church, Mr. Shannon?

SHANNON—I have been inactive in the Church for all but one year since I was ordained.

HANNAH—Well, that's quite a sabbatical.

SHANNON—I wasn't defrocked but I was . . . locked out of my church. . . . Fornication and heresy . . . in the same week. The fornication preceded the heresy by several days. . . . A very young Sunday school teacher asked to see me privately in my study: a pretty little thing—no chance in the world—only child, and both her parents were spinsters, almost identical spinsters wearing clothes of the opposite sexes. . . . Well, she declared herself to me—wildly. The natural, or unnatural attraction of one . . . lunatic for . . . another . . . that's all it was. I was the goddamnedest prig in those days that even you could imagine. I said, let's kneel down together and pray. We did, we knelt down, but all of a sudden the kneeling position turned to a reclining position on the rug of my study and . . . When we got up? I struck her in the face and called her a damned little tramp. So she ran home and cut herself with her father's straightblade razor . . . yeah, the paternal spinster shaved.

HANNAH—Fatally?

SHANNON—Just enough to bleed a little, but it made a scandal. . . . So the next Sunday when I climbed into the pulpit and looked down over all those smug, disapproving faces, I had an impulse to shake them. "Look here," I shouted, "I am tired of conducting services in praise and worship of a senile delinquent. All your Western theologies are based on a concept of God as an angry, petulant old man, the sort of old man in a nursing home that's putting together a jigsaw puzzle and can't put it together and gets furious at it and kicks over the table. All your theologies accuse God of brutally punishing all He created for His own faults in construction."

HANNAH (*smiling a bit*)—What was the upshot of it?

SHANNON—Well, I was locked out of the church in Pleasant Valley, Virginia, and put in a nice little private asylum to recuperate from a nervous breakdown as they preferred to regard it. And then I entered my present line: tours of God's world conducted by a minister of God. . . . Collecting evidence of my personal idea of God, not as a senile delinquent, but as a . . .

HANNAH—Incomplete sentence. (*Thunder and lightning in the distance.*)

SHANNON—It's going to storm tonight. Then you will see the Reverend T. Lawrence Shannon's conception of God Almighty, paying a visit to the world He created. I want to go back to the Church and preach the Gospel of God as Lightning and Thunder . . . and also stray dogs vivisected and . . . and . . . and . . . (*Suddenly pointing upward.*) THAT's HIM! There He is now! (*He is pointing at a majestic blaze of gold light shafting the sky.*) His oblivious majesty—and here am I on this . . . dilapidated verandah of a cheap hotel, out of season, in a country caught and destroyed in its flesh and corrupted in its spirit by its gold-hungry Conquistadors that bore the flag of the Inquisition along with the Cross of Christ.

HANNAH (*after a pause*)—Mr. Shannon, I have a strong feeling you will go back to the Church with this evidence you've been collecting, but when you do, you'll throw away the violent, furious sermon, and talk about . . . about nothing. Just lead them beside still waters because you know how badly they need the still waters, Mr. Shannon.

Hannah goes off to the annex to sell some of her paintings to the girls from the tour. There is a windy sound in the rain forest and then we hear the shouts of the Mexican boys, who appear carrying a just-captured Iguana in a bag. Maxine tells them to tie the Iguana under the verandah until they are ready to slaughter and eat it. A noise is heard from Nonno's cubicle, but it turns out to be only a minor accident. The Nazis enter with their portable radio to tell Frau Faulk of the super firebombs that are being dropped on London every night. Nonno tries to recite some poetry to them. Hannah returns and attempts to sell them some paintings, but there is no sale. Nonno keeps asking her: "How much was the take?" Shannon, in order not to disappoint the excited old man, gives him a five peso note, but tells him it is five dollars.

NONNO—MIGHTY GOOD FOR ONE POEM!

SHANNON—THE *PECUNIARY REWARDS* OF A *POEM* ARE *GROSSLY INFERIOR* TO ITS *MERITS, ALWAYS!*

Nonno's excitement, fed by Shannon, builds to a climax after which he subsides into half-sleep. Hannah, however, has to rouse him for supper and takes the opportunity to introduce Shannon as "a man of God—on vacation." Nonno tries to make a match between Shannon and Hannah, explaining that she was brought up to be a wonderful wife and mother, and it is only because of his selfishness that he has kept her all to himself. Hannah is most embarrassed and as Nonno's mind begins to wander she explains to Shannon that her grandfather was a "minor league poet with a major league spirit." She adds: "Sometimes I think that nineteenth century poets like Keats and Shelley who didn't outlive their talent were lucky." Nonno begins to talk about breakfast under the illusion that it is morning.

SHANNON—Fantastic—*fantastic*.

HANNAH—That word "fantastic" seems to be your favorite word, Mr. Shannon.

SHANNON—Yeah, well, you know we—live on two levels, Miss Jelkes, the realistic level and the fantastic level, and which is the real one, really. . . .

HANNAH—I would say both, Mr. Shannon.

SHANNON—But when you live on the fantastic level, as I have lately, but have got to operate on the realistic level, that's when you're spooked, that's the spook. . . . I thought I'd shake the spook here but conditions at the Costa Verde have changed. (MAXINE *enters carrying the cocktail shaker.*) It's being managed by a widow—a sort of black widow spider.

Maxine offers Hannah and Nonno cocktails, but Shannon reminds her that people don't drink cocktails between the fish course and the entrée. Maxine insists that Grandpa have one, "so he'll live through supper," and Nonno orders a Manhattan. Shannon tries to protect Hannah and Nonno from Maxine which leads to a ridiculous squabble in which Shannon and Maxine push the liquor cart at each other as if it were a battering ram. Hannah intercedes and Maxine turns on her, calling her "a deadbeat, using that dying old man for a front to get in places without the cash to pay one day in advance." Hannah, with forced calm, replies that she'll walk to town at daybreak, set up her easel and peddle her water colors and sketches. She even offers to put her grandfather in the wheelchair and push him back to town tonight. Maxine tries to calm her down and admits the real source of her irritation.

MAXINE—The trouble is Shannon. I want you to lay off him, honey. You're not for Shannon and Shannon isn't for you.

HANNAH—Mrs. Faulk, I'm a New England spinster who is pushing forty.

MAXINE—I got the vibrations between you. So just stop messing around with Shannon.

HANNAH—Mrs. Faulk, do I look like a *vamp?*

MAXINE—They come in all types. Of course, I suppose there isn't any sex in Nantucket unless they *catch* you at it!

Alan Webb, Margaret Leighton, Patrick O'Neal and Bette Davis in "The Night of the Iguana."

Shannon joins Hannah and Nonno, as Maxine exits. He asks Hannah if she would have gone through with her threat to push Nonno back to town in the wheelchair, or was it a poker player's bluff. She replies: "Let's say I was drawing to an inside straight." She asks Shannon what he would do if he were fired by Blake Tours. He answers: "Go back to the Church or take the long swim to China." She offers to help him. Suddenly the wind rises, and the electric lights go out because of the thunderstorm that is descending upon the Costa Verde. Everyone scatters for shelter. Hannah leads Nonno to his cubicle and turns back to speak to Shannon, who has not sought shelter.

HANNAH—Here is your God, Mr. Shannon.
SHANNON—Yes, I see him, I hear him, I know him. And if he doesn't know that I know him, let him strike me dead with a bolt of his lightning.

He moves to the edge of the verandah and catches in his hands the rain pouring off the roof. He bathes his forehead with it. Then he reaches out again as if he were reaching for something outside and beyond himself. There is a pure white flash of lightning which reveals Hannah and Nonno, against the wall, and Shannon, whose hands remain illuminated after the lightning has disappeared. The curtain falls slowly.

ACT II

It is several hours later. The sky has cleared after the rain and an almost full moon reflects off the drenched verandah and foliage. We can see Hannah reading in her cubicle, Nonno in his cubicle composing his new poems, and Shannon on the verandah working feverishly on the letter to his Bishop. Maxine enters with some burning smudge pots to drive away the mosquitoes. She begins to talk to Shannon about her dissatisfaction with her lonely life, which is relieved only by purely physical treatments from her Mexican bellboys.

MAXINE—When you let employees get too free with you, personally, they stop respecting you, Shannon. It's, well, it's . . . humiliating—not to be respected. I been thinking lately of selling out here and operating a tourist camp outside some live town like Houston or Dallas, and renting out cabins to business executives. Complimentary rum-cocos—bathrooms with bidets . . .

SHANNON—Does everything have to wind up on that level with you, Maxine?

MAXINE—Yes and no, baby. I know the difference between loving someone and just sleeping with someone. (SHANNON *starts to rise.*) We've both reached a point where we've got to settle for something that works for us in our lives—even if it isn't on the highest kind of level.

SHANNON—I don't want to rot.

MAXINE—You wouldn't. I wouldn't let you! I know your psychological history. I heard you tell Fred that your Mama used to send you to bed before you was ready to sleep, so you amused yourself with yourself. And once she caught you at it and whaled your backside. She said she had to punish you for it because it made God mad as much as it did Mama, and she had to punish you for it so God wouldn't punish you for it harder than she did. You said you loved God and Mama and so you quit it to please them, but you harbored a secret resentment against Mama and God for making you give it up, and so you got back at God by preaching atheistical sermons and you got back at Mama by starting to lay young girls. Did you mention the charge of statutory rape to the Divinity Dean?

Their conversation is interrupted when Shannon notices that his ladies are gathered around the bus. It develops that Blake Tours has sent Jake Latta to take over Shannon's party. Latta and the bus driver take the ignition key away from Shannon by force while Miss Fellowes gloats about her victory. Furthermore they leave Shannon broke and accuse him of having taken money from Charlotte, in order to take her to filthy places not in the Blake Tours brochure. Latta pompously informs Miss Fellowes that Blake Tours was deceived by Shannon, and will see to it that from now on he will be blacklisted "at every travel agency in the United States."

SHANNON—How about Africa, Asia, Australia? The whole world, Latta, God's world, has been the range of my travels. I haven't stuck to the schedules of the brochures and I've always allowed the ones that were willing to see, to SEE!—the underworlds of all places, and if they have hearts to be touched, feelings to feel with, I gave them a priceless chance to feel and be touched. And none will ever forget it, none of them, ever, never!

They go off and the frenzied Shannon runs after them down the hill. There is a great commotion and outraged shrieking and shocked laughter from below. Shannon returns panting, and it is clear that he has cracked up. Maxine tries to get him to lie down. Stunned by the realization that he is in danger of insanity he asks the Mexican boys to tell him what he has done, and they inform him that he has urinated over the girls' baggage. This and the sight of the bus leaving is too much for him and he starts for the beach "to swim to China." Maxine sends the Mexican boys after him, and they bring him back by force and tie him up in the hammock. Maxine tells Hannah that she's sending for the doctor to give him a knockout injection and that if he isn't better by tomorrow she's going to send him to the Casa de Locos. The Nazis enter and torment him about his behavior with the ladies' luggage, and Hannah begs them to leave him alone. Shannon asks her to untie him, but she refuses, and tells him that he is enjoying his suffering and atonement, "a luxurious crucifixion, with ropes instead of nails, and a hammock instead of a cross." Shannon tells her that she, like all women, takes pleasure in getting men in a tied-up situation. He notices that she is brewing some poppyseed tea with her little spirit lamp, and jokes that she ought to put some hemlock in the cup she gives to her grandfather. Hannah begs him to stop, saying: "I can't stand for a person I respect to talk like a small, cruel boy."

SHANNON—Respect? What have you found to respect in me, Miss . . . Thin-Standing-Up-Female-Buddha?

HANNAH—I respect a person that has had to fight and howl for his decency and his bit of goodness, much more than I respect the lucky ones that just had theirs handed out to them at birth and never afterwards snatched away from them by . . .

SHANNON—Will you untie me!

HANNAH—Not till I'm reasonably sure that you wouldn't swim out to China, because, you see, I think you think of the . . . "long swim to China" as another painless atonement.

Shannon asks her to light a cigarette for him and put it in his mouth. When she does, he grabs her wrist with one of his tied hands and twists it to force her to untie him. Instead she calls Maxine, who jumps on top of him and threatens him with the insane asylum. Hannah tells her that Shannon won't quiet down until he is left alone in the hammock, and that she is preparing some sedative tea for him. Maxine says it is against the rules for the guests to cook, and blows out the flame of Hannah's spirit lamp. A call from the Nazis on the beach ordering more beer necessitates Maxine's departure to the beach, and Hannah relights her spirit lamp and after a moment serves Shannon the poppyseed tea. Nonno calls from his cubicle and while Hannah leaves to answer it, Shannon struggles free of the ropes. She returns and is not surprised. They talk as he pours himself a rum-coco.

Hannah admits that she was once in danger of cracking up like Shannon, but that she didn't because she couldn't afford to, and that perhaps her occupation of painting, which forced her to look out of herself at others, helped her. Shannon remarks that she isn't operating on the realistic level any better than he is, and he offers her his gold cross to hock so that she'll be able to get her grandfather back to Laredo. When she refuses, he suggests the world's oldest profession, which she puts in her files under the heading of interesting but useless information. Hannah tells Shannon that she and her grandfather make a home for each other, not a stationary one, but "the kind that two people build between them, in which they can nest—rest—live in, emotionally speaking."

SHANNON—When a bird builds a nest, it builds it with an eye for the . . . the relative permanence of the location, and also for the purpose of propagating its species.

HANNAH—I'm not a bird, Mr. Shannon, I'm a human being and when a member of that fantastic species builds a nest in the heart of another, the question of permanence isn't the first or even the last thing that's considered . . . necessarily . . . always?

Shannon asks her what will happen when Nonno dies, and Hannah replies that she will probably go on alone, just as Shannon has gone it alone.

SHANNON—Alone? I never fail to make an intimate connection with someone in my parties.

HANNAH—Yes, the youngest young lady, and how lonely the intimate connection has always been for you. The episode in the cold, inhuman, hotel room, Shannon, for which you despise the lady almost as much as you despise yourself. Afterwards you either strike her or are so polite that it must chill her to the bone. Oh, no, Mr. Shannon, you have always traveled alone except for your spook, as you call it.

Hannah suggests that Shannon drink another cup of the bitter tasting poppyseed tea, and Shannon agrees provided she will answer one not nice question, namely: "Have you never had in all your life and travels any experience, any encounter, with what Larry the Crackpot Shannon thinks of as love life?"

HANNAH—Yes, two. And don't you say "fantastic" before I've told you both stories. When I was sixteen, your favorite age, Mr. Shannon, each Saturday afternoon my grandfather would give me thirty cents. Twenty-five cents for admission to the matinee at the Nantucket movie theatre and five cents extra for a bag of popcorn. I'd sit at the almost empty back of the theatre so that the popcorn munching wouldn't disturb the other movie patrons. Well . . . one afternoon a young man sat down beside me and pushed his . . . knee against mine and . . . I moved over two seats but he moved over beside me and continued this . . . pressure! I jumped up and screamed, Mr. Shannon. He was arrested for molesting a minor. But I told the police that it was a Clara Bow picture—and I was just overexcited.

SHANNON—Fantastic.

HANNAH—The second experience was only two years ago at the Raffles Hotel in Singapore. One evening we met this middle-aged, sort of nondescript Australian salesman there. You know—plump, bald-spotted, with a bad attempt at speaking with an upper-class accent, and terribly overfriendly. Grandfather said him a poem and I did a quick character sketch that was shamelessly flattering of him. He paid me more than my usual asking price and he even purchased one of my water colors. Then it was Nonno's bedtime. The Aussie salesman asked me out in a sampan with him. Well, he'd been so generous . . . I accepted and went out in the sampan with this ladies' underwear salesman. As the afterglow of the sunset faded out on the water he became more and more agitated. Finally he looked intensely, passionately into my eyes! (*She laughs with a delicate sadness.*) And he said to me: "Miss Jelkes? Will you do me a favor? Will you do something for me? If I turn my back, if I look the other way, will you take off some piece of your clothes and let me hold it, just hold it?" I gratified his request and threw him the part of my clothes. I looked the other way while his satisfaction took place. The moral is Oriental, "Accept whatever situation you cannot improve." The incident was embarrassing, not violent. I left and returned unmolested. Somehow the little experience had been rather touching. I'd known about loneliness—but not that degree or—depth of it.

SHANNON—You mean it didn't *disgust* you?

HANNAH—Nothing human disgusts me unless it's unkind, violent! (SHANNON *rises and touches* HANNAH.) Save it for the widow. It isn't for me.

SHANNON—Yes, you're right. (*Removes his hand from her.*) I could do it with Mrs. Faulk, but I couldn't do it with you.

HANNAH (*making light of it*)—Spinster's loss, widow's gain, Mr. Shannon.

SHANNON—But . . . I wonder something. . . . If we couldn't . . . *travel* together, I mean just *travel* together?

HANNAH—I think the impracticality of that idea will appear much clearer to you in the morning. Mr. Shannon, you're not well enough to travel anywhere with anybody right now.

SHANNON—You mean that I'm stuck here for good? With the . . . insatiable widow?

HANNAH—We all wind up with something or someone and if it's someone instead of something, we're lucky, perhaps . . . unusually lucky. (*She starts to take the tray into her room when she hears something and stops.*) What is making that constant, dry, scuffling sound beneath the verandah?

SHANNON—It's an Iguana. Do you want to see the Iguana? At the end of its rope? Trying to go on past the end of its goddam rope? Like *you!* Like *me!* Like Grampa with his last poem!

HANNAH—Why do they tie it up?

SHANNON—Because that's what they do. They tie them up and fatten them up and then eat them, when they're ready for eating. And the Mexican kids have a lot of fun with them, poking out their eyes with sticks and burning their tails with matches.

HANNAH—Mr. Shannon, please go down and cut it loose.

SHANNON—I can't. Mrs. Faulk wants to eat it. I've got to please Mrs. Faulk, I am at her mercy. I am at her disposal.

HANNAH—I don't understand how anyone can eat a big lizard.

SHANNON—Miss Jelkes, you're still not operating on the realistic level. You'd be surprised what people will eat when they're really hungry. They'll eat cold, greasy, frijoles at the Casa de Huespedes—they'll even—why I remember conducting a party of ladies . . . through a country that shall be nameless but in the world, we were passing by rubberneck bus along a tropical coast when we saw a great mound of . . . well, the smell was unpleasant. One of my ladies said, "Oh, Larry, what is that?" I didn't use the four letter word for what the great mound was. I didn't think it was necessary. Then she noticed, and I noticed too, a pair of very old natives, practically naked except for a few filthy rags, creeping and crawling about this mound of . . . and . . . occasionally stooping to pick something out of it, and pop it into their mouths! What? Bits of undigested . . . food particles, Miss Jelkes. (HANNAH *makes a gagging sound and rushes to the wooden steps and disappears.*) Disgusting? Nothing human disgusts you unless it's . . . Now why did I tell her that? Because it's true? That's no reason to tell her. Because it's true was a good reason not to tell her. Except . . . I think I first *faced* it in that nameless country. The gradual, rapid, natural, unnatural—predestined, accidental—cracking up and going to pieces of young Mr. T. Lawrence Shannon, by which rapid-slow process . . . his final tour of ladies through tropical countries. . . . It's always been tropical countries I took ladies through. Does that signify something, I wonder? Fast decay is a thing of steamy, hot, wet climates, and I run back to them like a. . . . Incomplete sentence. . . . Always seducing a lady or two in the party, but really ravaging her first by pointing out to her the horrors of the tropical country being conducted a tour through . . . Cruelty . . . pity. What is it? . . . Don't know, all I know is my brain is going out like a failing power.

HANNAH (*coming back to the verandah*)—I took a closer look at the Iguana down there. Its situation seems very human and so does its desperation. Mr. Shannon, will you please cut it loose. Because if you don't, I will.

SHANNON—Can you look at *me* and tell *me* truthfully that this reptilian creature, tied up down there, doesn't mostly disturb you because of its parallel situation to your Grampa's dying effort to finish one last poem, Miss Jelkes?

HANNAH—Yes, I . . .

SHANNON—Never mind completing that sentence. We'll play

God tonight like kids play house with old broken crates and boxes. All right? Now Shannon is going down there with his machete and cut the damn lizard loose because God won't do it. (SHANNON *takes a machete and goes off the verandah. Suddenly there is a shout from* NONNO'S *cubicle and* HANNAH *rushes to her grandfather.*)

NONNO—I! BELIEVE! IT! IS! *FINISHED!* Quick, before I forget it! (HANNAH *picks up a pad and pencil to take down the poem, as* NONNO *recites in a loud, exalted voice.*)

How calmly does the orange branch
Observe the sky begin to blanch
Without a cry, without a prayer,
With no betrayal of despair.

Sometime while night obscures the tree
The zenith of its life will be
Gone past forever, and from thence
A second history will commence.

A chronicle no longer gold,
A bargaining with mist and mould,
And finally the broken stem
The plummeting to earth; and then

An intercourse not well designed
For beings of a golden kind
Whose native green must arch above
The earth's obscene, corrupting love.

And still the ripe fruit and the branch
Observe the sky begin to blanch
Without a cry, without a prayer,
With no betrayal of despair.

O Courage, could you not as well
Select a second place to dwell.
Not only in that golden tree
But in the frightened heart of me?

Oh! God! Finally finished! (*To* HANNAH.) It is *good?*

HANNAH—It's beautiful, Grandfather. It was worth the long wait. I'll type it up and send it off to *Harper's* tomorrow.

Nonno, exhausted by his effort, falls asleep. Maxine enters and discovers the empty hammock. Then she sees Shannon as he climbs up onto the verandah.

MAXINE—What're you doing down there, Shannon?

SHANNON—I cut loose one of God's creatures at the end of his rope. A little act of grace, honey.

MAXINE—Let's go down and swim in that liquid moonlight.

SHANNON—Where'd you pick up that poetic expression?

MAXINE—Shannon, I want you to stay here with me.

SHANNON (*taking the rum-coco from her*)—You want a drinking companion?

MAXINE—No. I just need somebody to manage the place.

SHANNON (*looking at* HANNAH)—I want to remember that face. I won't see it again. Miss Jelkes, I cut loose the Iguana.

HANNAH—Thank you. Thank you, Larry.

SHANNON—Now another one of God's creatures is going down to swim in that liquid moonlight. (*He goes down to the beach followed by* MAXINE.)

MAXINE—You know something, baby! I've got five more years to make this place attractive to the middle-aged male clientele, and you can take care of the women with them. That's what you can do. (*Her voice and laughter fade out.*)

HANNAH (*talking to herself and to the sky*)—Oh, God, can't we stop now? Finally? Please let us. It's so quiet here, now.

She starts to put the shawl about Nonno, but his hand drops limply to his side. She places her hand before his mouth to see if he is still breathing. He isn't. In panic she looks around for someone to call. There's no one. Then she bends her head and presses it to Nonno's as the curtain falls.

THE EGG

A Play in Two Acts

BY FÉLICIEN MARCEAU

ADAPTED BY ROBERT SCHLITT

[FÉLICIEN MARCEAU *is the pen name of Louis Carrette. He was born in Cortenberg, Belgium, on September 16, 1913. In the world of letters he has made three careers for himself: as critic, as novelist, and as playwright. His critical works include "Balzac et Son Monde," and among his novels are "Bergère Légère" and "Les Elans du Coeur," both of which have been published here in translation. M. Marceau turned to the theatre in 1951 with his first play, "L'École des Moroses." Of the five plays he has written since, two, "La Bonne Soupe" and "L'Oeuf," have been presented on Broadway. His latest play, "Les Cailloux," is currently running in Paris. "The Egg" has played successfully in Paris, London, and Tel-Aviv. And in 1960 at Washington's Arena Stage—as directed by F. Cowles Strickland and with William Shust as Magis—it proved enchanting theatre. The colder and more extroverted Broadway production of this season was, alas, a failure.*

ROBERT SCHLITT *was born in New York City on July 24, 1933, and he attended Columbia University and the Sorbonne. He has directed plays in Paris, as well as adapting into English plays of Ionesco, Giraudoux, Anouilh, Achard, and Roussin. He has also written several original plays.*]

A GOOD-NATURED ordinary young Frenchman named Magis is working with a screwdriver on the back of a radio set. He notices the audience and explains that he is just fiddling around with the radio, when suddenly it blares forth music. Magis is astonished, but then a moment later it goes off again, and he resumes his tinkering. He casually explains to the audience.

MAGIS—It's just a question of figuring out the system. I mean the way it's all laid out, the way it all works. Like anything else . . . like life. With a radio it's something you can see . . . tubes, wiring . . . Scientific. But the system of life . . . well, it's not quite so simple, but I figured *it* out, too. All through one little sentence: "He got up fresh as a daisy." The whole system is right there. Everybody gets up fresh as a daisy. Every morning all over the world, people are getting up fresh as a daisy. Or at least they go around telling each other they got up fresh as a daisy. Except me, that is. I never once in my entire life got up fresh as a daisy. So I looked at the rest of them, and I figured *I* must be crazy. The whole world sitting there like an egg . . . and what's inside it? People who get up fresh as a daisy! I was on the outside, alone . . . different . . . a freak. I said well, there must be something wrong with me. So I went to a doctor.

We see Magis being examined by the doctor who tells him that although he is not a very imposing physical specimen, there is nothing at all the matter with him. Magis then asks him why he wakes up in the morning feeling worn out, and the doctor replies that he feels the same way himself, but that it doesn't mean a thing. Magis is astounded. He asks a few other people, and they all admit to not waking up fresh as a daisy either.

MAGIS (*to the audience*)—So what about my little magic sentence? What about the system? What about the egg? (*Shrugs.*) Or take the question of sex. When I was nineteen, I was still pure and undefiled. I used to listen to the fellows at work: "She dropped a package, I picked it up, I bought her a drink. I said, my place? She said, why not? And that's all there was to it." Well, it sounded easy. So the next day. . . .

We watch Magis try to pick up a girl, who brushes him off. Then another, who mocks his youth, and a third, who threatens to call a policeman. Finally he decides to court a girl slowly, having several dates with her, walking in the park, allowing the romance to grow. Then, when the time seemed ripe. . . .

MAGIS (*to the girl*)—There's a nice hotel nearby. I thought we might . . . go there for a little while.

GIRL (*insulted*)—Emile! You're just like all the others.

MAGIS—Well, I'm trying to be. (GIRL *goes off, and* MAGIS *turns to the audience.*) So what about the system? If I went after Brigitte Bardot, all right, I'd expect a little trouble. But these girls?

You saw. I tried them all, the hopeless cases. I must have been doing something wrong, but what? You just go into it blindly and when you fail, you start to lie. . . . The next day at work I'd say, "Chalk up another for Magis!" Until one day it suddenly hit me. If *I'm* lying . . . suppose *they're* lying too. If the system didn't work, then you had to lie about it . . . and each lie made the system that much stronger. I lied, just like the others. But why? To show off? No. I lied because if I hadn't lied, I'd have been the only one . . . I hadn't blamed the system. I'd blamed myself! Now do you see how it works? The system tells you the way things should be, and naturally the system is always right. So if it doesn't work out that way for you, then it's your fault! You're the exception to the rule, a menace to the system . . . and they shut you out. Well, it's just not true! There's no such thing as the system. Things work out or they don't work out, and that's all there is to it. Take stealing, for instance. According to the system crime does not pay, etc. Well, that's not true either. I know, I'm a criminal myself. I stole some money . . . just once.

We see Magis surreptitiously taking a 10,000-franc note by hoodwinking the middle-aged woman who is cashier in the store where he works. Afterwards, when she discovers that her cash is short, Magis is so sympathetic that she interprets it as an interest in her, and instead of ending up in jail, he ends up in bed.

Now Magis introduces us to his family. There is his mother, and his sister, Justine, who is engaged to marry a salesman named Gustave. However, one afternoon Gustave tells Justine that he's in love with somebody else, and that he's sorry but he can't marry her. Both Justine and Magis' mother insist that he do something about his jilted sister. Magis reluctantly has a talk with Gustave who tells him that he had thought he was in love with Justine, but since he has met Georgette he now realizes that it wasn't really love. Magis meets Georgette, who is very pretty and very jealous. After she has gone he tells Gustave that he understands perfectly, but that if Gustav could just come over to the house one night and explain it to Justine, letting her down gently, that would make all the difference. Gustave nervously agrees to come over the next night, but only that one time.

MAGIS (*to the audience*)—Now, when you hear what happened next, you're going to think I'm a bit of a stinker. But it's not so. What I did was experiment. The thing that had bothered me was something Gustave had said. "I thought that was love," he told me. And he was sincere about it. And if he hadn't met Georgette, he could have gone on for the rest of his life, thinking the way he felt about Justine was love. Because after all, how did he happen to meet Georgette? By accident. And there must be millions of people in the world who never do meet their Georgette, who go around yelling "love" all over the place. And here's another thing. Suppose you meet Georgette. But then along comes somebody else . . . and then another one . . . and another one . . .

Is that what love is supposed to be? Where's the beauty, the nobility in a thing like that? (*In a different tone.*) And what if the whole thing is really an enormous joke? . . . if love is nothing but a lie that people make up because they don't know . . . because they're not sure? (*Pauses.*) Now, I had nothing against Georgette. But I wanted to find something out, scientifically. If it was really love, then it ought to be able to stand a little experiment, a little test.

Magis relates how he telephoned Georgette and advised her that Gustave would be two-timing her the next evening. And he is genuinely disappointed to find that the resultant misunderstanding was all that was needed to destroy this "noble passion." He tells us that Gustave even returned to Justine and married her. "The guinea pigs," he comments, "took matters into their own hands."

Magis goes on to tell us about how if the human being is willing to live without such illusions as "love" and "purpose," he can be happy, and he proves his case by introducing us to Rose, a buxom married woman in her early forties, with whom he used to sleep. She is lying on her bed, as Magis unbuttons his shirt.

Magis (*to audience*)—We went to bed. Often. It was the only thing to do under the circumstances. A man and a woman alone in a room . . . there's a kind of magnetism in the air, a loneliness that pushes them together. What else were we there for? For conversation? Rose didn't appreciate my conversation. Oh, I used to talk to her every once in a while but . . .

Rose—It's better than if I was deaf.

Magis—And it was wonderful! That woman was a desert! Not a tree, not a shadow! And I began to realize that that's what life really is. No reasons, no excuses, no explanations, nothing to get in the way . . . And I owe it all to Rose. I moved, too. . . .

Rose—There's a room free in my building. On the sixth floor. Take it, it'll be less trouble.

Magis—Why was I sleeping with Rose? Because one of the fellows where I worked introduced me to her. And why was I working there? Because Gustave got me the job. And why Gustave? Because one day my sister got her umbrella caught in the door and Gustave got it out for her. Which means that every time I went to bed with Rose, it was all because of my sister. Now that's a lovely thought.

ROSE—You finished, Einstein?

MAGIS—Coming, Rosie . . . (*He lies on the bed next to* ROSE, *as the lights go out.*)

ROSE—Hey, how late do the stores stay open on Thursday? (*After a moment the lights come up, and we see* MAGIS *alone, putting on his tie, his shoes and his jacket.*)

MAGIS (*smiling*)—For the first time in my life I was happy. As soon as I stopped trying to figure things out, it all made sense. Because there wasn't any sense. That was the secret. Once you start looking for reasons, it's like a drug. You need more of them every day. To hide behind, to put between yourself and emptiness. And when you can't hide behind them anymore, then the nightmare begins. Well, Rose saved me from that. She taught me how to live in the desert. But I didn't know when I was well off. You know what ruined it? A silly little thing. I happen to be a good card player. And I got conceited about it. It was the cards and Rose's husband, Eugene. . . .

We watch a touching little domestic scene between Magis, Rose, and her good-naturedly stupid and fat husband, Eugene. Something in the conversation leads Magis to suspect that Eugene knows about him and Rose, and he asks her about it. She replies: "What the hell do you care? He doesn't bother you, don't you bother him." Then he and Magis go to a café to play cards with some other men. They all flatter Magis for his card-playing, which pleases him, but he turns away to tell the audience: "They made me feel important. That's a mistake. The trick in life is to feel as unimportant as possible. Once you begin to get impressed with yourself, you're through. You never know when to stop. Look at Napoleon. . . ." M. Berthoullet comes along and watches. He is so delighted with Magis' cleverness at cards, he suggests that Magis come to his house tomorrow night and play there with his uncle, who holds the important post of tax-collector at Amiens. Berthoullet himself worked in the Ministry and has three daughters. Magis is interested in them, and soon begins to go to play cards with the Berthoullets with increasing frequency, telling Rose: "Not tonight, Rose, I'm going over to the Berthoullets'."

ROSE (*indifferent*)—Again? The big bad wolf is after the three little pigs, huh? You've got a button loose. Give me your jacket.

MAGIS (*to audience, as* ROSE *sews his button on*)—You see With Rose there were no excuses, no lies, no reasons. But at the Berthoullets' there were reasons crawling all over the place. And as soon as you begin to think about the reasons, misery begins. You're happy, but you start asking yourself why. You could get sick . . . lose your job . . . no money in the bank. You worry whether things can last. . . .

We now observe another evening at the Berthoullets'. This time the card game is interrupted by the visit of M. Raffard, Berthoullet's department supervisor. Magis gives him his place at the card table as the girls invite him to play rummy with them. While he is enjoying himself with them, the supervisor inquires about his reliability, and reveals that there may be an opening in his department. He tells Berthoullet that he would like to hire Magis if he is interested. Berthoullet asks permission to announce this good news to Magis.

BERTHOULLET—My dear boy! M. Raffard is going to recommend you for a job in our department. The Ministry . . . The Civil Service.

MME. BERTHOULLET (*rapturously, sensing an eligible husband for one of her daughters*)—The Civil Service . . .

BERTHOULLET—A responsible position . . . steady income . . . full pension retirement benefits. This calls for a celebration! Charlotte, bring in the brandy. (CHARLOTTE *goes to the cupboard.*)

CHARLOTTE (*out of sight of the others*)—Monsieur Magis, would you come and help me carry the glasses? (MAGIS *crosses to her. She smiles longingly at him. Obligingly he takes her in his arms and kisses her.*)

ACT II

It is some months later, and in the comfortable middle-class apartment that he has acquired Magis is sitting in an armchair reading, while Hortense sews at the table. Magis finishes the paper, folds it, and rises to address the audience.

MAGIS—I'm married now. To Charlotte? Well, no. To Hortense, the oldest. She had seniority rights. Oh, well, basically, Charlotte or Hortense . . . what difference does it make? What I was really interested in was this new world I saw opening up in front of me, this egg with a crack in its shell. I wanted to get inside and make myself at home. I also started work at the Ministry

. . . and that was a new world too. I was somebody important, a civil servant, a member of the bureaucracy. I liked it. Because the work of a bureaucrat doesn't . . . . (*Pauses.*) Well, I was going to say it's useless, it doesn't serve any purpose, but that's not quite correct. It's just that nobody knows *what* purpose it serves. No problems, no decisions to make, no boss. Oh, technically I was working for Raffard, but it wasn't Raffard who handed me my paycheck. He was just sort of a link between me and the tax-payers. (*Reflecting.*) The whole world would be a better place if everybody was a government employee. All right, you say, who would do the work? Well, what people need isn't work, it's a job . . . a place to go in the morning.

Magis is interrupted by his in-laws who have come to pay "the lovebirds" a visit. With them is a young civil servant named Joseph, whom they are grooming to marry one of their other daughters. After discussing the new curtains and Aunt Helen's gallstones, they set up two card games, a serious one for the older people and a fun game for the younger ones. Magis wants to play with the young people, but Berthoullet insists he play with them and sends Joseph over to play rummy with the girls. After a moment of reluctant card-playing, Magis turns to the audience.

MAGIS—I ask you, is it fair? Why did I get married in the first place? (*Pointing to the second table.*) To get in there . . . inside that egg, where the young people are, where life is just a game of rummy. For a moment it opened up for me . . . and then it closed again. With me still outside. Well, I'll try one more time . . . . (MAGIS *goes over to* CHARLOTTE, *who has left her game for a minute to watch a parade out the door.*) Give me a kiss.

CHARLOTTE—What's the matter with you?

MAGIS—Can't you even kiss your own brother-in-law? (*She kisses him perfunctorily on the cheek, as she tries to get away.*) Not like that. The way you used to. (*He tries to take her in his arms.*)

CHARLOTTE—Let go of me! I'll tell Hortense.

She struggles with him, and he takes her handkerchief. Charlotte tells her parents what Magis has been up to, and Mme. Berthoullet rushes to Hortense's side in sympathy. However, Hortense minimizes the whole business, and the men are merely annoyed that their game is interrupted.

MAGIS—You'd think Hortense would have said something to me about it—a big, emotional scene. Oh, no. Not a word. The silent treatment. That was standard operating procedure with the Berthoullets. If something came up that bothered them, they just ignored it. Hortense went around that house as if I wasn't even there. Not a word. Like I was a piece of furniture. It began to get on my nerves. So (*Putting on his hat.*) I started going to see Rose again.

Magis goes to see Rose and her husband. They give him the old greeting, and after a while Rose suggests that Eugene go for a walk by himself. He doesn't really want to go, because there isn't anybody at the café this time of day, but he finally obliges.

Rose (*to* Magis)—Next time, we'll go to a hotel. I don't like to disturb Eugene like that. (*She heads for the bedroom.* Magis *doesn't move.*) You coming, or what?

Magis (*following her*)—Good old Rose! (*He re-enters immediately, putting on his jacket.*) And while we're on the subject, here's an interesting point. According to the system, love is a free spirit, capricious, unpredictable. Desire, too. It comes and it goes. For example, when you and your wife go home tonight, are you going to make love? Well, you don't really know . . . it all depends, right? Suppose the police came around and tried to make you. You'd say, just a minute now, desire is something you can't order around. No question about it. All right, so please explain to me how Rose used to say, Thursday, six-thirty . . . and on Thursday, six-thirty, boom! . . . we made love. Of course, if you have a woman for life or even for two weeks, it's different. You take your time. But when you have a woman for twenty-five minutes, then it's now or never. The desire is there, that's all there is to it.

Hortense enters wheeling a baby carriage. In it is Magis' baby girl, Alexandria, who has served to patch things up between Magis and the Berthoullets. Meanwhile, an old boy friend of Hortense, Victor Dugommier, has returned to France after a long spell in Indo-China. The following Sunday he comes to visit them. He is a pompous and dapper man.

Magis (*to the audience*)—You know . . . at first I didn't suspect a thing. Maybe I was stupid, but it just never occurred to me. Oh, I figured there'd been something between them, holding hands, kissing in the parlor, that sort of stuff. Victor went off to Indo-China, alone, and by the time he got back it was too late. She must have been sorry about it, too. I wasn't really her type. There he was, off in the wilderness, dreaming about the love of his life . . . and then he comes back and finds her married to a man he thinks is an idiot. Ah, that must be sad . . . I made it a point to annoy hell out of them.

MAGIS (*picks up package* DUGOMMIER *has put on the table*)—Ah, what have we here? This beautiful little box with the pink ribbon?

DUGOMMIER—Marrons glacés. I remembered how much Hortense likes them.

MAGIS (*unwrapping the box*)—Mmm, a real delicacy. I'm mad about them myself. (*Eats one.*) Delicious! (*Takes another.* DUGOMMIER *is annoyed.*) Well, Victor, why don't you tell us all about Indo-China and those native girls. We're broad-minded, right, honey? (*Leaving* DUGOMMIER *thoroughly exasperated,* MAGIS *puts on his hat and steps towards the audience and speaks to it.*) But I still didn't suspect anything. I knew Dugommier used to drop around sometimes on Friday afternoon, while I was at the office. But it still didn't worry me. I thought it was just exchanging memories, holding hands on the couch: he poured out his soul, she poured out the coffee. That kind of thing. It was Rose who finally put me wise. One day she said to me: "What about that Dugowhatshisname? He laid your wife yet?" Hmmm . . . I never thought of that . . . So, that Friday, I said I had a toothache, and I left the office early.

Magis describes how he listened and watched through the keyhole. The first Friday they just talked, with Dugommier telling Hortense that her marriage was a terrible mistake, and that Magis is an idiot, a complete fool. However, two weeks later Magis eavesdrops again, and this time he hears Dugommier woo her with florid romantic talk and eventually make love to Hortense.

MAGIS—The first couple of times it was very interesting. Funny . . . I thought I'd be seething with rage, jealousy, but I wasn't. (*Shrugs.*) After a while, though, it began to get on my nerves. It was that happy, sanctified air of theirs that annoyed me . . . that blissful togetherness of theirs. As far as they were concerned, I didn't even exist. I didn't like being ignored like that, so I decided to remind them I was still around. . . . (*He moves back into the room.*) You know, M'sieu Victor, you really ought to get married. Being single . . . that's no way to live.

DUGOMMIER—Please, Emile, you mustn't worry about me.

MAGIS—Now take me for instance. I come home from work and there's somebody to make my dinner, keep me company. And then when I get ready for bed, I just pull back the covers and what do I find? A nice, wholesome, healthy, desirable girl like Hortense. Isn't that wonderful?

DUGOMMIER (*gritting his teeth*)—Yes . . . I'm sure . . . it must be . . .

MAGIS—Or maybe you don't like women. Some men like other men.

DUGOMMIER—Really, Emile!

MAGIS—Oh, don't worry. I'm only kidding. I know your little secret. . . . (DUGOMMIER *and* HORTENSE *exchange a frightened look.*)

HORTENSE (*her voice trembling*)—What secret, Emile?

MAGIS—Well, once you've been to bed with those native girls, an ordinary woman doesn't mean anything to you any more.

DUGOMMIER (*relieved*)—I'm afraid I don't know what you're talking about.

MAGIS (*to audience*)—Until one day, I began to feel a sort of ache . . . in my chest. Every Sunday the three of us, and hanging over us like a cloud was love. Oh, I don't mean that nonsense between him and my wife. That was nothing. No, I mean real love, the three of us. Dugommier telling his stories to Hortense, Hortense darning my socks, and me eating Dugommier's marrons glacés. A perfect circle. But on Fridays it was different. They kept all that love for themselves, and for me nothing. They stole something that belonged to me, too. I was the one who married Hortense. Not him, me. To have and to hold. Dugommier came along, all right, I was willing to hold him too. But they wouldn't let me. They pushed me away, they shut me out. (*Finding himself pushed to a decision.*) All right. They weren't going to get rid of me that easily . . . (*During* MAGIS'S *speech,* DUGOMMIER *and* HORTENSE *have assumed their amorous position on* MAGIS'S *couch.* MAGIS *watches through the keyhole a moment and then enters.*) Great! Terrific!

HORTENSE (*terrified*)—Oh! (MAGIS *goes to* DUGOMMIER'S *jacket and takes out* DUGOMMIER'S *wallet.*)

DUGOMMIER—What are you doing?

MAGIS (*moving back toward the door with the wallet*)—I'm taking your wallet.

DUGOMMIER—What . . . What for?

MAGIS (*casually*)—Why, naturally, for the . . . entertainment, M'sieu Victor. (DUGOMMIER *and* HORTENSE *exchange a stupefied look, as* MAGIS *removes the money and puts it in his pocket.*) I'll keep the whole thing, all right?

DUGOMMIER (*agonized*)—But that's a week's pay.

MAGIS—Yes, I know. That's why Hortense told me to wait until today.

HORTENSE—It's not true! Don't listen to him, Victor.

MAGIS—M'sieu Victor, I'm surprised at you. You're the first one to make such a fuss about it.

DUGOMMIER (*shocked*)—The first one? (*Pushes* HORTENSE *away and starts to get up.*)

MAGIS (*at the door*)—Oh, don't bother to get up. I'm just leaving anyway. Go right ahead. (MAGIS *goes out.*)

A little later there is a scene between Magis and Hortense. She is upset that he disgraced her and took Dugommier's money. She explains her behavior by saying that she had thought there was nothing between her and Magis any more. They make up, and she pleads with him to give Dugommier back the money. Magis refuses, and she asks what Victor will think of her. He replies: "What difference does it make. You're not going to see him again." She swears that she won't.

MAGIS (*to the audience*)—Then after a few weeks, I realized the whole thing had started all over again. How did it happen? I don't know. But I was out in the cold again. I had to think of something else, so they wouldn't forget me.

Magis goes to visit Dugommier and tells him in a businesslike way that it is unfair of him to derive pleasure from a woman whose upkeep is being paid by someone else. He suggests a "service charge" of 15,000 francs a month, which he points out is less than a professional would cost him. Angry and terrified, Dugommier painfully gives him the money.

MAGIS (*to the audience*)—Now I was alive again. Now they remembered me. At 15,000 francs a month, I was hard to forget. I didn't care about the money. But for Dugommier it was a different story. It hurt. With his poor old mother . . . and the little things he had to do without. Each time he washed his own shirts, walked to work, cut down on his smoking, he thought of me. I was going to a lot of trouble to keep my presence felt. But as long as the three of us were together, I didn't mind. But there was one thing I couldn't forgive them for. They didn't understand . . . they thought I was crazy. I could tell by the way they looked at me . . . the way they always agreed with everything I said. Walling me up in a padded cell of politeness. The fear rolled out of them like a fog . . . a fog between them and me. One day I was looking for a handkerchief in Hortense's drawer when I came across . . . a gun! (*Reading off the pistol.*) "Picard Gunsmiths . . . Saigon, Indo-China." Dugommier's gun! Dugommier had given it to her, just in case. "You can't take any chances with a lunatic," he probably said. A gun . . . pointing at me . . . (*Almost in tears.*) like an animal. That changed everything, that gun. Until then I was just a joke, a deceived husband, like a thousand other people. But now it was different. Because now, if I didn't beat the system, the system would beat me. (*Craftily.*) And then I realized what I had to do.

Hortense comes in and Magis accuses her of seeing Dugommier again, which she denies. He insists that she write a letter to Dugommier, which he dictates. It is to the effect that Hortense has informed him that she wants nothing more to do with him, and asks him not to continue his unwelcome attentions and bring further misery into what was, before his arrival, a happy and united home. She further asks Dugommier to write her by return mail a letter which she can show her husband, giving her his word that he will never again try to see her. Magis keeps a copy of the letter, and also of Dugommier's obedient but hypocritical reply which Hortense gives him three days later. Then, a couple of weeks later, Magis tells Hortense he is going to take the next day, Friday, off, and take the 1:30 train to Lyons and visit his mother. About noon he sneaks the gun out of the drawer, puts it in his pocket, says goodbye to Hortense and pretends to leave. However, once outside he stays in the neighborhood and makes sure he is noticed by several people. When he spies Dugommier arriving, he waits a few minutes and then returns to his apartment. He puts on a pair of gloves, takes out the gun, throws open the door, fires the gun at Hortense, who falls, throws the gun at Dugommier's feet, and runs to the door removing his gloves, and shouting: "Help! Murder! He's killed my wife and now he's going to kill me."

Scene II

The courtroom. Dugommier is in the dock, and Magis is watching the proceedings with interest from a stool at one side.

Prosecutor (*rising to begin his summation to the jury*)—The facts in this case are simple. Spurned by his mistress, the defendant pursued her with protestations and threats. The deceased herself has told us that in a letter she left. Crazed by his evil passion for another man's wife, Dugommier went to her home to persuade her to take him back as her lover. But she resisted his entreaties. Suddenly the husband returns. Dugommier pulls out his revolver. He fires!

DUGOMMIER (*wearily*)—But it's not true. It was Magis who killed her.

PROSECUTOR—Why should he kill his wife for resisting your advances?

DUGOMMIER—But she didn't resist my advances.

PROSECUTOR—How courageous you are! Having murdered this poor woman, you now proceed to besmirch her memory.

DUGOMMIER—We loved each other.

PROSECUTOR (*to jury*)—The letters from the deceased and from Dugommier himself show conclusively that this "love affair" was quite finished.

DUGOMMIER—We didn't mean what we wrote in those letters. We were only pretending.

PROSECUTOR—Only pretending? Then why was it necessary for you to storm over to the deceased's apartment with a loaded revolver to convince her that you were, as you say, "only pretending"?

DUGOMMIER—She told me to come.

PROSECUTOR—A married woman? She invited you to her husband's home?

DUGOMMIER—We thought Magis wasn't suspicious any more. And he was at his office all day.

PROSECUTOR—Are you trying to convince this court that the deceased invited you to her home on the one day when her husband was *not* at his office? When he could come home any moment?

DUGOMMIER—She didn't know he wasn't working that day . . .

PROSECUTOR—Why, the whole neighborhood knew it. We have the testimony of the cleaning woman, the corner grocer, the owner of the café across the street, and you want us to believe that the man's own wife was the only one who didn't know it.

DUGOMMIER (*exasperated*)—But it was Magis who killed her.

PROSECUTOR—With your gun! Purchased in Indo-China.

DUGOMMIER—It was my gun. I gave it to Hortense. She was afraid of Magis.

PROSECUTOR (*reasonably*)—Why was she afraid of him? She had broken off her affair with you. Magis had forgiven her. (*To jury.*) You have heard the testimony of his superiors in the Ministry. He is a shy, easy-going young man.

DUGOMMIER—You don't know what he is really like. Magis is a lunatic . . . He's capable of anything.

PROSECUTOR—"Capable of anything"? His wife betrays him and he forgave her. The seducer returned a second time and he went to see him to beg Dugommier to leave his wife alone.

DUGOMMIER—He wanted me to give him money.

PROSECUTOR (*to jury*)—If Magis really did accept money from

Dugommier for his wife's favors, if he accepted dishonor, if he tolerated your affair with his wife, then why did he kill her? Why did he cut off his source of revenue?

The Prosecutor further confounds Dugommier by asking him why the gun bears Dugommier's fingerprints, and Dugommier points out that when he gave the case with the gun in it to Hortense it had his fingerprints on it, and that Magis had worn gloves so as not to leave the real murderer's fingerprints on it. The Prosecutor reminds the court that no one had ever seen Magis wear gloves, either on the day of the murder or before. Doggedly, Dugommier insists that Magis had put them on especially "to kill us."

PROSECUTOR—But you forget, according to your own testimony, that Magis thought your affair with his wife had already ended. So how could he have known in advance that he would find you in his apartment, and particularly on the one day when he was not at his office, the one day you would have been expected to stay away in any case? Or are we to assume that his wife was an accomplice to this "plot of Magis' "? That she conspired with him to lure you there and to be killed? You just said "to kill *us*," but you overlook one small point. You are still alive!

The jury retires, then returns quickly to give their verdict to the judge. It is "Guilty," and Dugommier is sentenced to forty-five years at hard labor. He is led off, and the court disperses leaving Magis standing alone.

MAGIS (*smiling innocently at the audience*)—And that's it. That's the system. (*He shuffles off as the curtain falls.*)

OH DAD, POOR DAD, MAMMA'S HUNG YOU IN THE CLOSET AND I'M FEELIN' SO SAD

A Pseudoclassical Tragifarce in a Bastard French Tradition in Three Scenes

BY ARTHUR L. KOPIT

[ARTHUR L. KOPIT *(pronounced "cope-it") was born on May 10, 1937, in New York City. He attended Lawrence (L. I.) High School and Harvard University where, as an undergraduate, he began to write plays. Nine of these were produced by various groups and included among others "The Questioning of Nick," "On the Runway of Life You Never Know What's Coming Off Next," "Across the River and into the Jungle," "Aubade," "Sing to Me Through Open Windows," and "To Dwell in a Place of Strangers." "Oh Dad, Poor Dad" was first produced by an undergraduate group at Cambridge, Mass., in January, 1960. During the summer of 1961 it achieved only a short run in its professional premiere in England. However, when recast and redirected at the Phoenix Theatre, it became the hit of the Off-Broadway season. Mr. Kopit is preparing two related short comedies about the inmates of a mental institution, which will be produced in the Fall of 1962 under the somewhat more economical title of "Asylum."*]

THE scene is the living room of a de luxe hotel suite in the Caribbean. The door opens and Bellboys 1 and 2 enter carrying a coffin. They are followed by Madame Rosepettle, who is wearing an elegant black dress and black veil, and by Jonathan, a seventeen-year-old boy dressed like a child of ten. Madame Rosepettle cruelly berates the Bellboys for their stupidity in not knowing where to put the coffin. Bellboy 3 comes in carrying black drapes and is in turn insulted for his lack of clairvoyance.

BELLBOY 3—Madame, I will have you know I am not a *common* bellboy. Notice, if you will, the stripes on my sleeve. I am a lieutenant in charge of other bellboys and thereby entitled to a little more respect from you.

MADAME ROSEPETTLE—Well, *you* may consider yourself a lieutenant, lieutenant, but if you're going to insist upon pulling rank, I'll have you know I'm a tourist. Notice, if you will, the money. And being a tourist I am in charge of you. You may begin by picking up the drapes, carrying them to the master bedroom and tacking them over the windowpanes. I am in mourning. And since the problems confronting civilization are ultimately moral ones, while I'm here in Port Royal no single speck of sunlight shall enter and brighten the mournful gloom of my heart. (*Short pause.*) At least, not while I'm in my bedroom. (BELLBOY 3 *takes drapes into the bedroom as other* BELLBOYS *enter carrying* JONATHAN'S *stamp collection, his coin collection, and a trunk containing his rare books.*)

JONATHAN (*stammering*)—Ca . . . ca . . . could they . . . open it?

MADAME ROSEPETTLE—You really want to see them again? That badly?

JONATHAN—Yyyyessssss.

MADAME ROSEPETTLE (*dramatically*)—Then let the trunk be opened! (*They open the trunk and* JONATHAN *falls on top of the books that have spilled out, like a starved man upon food.*)

JONATHAN (*caressing each book emotionally*)—Tra-Tra . . . Trollope . . . Ha-Haggard . . . Dau-Dau-Daudet . . . Gautier . . . Tur-Tur-Tur-genev . . . Ma-ma-my old fra-fra . . . friends.

The Bellboys bring in Madame's carnivorous tropical plants, placing them apart on the porch so they won't fight with each other. Bellboy 5 enters wearing thickly padded hockey gloves and carrying a huge fishbowl covered with a black cloth. He removes the cloth.

MADAME ROSEPETTLE (*looking at the fish inside the bowl*)—Ah, I see you fed it today. (*She takes a pair of tongs from her purse and plucks a cat's skeleton from the bowl.*) Siamese, I presume.

BELLBOY 4—No, madame. Alley.

MADAME ROSEPETTLE—WHAT! *A common alley cat?* Just who do you think I am? What kind of a fish do you think I have? (*To* JONATHAN.) Make note: we will dismiss this creature from the bellboy squad *first thing in the morning!*

BELLBOY 4—Madame, *please.* I have a wife.

MADAME ROSEPETTLE—And I have a fish. There are half a million men in Port Royal with wives. But show me another woman in Cuba with a silver piranha fish. You are common. While my piranha fish is *rare*. Now green piranhas can eat alley cats if they like, and red piranhas, I've been told, will often eat alley cats, tomcats, and even dogs; but my silver piranha has been weaned on Siamese, and Siamese it will be, sir. You have all behaved rudely. If the sunset over Guanabacoa Bay were not so full of magenta and wisteria blue I'd leave this place tonight. (BELLBOYS *start to leave.*) Wait. (*They stop.*) A question before you go. The yacht in the harbor. The pink one with lilacs draped about the railing. Who owns it?

BELLBOY 1—Commodore Roseabove, madame. It's a pretty sloop.

MADAME ROSEPETTLE—*Roseabove*. I like that name.

BELLBOY 1—He's a strange man, madame. A man who knows no master but the sea. (BELLBOYS *leave.*)

MADAME ROSEPETTLE (*dreamily, with a slight smile*)—*Roseabove.* I like that name.

ROSALINDA THE FISH (*gleefully*)—Gleep.

MADAME ROSEPETTLE—Ah, listen. My lovely little fish. She, too, is feeling better already.

SCENE II

It is two weeks later. Jonathan is in the same room talking to Rosalie, a nineteen-year-old girl dressed in girlish pink taffeta.

ROSALIE—But if you've been here two weeks, why haven't I seen you?

JONATHAN—I've . . . I've been in my room.

ROSALIE—Well, you must get out sometimes. I mean sometimes you simply must get out. You just couldn't stay inside all the time . . . could you?

JONATHAN—Yyyyyes.

ROSALIE—You never get out at all?

JONATHAN—Sometimes I do go out on the porch. M-Ma-Mother has some . . . Venus'-flytraps which she bra-brought back from the rain forests of Va-Va-Va-Venezuela. She ka-keeps them on the porch and I . . . I feed them.

ROSALIE—Oh. I don't think I've ever met anyone before who's fed . . . uh . . . Venus'-flytraps.

JONATHAN—Ma-Ma-Mother says everyone must have a vocation in life. (*Laughs nervously.*) I ga-guess that's . . . my job. I fa-feed them . . . ga-ga-green peas, chicken feathers, rubber bands.

They're . . . not very fussy. They're . . . nice, that way. (*There is an awkward silence while he stares at her.*) Sometimes, when I'm on the porch . . . I do other things. Other things besides feeding my mother's plants. Other things *besides* that. That's what I mean.

ROSALIE—What kind of things . . . *in particular?*

JONATHAN—Oh, like . . . watching.

ROSALIE—Watching? (*He giggles.*) *Watching what?*

JONATHAN—You. I . . . watch you from the porch. You want me to tell you how I watch you?

ROSALIE—How?

JONATHAN—*Guess.*

ROSALIE (*ponders*)—Through a telescope?

JONATHAN—How did you guess? I thought you were . . . ga-going to say I . . . I watch you with . . . with love in my eyes or some . . . thing like that. (*Excitedly.*) I made it out of lenses and tubing. The lenses I had because Ma-Ma-Mother gave me a set of lenses so I could see my stamps better. She suspected that some of the stamps were fake so she gave me the lenses so I might be . . . able to see. Well sir, I happen to have nearly a billion sta-stamps. So far I've looked closely at 1,352,769. I've discovered three actual fakes! Mother made me feed them immediately to her flytraps. The tubing came from an old blowgun Mother brought back from her last hunting trip to Zanzibar. So I built it. (*Takes it out and shows it to* ROSALIE.) My telescope. (*He hands it to her and she scans the horizon.*)

ROSALIE (*annoyed*)—There's nothing out there to see.

JONATHAN (*sadly*)—I know. That's the trouble. You take the time to build a telescope that can sa-see for miles, then there's nothing out there to see. Ma-Mother says it's a lesson in Life. (*Pause.*) But I'm not sorry I built my telescope. Because even if I didn't see anything else, I did see you. And . . . and I'm . . . very glad.

Jonathan inquires if the ten little children he saw her playing with were hers, and Rosalie explains that she is a baby sitter and that after she puts the children to bed she gets very lonesome.

ROSALIE—Perhaps . . . well, Jonathan, I thought that perhaps you might . . . visit me.

JONATHAN—Well . . . well . . . well, you . . . you see . . . I . . . I . . .

ROSALIE—Why are you trembling so? Are you afraid?

JONATHAN—Nnnnnnnnnnnnnnnnnnno. Whaaaaaaaaa-why . . . should I . . . be . . . afraid?

ROSALIE—I don't think you're allowed to go out. That's what I think. Why can't you go out, Jonathan? I want to know.

JONATHAN—I . . . I don't . . . know. I mean, I've . . . nnnnnnnever really thought . . . about going out. I . . . guess it's . . . just natural for me to . . . stay inside. You see . . . I've got so many things to do. All my sssssstamps and . . . things . . . like my future, for instance. Ma-Mother says I'm going to be great. That's . . . that's what she . . . says. Of course, she doesn't know exactly what I'm going to be great *in* . . . so she sits every afternoon for . . . for two hours and thinks about it. Na-na-naturally I've . . . got to be here when she's thinking in case she . . . thinks of an answer. Otherwise she might forget and I'd never know . . . what I'm ga-going to be great in. You . . . see what I mean . . . I've ggggggot so many things to do I . . . just couldn't possibly get *anything* done if I ever . . . went . . . outside. (*Pause.*) Besides, Mother locks the front door.

ROSALIE—I thought so.

JONATHAN—No! You-you don't understand. She doesn't lock the door to ka-ka-keep me in, which would be malicious. She . . . locks the door so I can't get out, which is for my own good and therefore . . . beneficent.

The Cuckoo Clock from the master bedroom starts to sound and Jonathan becomes agitated and tells Rosalie she must go now. Rosalie refuses and starts to question Jonathan as to why his mother asked her to come up here. The clock sounds again and Jonathan pushes her towards the door as she begs him to promise to come and see her. Rosalie breaks loose and starts for the bedroom door to investigate. Hysterically Jonathan tackles her, collapsing in tears at her feet.

JONATHAN (*sobbing uncontrollably*)—I love you. (*The Cuckoo Clock cackles and goes berserk. The bedroom door opens and* MADAME ROSEPETTLE *appears.*)

MADAME ROSEPETTLE—Harlot! I've seen you. Blind man's buff with the children in the garden. The redheaded boy—fifteen, I think. Behind the bushes while the others cover their eyes. Up with the skirt, one-two-three and it's done.

ROSALIE—That's a lie.

MADAME ROSEPETTLE—Life is a lie, my sweet. Not words but Life itself. It builds green trees that tease your eyes and draw you under them. Then when you're there in the shade and you say, "Oh, God, how beautiful," that's when the bird on the branch lets go his droppings and hits you on the head.

ROSALIE—Why don't you let Jonathan out of his room?

MADAME ROSEPETTLE—*I don't let him out because he is my son.* I don't let him out because his skin is as white as fresh snow and he would burn if the sun struck him. I don't let him out because outside there are trees with birds sitting on their branches waiting for him to walk beneath. I don't let him out because you're there, waiting behind the bushes with your skirt up.

ROSALIE—Then why did you come and get me?

MADAME ROSEPETTLE—Because, my dear, my stupid son has been watching you through that stupid telescope he made. Because, in short, he wanted to meet you and I, in short, wanted him to know what you were really like. Now that he's seen you, you may go.

ROSALIE—And if I choose to stay? (*Pause.*)

MADAME ROSEPETTLE (*slyly*)—Can you cook?

ROSALIE—Fairly well.

MADAME ROSEPETTLE—Not good enough! My son is a connoisseur. I cook him the finest. Recipes no one knows exist. So, go, my dear. You are garnished with garlic and turn our tender stomachs in disgust. (*She starts towards her room and* ROSALIE *moves towards the door, as* JONATHAN *grabs her hand in desperation.*)

JONATHAN (*whispering*)—Come back again. Pa-please . . . come back again. (ROSALIE *stops and looks at* JONATHAN. MADAME ROSEPETTLE *stops too, and looks back at both of them, and* ROSALIE, *sensing her glance, walks out the door. Curtain.*)

SCENE III

It is night, one week later. A table set for two is illuminated at one side of the stage, and we can hear a Viennese waltz playing romantically in the background. The music grows in brilliance and The Commodore and Madame Rosepettle waltz into the room.

THE COMMODORE—Oh, if only Madame knew how long I've waited for this moment. Tonight at last, we are alone, ready for romance. For the night was made for love. And tonight . . . we will love. (*They waltz liltingly around the room.*)

MADAME ROSEPETTLE—You're not paying enough attention to the music, Commodore.

THE COMMODORE—Then lead me, madame.

MADAME ROSEPETTLE (*very sweetly*)—Why certainly, Commodore, if that is what you want. (*They switch hands and she begins to lead him. He whirls madly about, spinning faster and faster.*) The waltz. The Dance of Lovers. I'm so glad you enjoy it so much. (*Suddenly he tries to kiss her. She pulls back.*) Commodore! You were supposed to spin just then. When I squeeze you in the side it means *spin!*

THE COMMODORE (*flustered*)—I thought it was a sign of affection. (*She laughs.*)

MADAME ROSEPETTLE—You'll learn. (*She squeezes him in the side again and he begins to spin faster and faster around* MADAME ROSEPETTLE, *who smiles serenely.*)

THE COMMODORE—Ho-ho. Stop. I'm dizzy. Too fast. Too dizzy. Weeeeeee! (*She grabs him and gives him a long predatory kiss. He breaks free, gasping for breath.*) Couldn't get any . . . air. You . . . surprised me. Wasn't . . . ready for that. Didn't expect you to kiss me.

MADAME ROSEPETTLE—I know. That's why I did it. (*She laughs.*) Perhaps you'd prefer to sit down for awhile, Commodore. Dancing can be tiring . . . when you're growing old. We could just sit and talk, and sip some pink champagne, eh? Champagne.

THE COMMODORE—Ah, champagne. (*She walks him towards the table.*)

MADAME ROSEPETTLE—And just the two of us. Alone. (*She takes his hand tenderly.*)

THE COMMODORE—Madame, you have won my heart. And easily.

MADAME ROSEPETTLE—No, Commodore. You have lost it. *Easily.* (*She smiles seductively and pours the champagne. They gaze wistfully into each other's eyes. The music builds to brilliance as they raise their glasses.*)

MADAME ROSEPETTLE and THE COMMODORE (*together*)—To us. (*The glasses break as they are clinked together.*)

THE COMMODORE (*furiously mopping up the mess*)—Pardon, madame! Pardon. J'étais emporté par l'enthousiasme du moment.

MADAME ROSEPETTLE—Pas de quoi. (*She snaps her fingers and a waiter appears with a new table already set with a tablecloth, two champagne glasses, two candelabra, which are already flickering, and substitutes it for the old one. She lifts a bottle from the ice bucket.*) Encore?

THE COMMODORE—S'il vous plait. (*She pours, as the music swells again. He clinks his glass to hers with extreme caution, as she speaks softly.*)

MADAME ROSEPETTLE—Tell me about yourself.

THE COMMODORE—My heart is speaking, madame. Doesn't it tell you enough?

MADAME ROSEPETTLE—Your heart, monsieur, is growing old. It speaks with a murmur. Its words are too weak to understand.

THE COMMODORE—But the feeling, madame, is still strong.

MADAME ROSEPETTLE—Feelings are for animals, monsieur.

Words are the specialty of Man. Tell me what your heart has to say.

THE COMMODORE—My heart says it loves you. You alone.

MADAME ROSEPETTLE—And pray, monsieur, just what is it that I've done to make you love me so?

THE COMMODORE—Nothing, madame. And that is why. You disregard me, madame, but never discourage. You treat my love with indifference . . . but never disdain. You've led me on, madame.

MADAME ROSEPETTLE—I've led you to my room, monsieur. That is all.

THE COMMODORE—To me, that is enough.

MADAME ROSEPETTLE—I know, that's why I did it.

THE COMMODORE (*with sudden soul-rendering passion*)—Madame, my heart is yours!

MADAME ROSEPETTLE—How much is it worth?

THE COMMODORE—A fortune, madame.

MADAME ROSEPETTLE—Good, I'll take it in cash.

THE COMMODORE—But the heart goes with it, madame.

MADAME ROSEPETTLE—And you with the heart, I suppose?

THE COMMODORE—Forever.

MADAME ROSEPETTLE—Sorry, monsieur. The money's enticing and the heart would have been nice, but you, I'm afraid, are a bit too bulky to make it all worth while.

THE COMMODORE—You make fun of my passion, madame.

MADAME ROSEPETTLE—But, monsieur, I've never taken your passion seriously enough to make fun of it.

THE COMMODORE (*leaning across the table and kissing her hand passionately and sobbing*)—Madame . . . I love you. Forever. Don't you understand? Oh, your husband . . . he must have been . . . a wonderful man . . . to deserve a woman such as you.

MADAME ROSEPETTLE (*nonchalantly*)—Would you like to see him?

THE COMMODORE—A snapshot?

MADAME ROSEPETTLE—No. My husband. He's inside in the closet. I had him stuffed. He's my very favorite trophy. I take him with me wherever I go.

THE COMMODORE (*shaken*)—Hah-hah. Yes. Very good. Very funny.

MADAME ROSEPETTLE—Life, my dear Commodore, is *never* funny. It's grim. It's there every morning breathing in your face the moment you open your red baggy eyes. Worst of all, it follows you wherever you go. Life, Mr. Roseabove, is a husband hanging from a hook in the closet.

THE COMMODORE (*weakly*)—How . . . how did he die?

MADAME ROSEPETTLE—Why, I killed him of course. Champagne? (*She smiles sweetly and fills his glass.* THE COMMODORE *tries to leave but discovers that his chair will not push back and that he is trapped by its arms.*) Now you don't *really* want to leave . . . do you, Commodore? (*He tries once more to push back his chair, but it won't move.*) Good. It would have been a shame if you'd have had to leave. For you see, Commodore, we are in a way united. We share something in common. . . . We share desire. For you desire me, with love in your heart. While I, my dear Commodore . . . desire your heart. (*She smiles sweetly.*) Tell me, Commodore, how would you like to hear a little story? A bedtime story? A fairy tale?

THE COMMODORE—No. I . . . I don't think so.

MADAME ROSEPETTLE—Good. Then I'll tell it. His name was Albert Edward Robinson Rosepettle III. All the others who had come to see me had been tall, but he was short. They had been rich, while he was poor. The others had been handsome, but Albert was as ugly as a humid day . . . (*She laughs sadly, distantly.*) and just about as wet, too. Oh, he was a fat bundle of sweat, Mr. Roseabove. And I must have been very susceptible indeed to have married him. I *was* twenty-eight and that *is* a susceptible year in a woman's life. And I *was* a virgin. Oh, I had spoken to men. I had observed their ways and habits. One night when I was walking home I saw a man standing in a window. I saw him take his contact lenses out of his eyes, and his hearing aid out of his ear. I saw him take his teeth out of his thin-lipped mouth. I saw him lift his snow-white hair off of his wrinkled head. And then I saw him take his clothes off. And when he was done I went home and wept. I stayed inside my room. I watched a world of lechery and lies and greed walk by my window, and I decided not to leave my room until this world came to me, *exactly* as I wanted it.

One day Albert came toddling up the stairs. He scratched on the door and said in a frail and very frightened voice, "Will you please marry me?" And so I did. Perhaps it's because one look at Albert's round, sad face and I knew he could be all mine, all mine—mine to love, mine to live with, mine to kill; *my very own.*

And so we were wed. That night I went to bed with a man for the first time in my life. The next morning I picked up my mattress and moved myself into another room. Oh, how easily is Man satisfied. How easily is his porous body saturated with "fun." All he asks is a little sex and a little food and there he is, asleep with a smile and snoring. Never the slightest regard for you, lying in bed next to him, your eyes open wide. Lean over to kiss him good night and he'll belch in your face.

His mind contained too many secrets. I wanted to find out certain things about him. What did he dream of while he slept? What did he think about when he stared out the window? At night I would listen at my door until I heard his door close. Then I'd tiptoe out and watch him through his keyhole. When his lights went out I'd creep across the floor to his bed. My ear was a stethoscope that recorded the fluctuations of his dream life. I listened but he only snored and smiled and slept on and on.

A month later I found that I was pregnant. It had happened that first horrible night. How like Albert to do something like that. But I never let on. Oh, no. Let him think I was simply getting fat, I said. And that's the way I did it, too. I, nonchalantly putting on weight; Albert nonchalantly watching my belly grow. If he knew what was happening to me he never let me know it. It was only at night that he changed. I found that the smile on his face . . . while he slept . . . had become a grin.

Twelve months later my son was born. He was so overdue that when he came out he was already teething. I took him home and put him in a cage in the darkest corner of my room—

THE COMMODORE—Was it a large cage?

MADAME ROSEPETTLE—Did I say cage? I meant crib. I set the crib where my husband would not see him. For until I found out exactly why he'd married me, I would not tell him that his son had been born.

Shortly after that, Rosalinda came. She was one of Albert's many secretaries. She was the only person I ever met who was equally as ugly as Albert. It seems her mother had once owned a laundromat, and at the tender age of five, Rosalinda, being a curious child, had taken an exploratory trip through the mangler.

Well, naturally I never let on. I said good night as politely as I could and left them alone—the monster and my husband, two soulmates expressing their souls through sin. And when they lay in bed I listened at the keyhole. Albert had begun to speak. He told her things he never told to me. Words of passion and love! I ask you, how much is a woman supposed to take?

But the signs of regret were beginning to show. And oh, how I laughed when I saw how tired he had begun to look, how little he ate, how slowly he seemed to move. Then one night he died. At one o'clock in the morning his heart stopped beating. (*She laughs softly.*) But it wasn't until dawn that she discovered he was dead. He was lying with her in bed for nearly six hours, *dead,* and she never knew it. What a lover he must have been! (*She laughs uproariously.*)

Don't you see? Their affair never even existed. He tried to make me jealous but there was nothing to be jealous of. He was impotent. He was *mine*. Mine all the time, even when he was in bed with another, even in death . . . *he was mine!* (THE COMMODORE *climbs out of his chair and walks weakly toward the door. In panic he twists the doorknob, which comes off. He falls to the floor.*) Why, Commodore, you're on your knees! How romantic. Don't tell me you're going to ask me to marry you again?

THE COMMODORE (*weakly*)—I . . . I-I . . . feel . . . sa-sorry for your . . . ssssson . . .

MADAME ROSEPETTLE—And I feel sorrier for you. For you are *nothing!* While my son is mine. His mind is pure. For I have saved him from the world beyond the door. The world of you. The world of his father. A world waiting to devour those who trust it; those who love. A world vicious under the hypocrisy of kindness, ruthless under the falseness of a smile. Well, go, Mr. Roseabove. Leave my room and enter your world again—your sex-driven dirt-washed waste of cannibals eating each other up while they pretend they're in the act of love. (*She turns with a flourish and enters her bedroom.*)

The Commodore staggers out. After an interval during which we hear church bells, the bedroom door reopens and Madame Rosepettle emerges wearing an immense straw hat, sunglasses and tight toreador pants. She carries a huge flashlight and she tiptoes out. Jonathan, who has overheard everything, emerges from behind the Venus-flytraps. He runs to the fire-extinguisher emergency axe, removes it from the wall, and proceeds to hack down the writhing flytraps. He is about to break the fishbowl when Rosalie enters dressed as the picture of innocence in childish pink party clothes.

ROSALIE—Jonathan! Jonathan! What *have* you done?

JONATHAN—I killed it.

ROSALIE—Ssh. Where did you put your mother's body?

JONATHAN—I haven't killed my mother. I've killed her plants.

ROSALIE (*with apologetic laugh*)—I thought you'd . . . killed your mother. (*The* PIRANHA FISH *giggles.*) JONATHAN *moves towards it with his axe raised.*) Jonathan, stop. (JONATHAN *smashes the fish bowl and strikes the flapping fish, killing it.* ROSALIE *walks over and touches* JONATHAN *consolingly.*) There's something bothering you, isn't there?

JONATHAN (*weakly*)—I never thought I'd see you again. She told me she'd never let you visit me again.

ROSALIE—But I had a key made.

JONATHAN—She doesn't let me do anything. She doesn't let me use her phone. She doesn't . . .

ROSALIE—Do you know why I had this key made? Do you know why I'm wearing this new dress?

JONATHAN—She doesn't let me stand in the window at noon because the sun is too strong. She . . .

ROSALIE—Try and guess why I'm all dressed up.

JONATHAN—She tells me I'm brilliant. She makes me read and reread books no one's ever read. She . . .

ROSALIE—Stop talking about that and pay attention to me!

JONATHAN—But I heard everything tonight.

ROSALIE—Jonathan, isn't my dress pretty?

JONATHAN—But she must have known I was here. I mean . . . where could I have gone? But . . . if that's the case . . . *why did she let me hear?*

ROSALIE—Jonathan, I do wish you'd pay more attention to me. Here, guess how many crinolines I have on.

JONATHAN—Maybe . . . it didn't make any difference to her . . . whether I heard or not. (*He suddenly turns and hugs her closely. She lets him hold her, and then steps back away from him as a determined look appears in her eyes.*)

ROSALIE (*in a deeper voice*)—Come with me.

JONATHAN (*fearfully*)—Where?

ROSALIE—Give me your hand and come with me. Just through the door. Then we can run far away, somewhere where she'll never find us.

JONATHAN—Well . . . can't we stay here?

ROSALIE—No. I want you *alone.* I want you, Jonathan. *I want you for my husband.*

JONATHAN—I . . . I . . . can't. I . . . I want to . . . go with you very much but I . . . I don't think . . . I can. I'm . . . sorry. (*He sobs quietly.*)

ROSALIE (*thinking and making a decision*)—What time will your mother be back?

JONATHAN—Na-not for a while. Every night at midnight she walks down to the beach searching for people making love. When she finds them she kicks sand in their faces, and walks on. Sometimes it takes her as much as three hours to chase everyone away. (ROSALIE *smiles and walks over to the bedroom door and opens it despite* JONATHAN'S *frenzied consternation. The alarm bell rings. She goes in.*) What have you done? GET OUT OF THERE!

ROSALIE—Come in and get me.

JONATHAN—Rosalie . . . ? I'll show you my stamp collection if you'll promise to come out.

ROSALIE—Bring it in here.

JONATHAN—If I come in, will you come out?

ROSALIE—If you don't come in I'll never come out.

JONATHAN—And if I do?

ROSALIE—Then I may.

JONATHAN—What if I bring my stamps in?

ROSALIE—Bring them and find out.

JONATHAN (*getting them*)—I'm bringing the coins, too.

ROSALIE—How good you are, Jonathan.

JONATHAN (*entering fearfully*)—Let me show you my stamps.

ROSALIE—Later, Jonathan. Let me show you something first. Why are you trembling so?

JONATHAN—Look, we've got to get out! Something terrible will happen if we don't.

ROSALIE—Then leave with me. I love you, Jonathan, and I won't give you up. I want you . . . all for myself.

JONATHAN (*softly, weakly*)—What do you want me to do?

ROSALIE—Forget about your mother. Look at me, Jonathan; my mouth, my hands, my skirt, my legs. (*She smiles and starts to unbutton her dress.*)

JONATHAN—What are you doing? No!

ROSALIE—Your mother is strong, but I am stronger. (*She lets her skirt fall about her feet.*) You're ashamed but you want me anyhow. (*She takes off a crinoline.*)

JONATHAN—PUT IT ON! *Please,* put it back on!

ROSALIE—Come, Jonathan. (*She takes off another crinoline.*) Lie down. Let me loosen your shirt.

JONATHAN—No . . . NO . . . NO! STOP! *Please,* stop! (*She takes off her last crinoline and sits on the bed to take off her socks.*) Get off my mother's bed.

ROSALIE (*lying down*)—The bed is soft. Lie here by my side. (*Meekly he sits on the edge of the bed. Suddenly the closet door swings open and the stuffed corpse of Albert Edward Robinson Rosepettle III tumbles onto the bed beside them.*) Who the hell is this!?

JONATHAN (*terrified*)—It-it-it-it . . . it . . . it's . . .

ROSALIE (*pushing corpse back into closet*)—Forget it, Jonathan. Everything's fine again.

JONATHAN—It's . . . it's my . . . my . . .

ROSALIE (*kneeling next to* JONATHAN *and starting to unbutton his shirt*)—It's all right, Jonathan. Sshh. Let me take off your clothes.

JONATHAN—It's . . . it's my . . . ffffather. (*The corpse falls out of the closet again, knocking* ROSALIE *off the bed and onto the floor.*)

ROSALIE (*without missing a beat and using the corpse's arm with which to gesture*)—LISTEN TO ME, JONATHAN! STOP LOOKING AT HIM AND LOOK AT ME! I love you, Jonathan, and I want you *now.* Not later and not as a partner with your mother but now and by myself. I want you to lie with me, to sleep with me, to be with me, to kiss me and touch me, to live with me, *forever.* Stop looking at him! He's dead! Listen to me. I'm alive. Now help me take my slip off.

JONATHAN—Ma-Mother was right! You *do* let men do anything they want to you.

ROSALIE—Of course she was right! Did you really think I was that sweet and pure? (*She laughs.*) Behind the bushes and it's done. Here's the money. Come again! (*Pauses.*) So what! It's only you I love. They make no difference.

JONATHAN—You're dirty!

ROSALIE—No. I'm pure. I want no one but you. I'm full of love and womanly feelings. I want children. I want a husband. Is that dirty? Take off your clothes.

JONATHAN—NO!

ROSALIE—Forget about your father. Drop your pants on top of him, then you won't see his face. Forget about your mother. She's gone. Come on and let me love you. Come and let me keep you mine. Mine to love when I want, mine to kiss when I want, mine to have when I want. Come. Let me show you how beautiful it is . . . love.

Rosalie lies back on the bed and slowly starts to raise her slip. Jonathan stares at her legs in horror. Suddenly he seizes her skirt and throws it over her face. He smothers her to death. Then he dumps his stamps and coins over her limp body. He starts to run, but his father's lifeless arms somehow come to life for an instant and tackle him to the floor. The lights go out as the scene changes back to the living room. Jonathan is out on the porch as Madame Rosepettle enters. She notices the chaotic state of the room and shrieks slightly.

MADAME ROSEPETTLE—What has happened? My plants! Rosalinda! Great gods, my fish has lost her water! (JONATHAN *enters from porch.*) What are you doing out there when Rosalinda is lying there dead? (*He doesn't answer, as* MADAME ROSEPETTLE *attempts to give the fish artificial respiration. Seeing it is futile she goes off into her bedroom, returning almost immediately.*) I went to lie down and I stepped on your father. I lay down and I lay on some girl. Jonathan, there is a woman on my bed and I do believe she's stopped breathing. What is more, you've buried her under your fabulous collection of stamps and coins. I ask you, Jonathan. As a mother to a son I ask you. *What is the meaning of this?* (*Blackout and curtain.*)

A THOUSAND CLOWNS

A Play in Three Acts

By Herb Gardner

[Herb Gardner *was born in Brooklyn on December 28, 1934. While attending New York City's High School of the Performing Arts, he wrote his first play, a one-acter called "The Elevator," which in twelve years has now earned him some $32 in royalties. He attended Carnegie Tech, where he studied sculpture and playwriting, and Antioch. He abandoned sculpture for commercial art, doing such odd jobs as selling orange drinks in Broadway theatres and drawing the "in-between" parts of a TV commercial. His first success came when he created a group of cartoon characters called "The Nebbishes" which finally earned him enough money to enable him to quit cartooning and devote his full time to the writing of "A Thousand Clowns." This play took him two-and-a-half years to write and went through many versions.* (*One of them was a tragedy in which we see Murray completely defeated by society.*) *Some of the play started in a short story he wrote in 1956 called "The Man Who Thought He Was Winston Churchill." And much of Murray—for instance, the shouting out of the window—is a projection of things the author has actually done. Mr. Gardner continued revising the play even after its successful opening night, and it is his private belief that Murray will somehow stick to his TV job, but not necessarily to Sandra.*]

IN a messy old apartment on New York's lower West Side live a man and a twelve-year-old boy. The boy, Nick, is listening to a nauseating and noisy TV program for kidderoonies called Chuckles, the Chipmunk. The man, Murray Burns, enters from the kitchen half-dressed and carrying a cup of coffee. He tells Nick to shut off the program, which it turns out he used to write. He pulls up the window blind to reveal the wall of another building a few feet away. He opens the window and cranes his head out to look up at the sky.

MURRAY—Can't see a thing. (*Pulls his head back in.*) No matter what time of day or what season, we got a permanent fixture out there; twilight in February.

NICK (*pouring* MURRAY *a second cup of coffee*)—You better call the weather record like always.

MURRAY (*dialing phone*)—Using a machine to call up another machine! (*Into phone.*) Hello, Weather-Lady! Well, I'm just fine, and how is your nasal little self this morning? What's the weather? That high? And the wind, which way does the wind blow this morning? Ah, all the way to East Point and Block Island. Humidity? Very decent. Whoops, there you go again. You simply *must* learn not to repeat yourself. (*Hangs up and goes to window, leans out and shouts.*) Neighbors, I have an announcement for you. I have *never seen* such a collection of dirty windows. Now I want to see you all out there on the fire escape with your "Mr. Clean" bottles, and let's snap it up. . . . (*Pulling his head back in.*) Hey, why aren't you in school today?

NICK—It's a holiday. It's Irving R. Feldman's Birthday, like you said.

MURRAY—Irving R. Feldman's Birthday is my own personal national holiday. I did not open it up for the public.

It turns out that Irving R. Feldman is the proprietor of the most distinguished kosher delicatessen in the neighborhood, and that Nick's real reason for staying home is that the Child Welfare Bureau is sending someone to investigate Nick's living quarters and his guardian. It appears that Nick has submitted pictures of a night club that Murray took him to, as part of a class project, and he has also been quoting Murray's unorthodox opinions in his talk and creative writing assignments. Nick urges Murray to shave and look through the Help Wanted ads so that they can at least tell the investigators about his prospects. Nick picks up a *Times* but notices that it's three days old. He starts to put it down to get a newer one.

MURRAY—We do *not need* a newer paper. All the really important jobs stay forever. Now read.

NICK—O.K. (*Reading aloud.*) "Administ. Ex. Oppty. To 90 dollars." What's that?

MURRAY—Administrative Assistant, excellent opportunity. Nothing.

NICK—But, 90 dollars . . .

MURRAY—You go be an Administ Exoppty. Do I look like a 90-dollar brain? Read further.

NICK—"Versatile Junior, traffic manager, industrial representative organization. 100 to 125 dollars. Call Mr. Shiffman."

MURRAY (*picking up telephone and talking into it*)—Hello, Mr. Shiffman? I am a stupid, brainless, half-assed, versatile Junior and I would like to manage your traffic for you. You see, sir, it has long been my ambition to work in a pointless job, with no future and a cretin like you as my boss . . .

NICK—You want to be your own boss, but the trouble with that is you don't pay yourself anything. (*Taking off his glasses.*) Look, Murray, I am upset. For me as an actual child, the way you live in this house and we live is a dangerous thing for my later life when I become an actual person. An unemployed person like you are for so many months is bad for you as the person involved and is definitely bad for me who he lives with in the same house where the rent isn't paid for months sometimes. And I wish you would get a job, Murray. Please.

MURRAY (*unable to hide his laughter, but stopping when he sees he has offended* NICK)—Kid, I know. I'm sorry. You're right.

Murray admits that he has been starting out looking for a TV writing job, but going to the movies instead. He describes getting in off the daytime street to the dark "Safetyville, U.S.A."

MURRAY—Once you sit down, there is no doubt how much better this is than being outside. And you snuggle down and unwrap your nut-fudge caramel sticky surprise, take a bite, and lift thine eyes unto the Lord Grade-B-whatsis or adult-western-psycho-whosis or spicy-dubbed-Italian-nipple picture and you are sailing. The Aficianadoes have their moment of truth, while we quiet patrons, devotees of the art of the afternoon film, have our moment of untruth, the big dark lie.

Nick sees that Murray is becoming more and more depressed and attempts to cheer him up by agreeing to go to the Statue of Liberty with him. But just as they are about to leave, the doorbell rings and it is the investigating team from the Child Welfare Bureau. The first to enter is Albert Amundson, a very correct and pedantic young man who wears glasses and carries a portfolio. He is followed by Sandra Markowitz, a soft and pretty woman dressed severely and carrying a huge handbag. Albert explains that they have come to ask Murray a few questions and that it would perhaps be better if Nick were sent out to play. Murray counters by asking Albert if he is going to talk dirty, and insists that the child stay, because otherwise he might become suspicious.

MURRAY (*to* SANDRA)—You are the psychologist part of this team?

SANDRA—That's right, Mr. Burns.

MURRAY (*to* ALBERT)—And you, I take it, are the brawn of the outfit?

ALBERT (*ignoring the insult*)—Mr. Burns, it is not easy to define those elements, those influences and problems which go into the make-up of a young boy.

MURRAY—I thought it was just frogs and snails and puppy-dogs' tails.

Murray and Nick continue to frustrate Albert and Sandra in their attempts to get down to serious business as they start to guess where their guests come from by their accents. Sandra is quite impressed with their accuracy and asks Nick if he and Murray play many games like this together. Nick senses what she is thinking and replies: "Oh, yes. We play many wholesome and constructive-type games together." Albert doggedly returns to the questioning only to have Nick guess his accent. He is annoyed not only by this but by Sandra's further interrupting to enthuse about the child's remarkable ability, in what he considers an irrelevant area. To make matters worse the front door opens and a well-dressed man enters carrying a carton of fruit which he deposits and leaves. It is Murray's brother who drops fruit off every day on his way to the office. "He's a fruit nut," explains Murray. Albert mentions that their research team has spoken to his brother, as well as to his last employer, an N.B.C. television program.

MURRAY—I was chief writer for Leo Herman, better known as Chuckles, the Chipmunk, friend of the young'uns, and seller of Chuckle-Chips the potato chips your friend Chuckles the Chipmunk eats and chuckles over.

ALBERT—And the circumstances under which you left the employ of . . .

MURRAY—I quit. I felt that I was not reaching all the boys and girls out there in Televisionland. Actually it was not so much that I wasn't reaching the boys and girls, but the boys and girls were starting to reach *me*. Six months ago a perfectly adult bartender asked me if I wanted an onion in my martini, and I said, "Gosh n' gollies, you betcha." I knew it was time to quit.

Murray is becoming increasingly irritated by the whole investigation and Albert's lack of understanding and humor. Sandra tries to help the situation and persuades Albert to let her talk to Nick for a while. Nick eagerly shows her the Peter Lorre imitation Murray has taught him, and Albert interrupts to bring Nick back to the investigation. This annoys Sandra, who tells Albert that this is her part of the investigation. She then asks Nick about his favorite games and toys, and Nick proudly brings out "Bubbles," a huge statue of a bare-chested hula girl, whose breasts blink on and off when he turns the switch. Sandra attempts to keep her composure and pursue her questioning.

SANDRA—Nick, tell me . . . do you like best the fact that the chest of the lady lights up? Does "Bubbles" in any way remind you of . . . your mother, for example.

MURRAY—Sandra, his mother's chest did not light up. Why don't I save you a lot of time. Nick is a fairly bright kid and he knows girls are *not* boys. Other than that his interest in ladies is confined right now to ones that light up. He doesn't have any unusual fixations, Sandy. He is no more abnormally interested in your bust than Mr. Amundson is.

ALBERT—Mr. Burns, it is not necessary to . . .

MURRAY—Of course, I might be wrong about that.

ALBERT—Our interest in that doll . . .

MURRAY—You really *are* interested in that doll, Albert.

Nick immediately offers to sell the doll to Albert, which amuses Sandra and infuriates Albert. By now Murray sees that there really is a personal relationship between his two investigators and starts to advise Albert on how to treat Sandra. Nick goes out to get some books to show them, and the hostility between Albert and Sandra reaches a boil. The embarrassed sociologist asks Murray to excuse them and takes Sandra aside for a conference. He tells her that she gets too emotionally involved in these cases. Meanwhile Murray, on the other side of the room, shouts advice to the lovelorn through a megaphone. Albert finally breaks down and tells Murray point blank that unless he cooperates, the Child Welfare Bureau will have to separate him and Nick, who is not his legal ward. Murray angrily exclaims: "Do you mean to tell me that four years at N.Y.U. has made you my judge?" Albert and Sandra start to leave, but Murray stops them and says he will cooperate, and tells them the facts about Nick's mother.

MURRAY—For five years she did everything she could for Nick . . . but get married. She used to get married to *everybody*. But having Nick matured her, she felt a responsibility not to get married to just *any*body anymore, so she didn't marry Nick's father.

SANDRA—Well, how did you . . .

MURRAY—My sister Elaine showed up here one day with two suitcases, a neurotic parakeet, and a five-year-old child. Three days later she went downstairs to buy a pack of filter-tip cigarettes. (MURRAY *shrugs.*) Six years later she returned for the suitcases . . . the parakeet I had given away; I had taught it to say "Stand back, I'm an eagle" and it had become completely unmanageable, and the five-year-old child had become six years older. I reminded her of the child and the pack of filter-tip cigarettes and suggested that this was perhaps the longest running practical joke in recent history. Sister then proceeded to explain to me her well-practiced theory on the meaning of life, a philosophy falling somewhere to the left of Karl Marx. Then we laughed and said "goodbye." That was almost a year ago, and I've still got Nick.

SANDRA—But she must have had *some* concern about Nicholas . . .

MURRAY—His name is not Nicholas. I will admit that he has stayed with that name longer than the others . . .

SANDRA—I'm sure, on his birth certificate . . .

MURRAY—Certainly an elusive document. Not having given him a last name, Elaine felt reticent about assigning him a first one. I made a deal with him when he was six, that he could try out any name he wished, for however long he wished, until his thirteenth birthday, at which point he'd have to decide on a name he liked permanently. He went through a long period of dog's names. He received his library card last year in the name of Rafael Sabatini, his Cub Scout membership lists him as Barry Fitzgerald, and only last week a friend of his called asking if Toulouse could come over to his house for dinner.

SANDRA—His mother . . . ?

MURRAY—His mother, when last heard of, was studying Mime in Paris, having been given a sort of scholarship by a twenty-two-year-old hand-bag heir named Myron, who seems to believe strongly in the development of talent and student exchange.

Albert asks where the child is and Sandra reminds him that he was the one who preferred not having him around during the questioning. Albert's anger at her leads him into attempting to dominate her as he suggests they leave and move on to their next case, the Ledbetters, in Queens. Sandra stands her ground by saying that she doesn't feel that it is advisable to leave the Burns case at this point, hands him the Ledbetter file and announces that she is staying here. Albert and Sandra argue violently, with Sandra on the verge of tears and Albert walking out with the formal announcement to Murray that "Miss Markowitz is no longer involved with the Burns case,"

Barry Gordon, Jason Robards, Jr. and Sandy Dennis in "A Thousand Clowns."

and that any discussion that takes place between Murray and her after he goes will be "entirely unofficial."

Sandra attempts a formal apology to Murray, but in the middle of it bursts into tears. She tells her troubles to Murray, beginning with her anxiety about her job, as her family spent so much money putting her through college; the fact that she loves some of her cases and hates others, like the Ledbetter one: "I didn't like Raymond Ledbetter so I tried to understand him, and now that I understand him I hate him." She finally tells of her engagement to marry Albert, who is "really very nice when he's not on cases," but who puts her to sleep sometimes when he is talking. She starts to cry again at her own incompetence and Murray cheers her up by turning on the "Bubbles" statue. She laughs.

MURRAY—Miss Markowitz, you are well rid of Albert. You have been given a rare opportunity to return the unused portion and have your money refunded.

SANDRA—But . . . my work . . .

MURRAY—Dr. Markowitz, you are a lover of things and people so you took up work where you could get at as many of them as possible, and it just turned out that there were too many of them and too much that moves you. Be glad that you are not reasonable and sensible, that you are capable of embarrassment and joy and are a marathon crier.

SANDRA—There is a kind of relief that it's gone . . . the job, and even Albert. . . . But I don't have the vaguest idea who I am.

MURRAY—It's just there's all these Sandras running around who you never met before. Like in the circus, this tiny red car comes out and putters around, suddenly its doors open and out come a thousand clowns, whooping and hollering and raising hell. (*He takes her hand.*) Would you like to go to the Empire State Building with me?

SANDRA—No, not really.

MURRAY—Well, then how about the Zoo?

SANDRA—Not just now.

MURRAY—Well, then will you marry me?

SANDRA—Huh?

MURRAY—Just a bit of shock treatment. It's the quickest way to get a woman's attention when her mind wanders.

SANDRA—Well, Murray, to sort of return to reality . . .

MURRAY—I will go only as a tourist.

SANDRA—The Child Welfare Board could really take Nick away.

They are interrupted by Nick who has blown his allowance money to buy some educational books with which to impress the investigators. He is disappointed that things have gone badly and that Sandra is no longer on the case. Seeing the child's anxiety, Murray lifts him out of it by suggesting that they do their duet for their guest. Each take a ukelele and play and sing "Yessir, That's My Baby," and they do a soft-shoe dance together, while Sandra watches from her position on the bed. Nick drops out as Murray sits beside Sandra and serenades her. Nick gets his school briefcase and pajamas and starts for the door.

NICK (*to* SANDRA)—Nice to meet you, lady. I'll see you around.

MURRAY (*stops singing*)—Where you off to, Nick?

NICK—Gonna leave my stuff up at Mrs. Myers. (*Opens the door.*) I figure I'll be staying over there tonight. (*He waves a pleasant goodbye and goes out as* MURRAY *resumes the song and the curtain falls.*)

ACT II

It is eight o'clock the next morning. There is now a folding screen that hides the bed from the audience. The phone rings and Murray emerges from the bathroom, toothbrush in mouth, and charges across the room to answer it curtly with: "Is this somebody with good news or money? No? Goodbye." He dials for the weather report, repeating the routine we saw the morning before. After he has hung up the phone rings again and he answers by giving an imitation of the weather report he has just received, and whoever is calling hangs up on him. Murray shrugs it off and goes again to the window and leans out to give his daily exhortation to the troops.

MURRAY—This is your neighbor speaking! Something must be done about your garbage cans in the alley here. It is definitely second-rate garbage! By next week I want to see a better class of garbage, more empty champagne bottles and caviar cans! So let's *snap* it up and get on the *ball!*

This wakes up Sandra who has been sleeping behind the screen. She pokes her head above the top of the screen and attempts formal dignified conversation with Murray. He tosses her Nick's bathrobe and she talks with him impersonally while she puts it on, asking him why he didn't wake her up when he got up. He replies: "Because you were smiling, and how do you tell somebody who smiles when they sleep that another day has just sneakered in down the elevator shaft?" Embarrassedly Sandra makes a mad dash for what she thinks is the bathroom, where her clothes are, and slams the door. It turns out to be the kitchen, so reluctantly she is handed her clothes by Murray. As she dresses she tries to make small talk, despite Murray's suggestion that they broaden the discussion. She talks about the soap, the toothpaste, the coffee, and about the Statue of Liberty which they visited together yesterday. Finally she emerges fully clothed, picks up her files and her handbag, says goodbye politely and walks out of the apartment closing the door behind her. Murray stands alone looking mournfully at it for a moment, and then rushes to it and pulls it open thereby dragging Sandra, who has held onto the doorknob, back into the room.

MURRAY (*laughing*)—You nut. I was ready to kill you.

SANDRA (*throwing her arms around him*)—I was waiting for you to say something or kiss me or . . . (*He kisses her.*) Murray, I thought about it and I probably love you.

MURRAY—That's very romantic. I probably love you too.

SANDRA (*kisses him again and then starts to walk up and down excitedly*)—I didn't go to work this morning and I simply can't tell you how fantastic that makes me feel. I'm not going to do a *lot* of things anymore. Do you realize that I feel more at home here after twenty-four hours than I do in my parents' house after twenty-five years? . . . Of course, we'll have to do something about the curtains. (*She puts her files away neatly in the closet and starts to "move in."*) Oh, there are so many wonderful tricks you can try with a one-room apartment, if you use your imagination. (*She kisses him again.*) I was here with you last night and I don't give a damn who knows it or what anybody thinks. . . . (*The doorbell rings.*)

MURRAY (*preparing to answer it*)—Sandra, would you prefer to . . .

SANDRA—I've got no reason to hide from anybody. (MURRAY *goes to the door and opens it half-way. It is* ALBERT, *and* SANDRA, *recognizing his voice, beats a hasty retreat into the closet. Then* ALBERT *enters. He is disturbed that neither he nor* SANDRA'S *parents have heard from her.*)

ALBERT—Where is she?

MURRAY—She's hiding in the closet.

ALBERT (*annoyed at* MURRAY'S *apparent joke*)—We're really all quite anxious to know where she is.

MURRAY—I'm not kidding. She's in the closet. (*Not really believing him* ALBERT *goes to the closet, opens the door, sees* SANDRA, *and closes the door again quickly.*)

ALBERT—She *is* in the closet. (*He sits down, perplexed.*) That's a very silly thing for her to be in the closet.

MURRAY—Don't knock it till you've tried it. Now what else can I do for you?

Albert fights down his personal feelings about Sandra and Murray's having spent the night together, and speaks in his official capacity. He informs Murray that the Child Welfare Bureau has come to the decision that he is unfit to be the guardian of his nephew, and that the child will be removed from this home on Friday.

MURRAY—Where'd they get this routine from, Charles Dickens? Look, Albert, there must be some kind of a hearing or something . . .

ALBERT—You will have the opportunity Thursday to state your case. If there is some substantial change in your circumstances, if you can demonstrate that you are a responsible member of society . . .

MURRAY—It's Tuesday; what the hell am I supposed to do in two days, win the Nobel Peace Prize?

ALBERT—You were to be informed by the court, but in view of . . .

MURRAY—Buddy, you speak like you write everything down before you say it.

ALBERT—Yes, I do speak that way, Mr. Burns. I wish that I spoke more spontaneously. I will always appear foolish in a conversation with a person of your imagination. Please understand there is no vengeance in my activities here. I admire you for your warmth, Mr. Burns, and for the affection the child feels for you. I admire this because I am one for whom children do not easily feel affection. I am not one of the warm people. But your feeling for the child does not mollify the genuinely dangerous emotional climate you have made for him. For yours is, I believe, a distorted picture of this world.

Albert leaves and Murray springs Sandra from the closet. He talks to her about Nick, saying that Nick shouldn't go for a couple of years yet, because he hasn't quite reached the point where he is unashamed of being original and bright. Nick has the dangerous weakness of sitting down and writing out lists of things he's going to do, etc., and Murray is afraid that they may send him to live with a family of listmakers who will encourage this terrible habit.

MURRAY—I just want him to stay with me till I can be sure he won't turn into another carbon copy of that ever-popular modern hero, Norman Nothing. I want to be sure he'll know when he's chickening out on himself. I want him to stay awake and know who the phonies are. I want him to know how to holler and put up an argument. I want to be sure he sees all the wild possibilities. I want him to know it's worth all the trouble just to give the world a little goosing when you get the chance. And I want him to know the subtle, sneaky, important reason why he was born a human being and not a chair. (*Pause.*) I will be very sorry to see him go. That kid was the best straight-man I ever had. He is a laugher, and laughers are rare. I mean you tell that kid something funny, and he'll give you your money's worth. And in addition to that . . . besides that. . . . (*Sharply, shouting loudly.*) Sandy, I don't want

him to go. I like having him around here. What should I do, Sandy? Help me out.

Sandra suggests that if he can get a job before Thursday, she knows the Board and that they will consider that proof of his desire to become reliable. Murray brightens up, calls his brother, who is a TV agent, and tells him that he wants a job and that he is on his way down to his office. He kisses Sandra goodbye and is off.

Scene II

We are in Arnold Burns' office on the twenty-second floor of a skyscraper. Arnold is alone and talking to Leo Herman (Chuckles, the Chipmunk) on a speaker-phone. Leo wants Murray to come back to work writing for him, but Arnold holds him off, telling him that Murray is considering another good offer. Murray comes in and relates the details of his interview with Jimmy Sloane, a TV producer.

Murray—Sloane lunches beautifully, can out-lunch anybody. Told me this idea he had where I'd be a lovable eccentric on his panel show. This somehow led him very logically to his conception of God, who he says is "probably a real fun guy."

Arnold—What'd you tell him about the offer?

Murray—I told him goodbye. I don't think he noticed when I left; he focuses slightly to the right of you when he talks, just over your shoulder, so if you stay out of range he can't tell that you're gone. Probably thinks I'm still there.

Arnold reminds Murray that this means he has only Leo Herman left, and warns him "no fun and games" like the time Leo came up to his apartment and Murray left him standing in the living room while he went in the kitchen and started singing "Yessir, That's My Baby." Arnold has checked with the Child Welfare Board who will give Murray a probationary year with Nick, if he has and keeps his job, and they will be checking on him every week. Murray is depressed but promises not to say the wrong thing to Leo. Arnold then phones Leo whom we hear on the speaker-phone.

Leo tells Murray he wants him back writing the Chipmunk show, but that he's got to watch his joking. He reminds him of the time he sent out hundreds of form letters to the kids who wrote in asking for a definition of a chipmunk. "A cute rat," Leo recalls, and self-righteously informs Murray that "we can't fool with the innocence of children, who believe in the little chipmunk." He continues outlining his plan to have some fifteen minute fairy tales on the show.

LEO'S VOICE—You've got your Hans Christian Andersens, your Grimm Brothers, your Goldilocks, your Sleepin' Beauties, your Gingerbread Men, your Foxy-Loxies . . . do I reach ya, Murr'?

MURRAY (*quietly, controlling himself*)—Yeah, Leo . . .

LEO'S VOICE—I want you to give 'em five minutes a action, five minutes a poignancy, and then five minutes of the *moral message:* race-relations-thing, world-peace-thing, understanding-brings-love-thing. I don't know. Kid's show with something to *say.*

MURRAY—Hey, Leo, I might show up one day with eleven minutes of poignancy, no action, and a twelve-second moral message . . . (*Suddenly shouting into speaker-phone.*) *and then where would we be?*

To rebut Murray's mocking of him, Leo starts to tell a nauseous story, which Murray has heard many times before, about how Chuckles, the Chipmunk is real to him and he pontificates about the sacredness of the laughter of children. Murray stands as much as he can of this and finally dumps the speaker-phone into the wastepaper basket. He explains to Arnie.

MURRAY—Arnie, I quit that nonsense five months ago . . .

ARNOLD—Murray, you're a *nut;* a man has a job for you, there's a hearing on Thursday . . .

MURRAY—A fool in a box telling me what's funny, a Welfare Board checking my underwear every week . . . and *I'm* the nut?

ARNOLD—Murray, you float like a balloon and everybody's waitin' for ya with a pin. I'm trying to put you in *touch,* Murray . . . with *real things;* with . . .

MURRAY (*angrily*)—You mean *real* things, like this office? The world could come to an end and you'd find out about it on the phone. . . . (*Pointing at framed photographs on* ARNOLD'S *desk.*) Pictures of your wife six years ago when she was still a piece and your kids at their cutest four years ago when they looked best for the office . . . Oh, you're in *touch* all right. (*He leaves.*)

SCENE III

It is early evening of the same day, and back at Murray's apartment Sandra has cleaned up all the disorder and added curtains, bedspreads, tablecloths, flowers, etc. Nick comes in and Sandra tells him the good news that Murray has gone downtown to get a job through his Uncle Arnold. Nick is happy but doesn't want to hang around to hear Murray's response to the redecoration. He leaves, and a moment later Murray arrives.

MURRAY—Oh God, I've been attacked by the Ladies' Home Journal.

SANDRA—Murray, don't keep me in suspense, which one of the jobs did you take?

MURRAY—I shall now leave you breathless with the strange and wondrous tale of this sturdy lad's adventures today in downtown Oz. I am walking on East Fifty-first street an hour ago, and I decided to construct a general-all-purpose Apology. Not complicated, just the words "I'm sorry" said with a little style. Well, y'know when you're talking to yourself how sometimes you suddenly say a coupla words out loud? So I said "I'm sorry" and this fellah, complete stranger, looks up a second and says, "That's all right, Mac," and goes on. I communicated! (SANDRA *and* MURRAY *laugh.*) So I decided to test the whole thing out scientifically by just saying "I'm sorry" to everybody that went by . . . Of course, some people gave me a funny look, but Sandy, I *swear,* seventy-five percent of them *forgave* me. I had tapped some vast reservoir. Something had happened to all of them for which they felt somebody should apologize. If you went up to people on the street and offered them money, they'd refuse it. But everybody accepts apology immediately. It is the most negotiable currency.

SANDRA (*after a pause*)—Murray, you didn't take any of the jobs.

MURRAY (*quietly*)—Sandy, I took whatever I am and put a new suit on it and gave it a haircut and took it outside and that's what happened. I'm sorry, I'm very sorry. (SANDRA *just looks at him.*) That's the most you should expect from life, Sandy, a really good apology for all the things you won't get.

SANDRA—Murray, what happens to Nick?

MURRAY—Nick, he's a wonderful kid, but he's brought the God-damned *world* in on me. Don't you understand, they'd be checking on me every week; being judged by people I don't know and who don't know me. Gimme a month of that and I'd turn into an ashtray. I wouldn't be of any use to Nick or you or anybody. . . .

Sandra blames her own ineptness for not having convinced Murray to accept his responsibility. She tells him she is leaving, although she can see why Nick liked it here, and that she might like it too if she was twelve years old. Murray begs her to stay, but she refuses, calling him "the most extraordinarily selfish person" she's ever met. Murray gets mad and predicts that: "It's really gonna be quite thrilling, you and Albert, guarding the Lincoln Tunnel together." She goes.

MURRAY (*looking around at the redecorated apartment*)—And what the hell did you do to my apartment? What've we got here; God-damn Sunnybrook Farm?! (*Suddenly realizing he is still wearing a new suit, he pulls off his jacket, rolls it in a ball and throws it across the room. Then he relaxes, puts on his favorite hat and wanders over to the open window. He smiles, and then leans out the window and speaks loudly.*) Campers . . . The entertainment committee was quite disappointed by the really poor turn-out at this morning's community sing. I mean, where's all that old Camp Chickawattamee spirit? Now I'd like to say that I . . . (*Faltering.*) I'd like to say right now that I . . . that . . . that I . . . (*Softly.*) Campers, I can't think of anything to say. . . .

ACT III

It is the same evening, and Murray is busy taking the curse off his apartment by redistributing some of his treasured junk around it. The door opens and Arnold enters, this time without fruit. He asks Murray to turn off the record-player, and when Murray ignores him, he angrily does it himself.

ARNOLD—You walked out of my office. That wasn't a nice thing to do to me, Murray. You came into my office like George God; everybody's supposed to come up and audition for Human Being in front of you. (*Gently takes* MURRAY'S *arm*). Murray, I called Leo back, I apologized, told him my phone broke down. I got him to come over here tonight. He's anxious to see you, everything's O.K. Listen, if you love this kid then you gotta take any kinda stupid job to keep him. (*Sees he is making no impression.*) Have you told him yet?

MURRAY—Arnie, don't worry. I've got a coupla days to tell him. And don't underrate Nick. He's gonna understand this a lot better than you think he is.

ARNOLD (*disappointed at* MURRAY'S *weak attitude*)—Murray, I finally figured out your problem. There's only one thing that really bothers you . . . (*Mockingly.*) Other people. Well, watch out, Murray, they're *every*where . . .

MURRAY (*stung a little*)—Go ahead, Arnie, give me advice. At thirty thousand a year you can afford it.

ARNOLD—Oh, I get it. If I'm so smart why ain't I poor? What's this game you play gonna be like ten years from now, without youth?

MURRAY (*counterattacking*)—Arnie, remember when you quit

"Harry the Fur King" on Thirty-eighth Street. You told me you were going to be in twenty businesses in twenty years if you had to, till you found out what you wanted. You weren't going to take crap from *any*body. So what's the business you finally picked? Taking crap from *every*body.

ARNOLD (*hurt, he makes a futile attempt to get back to* MURRAY'S *problem*)—Murray, the Welfare Board has these specifications; all you have to do is meet a couple of specifications. . . .

MURRAY (*cornering him*)—Oh, Arnie, you don't understand anymore. You got that wide stare that people stick in their eyes so nobody'll know their head's asleep. You want me to come with you and drag and stumble with the rotten weight of all the people who should have been told off, all the things you should have said, all the specifications that aren't yours. Arnold, five months ago I forgot what *day* it was and it scared the hell out of me. You got to know what day it is. You have to own your days and name them, each one of them, or else the years go right by and none of them belong to you. (MURRAY *turns away from him, apparently having proved his point. After a moment, however,* ARNOLD *rises and shouts in a voice stronger than we have ever heard from him.*)

ARNOLD—*Murray!* (MURRAY *turns, startled.*) I have long been aware that you don't respect me much. Unfortunately I am willing to deal with the available world and I do not choose to shake it up but to live with it. There's the people who spill things, and the people who get spilled on; I do not choose to notice the stains. I have a wife, and I have children, and business like they say is business. I am not an exceptional man, so it is possible for me to stay with things the way they are. I'm lucky. I'm gifted. I have a talent for surrender. I'm at peace. But you are cursed; and I like you so it makes me sad you don't have the gift. All I can do is worry for you. But I will not worry for myself. I get up, I go, I lie a little, I peddle a little, I watch the rules, I talk the talk. But, and I will not apologize for it, I take pride; I am the best possible Arnold Burns. (*He starts to leave.*)

MURRAY (*genuinely moved,* MURRAY *goes to stop him*)—Arnold . . .

ARNOLD—Please, Murray. (*He holds up his hand.*) Allow me once to leave a room before you do. (*To give his knife a final twist he flicks on the record-player, and walks out.*)

Murray stands looking at the record-player as "The Stars and Stripes Forever" plays grotesquely out of the speaker. Slowly he is coming to a decision. Nick enters from the fire escape. He still thinks Murray got the job downtown and tells Murray that since he has taken his decisive step, Nick has also figured that it was time for him to finish a certain matter he had been putting off, the selecting of a permanent first name. He doesn't like "Nick" because it is a name for a short person, and even though he is short, he doesn't want to call attention to it.

NICK—So I considered various tall names. I considered for a while "Zachary," but I figured there was a chance Zachary could turn into a short, fat, bald name. Then I thought about "Richard," which is not really tall, just very thin with glasses. Then last week I finally, really, decided. I took out a new library card to see how it looks. And today I figured I would make it definite and official. (*He hands library card to* MURRAY.)

MURRAY (*looking at it, confused*)—This is *my* library card.

NICK—No, that's the whole thing; it's mine.

MURRAY—But it says "*Murray* Burns" on it . . .

NICK—Right, that's the name I picked.

MURRAY (*moved and astonished by this indirect expression of* NICK's *feelings for him, and aware now of the dependency on him of this child he had been treating as a man*)—Well, Nick, I'm flattered . . . I want you to know that I'm very flattered by . . . this.

Nick plays it cool and goes to put his schoolbooks away while Murray tries to make light of it by asking him why he didn't pick this or that other name, but each time he asks he recognizes again how much keeping Nick means to both of them.

They are interrupted by a knock on the door. It is Leo Herman. He is carrying a paper bag containing two "Chuckles" hats and a huge cardboard cutout of himself as Chuckles, the Chipmunk. He gives the cutout and one cap to Nick while he puts on the other, and urges Nick to give him the "Chip-chip Chippermunkie" hello, which Nick does reluctantly but obligingly. He suggests that Nick take the potato chips he has brought into the kitchen, so he can talk to Murray. As the kid goes out Leo turns to Murray and says paranoiacally: "The kid hates me. I can tell." He goes on to confess to Murray that since Murray left the show, he's been "bombing out" in front of the kids. He knows that with Murray back that will all change. Leo keeps deprecating himself, saying that he forgives Murray for hanging up on him, that he *is* boring and phony, cowardly and immodest. Nick returns with the potato chips in a bowl, and Leo can't resist the temptation to go into his act. Nick doesn't respond, so Leo tries another routine and bombs out again. Nick decides that he and Murray ought to show Leo something really funny and they do their imitation of Alexander Hamilton and Thomas Jefferson, which Leo refuses to find funny, because "you can't do an imitation of Alexander Hamilton; nobody knows what he *sounds* like. . . ."

LEO—It's oddness here, Murray, *odd*ness. Alexander *Ham*ilton imitations! Jaded jokes for old men. Murray, what've you done to this kid? This grotesque atmosphere, *unhealthy,* and you're not even guilty about it. The routine I did for him was *funny.* Had he been brought up by a normal person and not in this madhouse . . .

NICK—Hey, don't say that . . .

LEO—. . . a certain kind of freakish way of growing up. . . .

NICK—Hey, are you calling me a freak? Take back what you said.

LEO (*walks away from* NICK, *mumbling*)—On June third I will be forty-two years old and I'm standing here arguing with a twelve-year-old kid. (*Quiets down.*) See, Nicky, humor is a cloudy, wonderland thing, but simple and clear like the blue, blue sky. All I want is your simple, honest, child's opinion of my routine.

NICK (*looking directly at* LEO; *calmly, slowly*)—My simple, child's reaction to what you did is that you are not funny. What is also not funny is to call us names and what is mostly not funny is how sad you are. I would feel sorry for you if it wasn't for how dull you are and those are the worst tasting potato chips I ever tasted. And that is my opinion from the blue, blue sky. (MURRAY *laughs uproariously.*)

Leo is furious and starts to leave, as Murray, realizing what's at stake, tries to stop him. Nick complicates matters by getting the uke and playing "Yessir, That's My Baby," and then kicking Leo's "crummy" cardboard statue. Murray somehow quiets Nick down and sends him to his alcove, and then convinces Leo that Nick's whole performance was just a practical joke. Murray even lies a little and tells Leo that the bit he did was funny, and so it is arranged that Murray will report for work tomorrow morning, and Leo leaves. Murray now tries to make peace with Nick who is still angry that Murray didn't let "that moron" go. While they are talking, Sandra enters. She immediately starts picking up and enlists Nick's help in putting Murray's junk out of sight. Murray realizes that they are taking over and tries to stop them. Then he gives up, good-naturedly. As they continue, he goes over to the window, leans out, and begins to talk.

MURRAY—Everybody on stage for the Hawaiian number, please. . . . Well, then if you're not ready, we better work on the Military March number. Now the last time we ran this, let's admit it was pretty ragged. I mean the whole "Spirit of '76" float was in dis*grace*ful shape yesterday . . . O.K. now, let's go, everybody ready . . . (NICK *looks up from his work with* SANDRA *and turns on the record-player.*) Grenadiers ready, Cavalry ready, Cossacks ready, Rough Riders ready, Minute Men ready . . . (*The record-player has warmed up and we hear "The Stars and Stripes Forever."* MURRAY *smiles, acknowledging* NICK's *assistance and then continues his harangue out the window as* NICK *hums along with the music and* SANDRA *laughs and the curtain falls.*)

A GRAPHIC GLANCE

Patricia Harty, Grover Dale, Elaine Stritch, Alice Pearce, Paul O'Keefe (with the match) and James Hurst in "Sail Away"

Elizabeth Allen, Loring Smith, Walter Chiari, Barbara Cook and Jules Munshin in "The Gay Life"

Molly Picon, Robert Weede, Mimi Benzell, Albert Marre (director) and Max Goberman (musical director) rehearse "Milk and Honey"

Robert Lewis (director) reads from the script while Richard Adler (composer and lyricist) sings the songs for the cast of "Kwamina": Ethel Ayler, Terry Carter, Rex Ingram, Brock Peters and Sally Ann Howes. The man at the piano is Colin Romoff, the musical director.

Wendy Hiller (England)
in "The Aspern Papers"

Paul Scofield (England)
in "A Man for All Seasons"

Zia Mohyeddin (Pakistan) in "A Passage to India"

Margaret Leighton (England) in "The Night of the Iguana"

John Mills (England) in "Ross"

Zero Mostel, Jack Gilford and David Burns in

"A Funny Thing Happened on the Way to the Forum"

Noelle Adam, Alvin Epstein, Diahann Carroll and Richard Kiley in "No Strings"

James Jamieson (choreographer), John Fearnley (director with script), Walter Blocher, Peter Palmer and Sally Ann Howes rehearse the City Center revival of "Brigadoon"

Carrie Nye and Ted van Griethuysen as the two lovers in "Troilus and Cressida," as performed at the Connecticut Shakespeare Festival

Shakespeare in New York's Central Park. Joseph Papp (center) directs J. D. Cannon and Nan Martin in "Much Ado About Nothing"

Students from nearby states attending a preview matinee at the Connecticut Shakespeare Festival in Stratford, Conn.

PLAYS PRODUCED IN THE UNITED STATES

PLAYS PRODUCED ON BROADWAY

June 1, 1961—May 31, 1962

(Plays marked "Continued" were still running on June 1, 1962)

THE BILLIE BARNES PEOPLE

(7 performances)

Revue with sketches by Bob Rodgers; music and lyrics by Billy Barnes. Produced by John Pool at the Royale Theatre, June 13, 1961.

Joyce Jameson	Ken Berry
Dick Patterson	Jackie Joseph
Patti Regan	Jack Grinnage
Dave Ketchum	Jo Anne Worley

Staged by Mr. Rodgers; settings by Spencer Davies; costumes by Grady Hunt; musical arrangements and supervision by Ray Henderson; cartoons by William Box; stage manager, Allen Kramer; press, Bill Doll.

ACT I

"If It Wasn't for People" .... Entire Company
"There's Nothing Wrong With Our Values" ...... Joyce Jameson, Patti Regan, Dave Ketchum, Dick Patterson
Vegas Revisited
  Barker .... Jack Grinnage
  Statue .... Jackie Joseph
  Chorus Girl .... Patti Regan
  Herman Hepplewhite .... Dave Ketchum
  Fellas .... Dick Patterson, Jack Grinnage
  Opera Diva .... Jo Anne Worley
"Don't Bother" .... Jackie Joseph and Ken Berry
I Wrote a Book
  Authoress .... Joyce Jameson
  Fans .... Jo Anne Worley, Dick Patterson
If It Makes You Happy
  The Boss .... Dave Ketchum
  His Girl .... Jackie Joseph
  The Boys .... Jack Grinnage, Ken Berry
"Damn-Alot"
  Introduced by .... Jack Grinnage
  Guenevere .... Patti Regan
  Morgan O'Fey .... Joyce Jameson
  King Arthur .... Dave Ketchum
  Lancelot .... Dick Patterson
"What Do We Have to Hold on To?" .... Jo Anne Worley
"I Like You"
  Romantic Couple .... Jackie Joseph and Ken Berry
  Neurotic Couple .... Jo Anne Worley and Jack Grinnage
  Sophisticated Couple ... . Joyce Jameson and Dick Patterson
"Before and After" .... Dave Ketchum and Dick Patterson
"Let's Get Drunk" .... Ken Berry
"It's Not Easy"
  Ethel .... Patti Regan
  Janet .... Joyce Jameson
  Adele .... Jo Anne Worley

The Speech Teacher
Teacher ....Dick Patterson
Client ....Jack Grinnage
"The Matinee" ....Entire Company

ACT II

"If It Wasn't for People" (Reprise) ....Jack Grinnage
The Couch ....Jackie Joseph and Dick Patterson
The Balcony ....Jo Anne Worley and Dave Ketchum
Bus Stop ....Patti Regan and Ken Berry
Liberated Woman
Sally O'Toole ....Joyce Jameson
Johnny, her boy friend ....Jack Grinnage
Narrator ....Dick Patterson
"What Do We Have to Hold on To?" ....Jo Anne Worley
"The End?" ....Dick Patterson, Ken Berry and Dave Ketchum
Alice
Alice ....Jackie Joseph
Felicia Fashion ....Patti Regan
Marty Market ....Dick Patterson
Housewife ....Jo Anne Worley
Mrs. Karr ....Joyce Jameson
Mr. Karr ....Ken Berry
Mr. Big Business, Sr. ....Dave Ketchum
Mr. Big Business, Jr. ....Jack Grinnage
Grauman's Chinese .....Dick Patterson, Patti Regan and Ken Berry
"Second Best" ....Joyce Jameson
"What Do We Have to Hold on To?" ....Jo Anne Worley
"Dolls" ....Dave Ketchum, Dick Patterson and Patti Regan
"Where Is the Clown?" ....Joyce Jameson and Ken Berry
"Marital Infidelity" ....Entire Company
"I Like You" (Reprise) ....Entire Company

(Closed June 17, 1961)

RHINOCEROS

(16 performances)

Play by Eugene Ionesco, translated by Derek Prouse. Produced by Leo Kerz, in association with Seven Arts Associates Corp., at the Longacre Theatre, September 18, 1961.

Waitress ....Elisa Loti
Logician ....Dolph Sweet
Grocer ....Robert Jacquin
Grocer's Wife ....Eulalie Noble
Housewife ....Aza Bard
Berrenger ....Alfred Ryder
John ....Zero Mostel
Old Gentleman ....Leslie Barrett
Cafe Proprietor ....William Putch
Daisy ....Flora Elkins
Mr. Nicklebush ....Will Hussung
Dribble ....Salem Ludwig
Shiftor ....William Myers
Mrs. Ochs ....Jean Stapleton
Fireman ....Dolph Sweet

Staged by Joseph Anthony; settings and lighting by Leo Kerz; costumes by J. Michael Travis; sound engineered by Saki Oura; production stage manager, Bill Ross; stage manager, Ken Paine; press, Barry Hyams. "Rhinoceros" was first produced by Leo Kerz at the Longacre Theatre, January 9, 1961, for 240 performances.

(Closed September 30, 1961)

GREEK TRAGEDY THEATRE

(16 performances)

Two week limited engagement of three Greek tragedies: "Electra" by Sophocles and "The Choephori" and "The Eumenides" by Aeschylus. Produced by the City Center of Music and Drama, Inc., in association with the Greek Theatre Association (Los Angeles), at the New York City Center, September 19, 1961.

ELECTRA

The Tutor .... Ph. Taxiarchis
Orestes .... D. Veakis
Electra .... A. Papathanassiou
Clytemnestra .... K. Pappa
Chryothemis .... N. Debonera, A. Kariofylli
Aegisthus .... A. Xenakis
Pylades .... K. Georgoussopoulos

Leading women of the chorus: M. Vassiliou, E. Zerva, A. Kariofylli, N. Debonera.

THE CHOEPHORI
(The Libation Pourers)

Orestes .... D. Veakis
Electra .... K. Pappa
Servant .... A. Xenakis
Clytemnestra .... A. Papathanassiou
Nurse .... M. Vassiliou, N. Debonera
Aegisthus .... Ph. Taxiarchis
Pylades .... K. Georgoussopoulos

Leading women of the chorus: N. Debonera, E. Zerva, A. Kariofylli.

THE EUMENIDES

Pythia .... E. Zerva
Apollo .... A. Xenakis
Orestes .... D. Veakis
Clytemnestra's shadow .... A. Papathanassiou
Pallas Athene (Minerva) .... K. Pappa, A. Papathanassiou

Leading women of the chorus: M. Vassiliou, A. Kariofylli, N. Debonera.

Chorus for the three tragedies: M. Anapliotou, N. Emmanouilidou, K. Zakka, I. Korobilli, I. Konstandinou, N. Margari, E. Papdimopoulou, H. Paralopoulou, K. Romanou, H. Stefanidou, M. Xyrafidou.

For the Greek Tragedy Theatre: direction by D. Rondiris; translation by J. Gryparis; choreography by Loukia; music by K. Kydoniatis; press, Phillip Bloom.

(Closed October 1, 1961)

FROM THE SECOND CITY

(87 performances)

Revue with scenes and dialogue created by the company; music by William Mathieu. Produced by Max Liebman, Bernard Sahlins, Howard Alk and Paul Sills at the Royale Theatre, September 26, 1961.

Howard Alk	Alan Arkin
Severn Darden	Andrew Duncan
Barbara Harris	Mina Kolb
Paul Sand	Eugene Troobnick

Staged by Paul Sills; setting and lighting by Frederick Fox; production stage manager, Gordon Davidson; press, Frank Goodman, Ben Washer and Arlene Wolf.

ACT I

Max and Moritz ...... Severn Darden, Howard Alk, Barbara Harris
Great Books .... Eugene Troobnick, Barbara Harris, Andrew Duncan, Mina Kolb, Severn Darden
Hollywood Ten .... Alan Arkin, Mina Kolb, Severn Darden
Phono Pal .... Paul Sand, Eugene Troobnick
The Hoboken Story .... Paul Sand, Barbara Harris, Mina Kolb, Andrew Duncan, Alan Arkin, Howard Alk, Severn Darden
The Silent Film ...... Severn Darden, Eugene Troobnick, Paul Sand
The Bergman Film ...... Severn Darden, Paul Sand, Barbara Harris
Interview: West Germany .... Eugene Troobnick, Alan Arkin
Interview: Louisiana .... Andrew Duncan, Severn Darden
A Short Message .... Mina Kolb, Eugene Troobnick
Football Comes to the U of C .... Andrew Duncan, Howard Alk, Eugene Troobnick, Severn Darden
Museum Piece .... Barbara Harris, Alan Arkin
Second City Symphony .... The Company

ACT II

Tempo .... The Company
Laos .... Paul Sand, Andrew Duncan
I Got Blues .... Barbara Harris, Severn Darden, Howard Alk
Minstrel Show .... Eugene Troobnick, Andrew Duncan, Paul Sand, Howard Alk
A Piece of String .... Severn Darden, Paul Sand
No George Don't .... Alan Arkin, Mina Kolb
News Broadcast—1965 .... Eugene Troobnick
First Affair .... Barbara Harris, Severn Darden
Mountain Climbing .... Howard Alk, Alan Arkin, Paul Sand, Andrew Duncan, Eugene Troobnick
Caesar's Wife .... Mina Kolb, Barbara Harris, Howard Alk
Noah .... The Company

(Closed December 9, 1961)

PURLIE VICTORIOUS

(261 performances)

Play by Ossie Davis. Produced by Philip Rose at the Cort Theatre, September 28, 1961.

Purlie Victorious Judson .... Ossie Davis
Lutiebelle Gussie Mae Jenkins .... Ruby Dee
Missy Judson .... Helen Martin
Gitlow Judson .... Godfrey M. Cambridge
Charley Cotchipee .... Alan Alda
Idella Landy .... Beah Richards
Ol' Cap'n Cotchipee .... Sorrell Booke
The Sheriff .... Ci Herzog
The Deputy .... Roger C. Carmel

Time: the recent past. Place: the cotton plantation country of the Old South.

Staged by Howard Da Silva; settings and lighting by Ben Edwards; costumes by Ann Roth; stage manager, Leonard Auerbach; press, James D. Proctor. Parody of social discrimination in rural Georgia.

(Closed May 13, 1962)

SAIL AWAY

(167 performances)

Musical with book, music and lyrics by Noel Coward. Produced by Bonard Productions, in association with Charles Russell, at the Broadhurst Theatre, October 3, 1961.

Joe, the ship's purser .... Charles Braswell
Shuttleworth, a steward .... Keith Prentice
Rawlings, a passenger who drinks .... James Pritchett
Sir Gerard Nutfield .... C. Stafford Dickens
Lady Nutfield .... Margaret Mower
Barnaby Slade .... Grover Dale
Elmer Candijack .... Henry Lawrence
Maimie Candijack, his wife .... Betty Jane Watson
Glen Candijack, their son .... Alan Helms
Shirley Candijack, their daughter .... Patti Mariano
Mr. Sweeney .... Jon Richards
Mrs. Sweeney .... Paula Bauersmith
Elinor Spencer-Bollard .... Alice Pearce
Nancy Foyle, her niece .... Patricia Harty
Alvin Lush .... Paul O'Keefe
Mrs. Lush, his mother .... Evelyn Russell
John Van Mier .... James Hurst
Mrs. Van Mier, his mother .... Margalo Gillmore
Mimi Paragon .... Elaine Stritch
Ali, an Arab guide .... Charles Braswell
Man from American Express .... Richard Woods

Arabs, Italians, passengers, stewards and children: Jere Admire, Bobby Allen, Don Atkinson, Gary Crabbe, David Evans, Pat Ferrier, Dorothy Frank, Ann Fraser, James Frasher, Gene Gavin, Paul Gross, S. Curtis Hood, Wish Mary Hunt, Cheryl Kilgren, Bridget Knapp, Nancy Lynch, Patti Mariano, Mary Ellen O'Keefe, Alan Peterson, Dennis Scott, Alice Shanahan, Dan Siretta, Gloria Stevens, Christopher Votos.

Time: the present. Place: various parts of the Cunard steamship "Coronia," with additional scenes in Tangier, Italy and the Parthenon.

Staged by Mr. Coward; musical numbers and dances staged by Joe Layton; settings by Oliver Smith; costumes by Helene Pons and Mr. Smith; lighting by Peggy Clark; musical direction and dance arrangements by Peter Matz; orchestrations by Irwin Kostal; vocal arrangements by Fred Werner; stage manager, Joe Dooley; press, Frank Goodman and Ben Washer. Satire on the "pleasures" of travel as seen by a cruise hostess.

ACT I

"Come to Me" .... Mimi and the Stewards
"Sail Away" .... Johnny
"Come to Me" (Reprise) .... Mimi
"Sail Away" (Reprise) .... Johnny and the Company
"Where Shall I Find Him?" .... Nancy
"Beatnik Love Affair" .... Barnaby, Nancy and the Passengers
"Later Than Spring" .... Johnny
"The Passenger's Always Right" .... Joe and the Stewards
"Useful Phrases" .... Mimi
"Where Shall I Find Her?" (Reprise) .... Barnaby
"Go Slow, Johnny" .... Johnny
"You're a Long, Long Way From America" .... Mimi and Company

ACT II

"The Customer's Always Right" ....Ali and the Arabs
"Something Very Strange" ....Mimi
Italian Interlude ....The Company
"The Little Ones' ABC" ....Mimi, Alvin and the Children
"Don't Turn Away From Love" ....Johnny
"When You Want Me" ....Barnaby and Nancy
"Later Than Spring" (Reprise) ....Mimi
"Why Do the Wrong People Travel?" ....Mimi
"When You Want Me" (Reprise) ....The Company

(Closed February 24, 1962)

THE CARETAKER

(165 performances)

Play by Harold Pinter. Produced by Roger L. Stevens, Frederick Brisson and Gilbert Miller at the Lyceum Theatre, October 4, 1961.

Mick ....Alan Bates
Aston ....Robert Shaw
Davies ....Donald Pleasence

Time: the present. Place: a house in West London.

Staged by Donald McWhinnie; setting by Brian Currah; supervision and lighting by Paul Morrison; production stage manager, Fred Hebert; stage manager, Charles Forsythe; press, Harvey B. Sabinson.

See page 49.

(Closed February 24, 1962)

BLOOD, SWEAT AND STANLEY POOLE

(84 performances)

Play by James and William Goldman. Produced by Roger L. Stevens and Fields Productions, in association with Lyn Austin, at the Morosco Theatre, October 5, 1961.

Pfc. Rooney ....Gene Roch
Cpt. Mal Malcolm ....John McMartin
1st Lt. Stanley Poole ....Darren McGavin
Master Sgt. Florence Denzil ....Elisabeth Fraser
Pvt. Robert Oglethorpe ....Peter Fonda
Col. Egan ....Nat Polen
Master Sgt. David Bell ....Reed Brown, Jr.
Master Sgt. Angelo Bucci ....Robert Weil
Master Sgt. Lucious Snow ....J. Talbot Holland
Master Sgt. Jerry Wheeler ....Richard Hamilton
Master Sgt. J. J. LaRue ....Hy Anzel
Mrs. Bucci ....Peg Murray

Time: Indian Summer. Place: the supply room of Headquarters Company of an old established army post in the Middle West.

Staged by Jerome Chodorov; setting and lighting by Donald Oenslager; costumes by J. Michael Travis; production stage manager, Charles Atkin; stage manager, Frank Hamilton; press, Arthur Cantor.

Comedy about a not too bright lieutenant who helps and is helped by a smart private in a struggle to get rid of a blackmailing officer.

(Closed December 16, 1961)

MILK AND HONEY

(268 performances)
(Continued)

Musical with book by Don Appell; music and lyrics by Jerry Herman. Produced by Gerard Oestreicher at the Martin Beck Theatre, October 10, 1961.

Porter ....Burt Bier
Shepherd Boy ....Johnny Borden
Policeman ....Ronald Holgate
Ruth ....Mimi Benzell
Phil ....Robert Weede
Clara Weiss ....Molly Picon
The Guide ....Ellen Berse
Mrs. Weinstein ....Addi Negri
Mrs. Strauss ....Dorothy Richardson
Mrs. Breslin ....Rose Lischner
Mrs. Segal ....Diane Goldberg
Mrs. Kessler ....Ceil Delli
Mrs. Perlman ....Thelma Pelish
Barbara, Phil's daughter ....Lanna Saunders
David, Barbara's husband ....Tommy Rall
Adi ....Juki Arkin
Zipporah ....Ellen Madison
The Cantors ....Lou Polacek, David London
Maid of Honor ....Matt Turney
Wedding Couples ....Jose Gutierrez, Linda Howe, Michael Nestor, Jane Zachary
Cafe Arab ....Renato Cibelli
Man of the Moshav ....Art Tookoyan
Mr. Horowitz ....Reuben Singer

Hassidim, soldiers, Arabs, tourists, waiters, tradesmen and farmers: Marceline Decker, Urylee Leonardos, Terry Marone, Sandra Stahl, Marilyn Stark, Patti Winston, Myrna Aaron, Nina Feinberg, Penny Ann Green, Judith Haskell, Linda Howe, Susan May, Matt Turney, Jane Zachary, Burt Bier, Gerald Cardoni, Renato Cibelli, Murray Goldkind, David London, Ed Mastin, Lou Polacek, Robert Rue, Art Tookoyan, Anthony De Vecchi, Louis Gasparinetti, Jose Gutierrez, Stuart Hodes, Alex Kotimski, Carlos Macri, John Mandia, Michael Nestor, Dom Salinaro, Walter Stratton, Eddie Roll, Ronald Holgate.

Time: the present. Place: Jerusalem and its environs.

Staged by Albert Marre; choreography by Donald Saddler; settings and lighting by Howard Bay; costumes by Miles White; orchestrations by Hershy Kay and Eddie Sauter; choral arrangements by Robert de Cormier; musical direction by Max Goberman; dance arrangements by Genevieve Pitot; production stage manager, James S. Gelb; stage manager, Burry Fredrik; press, Dick Weaver. A middle-aged American and a young American widow fall in love during their visit to modern Israel.

ACT I

"Shepherd's Song" ....Shepherd Boy and Phil
"Shalom" ....Phil and Ruth
"Independence Day Hora" ....The Company
"Milk and Honey" ....David, Adi and Company
"There's No Reason in the World" ....Phil
"Chin Up, Ladies" ....Mrs. Weiss and Widows
"That Was Yesterday" ....Ruth, Phil, Adi and Company
"Let's Not Waste a Moment" ....Phil
"The Wedding" ....Ruth, Phil and Company

ACT II

"Like a Young Man" ....Phil
"I Will Follow You" ....David

"Hymn to Hymie" .... Mrs. Weiss
"There's No Reason in the World (Reprise) .... Ruth
"Milk and Honey" (Reprise) .... Adi and Company
"As Simple as That" .... Ruth and Phil
"Shalom" (Reprise) .... Ruth, Phil and Company

EVERYBODY LOVES OPAL

(21 performances)

Play by John Patrick. Produced by Roger L. Stevens, in association with Seven Arts Productions, at the Longacre Theatre, October 11, 1961.

Opal .... Eileen Heckart
Mister Tanner .... Himself
Gloria .... Brenda Vaccaro
Bradford .... Donald Harron
Solomon .... Stubby Kaye
Officer .... John Napier
Doctor .... James Coco

The action of the play takes place in Opal's house over a period of three months.

Staged by Cyril Ritchard; setting and lighting by Jo Mielziner; costumes by Noel Taylor; production stage manager, Gerald O'Brien; stage manager, Robert Gothie; press, Shirley E. Herz. Comedy about a female junk collector and three drifters who plot to kill her for her insurance money.

(Closed October 28, 1961)

LET IT RIDE!

(68 performances)

Musical based on "Three Men on a Horse" by John Cecil Holm and George Abbott; book by Abram S. Ginnes; music and lyrics by Jay Livingston and Ray Evans; additional material by Ronny Graham. Produced by Joel Spector at the Eugene O'Neill Theatre, October 12, 1961.

Erwin .... George Gobel
Audrey .... Paula Stewart
Carver .... Stanley Grover
Harry .... Harold Gary
Charlie .... Albert Linville
Frankie .... Larry Alpert
Mabel .... Barbara Nichols
Patsy .... Sam Levene
Birthday Girls .... Pat Turner, Sandra Devlin, Ann Johnson, Sandy Walsh, Rae McLean, Carol Glade, Sally Lee, Sally Kirk, Barbara Marcon
Nice Nose Brophy .... Dort Clark
Mother .... Maggie Worth
Chief Schermerhorn .... Ted Thurston
Repulski .... Stanley Simmonds
First Cop .... John Ford
Announcer's Voice .... Ted Thurston

Dancers: Ted Adkins, Robert Bakanic, Rhett Dennis, Sandra

Devlin, Bob Evans, Dick Gingrich, Ann Johnson, Sally Kirk, Sally Lee, Jack Leigh, Vernon Lusby, Rae McLean, Barbara Marcon, Pat Turner, Sandra Walsh, Marty Allen, Marc West.

Singers: Helen Baisley, Francine Bond, Austin Colyer, Clifford Fearl, John Ford, Carol Glade, Robert Lenn, Virginia Perlowin, Michael Roberts, Maggie Worth.

Time: the present. Place: the offices of the Modern Greeting Card Co., the Hotel Lavillere, a bar and Erwin's island.

Staged by Stanley Prager; dances and musical numbers staged by Onna White; settings and lighting by William and Jean Eckart; costumes by Guy Kent; musical director, Jay Blackton; vocal director, Jerry Packer; orchestrations by Raymond Jaimes; dance music arranged by Billy Goldenberg; production stage manager, Terence Little; stage manager, Ralph Linn; press, David Lipsky and Chester Fox. A meek little man, whose profession is writing poems for greeting cards, discovers he has a knack for picking winning horses, and is exploited by a group of shady characters.

ACT I

"Run, Run, Run" .... Singers and Dancers
"The Nicest Thing" .... Audrey
"Hey, Jimmy, Joe, John, Jim, Jack" .... Erwin
"Broads Ain't People" .... Erwin, Harry, Frankie, Charlie
"Let It Ride" .... Patsy, Singers and Dancers
"I'll Learn Ya" .... Erwin and Patsy
"Love Let Me Know" .... Audrey and Carver
"Happy Birthday" .... Birthday Girls
"Everything Beautiful" .... Erwin and Birthday Girls
"Who's Doing What to Erwin" .... Audrey, Chief Schermerhorn, Carver, Mother
"I Wouldn't Have Had To" .... Mabel

ACT II

"There's Something About a Horse" .... Singers and Dancers
"He Needs You" .... Erwin, Frankie, Charlie
"Just an Honest Mistake" .... Chief Schermerhorn, Repulski and Cops
"His Own Little Island" .... Erwin
"If Flutterby Wins" .... Erwin, Patsy, Frankie, Charlie, Harry, Hoods

(Closed December 9, 1961)

HOW TO SUCCEED IN BUSINESS WITHOUT REALLY TRYING

(262 performances)
(Continued)

Musical based on the novel by Shepherd Mead; book by Abe Burrows, Jack Weinstock and Willie Gilbert; music and lyrics by Frank Loesser. Produced by Feuer and Martin, in association with Frank Productions Inc., at the Forty-sixth Street Theatre, October 14, 1961.

Finch .... Robert Morse
Gatch .... Ray Mason
Jenkins .... Robert Kaliban
Tackaberry .... David Collyer
Peterson .... Casper Roos
J. B. Biggley .... Rudy Vallee
Rosemary .... Bonnie Scott
Bratt .... Paul Reed

Smitty .... Claudette Sutherland
Frump .... Charles Nelson Reilly
Miss Jones .... Ruth Kobart
Mr. Twimble .... Sammy Smith
Hedy .... Virginia Martin
Scrubwomen .... Mara Landi, Silver Saundors
Miss Krumholtz .... Mara Landi
Toynbee .... Ray Mason
Ovington .... Lanier Davis
Policeman .... Bob Murdock
Womper .... Sammy Smith

Singers: David Collyer, Lanier Davis, Robert Kaliban, Bob Murdock, Casper Roos, Charlotte Frazier, Mara Landi, Fairfax Mason, Silver Saundors, Maudeen Sullivan.

Dancers: Nick Andrews, Tracy Everitt, Stuart Fleming, Richard Korthaze, Dale Moreda, Darrell Notara, Merritt Thompson, Carol Jane Abney, Madilyn Clark, Elaine Cancilla, Suzanne France, Donna McKechnie, Ellie Somers, Rosemary Yellen.

Time: the present. Place: the Park Avenue offices of World Wide Wickets Company, Inc.

Staged by Mr. Burrows; musical staging by Bob Fosse; settings and lighting by Robert Randolph; costumes by Robert Fletcher; choreography by Hugh Lambert; musical direction by Elliot Lawrence; orchestrations by Robert Ginzler; production stage manager, Phil Friedman; stage manager, Lawrence N. Kasha; press, Merle Debuskey and Seymour Krawitz.

ACT I

"How To" .... Finch
"Happy to Keep His Dinner Warm" .... Rosemary
"Coffee Break" .... Frump, Smitty and Office Staff
"The Company Way" .... Finch and Mr. Twimble
"The Company Way" (Reprise) .... Frump, Mr. Twimble and Office Staff
"A Secretary Is Not a Toy" .... Bratt, Frump and Office Staff
"Been a Long Day" .... Finch, Rosemary and Smitty
"Been a Long Day" (Reprise) .... Biggley, Hedy and Frump
"Grand Old Ivy" .... Finch and Biggley
"Paris Original" .... Rosemary, Smitty, Miss Jones and Secretaries
"Rosemary" .... Finch and Rosemary
Finaletto .... Finch, Rosemary and Frump

ACT II

"Cinderella, Darling" .... Rosemary, Smitty and Secretaries
"Happy to Keep His Dinner Warm" (Reprise) .... Rosemary
"Love From a Heart of Gold" .... Biggley and Hedy
"I Believe in You" .... Finch, Frump, Bratt and Executives
"The Yo Ho Ho" .... The Jolly Wickets and Wickettes
"I Believe in You" (Reprise) .... Rosemary
"Brotherhood of Man" .... Finch, Biggley, Frump, Bratt, Womper, Miss Jones and Office Staff
Finale .... The Company

See page 64.

DO YOU KNOW THE MILKY WAY?

(16 performances)

Play by Karl Wittlinger. Produced by Ninon Tallon, Paul Feigay and Dick Button, by arrangement with the Vancouver International Festival, at the Billy Rose Theatre, October 16, 1961.

Dr. Neuross .... George Voskovec
The Man .... Hal Holbrook

The entire action of the play takes place in a sanatorium.

Staged by Herbert Berghof; setting by Colin Low; supervision and lighting by Lee Watson; costumes by Edith Lutyens Bel Geddes; music by Alex Fry; lyrics by Lyon Phelps; stage manager, Joseph Keating; press, Harvey B. Sabinson. A legally dead soldier of World War II returns home to find himself unwanted and is eventually destroyed by the cutthroat society that has taken over.

(Closed October 28, 1961)

A SHOT IN THE DARK

(258 performances)
(Continued)

Play by Marcel Achard, adapted by Harry Kurnitz. Produced by Leland Hayward at the Booth Theatre, October 18, 1961.

Paul Sevigne .... William Shatner
Morestan .... Gene Saks
Leblache .... Hugh Franklin
Antoinette Sevigne .... Diana van der Vlis
Josefa Lantenay .... Julie Harris
Dominique Beaurevers .... Louise Troy
Benjamin Beaurevers .... Walter Matthau
Guard .... Pierre Epstein

Time: the present. Place: the chamber of an examining magistrate in Paris.

Staged by Harold Clurman; setting and lighting by Ben Edwards; costumes by Noel Taylor; production stage manager, David Gray, Jr.; stage manager, Pierre Epstein; press, Frank Goodman and Ben Washer. Farce about a maid suspected of killing a chauffeur and an idealistic magistrate who believes her to be innocent.

A COOK FOR MR. GENERAL

(28 performances)

Play by Steven Gethers. Produced by William Darrid, Eleanore Saidenberg and Leonard Ruskin at the Playhouse, October 19, 1961.

General Rivers .... Roland Winters
Cook .... William Duell
Lt. Farley .... Thomas Carlin
Cpt. Chalmers .... Alan Bunce
Sgt. Potter .... Richard X. Slattery
Thomas Agganis .... Bill Travers
Thompson .... Otis Bigelow
Ridzinski .... Dustin Hoffman
Frank .... Fred Kareman
Sullivan .... Jonathan Lippe
Jordan .... George Furth
Walker .... Leo Morrell
Kroy .... Roberts Blossom
Arturi .... Allen F. Collins
Abrams .... Sam Lloyd
Fishwick .... Joe Gentry

Bradford .... Mike Gentry
Richards .... Paul B. Price
Goober .... Gerald O'Loughlin
Black .... Alek Primrose
Cpl. Mason .... Ed Maxcy
General Rivers' Aide .... Taugh O'Faillon
Guard .... Felix Munso
General Clayton .... John McGiver
Cpt. Moss .... James Karen
Law Officer .... Douglas Gordon
Prosecuting Captain .... Paul Sparer

Time: Summer, 1944. Place: Port Marino, an island in the Pacific.

Staged by Fielder Cook; settings and lighting by Will Steven Armstrong; costumes by J. Michael Travis; stage manager, Julian Barry; press, Abner D. Klipstein. The zany goings on in a Pacific rehabilitation center.

(Closed November 11, 1961)

KWAMINA

(32 performances)

Musical with book by Robert Alan Aurthur; music and lyrics by Richard Adler. Produced by Alfred de Liagre, Jr. at the Fifty-fourth Street Theatre, October 23, 1961.

Obitsebi .... Brock Peters
Blair .... Norman Barrs
Ako .... Robert Guillaume
Eve .... Sally Ann Howes
Naii .... Ethel Ayler
Akufo .... Joseph Attles
Kwamina (Peter) .... Terry Carter
Kojo .... Ainsley Sigmond
Children .... Vaughn Fubler, Renaye Fubler
Nana Mwalla .... Rex Ingram
Alla .... Rosalie Maxwell
Mammy Trader .... Lillian Hayman
Policemen .... Ronald Platts, Edward Thomas

Singers: Issa Arnal, Doreese DuQuan, Victoria Harrison, Lillian Hayman, Lee Hooper, Mary Louise, Rosalie Maxwell, Helen Phillips. Joseph Crawford, Scott Gibson, Wanza King, James Lowe, John Miles, Clark Morgan, Mal Scott, Rawn Spearman, George Tipton, Gordon Watkins, Arthur Wright.

Dancers: Hope Clarke, Doris deMendez, Altovise Gore, Minnie Marshall, Joan Peters, Lucinda Ransom, Joan Seabrook, Barbara Teer, Glory Van Scott, Myrna White, Camille Yarborough, Pepsi Bethel, Zebedee Collins, Julius Fields, Frank Glass, Louis Johnson, Charles Moore, Ronald Platts, Mike Quashie, Charles Queenan, Philip Stamps, Edward Thomas.

Drummers: Montego Joe, Robert Crowder.

Time: the present. Place: a village in West Africa.

Staged by Robert Lewis; dances and musical numbers staged by Agnes de Mille; setting and lighting by Will Steven Armstrong; costumes by Motley; music and choral direction by Colin Romoff; dance arrangements by John Morris; orchestrations by Sid Ramin and Irwin Kostal; technical consultant, Albert Opoku; production stage manager, James E. Wall; stage managers, Arthur Marlowe and William Weaver; press, Frank Goodman and Ben Washer. A miscegenatory love affair and the struggle of superstitious natives of a new African country to adjust to a modern way of life.

Sally Ann Howes and dancers in "Kwamina."

ACT I

"The Cocoa Bean Song" .... Robert Guillaume, Scott Gibson, Gordon Watkins and the Company
"Welcome Home" .... Scott Gibson, Mal Scott, Lee Hooper, Mike Quashie and the Company. Spear Dancers: Charles Moore, Charles Queenan. Fonga: Joan Seabrook, Barbara Teer, Glory Van Scott, Myrna White
"The Sun Is Beginning to Crow" .... The Company
"Did You Hear That?" .... Sally Ann Howes and Terry Carter
"You're As English As" .... Sally Ann Howes
"Seven Sheep, Four Red Shirts, and a Bottle of Gin" ...... Joseph Attles, Scott Gibson, Charles Queenan, George Tipton and the Company
"Nothing More to Look Forward To" .... Robert Guillaume and Ethel Ayler
"What's Wrong With Me?" .... Sally Ann Howes
"Something Big" .... Terry Carter and the Company
"Ordinary People" .... Sally Ann Howes and Terry Carter
Mammy Traders .... Glory Van Scott, Charles Moore, Zebedee Collins and Dancers
"A Man Can Have No Choice" .... Brock Peters
"What Happened to Me Tonight?" .... Sally Ann Howes

ACT II

Naii's Nuptial Dance .... Ethel Ayler, Hope Clarke and the Company

"One Wife" .... Lillian Hayman, Rosalie Maxwell, Issa Arnal, Victoria Harrison, Lee Hooper, Mary Louise, Helen Phillips and Dancers
"Nothing More to Look Forward To" (Reprise) .... Ethel Ayler
"Something Big" (Reprise) .... The Company
"Another Time, Another Place" .... Sally Ann Howes
Fetish .... Brook Peters, Zebedee Collins, Frank Glass, Charles Moore, Mike Quashie, Charles Queenan, Philip Stamps

(Closed November 18, 1961)

AN EVENING WITH YVES MONTAND

(55 performances)

A program of songs performed by M. Montand. Produced by Norman Granz, in association with Jacques Canetti and Alexander H. Cohen, and Salle Productions, Inc., at the John Golden Theatre, October 24, 1961.

Je Suis Venu a Pieds
Battling Joe
La Tete a l'Ombre
Une Demoiselle sur une Balancoire
Just in Time
Gilet Raye
Sous le Ciel de Paris
Le Carrosse
Les Grands Boulevards
Flamenco of Paris
Un Garçon Dansait
Mais Qu'Est-Ce Que J'Ai
I've Grown Accustomed to Her Face
Dis-Moi Jo
La Marie Vison
Planter Cafe
Le Chef d'Orchestre Est Amoureux
C'Est a l'Aube
Barbara (poem)
A Paris
Il Fait Des . . . le Fanatique du Jazz
Mon Manege a Moi

Staged and lighted by M. Montand; stage manager, John Effrat; press, Richard Maney and Martin Shwartz.

(Closed December 16, 1961)

LOOK: WE'VE COME THROUGH

(5 performances)

Play by Hugh Wheeler. Produced by Saint-Subber and Frank Prince, in association with David Black, at the Hudson Theatre, October 25, 1961.

Belle Dort .... Collin Wilcox
Jennifer Lewison .... Zohra Lampert
Wain Dumke .... Clinton Kimbrough
Miltie Mizer .... Zack Matalon
Bobby Kraweig .... Ralph Williams
Skip .... Burt Reynolds

Time: the present. Place: Bell's and Jennifer's apartment in Chelsea, Manhattan.

Staged by José Quintero; setting and lighting by David Hays; costumes by Ann Roth; production stage manager, Joseph Olney; stage manager, Ian Cadenhead; press, Harvey B. Sabinson. Two young people fall in love despite their knowledge that each has just suffered sordid sexual experiences.

(Closed October 28, 1961)

WRITE ME A MURDER

(196 performances)

Play by Frederick Knott. Produced by Compass Productions, Inc. at the Belasco Theatre, October 26, 1961.

The Hon. Clive Rodingham .... Denholm Elliott
Dr. Elizabeth Woolley .... Ethel Griffies
The Hon. David Rodingham .... James Donald
Charles Sturrock .... Torin Thatcher
Julie Sturrock .... Kim Hunter
Mr. Tibbit, the builder .... Robert Milli
Constable Hackett .... Herbert Voland
Two Men .... John D. Irving, Robert Milli

Time: the present. Place: Rodingham Manor, about two hours from London.

Staged by George Schaefer; setting by Warren Clymer; costumes by Noel Taylor; production stage manager, William Dodds; stage manager, Robert Milli; press, Sol Jacobson and Lewis Harmon. A professional writer concocts an ingenious murder to save an English estate.

(Closed April 14, 1962)

THE GARDEN OF SWEETS

(1 performance)

Play by Waldemar Hansen. Produced by Ben Frye and Irving Squires at the ANTA Theatre, October 31, 1961.

Stavro .... Lou Antonio
Ida .... Madeleine Sherwood
Alex .... Morgan Sterne
Helen .... Martine Bartlett
Nicky .... Ted Beniades
Sophie .... Eleni Kiamos
Penny .... Leslye Hunter
Ana Zachariadis (Manna) .... Katina Paxinou
Costa .... John Balzac
Father Athanasios .... Boris Tumarin
A Boy .... Alan Howard

Time: the present. Place: the Garden of Sweets, a Greek-American candy store and ice cream parlor, in a city on the Great Lakes.

Staged by Milton Katselas; setting by Boris Aronson; costumes by Patricia Zipprodt; lighting by Tharon Musser; music by John Balamos; production stage manager, Richard Blofson; stage manager, William Woodman; press, Harvey B. Sabinson. The owner of a confectionery store faces some unpleasant truths about her grown-up children.

(Closed October 31, 1961)

THE COMPLAISANT LOVER

(101 performances)

Play by Graham Greene. Produced by Irene Mayer Selznick, in association with H. M. Tennent Ltd., Donald Albery and F.E.S. Plays Ltd., at the Ethel Barrymore Theatre, November 1, 1961.

Victor Rhodes ....Michael Redgrave
William Howard ....George Turner
Clive Root ....Richard Johnson
Ann Howard ....Sandy Dennis
Margaret Howard ....Christine Thomas
Mary Rhodes ....Googie Withers
Robin Rhodes ....Nicholas Hammond
Hotel Valet ....Gene Wilder
Dr. Van Droog ....Bert Nelson

Time: the present. Place: the Rhodes' home in London and a hotel in Amsterdam.

Staged by Glen Byam Shaw; settings and costumes by Motley; lighting by Paul Morrison; production stage manager, Del Hughes; stage manager, Eugene Stuckmann; press, Arthur Cantor.

See page 92.

(Closed January 27, 1962)

KEAN

(92 performances)

Musical based on the play by Jean-Paul Sartre and the play by Alexandre Dumas; book by Peter Stone; music and lyrics by Robert Wright and George Forrest. Produced by Robert Lantz at the Broadway Theatre, November 2, 1961.

Christie ....Alfred DeSio
Barnaby ....Christopher Hewett
Edmund Kean ....Alfred Drake
Stage Manager ....Alfred Toigo
Ben ....Robert Penn
Francis ....Arthur Rubin
Solomon ....Truman Smith
Lord Neville ....Roderick Cook
Countess Elena De Koeberg ....Joan Weldon
Lady Amy Goswell ....Patricia Cutts
Count De Koeberg ....Patrick Waddington
Lord Delmore ....John Lankston
Major-Domo ....Martin Ambrose
Prince of Wales ....Oliver Gray
Anna Danby ....Lee Venora
Prop Boy ....Eddie Ericksen
Secretary ....Joseph McGrath
Maxwell ....Larry Shadur
Henchman ....Martin Ambrose
Pott ....George Harwell
St. Albands ....Rene Jarmon
Sparrow ....Margaret Gathright
Bolt ....Gloria Warner

Alfred Drake in "Kean."

Tim .... Randy Doney
David .... John Jordan
Pip .... Paul Jordon
Patrick .... Charles Dunn
Guards .... Larry Shadur, John Wheeler

Lords, ladies, stage hands, sailors, barmaids, prostitutes, street hawkers, servants and citizens of London.

Dancers: John Aristides, Barbara Beck, Johanna Carothers, Lois Castle, Charles Corbett, Kenneth Creel, Randy Doney, Judy Dunford, Larry Fuller, Mickey Gunnersen, Pamela Hayford, Jim Hutchison, Lisa James, Rene Jarmon, Richard Lyle, George Martin, Roger Puckett, Suanne Shirley.

Singers: Martin Ambrose, Charise Amidon, Charles Dunn, Eddie Ericksen, Nancy Foster, Margaret Gathright, Maggie Goz, George Harwell, John Lankston, Joseph McGrath, Lispet Nelson, Mary Nettum, Larry Shadur, Susan Terry, Alfred Toigo, Gloria Warner, John Wheeler.

Place: London. Time: early 19th Century.

Staged and choreographed by Jack Cole; settings and costumes by Ed Wittstein; lighting by John Harvey; musical direction and vocal arrangements by Pembroke Davenport; orchestrations by Philip J. Lang; ballet and incidental music by Elie Siegmeister; production stage manager, Peter Bronte; stage managers, Walter Neal and Malcolm Marmorstein; press, Harvey B. Sabinson. The famous 19th Century Shakespearean actor Edmund Kean shruggles for recognition and social acceptance as a human being rather than as a renowned actor.

ACT I

"Penny Plain, Twopence Colored" .... Christie
"Man and Shadow" .... Kean
"Mayfair Affair" .... Elena, Amy, Dancing and Singing Ensemble
"Sweet Danger" .... Elena and Kean
"Queue at Drury Lane" .... Barnaby, Ben, Francis, Ensemble
"King of London" .... Barnaby, Ben, Francis, Ensemble
"To Look Upon My Love" .... Kean and Solomon
"Let's Improvise" .... Kean and Anna

"Elena" .... Kean, Francis, Ensemble
"Social Whirl" .... Elena, Amy, Prince, Count
"The Fog and the Grog" .... Barnaby, Ben, Francis, Kean, Ensemble

ACT II

"Civilized People" .... Kean, Anna, Elena
"Service for Service" .... Elena and Kean
"Willow, Willow, Willow" .... Anna
"Fracas at Old Drury"... Barnaby, Ben, Francis, Christie, Ensemble
"Chime In!" .... Christie, Barnaby, Ben, Francis, Ensemble
"Swept Away" .... Elena and Kean
"Domesticity" .... Anna and Kean
"Clown ot London" .... Ensemble
"Apology?" .... Kean

(Closed January 20, 1962)

GIDEON

(233 performances)
(Continued)

Play by Paddy Chayefsky. Produced by Fred Coe and Arthur Cantor at the Plymouth Theatre, November 9, 1961.

Joash .... Mitchell Jason
Helek .... Martin Garner
Ahimelech .... Victor Kilian
Jether .... Robert Weiss
Gideon .... Douglas Campbell
Angel .... Fredric March
Shillem .... Eric Berry
Jahleel .... David Hooks
Hezekiah .... Alan Manson
Malchiel .... Mark Lenard
Purah .... George Segal
Zebah .... Alan Bergmann
Zalmunna .... Paul Marin
Shethulah .... Edward K. Holmes
Ozni .... David Hooks
Orpah .... Lorraine Egypt

Soldiers and women of Manasseh and Succoth: Bernard Chessler, Tom Klunis, Amnon Meskin, Meir Ovadia, Florence Anglin, Anna Berger, Bathsheba Garnett, Gubi Mann, Ilene Tema.

Time: 1100 B.C. The action of the play takes place in the tent of Joash, a hill at Harod, the ford at Beth Barah and near the city of Succoth.

Staged by Tyrone Guthrie; settings and lighting by David Hays; costumes by Domingo A. Rodriguez; production stage manager, Porter Van Zandt; stage manager, George Thorn; press, Gertrude Kirschner and Tony Geiss.

See page 109.

THE GAY LIFE

(113 performances)

Musical suggested by Arthur Schnitzler's "Anatol"; book by Fay and Michael Kanin; music and lyrics by Arthur Schwartz and Howard Dietz. Produced by Kermit Bloomgarden at the Sam S. Shubert Theatre, November 18, 1961.

Max .... Jules Munshin
Usher .... Sterling Clark
Anatol .... Walter Chiari
Franz .... Leonard Elliott
Helene .... Jeanne Bal
Liesl Brandel .... Barbara Cook
Herr Brandel .... Loring Smith
Frau Brandel .... Lu Leonard
Mimi .... Yvonne Constant
Proprietor .... Michael Quinn
The Great Gaston .... Jack Adams
Otto .... Rico Froehlich
Waiters .... Ted Lambrinos, Russell Goodwin
Anna .... Joanne Spiller
Grandmother .... Aura Vainio
Photographer .... Gerald Teijelo
Doorman .... Rico Froehlich
Headwaiter .... Carl Nicholas
Waiters .... Hal Norman, Ted Lambrinos
Magda .... Elizabeth Allen

Singers: Ken Ayers, Russell Goodwin, Tony LaRusso, Ted Lambrinos, Carl Nicholas, Hal Norman, Michael Quinn, Loyce Baker, Joan Bishop, June Card, Luce Ennis, Jeanne Grant, Carole O'Hara, Nancy Radcliffe, Joanne Spiller.

Dancers: Kip Andrews, Karoly Barta, Sterling Clark, Thatcher Clarke, Ray Kirchner, Louis Kosman, Michel Stuart, Gerald Teijelo, Patrick King, Bonnie Brandon, Carolyn Clark, Marion Fels, Carol Flemming, Leslie Franzos, Bettye Jenkins, Doris Ortiz, Eleanore Treiber, Aura Vainio, Jenny Workman.

Time: 1904. Place: Venice.

Staged by Gerald Freedman; musical numbers and dances staged by Herbert Ross; settings by Oliver Smith; costumes by Lucinda Ballard; lighting by Jean Rosenthal; orchestrations by Don Walker; vocal arrangements and musical director, Herbert Greene; dance arrangements by Robert Starer; production stage manager, Kermit Kegley; stage manager, Cliff Cothren; press, Dick Weaver. A Viennese playboy subsides into marriage.

ACT I

"What a Charming Couple" .... Ensemble
"Why Go Anywhere at All?" .... Helene
"Bring Your Darling Daughter" .... Max and Ensemble
"Now I'm Ready for a Frau" .... Anatol and Max
Frau Ballet .... Shy Girl, Tennis Girl, Mountain Climbers and Girl on Horseback
"Magic Moment" .... Liesl
"Who Can? You Can" .... Anatol and Liesl
"Oh, Mein Liebchen" .... Ensemble
Liebchen Waltz .... Jenny Workman, Leslie Franzos, Thatcher Clarke, Aura Vainio, Louis Kosman, Sterling Clark and Ensemble
"The Label on the Bottle" .... Liesl
(Danced by Louis Kosman, Ray Kirchner, Michel Stuart)
"This Kind of a Girl" .... Anatol and Liesl
"The Bloom Is Off the Rose" .... Max and Male Ensemble
"Who Can? You Can" (Reprise) .... Ensemble
"Now I'm Ready for a Frau" (Reprise) .... Anatol
"Magic Moment" (Reprise) .... Liesl

ACT II

"I'm Glad I'm Single" .... Max and Male Ensemble
"I'm Glad I'm Single" (Reprise) .... Male Ensemble
"Now I'm Ready for a Frau" (Reprise) .... Anatol and Max
"Something You Never Had Before" .... Liesl
"You Will Never Be Lonely" .... Frau Brandel, Herr Brandel and Ensemble
"You're Not the Type" .... Anatol and Liesl

"Come A-Wandering With Me" .... Magda and Male Dancers
"I Never Had a Chance" .... Anatol
"I Wouldn't Marry You" .... Liesl
"For the First Time" .... Anatol

(Closed February 24, 1962)

A MAN FOR ALL SEASONS

(218 performances)
(Continued)

Play by Robert Bolt. Produced by Robert Whitehead and Roger L. Stevens, by arrangement with H. M. Tennent, Ltd., at the ANTA Theatre, November 22, 1961.

The Common Man .... George Rose
Sir Thomas More .... Paul Scofield
Richard Rich .... William Redfield
The Duke of Norfolk .... Albert Dekker
Alice More .... Carol Goodner
Margaret More .... Olga Bellin
Cardinal Wolsey .... Jack Creley
Thomas Cromwell .... Leo McKern
Signor Chapuys, the Spanish Ambassador .... David J. Stewart
His Attendant .... John Colenback
William Roper .... Peter Brandon
King Henry VIII .... Keith Baxter
The Woman .... Sarah Burton
Cranmer, Archbishop of Canterbury .... Lester Rawlins

Time: the 16th Century. Place: England.

Staged by Noel Willman; settings and costumes by Motley; lighting by Paul Morrison; production stage manager, Frederic de Wilde; stage manager, Howard Fischer; press, Barry Hyams.

See page 124.

SUNDAY IN NEW YORK

(188 performances)

Play by Norman Krasna. Produced by David Merrick at the Cort Theatre, November 29, 1961.

Adam Taylor .... Conrad Janis
Eileen Taylor .... Pat Stanley
Man .... Pat Harrington, Sr.
Woman .... Sondra Lee
Mike Mitchell .... Robert Redford
Russell Wilson .... Ron Nicholas

Time: the present. Place: New York City.

Staged by Garson Kanin; settings and lighting by David Hays; costumes by Patricia Zipprodt; production stage manager, David M. Pardoll; stage manager, Richard Roat; press, Harvey B. Sabinson.

A young girl, who has successfully resisted her fiance's attempts to seduce her, comes to New York and is seduced by a newspaper reporter.

(Closed May 12, 1962)

Emlyn Williams, Rip Torn, Janet Margolin and William Hansen in "Daughter of Silence."

DAUGHTER OF SILENCE

(36 performances)

Play by Morris L. West, adapted from his novel of the same name. Produced by Richard Halliday at the Music Box Theatre, November 30, 1961.

Gianbattista Rosati	Norman Shelly
Sergeant Manzoni	Vincent Gardenia
Carrese	Jeremiah Morris
Fra Bonifacio	William Hansen
Anna Albertini	Janet Margolin
Maria Rosati	Ruth Volner
Valeria	Joanne Linville
Louisa	Barbara Scaasi
Antonio	Al Viola
Carlo	Rip Torn
Ascolini	Emlyn Williams
Francesco	Dino Terranova
Deodato	Paul Rufo
The Prosecutor	Frederic Tozere
President of the Court	Geoffrey Lumb
Clerk of the Court	V. D. Hughe
Luigi	Vincent Baggetta

Professor Emilio Galuzzi ....Joe De Santis
Maddalena Barone ....Barbara Hayes
Judges ....Robert J. Lance, Allan Frank
Assistant to the Prosecutor ....Daniel Ades
Assistant to the Defense ....Frank Savino

Villagers: Lynn Morris, Frank Savino, Robert J. Lance, Daniel Ades, Salvatore Lombardo.

Time: the present. Place: San Stefano, Tuscany.

Staged by Vincent J. Donehue; settings by Oliver Smith; costumes by Helene Pons and Mr. Smith; lighting by Jean Rosenthal; production stage manager, Randall Brooks; stage manager, Paul Bertelsen; press, Frank Goodman and Ben Washer. A young lawyer undertakes as his first case the defense of a girl on trial for the revenge murder of the town mayor, and by winning an acquittal he also wins the respect of his wife and peers.

(Closed December 30, 1961)

TAKE HER, SHE'S MINE

(185 performances)
(Continued)

Play by Phoebe and Henry Ephron. Produced by Harold S. Prince at the Biltmore Theatre, December 21, 1961.

Principal ....Nicholas Saunders
Mollie Michaelson ....Elizabeth Ashley
Frank Michaelson ....Art Carney
Anne Michaelson ....Phyllis Thaxter
Liz Michaelson ....June Harding
Airline Clerk ....Ron Welsh
Emmett ....Stephen Paley
Adele McDougall ....Jean McClintock
Sarah Walker ....Louise Sorel
Donn Bowdry ....Tom Brannum
First Freshman ....Marty Huston
Second Freshman ....Ron Welsh
Richard Gluck ....Walter Moulder
Alfred Greiffinger ....Paul Geary
Alex Loomis ....Richard Jordan
Mr. Whitmyer ....Heywood Hale Broun
Linda Lehman ....Susan Stein
Clancy ....Joe Ponazecki
Mr. Hibbetts ....Ferdi Hoffman

Time: the present. Place: Southern California and New England.

Staged by George Abbott; settings and lighting by William and Jean Eckart; costumes by Florence Klotz; production stage manager, Ruth Mitchell; stage manager, Paul J. Phillips; press, Sol Jacobson and Lewis Harmon. Comedy about a father's frustrations and bewilderment when his daughter goes away to college.

FIRST LOVE

(24 performances)

Play by Samuel Taylor, based on the memoir "Promise at Dawn" by Romain Gary. Produced by Roger L. Stevens and Frederick

Brisson, in association with Samuel Taylor, at the Morosco Theatre, December 25, 1961.

Romain .... Hugh O'Brian
The Boy .... Claude Gersene
Nina Kacew .... Lili Darvas
A Police Sergeant .... Bert Conway
A Policeman .... Peter Gumeny
First Schoolboy .... Dale Whitman
Second Schoolboy .... Peter de Vise
First Moving Man .... Brendan Fay
Second Moving Man .... Dale Johnson
Violin Master .... Guy Arbury
Shooting Master .... Dan Keyes
Fencing Master .... Chet London
The Grand Duke .... Boris Marshalov
The Adolescent .... Rex Thompson
Mariette .... Sasha von Scherler
The Tennis Club Secretary .... Dan Keyes
The King of Sweden .... Reynolds Evans
A Tennis Coach .... Chet London
Ivan Malekhine .... Sandor Szabo
A Waiter .... Guy Arbury
Rene Bouchard .... Tim O'Connor
Ilyena .... Zohra Lampert
Rinaldi .... Jack Bittner
First Airman .... Bert Conway
Second Airman .... Dan Keyes
Third Airman .... Guy Arbury
Captain Moulignat .... Dale Johnson
Fourth Airman .... Peter Gumeny
Fifth Airman .... Chet London
Sixth Airman .... Brendan Fay
Hotel Proprietor .... Guy Arbury
Hotel Waiter .... Dan Keyes

Place: Poland, France, the World. Time: present and past.

Staged by Alfred Lunt; settings and lighting by Donald Oenslager; costumes by Theoni V. Aldredge; dramatic sound-score composed by Charles Paul; production stage manager, Fred Hebert; stage manager, Robert Crawley; press, Samuel Lurie. Autobiographical play in which we are shown how Gary's mother by ruthless determination made her son what he is today.

(Closed January 13, 1962)

ROSS

(159 performances)

Play by Terence Rattigan. Produced by David Merrick, by arrangement with H. M. Tennent, Ltd., at the Eugene O'Neill Theatre, December 26, 1961.

Flight Lieutenant Stoker .... Robert Milli
Flight Sergeant Thompson .... Ted Gunther
Aircraftman Parsons .... Bill Glover
Aircraftman Nolan .... Dennis Cooney
Aircraftman Dickinson .... Francis Bethencourt
Aircraftman Ross .... John Mills
Franks, the lecturer .... Kenneth Ruta
General Allenby .... John Williams
Ronald Storrs .... Anthony Nicholls
Colonel Barrington .... Court Benson
Auda Abu Tayi .... Paul Sparer

The Turkish Military Governor, Deraa District ...... Geoffrey Keen
Hamed ...... Cal Bellini
Rashid ...... Joseph Della Sorte
A Turkish Captain ...... Eric Van Nuys
A Turkish Sergeant ...... Thomas Newman
A British Corporal ...... Del Tenney
A.D.C. ...... Nicolas Coster
A Photographer ...... Scott Graham
An Australian Soldier ...... John Hallow
Flight Lieutenant Higgins ...... James Valentine
Group Captain Wood ...... James Craven

The action of the play begins and ends at a Royal Air Force depot near London, on an afternoon, the same night and the following morning of a day in winter, 1922. The central passages cover the period 1916-1918 and are set in the Middle East.

Staged by Glen Byam Shaw; settings and costumes by Motley; lighting by Al Alloy; production stage manager, Ross Bowman; stage manager, Edward Hastings; press, Harvey B. Sabinson. The life and career of Laurence of Arabia showing how he succeeded in organizing the Arabs against the Turks, his painful discovery of his latent homosexuality, and his subsequent attempts to escape from public attention by enlisting in the RAF as a private.

(Closed May 12, 1962)

SUBWAYS ARE FOR SLEEPING

(178 performances)
(Continued)

Musical suggested by the book by Edmund G. Love; book and lyrics by Betty Comden and Adolph Green; music by Jule Styne. Produced by David Merrick at the St. James Theatre, December 27, 1961.

The Sleepers .... Gene Varrone, Cy Young, Bob Gorman, John Sharpe
Myra Blake ...... Grayson Hall
Angela McKay ...... Carol Lawrence
Tom Bailey ...... Sydney Chaplin
Station Guard ...... Robert Howard
J. Edward Sykes ...... Joe Hill
Bill ...... Anthony Saverino
Harry Shelby ...... Eugene R. Wood
Gus Holt ...... Cy Young
Charlie Smith ...... Orson Bean
Jack ...... Gene Varrone
A Drunk ...... Jim Weiss
Max Hillman ...... Gene Varrone
Martha Vail ...... Phyllis Newman
Mr. Pitman ...... Gordon Connell
A Delivery Boy ...... Michael Bennett
Lancelot Zuckerman ...... Horase
Freddie ...... Bob Gorman
Mac, a caretaker ...... John Sharpe
Social Worker ...... Joe Hill
Photographer ...... John Sharpe
The Models ...... Sari Clymas, Diane Ball
Teenagers ...... John Sharpe, Michael Bennett
Zack Flint ...... Lawrence Pool
Lt. Pilsudski ...... Robert Howard
Mary Tompkins ...... Dean Taliaferro
Joe, the museum guard ...... Anthony Saverino
Relief Doorman ...... Robert Howard

Orson Bean, Sydney Chaplin, Carol Lawrence and Phyllis Newman in "Subways Are for Sleeping."

Mr. Barney .... Joe Hill

Singers: Helen Baisley, Vicki Belmonte, Bob Gorman, Stokely Gray, Joe Hill, Robert Howard, Jeannine Michael, Bruce Payton, Anthony Saverino, Joan Sheller, Ruth Shepard.

Dancers: Diane Ball, Carlos Bas, Michael Bennett, Pepe de Chazza, Sari Clymas, Joel Craig, Robert Evans, Ted Forlow, Valerie Harper, Reby Howells, Gene Kelton, Victoria Mansfield, Wendy Nickerson, Larry Roquemore, Sandra Roveta, Ron Stratton, Dean Taliaferro, Jim Weiss.

Time: the present. Place: around New York City.

Staged and choreographed by Michael Kidd; settings and lighting by Will Steven Armstrong; costumes by Freddy Wittop; musical direction by Milton Rosenstock; orchestrations by Philip J. Lang; associate choreographer, Marc Breaux; dance music arranged by Peter Howard; production stage manager, Howard Whitfield; stage manager, Joe Calvan; press, Harvey B. Sabinson. A romance between a fashion magazine reporter and a gentleman hobo.

ACT I

"Subways Are for Sleeping" .... The Sleepers
"Girls Like Me" .... Angie
"Station Rush" .... People Who Are Going Places
"I'm Just Taking My Time" .... Tom
"I Was a Shoo-In" .... Martha
"Subway Directions" .... Tom, Angie and Subway Riders
"Ride Through the Night" .... Tom, Angie and Subway Riders
"Who Knows What Might Have Been" .... Angie and Tom
"Swing Your Projects" .... Tom
"Strange Duet" .... Martha and Charlie
"I Said It and I'm Glad" .... Angie
"Be a Santa" .... Tom, Angie, Shoppers and Santas

ACT II

"Subway Incident" .... Angie and Teenagers
"How Can You Describe a Face?" .... Tom

"I Just Can't Wait" .... Charlie
"Comes Once in a Lifetime" .... Angie and Tom
"What Is This Feeling in the Air?" .... Tom, Angie, Charlie and Entire Company

THE NIGHT OF THE IGUANA

(177 performances)
(Continued)

Play by Tennessee Williams. Produced by Charles Bowden, in association with Violla Rubber, at the Royale Theatre, December 28, 1961.

Pancho .... Christopher Jones
Maxine Faulk .... Bette Davis
Pedro .... James Farentino
The Reverend T. Lawrence Shannon .... Patrick O'Neal
Wolfgang .... Bruce Glover
Hilda .... Laryssa Lauret
Herr Fahrenkopf .... Heinz Hohenwald
Frau Fahrenkopf .... Lucy Landau
Hank .... Theseus George
Miss Judith Fellowes .... Patricia Roe
Hannah Jelkes .... Margaret Leighton
Charlotte Goodall .... Lane Bradbury
Nonno (Jonathan Coffin) .... Alan Webb
Jake Latta .... Louis Guss

Time: Summer, 1940. Place: the Costa Verde Hotel in Puerto Barrio, on the west coast of Mexico.

Staged by Frank Corsaro; setting by Oliver Smith; costumes by Noel Taylor; lighting by Jean Rosenthal; audio effects by Edward Beyer; stage manager, John Maxtone-Graham; press, Frank Goodman and Ben Washer.

See page 170.

THE CAPTAINS AND THE KINGS

(7 performances)

Play by Leo Lieberman. Produced by Theatre Guild Productions, Inc. and Joel Schenker, by arrangement with John Gerstad, at the Playhouse Theatre, January 2, 1962.

Lt. Endicott .... Robert Kenneally
Richard Kohner .... Dana Andrews
Carl Romano .... Joseph Campanella
Jordan .... Joseph Sullivan
Rose Collins .... Lee Grant
Joe Bradley .... Peter Graves
Shore Patrolman .... Thomas Ruisinger
Admiral Howard Bradley .... Conrad Nagel
Senator Norris Wrightson .... Charlie Ruggles
Admiral Cook .... Robert N. Terry
Admiral Swanson .... William Swetland
Admiral Gregg (Ret.) .... Warren Wade
Admiral Benton .... Stephen Chase

Dana Andrews, Charlie Ruggles, Conrad Nagel, Lee Grant and Peter Graves in "The Captains and the Kings."

Admiral Hall .... Alexander Clark
Admiral Riggs .... Wayne Wilson
Harry Locke .... Gavin MacLeod
Lt. Whitmore .... Thomas Ruisinger

Time: 1956. Place: the office room of Project L J 8 and the Army-Navy Club.

Staged by Joseph Anthony; settings, costumes and lighting by James Trittipo; production stage manager, Bill Ross; stage manager, Loy Nilson; press, Karl Bernstein and Ben Kornzweig. An unpopular Admiral tries to make the Navy believe in the effectiveness of nuclear submarine warfare.

(Closed January 6, 1962)

SOMETHING ABOUT A SOLDIER

(12 performances)

Play by Ernest Kinoy, based on the novel by Mark Harris. Produced by the Theatre Guild and Dore Schary, by arrangement with Herbert Brodkin, at the Ambassador Theatre, January 4, 1962.

Jacob ....Sal Mineo
Ananoka ....David Doyle
Toat ....Ralph Meeker
Captain Dodd ....Kevin McCarthy
Joleen Davis ....Gretchen Walther
Carmichael ....Ken Kercheval
Pop Davis ....Robert Donley
M.P. ....Carl Reindel
Candy Butcher ....Sid Raymond
Air Cadet ....Anthony Roberts
Intelligence Officer ....Alan Mixon
Ward Boy ....John Crowther

Soldiers: Murray Levy, Jeb Schary, John Crowther, Carl Reindel, Anthony Roberts.

Time: Spring to Winter, 1942. Place: Fort Smeed, Georgia.

Staged by Mr. Schary; settings and costumes by William Pitkin; lighting by Klaus Holm; stage manager, Harry Young; press, Nat Dorfman. Comedy about a World War II army training center and an awkward recruit with a high I.Q.

(Closed January 13, 1962)

GIANTS, SONS OF GIANTS

(9 performances)

Play by Joseph Kramm. Produced by Charles A. Totero and William F. Cioffi at the Alvin Theatre, January 6, 1962.

George ....Perry Skaar
Marianne ....Peggy Lang
Bennett ....Alfred Toigo
Myra Brisset .... Nancy Kelly
Mrs. Elder ....Eda Heinemann
Mr. Maguire ....Harry Gresham
Frank Brisset ....Claude Dauphin
Logan Harvey ....Franklin Cover
Alex Wilkins ....Paul McGrath
Edward Fenner ....Tom Shirley
Libby ....Robin Adair
Klinger ....Woodrow Parfrey
Lucy Harvey ....Lori March
Gensup ....Al Saxe
Mrs. Gensup ....Bette Henritze
Burke Harrison ....John Call
Maid ....Renne Jarrett
Club Attendant ....Glenn Walken

The action of the play takes place in a small American city.

Staged by Mr. Kramm; settings by Peter Larkin; lighting by Tharon Musser; costumes by Edith Lutyens Bel Geddes; production stage manager, Ben Janney; stage manager, Converse M. Converse; press, Abner D. Klipstein. A doctor has an ambition to build a great clinic, but he destroys the project just as it is being realized.

(Closed January 13, 1962)

THE EGG

(8 performances)

Play by Felicien Marceau, translated by Robert Schlitt. Produced by Zev Bufman, Alexander Ince and Pierre Cossette at the Cort Theatre, January 8, 1962.

Emile Magis ....Dick Shawn
The Doctor ....Frederick Rolf
Barbedart ....Lou Gilbert
Jacques ....Arnold Soboloff
Girl in Park ....Vilma Auld
Woman in Subway ....Mabel Albertson
Woman in Cafe ....Janet Ward
Young Girl ....Marcia Levant
Customer ....James Beard
Dufiquet ....Michael Vale
Mlle. Duvant ....Mabel Albertson
Justine ....Sudie Bond
The Mother ....Paddy Edwards
Gustave ....Michael Constantine
Waiter ....James Beard
Georgette ....Marcia Levant
Rose ....Janet Ward
Eugene ....Michael Constantine
Card Player ....Arnold Soboloff
Berthoullet ....Michael Vale
Mme. Berthoullet ....Mabel Albertson
Charlotte ....Marcia Levant
Lucy ....Lola Lynch
Heloise ....Paddy Edwards
Uncle ....Lou Gilbert
Raffard ....Frederick Rolf
Joseph ....Arnold Soboloff
Dugommier ....Frederick Rolf
Concierge ....Lola Lynch
Prosecutor ....Arnold Soboloff
Defense Attorney ....Michael Vale
Judge ....Lou Gilbert
Photographer ....James Beard
Gendarmes ....George Poulas, Harold Spelvin
Court Clerk ....Don Dwyer

Staged by Lamont Johnson; production designed by Robert Kelly; costumes by Ray Aghayan; lighting by Bob Brannigan; background music by Gerald Fried; stage manager, Chris Ryan; press, Bill Doll.

See page 188.

(Closed January 13, 1962)

ROMULUS

(69 performances)

Play by Friedrich Duerrenmatt, adapted by Gore Vidal. Produced by Roger L. Stevens, in association with Henry Guettel, at the Music Box Theatre, January 10, 1962.

Titus .... James Olson
Pyramus .... Francis Compton
Achilles .... Russell Collins
Romulus .... Cyril Ritchard
Chef .... Dolph Sweet
Tullius .... William Le Massena
Apollonius .... Graham Jarvis
Julia .... Cathleen Nesbitt
Rea .... Suzanne Osborne
Metellus .... George S. Irving
Zeno .... Earl Montgomery
Aemilian .... Ted van Griethuysen
Otto Rupf .... Fred Stewart
Ottaker .... Howard Da Silva
Theodoric .... Edwin Sherin
First Gothic Soldier .... Allan Miller
Second Gothic Soldier .... Dolph Sweet
Other Gothic Soldiers .... Drew Elliott, Michael O'Reilly, Harvey Vincent

Time: March, 476 A.D. Place: the villa of the Emperor Romulus at Tivoli, near Rome.

Staged by Joseph Anthony; settings by Oliver Smith; costumes by Lucinda Ballard; lighting by Peggy Clark; production stage manager, Leonard Patrick; stage manager, Michael Sinclair; press, Samuel Lurie. A Roman emperor allows his country to be conquered because he is disgusted with its decay.

(Closed March 10, 1962)

A FAMILY AFFAIR

(65 performances)

Musical with book, music and lyrics by James Goldman, John Kander and William Goldman. Produced by Andrew Siff at the Billy Rose Theatre, January 27, 1962.

Sally Nathan .... Rita Gardner
Gerry Siegal .... Larry Kert
Alfie Nathan .... Shelley Berman
Morris Siegal .... Morris Carnovsky
Tilly Siegal .... Eileen Heckart
Mrs. Forsythe .... Paula Trueman
Mother Lederer .... Lulu Bates
Babs Sanditz .... Beryl Towbin
Selma Siegal .... Barbara Ann Walters
Cindy .... Joan Lowe
Jenny Stone .... Cathryn Damon
Irma .... Kelli Scott
Wilma .... Linda Lavin
Betty Jane .... Carolsue Shaer
Marie Rose .... Judi West
Crying Daughter .... Linda Lavin
Mother .... Alice Nunn
Christopher Sanditz .... Randy Garfield
Mr. Weaver .... Jack De Lon
Wolfgang Demott .... Sam Greene
Kenwood Sanditz .... Bill McDonald
Morton Lederer .... Ferdinand Hilt
Bernice Lederer .... Lynne Charnay
Milton Lederer .... Bill Linton
Helene Lederer .... Yettanda Enelow
Simon Lederer .... Don Crabtree
Emil Lederer .... Eddie Becker

Big Sadie Lederer .... Jean Bruno
Little Sadie Lederer .... Maggie Task
Sports Announcer .... Sam Greene
Miss Lumpe .... Bibi Osterwald
Harry Latz .... Gino Conforti
Fifi of Paris .... Linda Lavin
Brash Girl .... Charlene Carter
Quiet Girl .... Linda Lavin
Stop and Shop Answering Service .... Alice Nunn

Singers: Eddie Becker, Theodora Brandon, Jean Bruno, Yettanda Enelow, Sam Greene, Linda Lavin, Gary Leatherman, Ripple Lewis, Alice Nunn, Kelli Scott, Maggie Task, Barbara Ann Walters.

Dancers: Tom Abbott, Robert Bishop, Charlene Carter, Jeremy Ives, Bob La Crosse, Carolsue Shaer, Judi West.

Time: the present. Place: Chicago and its suburbs.

Staged by Harold Prince; choreography by John Butler; musical numbers staged by Bob Herget; settings and lighting by David Hays; costumes by Robert Fletcher; musical and vocal direction by Stanley Lebowsky; orchestrations by Robert Ginzler; dance music arranged by Gerald Alters; production stage manager, Richard Evans; stage manager, James Bronson; press, Harvey B. Sabinson. A comic battle between the guardian of a prospective bride and the parents of the groom over the wedding preparations.

ACT I

"Anything for You" .... Gerry and Sally
"Beautiful" .... Alfie
"Beautiful" (Reprise) .... Tilly
"My Son, the Lawyer" ..... Tilly, Mother Lederer, Babs and Ladies
"Every Girl Wants to Get Married" .... Sally and Babs
"Right Girls" ..... Alfie, Mr. Weaver and the Gentlemen of the Gym
(Staged by John Butler)
"Kalua Bay" .... Tilly and Morris
"There's a Room in My House" .... Gerry and Sally
"Siegal Marching Song" .... Babs and her Family
"Nathan Marching Song" .... Alfie and his Friends
"Harmony" .... Miss Lumpe, Mr. Weaver, Harry and Fifi

ACT II

"Now, Morris" .... Morris
"Wonderful Party" .... Gerry and Kenny
"Revenge" .... Alfie and the Voices
(Staged by John Butler)
"Summer Is Over" .... Tillie
"Harmony" (Reprise) ..... Alfie, Tilly, Miss Lumpe and their Staffs
"I'm Worse Than Anybody" .... Tilly, Morris and Alfie
"What I Say Goes" .... Gerry
"The Wedding" .... Everybody

(Closed March 25, 1962)

A PASSAGE TO INDIA

(109 performances)

Play by Santha Rama Rau, adapted from the novel by E. M. Forster. Produced by Theatre Guild Productions, Inc., Robert Fryer, Lawrence Carr and John Herman, by arrangement with Donald Albery and Tennent Productions, Ltd., London, at the Ambassador Theatre, January 31, 1962.

Dr. Aziz .... Zia Mohyeddin
Mr. Fielding .... Eric Portman

Mrs. Moore .... Gladys Cooper
Miss Adela Quested .... Anne Meacham
Professor Godbole .... Saeed Jaffrey
Ronny Heaslop .... Louis Edmonds
A Guide .... Wally Peterson
Mr. McBryde .... Donald Moffat
Mrs. Callendar .... Dorothy Blackburn
Mrs. Turton .... Joan White
Mrs. Burton .... Margaret Braidwood
A Lieutenant .... David O'Brien
Mrs. McBryde .... Maureen Hurley
Dr. Callender .... Patrick Hines
Mr. Turton .... Robin Craven
Mr. Burton .... Albert Quinton
Mr. Hamidullah .... James Coco
Mr. Amritrao .... Noel Davis
Mr. Das .... Leonardo Cimino

Servants, guards and spectators: Frank Lauria, Ralph Lee, Philip Magdalany, Valerie Paone, Tony Converse, Hugh Faegan, Gene Gordon, Larry Kamm, David Kurzon, Joan Lauria, Nick Malekos.

Time: April of a year in the early 1920's. Place: the small provincial town of Chandrapore in Eastern India.

Staged by Donald McWhinnie; settings and costumes by Rouben Ter-Arutunian; lighting by John Harvey; stage managers, Edward Stevlingson and Kenneth Mays; press, Nat Dorfman. A young Indian doctor tries to make friends with some sympathetic Britishers and learns through sad experience that the British are his enemy.

(Closed May 5, 1962)

NEW FACES OF 1962

(28 performances)

Revue with music and lyrics mostly by June Carroll, Arthur Siegel, David Rogers, Mark Bucci, Jack Holmes and Ronny Graham; sketches mostly by Ronny Graham, Paul Lynde, Jean Shepherd, Richard Maury, Joey Carter and R. G. Brown. Produced by Carroll and Harris Masterson at the Alvin Theatre, February 1, 1962.

Tom Arthur	Patti Karr
Charles Barlow	Sylvia Lord
R. G. Brown	Erin Martin
Joey Carter	Marian Mercer
Jim Corbett	James Moore
Juan Carlos Copes	Maria Nieves
Michael Fesco	Sylvia
Travis Hudson	Joan Thornton
Helene Kardon	Mickey Wayland

Entire production conceived and directed by Leonard Sillman; sketches co-staged by Richard Maury; choreography mostly by James Moore; settings and lighting by Marvin Reiss; costumes by Thomas Becher; orchestrations by Jay Bower, Mark Bucci, Sy Oliver, Ted Royal, David Terry; dance arrangements by Jack Holmes; musical director, Abba Bogin; stage manager, Lo Hardin; press, Betty Lee Hunt.

ACT I

"Opening" .... The Entire Company
(Lyrics and music by Ronny Graham; dialogue by Joey Carter; introduction by Jim Corbett; choreography by James Moore)

Quickies
The Reds Visit Mount Vernon (By Paul Lynde)
(Introduction) .... Patti Karr
Father .... R. G. Brown
Mother .... Marian Mercer
George .... Joey Carter
"Moral Rearmament" ..... Travis Hudson, James Moore, Tom Arthur
(Lyrics and music by Jack Holmes)
"Pi in the Sky" (By Jean Shepherd; music by Mark Bucci)
(Introduction) .... Sylvia
Pilot .... Michael Fesco
Stewardesses .... Maria Nieves, Mickey Wayland
Passengers .... Patti Karr, James Moore, Erin Martin, Charles Barlow, Joan Thornton, R. G. Brown, Marian Mercer, Michael Fesco, Helen Kardon, Jim Corbett
"In the Morning" .... Sylvia Lord
(Lyrics and music by Ronny Graham)
"Happiness" (Lyrics by David Rogers; music by Marie Gordon)
Man .... R. G. Brown
Happiness Girls .... Joan Thornton, Helen Kardon, Sylvia, Marian Mercer, Travis Hudson, Mickey Wayland
Impressions and Folk Songs .... Joey Carter
"Togetherness" (Lyrics and music by Mavor Moore)
Cardinal .... R. G. Brown
Bishop .... Charles Barlow
Patriarch .... Michael Fesco
Moderator .... James Moore
"A Moment of Truth" .... Patti Karr
(Suggested by Ronny Graham; music and lyrics by Jack Holmes)
"I Want You to Be the First to Know" (Lyrics by June Carroll; music by Arthur Siegel)
Sung by .... Mickey Wayland, Charles Barlow, Michael Fesco
First Couple .... James Moore, Erin Martin
Second Couple .... Juan Carlos Copes, Maria Nieves
Third Couple .... Jim Corbett, Patti Karr
Young Man .... Tom Arthur
"Lemon Coke" (By R. G. Brown)
Boy .... R. G. Brown
Girl .... Marian Mercer
"ABC's" (Lyrics by David Rogers; music by Mark Bucci)
Girl .... Helen Kardon
Children .... Erin Martin, Maria Nieves, Jim Corbett, Juan Carlos Copes, James Moore
"It Depends on How You Look at Things" (Lyrics by June Carroll; music by Arthur Siegel)
Husband .... R. G. Brown
Wife .... Travis Hudson
Things .... Helen Kardon, Joan Thornton, Mickey Wayland, Erin Martin, Patti Karr, Maria Nieves, Sylvia
It Takes a Heap (By Tony Geiss and Paul Lynde)
(Introduction) .... Patti Karr
Foreman .... Joey Carter; and Michael Fesco, Helen Kardon, Jim Corbett, Patti Karr, Mickey Wayland, Maria Nieves, Erin Martin
"Freedomland" .... Marian Mercer
(Lyrics and music by Jack Holmes)
"Over the River and Into the Woods" .... Sylvia Lord
(Lyrics and music by Jack Holmes)
Nose Cone (By R. G. Brown)
Reporter .... Michael Fesco
Mr. Thurman .... R. G. Brown
Mrs. Thurman .... Marian Mercer
"Johnny Mishuga" (Sketch by David Rogers; lyrics by David Rogers and Mark Bucci; music by Mark Bucci)
(Introduction) .... Tom Arthur
Momma .... Travis Hudson
Hymie .... Joey Carter
Waiter .... Jim Corbett
Gringo .... Charles Barlow
Johnny .... R. G. Brown
Yasmin .... Marian Mercer

Deputy ....James Moore
Customers ....Erin Martin, Patti Karr, Sylvia, Maria Nieves, Helen Kardon, Michael Fesco

ACT II

"Entré Act" (Choreography by James Moore)
(Introduction) ....Joan Thornton and Sylvia
Dancers ....Jim Corbett, Juan Carlos Copes, Michael Fesco, Patti Karr, Erin Martin, James Moore, Maria Nieves

Quickies
The Scarsdale Sentence (By David Rogers)
(Introduction) ....Patti Karr
Bettina ....Marian Mercer
Warren ....R. G. Brown
Madison Avenue Executive (By Ronny Graham)
Executive ....James Moore
"Collective Beauty" (Lyrics by Michael McWhinney; music by William Roy)
Lady ....Travis Hudson
Revlonites ......Helen Kardon, Mickey Wayland, Charles Barlow, Jim Corbett, Maria Nieves, Patti Karr
Customers ....Erin Martin, Sylvia, Joan Thornton
Happy Person (By Herbert Hartig)
Girl ....Marian Mercer
Boy ....R. G. Brown
Untouchables ....Erin Martin and Charles Barlow
(By Joey Carter)
"The Other One" (Lyrics by June Carroll; music by Arthur Siegel)
Woman ....Marian Mercer
Man ....Jim Corbett
Dancers ....Patti Karr, Sylvia, Joan Thornton, Mickey Wayland, Tom Arthur, Charles Barlow, Michael Fesco, Juan Carlos Copes
"Our Models" ....Joan Thornton and Sylvia
"The Untalented Relative" (Lyrics by Joey Carter and Richard Maury; music by Arthur Siegel)
(Introduction) ....Patti Karr
Folk Singer ....Joey Carter
Folk ....Patti Karr, Juan Carlos Copes, Marian Mercer, Mickey Wayland, James Moore, Michael Fesco, Charles Barlow, Helen Kardon, Erin Martin, Jim Corbett
It's All in a Day's Work (By Joey Carter)
Girl ....Joan Thornton
"Love Is Good for You" ....Sylvia Lord
(Lyrics by June Carroll; music by Arthur Siegel)
Where Are Our Parents? (By Ronny Graham, Arnie Sultan and Marvin Worth)
Father ....Joey Carter
Mother ....Marian Mercer
Roger ....R. G. Brown
Mary ....Mickey Wayland
Cop ....Jim Corbett
"Wall Street Reel" ....Entire Company
(Lyrics by Jim Fuerst; music by Arthur Siegel; introduction written by Richard Maury)

(Closed February 24, 1962)

THE OLD VIC COMPANY

(48 performances)

Repertory of two dramas by William Shakespeare and one play by Bernard Shaw: "Macbeth" (premiere February 6, 1962), "Romeo and Juliet" (premiere February 13, 1962) and "Saint Joan" (premiere February 20, 1962). Produced, under the management of S. Hurok, by the Old Vic Trust Ltd. and the Arts Council of Great Britain at the New York City Center.

MACBETH

Witches ....Rosalind Atkinson, George Howe, Edward Atienza
Duncan, King of Scotland ....Andre Van Gyseghem
His Sons { Malcolm ....John Stride
{ Donalbain ....Dan MacDonald
Noblemen of Scotland { Macduff ....William Sylvester
{ Lennox ....Michael Meacham
A Sergeant ....Oswald Laurence
Ross, another Noble ....Hugh Manning
Generals of the King's Army { Macbeth ....John Clements
{ Banquo ....Nicholas Meredith
Fleance, son to Banquo ....Victoria Watts
Seyton, servant to Macbeth ....Job Stewart
Lady Macbeth ....Barbara Jefford
A Porter ....Edward Atienza
A Doctor ....Gerald James
Murderers ....Michael Graham Cox, Peter Rocca
Apparitions ....Sarah Long, Dan MacDonald, Linda Brandham
Lady Macduff ....Irene Sutcliffe
Boy, son to Macduff ....Elric Hooper
Messengers ....John Wackett, Peter Baldwin, Tim Wylton
Gentlewoman, attending Lady Macbeth ....Diana Scougall

Apparitions, attendants, nobles, messengers, soldiers: Peter Baldwin, Linda Brandham, John Broster, Michael Graham Cox, Julian Curry, Peter Forest, John Harwood, Oswald Laurence, Martin Lawton, Fiona Leland, Sarah Long, Michael Martin, Michael Pemberton, John Quentin, Malcolm Reid, Peter Rocca, John Wackett, Tim Wylton.

Staged by Michael Benthall; decor and costumes by Michael Annals; music and sound effects by Tristram Cary; fights staged by William Hobbs; stage managers, Nigel Stannard and Peter Hodgson; press, Martin Feinstein.

ROMEO AND JULIET

Chorus ....George Howe
Abraham, servant to Montague ....Peter Baldwin
Balthasar, servant to Romeo ....Elric Hooper
Servants to Capulet { Sampson ....Oswald Laurence
{ Gregory ....John Harwood
Benvolio, nephew to Montague and friend to Romeo .....Job Stewart
Tybalt, nephew to Lady Capulet ....Michael Meacham
Montague ....Andre Van Gyseghem
Capulet ....Peter Forest
Lady Montague ....Diana Scougall
Lady Capulet ....Irene Sutcliffe
Escalus, Prince of Verona ....Hugh Manning
Romeo, son to Montague ....John Stride
Paris, a young Nobleman ....John Quentin
Peter, servant to Juliet's nurse ....Michael Graham Cox
Nurse to Juliet ....Rosalind Atkinson
Juliet, daughter to Capulet ....Joanna Dunham
Mercutio, friend to Romeo ....Edward Atienza
A Singer ....Elric Hooper
Friar Laurence ....Gerald James
An Apothecary ....George Howe
Friar John ....Michael Pemberton

Citizens of Verona, guards, kinsfolk of both houses: Linda Brandham, John Broster, Julian Curry, Martin Lawton, Fiona Leland, Sarah Long, Dan MacDonald, Michael Martin, Michael Pemberton, Malcolm Reid, Peter Rocca, John Wackett, Victoria Watts, Tim Wylton.

Staged and designed by Franco Zeffirelli; costumes by Peter Hall; music by Nino Rota; dances arranged by Pirmin Trecu; fights arranged by William Hobbs.

SAINT JOAN

Robert de Boudricourt ....Michael Graham Cox
Steward ....Tim Wylton
Joan ....Barbara Jefford
Bertrand de Poulengey ....Peter Baldwin
Mgr. de la Tremouille ....Gerald James
Archbishop of Rheims ....Hugh Manning
Court Page ....Malcolm Reid
Gilles de Rais ....Oswald Laurence
Captain La Hire ....John Harwood
The Dauphin, later Charles VII ....Job Stewart
Duchess de la Tremouille ....Diana Scougall
Dunois, Bastard of Orleans ....William Sylvester
Dunois' Page ....Elric Hooper
Richard de Beauchamp, Earl of Warwick ....John Clements
Chaplain de Stogumber ....Nicholas Meredith
Warwick's Page ....Dan MacDonald
Peter Cauchon, Bishop of Beauvais ....Andre Van Gyseghem
The Inquisitor ....George Howe
Canon D'Estivet ....Edward Atienza
Canon de Courcelles ....John Broster
Brother Martin Ladvenu ....Michael Meacham
Executioner ....Peter Forest
A Soldier ....Gerald James
Gentleman ....Julian Curry

Lords, ladies, monks, soldiers: Peter Baldwin, Linda Brandham, John Broster, Michael Graham Cox, Julian Curry, Peter Forest, Martin Lawton, Fiona Leland, Dan MacDonald, Michael Martin, Michael Pemberton, John Quentin, Peter Rocca, John Wackett, Victoria Watts, Tim Wylton.

Staged by Douglas Seale; decor and costumes by Leslie Hurry; music by John Lambert.

(Closed March 18, 1962)

THE ASPERN PAPERS

(93 performances)

Play by Michael Redgrave, based on the story by Henry James. Produced by David Black, by arrangement with Peter Daubeny, Michael Redgrave Productions and F.E.S. Plays, Ltd., at the Playhouse, February 7, 1962.

Assunta ....Augusta Merighi
Mrs. Prest ....Jen Nelson
"H.J." ....Maurice Evans
Miss Tina ....Wendy Hiller
Miss Bordereau ....Francoise Rosay
Pasquale ....Clifford David

Time: the 1890's. Place: the sala of Miss Bordereau's house in Venice.

Staged by Margaret Webster; setting and lighting by Ben Edwards; costumes by Alvin Colt; production stage manager, Jose Vega; stage manager, Alan Foster; press, Sol Jacobson and Lewis Harmon.

The spinster niece of an old lady is encouraged to fall in love with a publisher, whose only interest is in acquiring some letters in her aunt's possession.

(Closed April 28, 1962)

Henry Fonda and Olivia de Havilland in "A Gift of Time."

A GIFT OF TIME

(92 performances)

Play by Garson Kanin, based on "Death of a Man" by Lael Tucker Wertenbaker. Produced by William Hammerstein, in association with David Shaber and William Snyder, Jr., at the Ethel Barrymore Theatre, February 22, 1962.

Charles Christian Wertenbaker	Henry Fonda
Lael Tucker Wertenbaker	Olivia de Havilland
A Nursing Mother	Anne Drapper
Dr. Cartier	Guy Sorel
Dr. Barcet	John MacKay
A Patient	Virginia Downing
A One-Armed Man	Philip Huston
A Waiter	Guy Danfort
A News Vendor	Kris Davis
Madame Oyarzabel (Ama)	Lucretia Gould
Mirentchu Etchegarry	Nicola Lubitsch
Christian Wertenbaker	Gary Morgan
Timberlake Wertenbaker	Leslye Hunter
Michel Etchegarry	Alan Howard
Ginette Hirribarren	Sindee Anne Richards
Frédéric Etchegarry	Sol Frieder

Dr. Ross .... Philip Huston
Dr. James Danielson .... Rufus Smith
Dr. Martinez .... Peter Levin
Dr. Sala .... Cliff Miller
Dr. Gershkorn .... Guy Danfort
Two Orderlies .... Guy Danfort, Jon Paul
Thomas Loring .... John MacKay
Susan Loring .... Marian Seldes
Miss Wills .... Carol Joplin
Miss Pieroni .... Anne Draper
Two Countermen .... Perry Kirk, Sol Frieder
A Visitor .... Virginia Downing
A Patient .... Sol Frieder
Carlos .... Leo Bloom
The Purser .... Daniel Evan
A Deck Steward .... Philip Huston
Mrs. Allen .... Anne Draper
Mr. Allen .... Guy Danfort
The Ship's Nurse .... Virginia Downing
Miguel Telleria .... Philip Huston
A Very Old Man .... Sol Frieder
Daniel Stein .... Joseph Campanella
Two Monks .... Alex Easton, Dan Henry
A Man .... Philip Huston
His Wife .... Virginia Downing

The action of the play takes place in St. Jean-de-Luz, Ciboure, New York and at sea. The time is 1954.

Staged by Mr. Kanin; settings by Boris Aronson; costumes by Edith Lutyens Bel Geddes; lighting by Jean Rosenthal; stage manager, Paul Leaf; press, James D. Proctor. A man dying of cancer decides to live fully for a few months, rather than suffer a prolonged bed-ridden illness.

(Closed May 12, 1962)

GENERAL SEEGER

(2 performances)

Play by Ira Levin. Produced by the Theatre of Michigan Company, Inc. and Theodore Mann at the Lyceum Theatre, February 28, 1962.

A Corporal .... Roscoe Lee Browne
A Woman .... Dolores Sutton
Captain Peck .... Gerald Richards
Captain Thibaudeau .... Paul Stevens
Lt. Colonel Bonney .... Lonny Chapman
Major General Vohs .... John Leslie
Boyd McKay .... Tim O'Connor
Major General Seeger .... George C. Scott
Rena Seeger .... Ann Harding
Color Guards .... Johnny Cosgrove, Matt Bennett

Reporters and photographers: Charles Dierkop, J. Nathan French, Elaine Hyman, John O'Leary, Loree Marks, Thomas Maxwell, Martin Priest, Tom Signorelli, Frank Simpson.

Time: the present. Place: the Commanding General's office on a New England army post.

Staged by George C. Scott; setting by Gerald Parker; costumes by Noel Taylor; lighting by Ralph Holmes; production stage manager, William Armitage; stage manager, Robert Crawley; press, James D. Proctor. The disillusionment of an idealistic career officer on discovering that he drove his son to suicide, which the army for its own reasons reported as a hero's death.

(Closed March 1, 1962)

NO STRINGS

(89 performances)
(Continued)

Musical with book by Samuel Taylor; music and lyrics by Richard Rodgers. Produced by Richard Rodgers, in association with Samuel Taylor, at the Fifty-fourth Street Theatre, March 15, 1962.

Barbara Woodruff .... Diahann Carroll
David Jordan .... Richard Kiley
Jeanette Valmy .... Noelle Adam
Luc Delbert .... Alvin Epstein
Mollie Plummer .... Polly Rowles
Mike Robinson .... Don Chastain
Louis dePourtal .... Mitchell Gregg
Comfort O'Connell .... Bernice Massi
Gabrielle Bertin .... Ann Hodges
Marcello Agnolotti .... Paul Cambeilh

Dancers: Alan Johnson, Susanne Cansino, Julie Drake, Jean Eliot, Ginny Gan, Ellen Graff, Kay Hudson, Ann Hodges, Diana Hrubetz, Sandy Leeds, Anna Marie Moylan, Patti Pappathatos, Janet Paxton, Dellas Rennie, Bea Salten, Carol Sherman, Mary Zahn, Gene Gebauer, Scott Hunter, Larry Merritt, Michael Maurer, David Neuman, Wakefield Poole, Calvin van Reinhold.

Time: the present. Place: Paris, Monte Carlo, Honfleur, Deauville and St. Tropez.

Staged and choreographed by Joe Layton; settings and lighting by David Hays; costumes by Fred Voelpel and Donald Brooks; musical direction and dance arrangements by Peter Matz; orchestrations by Ralph Burns; associate choreographer, Buddy Schwab; production stage manager, Charles Atkin; stage manager, Fred Smith; press, Frank Goodman, Ben Washer and Arlene Wolf. Romance between an author and a Paris model.

ACT I

"The Sweetest Sounds" .... Barbara and David
"How Sad" .... David
"Loads of Love" .... Barbara
"The Man Who Has Everything" .... Louis
"Be My Host" .... David, Comfort, Mike, Luc, Gabrielle and Dancers
"La La La" .... Jeanette and Luc
"You Don't Tell Me" .... Barbara
"Love Makes the World Go" .... Mollie, Comfort and Dancers
"Nobody Told Me" .... David and Barbara

ACT II

"Look No Further" .... David and Barbara
"Maine" .... David and Barbara
"An Orthodox Fool" .... Barbara
"Eager Beaver" .... Comfort, Mike and Dancers
"No Strings" .... David and Barbara
"Maine" (Reprise) .... Barbara and David
"The Sweetest Sounds" (Reprise) .... David and Barbara

ISLE OF CHILDREN

(11 performances)

Play by Robert L. Joseph. Produced by Lester Osterman, in association with Shirley Bernstein, at the Cort Theatre, March 16, 1962.

Deirdre Striden .... Patty Duke
Eugene Striden, her father .... Noel Willman
Ruth Striden, her mother .... Norma Crane
Philip Anding, a boy from the neighborhood .... James Aubrey
Sara Paulson, a tutor .... Louise Latham
Leon Hallett, a doctor .... Stefan Gierasch
Kathy Lanen, a girl from the neighborhood .... Bonnie Bedelia

Time: the present. Place: New York City.

Staged by Jules Dassin; setting and lighting by Howard Bay; costumes by Ann Roth; incidental music by Victor Ziskin; production stage manager, Harry Young; stage manager, Nicholas Gray; press, Harvey B. Sabinson. Young girl with incurable heart ailment tries to find some sense of meaning in her life.

(Closed March 24, 1962)

ALL AMERICAN

(86 performances)

Musical based on the novel "Professor Fodorski" by Robert Lewis Taylor; book by Mel Brooks; music by Charles Strouse; lyrics by Lee Adams. Produced by Edward Padula, in association with L. Slade Brown, at the Winter Garden Theatre, March 19, 1962.

Airline Stewardess .... Lori Rogers
Flight Attendant .... Robert Lone
Head Immigration Officer .... Barney Martin
Immigration Officer .... Michael Gentry
Fleisser .... Mort Marshall
Shindler .... David Thomas
Feinschveiger .... Bernie West
Katrinka .... Betty Oakes
Professor Fodorski .... Ray Bolger
Taxis .... Michael Gentry, Barney Martin, Fred Randall, Norman Riggins, Will B. Able
Policeman .... Jed Allan
Gorilla .... Bob Bakanic
Bride .... Bonnie Brody
Mannikin .... Mary Jane Ferguson
Peddler .... Will B. Able
Chewing Gum Girl .... Bonnie Brody
Drunk .... Mort Marshall
Con Ed Worker .... Joseph Gentry
Cowboys .... Bill Burns, Robert Lone
Park Avenue Couple .... Betty Oakes, David Thomas
Sightseeing Tour Guide .... Bernie West
Second Sightseeing Tour Guide .... George Lindsey
Elizabeth Hawkes-Bullock .... Eileen Herlie
Susan .... Anita Gillette
Edwin Bricker .... Ron Husmann

Eileen Herlie and Ray Bolger in "All American."

Dr. Snopes .... Bernie West
Coach Hulkington (Hulk) Stockworth .... Mort Marshall
Assistant Coach .... Barney Martin
Moose .... George Lindsey
President Piedmont .... Will B. Able
Professor Dawson .... David Thomas
Professor White .... Warren Hays
First Boy .... Robert Lone
First Girl .... Trudy Carole
Second Girl .... Karen Sargent
Second Boy .... Ed Kresley
House Mother .... Betty Oakes
Baton Twirler .... Karen Sargent
Red Stern .... Barney Martin
Henderson .... Fritz Weaver
Whistler's Mother .... Betty Oakes
Craven .... Jed Allan
Phillips .... Anthony Falco
Wyler .... Bill Burns
Homecoming Queen .... Sharon Vaughn
Secretary .... Betty Oakes
Farquar .... Bill Starr
Fountainhead .... Bob Bakanic

Immigrants: Will B. Able, Jed Allan, Don Atkinson, Vicki Belmonte, Bonnie Brody, Bill Burns, Trudy Carole, John Drew, Anthony Falco, Mary Jane Ferguson, Catherine Gale, Joseph Gentry, Linda Rae Hager, Warren Hays, Jerry Howard, Bill Landrum, George Lindsey, Selma Malinou, Joe McWherter, Norman Riggins, Bill Starr, Sharon Vaughn.

Football players: Jed Allan, Bill Burns, John Drew, Joseph Gentry, Michael Gentry, Jerry Howard, Bill Landrum, Joseph McWherter, Fred Randall, Bill Starr.

Singers: Vicki Belmonte, Bonnie Brody, Catherine Gale, Selma Malinou, Lori Rogers, Sharon Vaughn, Jed Allan, Bill Burns, John Drew, Anthony Falco, Warren Hays, Norman Riggins.

Dancers: Trudy Carole, Cathy Conklin, Mary Jane Ferguson, Linda Rae Hager, Charlene Mehl, Karen Sargent, Don Atkinson, Bob Bakanic, Ed Kresley, Bill Landrum, Robert Lone, Kip Watson.

Time: the present. Place: the U.S.A.

Staged by Joshua Logan; choreography by Danny Daniels; settings and lighting by Jo Mielziner; costumes by Patton Campbell; dance arrangements and musical direction by John Morris; orchestrations by Robert Ginzler; musical continuity by Trude Rittman; stage manager, George Wagner; press, Bill Doll. A European professor attempts to adjust himself to the American way of life.

ACT I

"Melt Us" .... Fodorski and Immigrants
"What a Country!" .... Fodorski and Company
"Our Children" .... Fodorski and Elizabeth
"Animal Attraction" .... Susan and Bricker
"Our Children" (Reprise) .... Fodorski and Elizabeth
"We Speak the Same Language" .... Fodorski and Bricker
"I Can Teach Them!" ..... Fodorski, Elizabeth, Bricker and Dawson
"It's Fun to Think" .... Fodorski, Professors and Students
"Once Upon a Time" .... Fodorski and Elizabeth
"Nightlife" .... Susan and Girls
"I've Just Seen Her" .... Bricker
"Once Upon a Time" (Reprise) .... Elizabeth
"Physical Fitness" .... The Football Team
"The Fight Song" .... Fodorski and the Football Team
"What a Country!" (Reprise) .... Fodorski and Company

ACT II

"I Couldn't Have Done It Alone" .... Bricker and Susan
"If I Were You" .... Fodorski and Elizabeth
"Have a Dream" .... Fodorski, Henderson and Company
"I've Just Seen Him" .... Susan
"I'm Fascinating" .... Fodorski
"Once Upon a Time" (Reprise) .... Elizabeth
"The Real Me" .... Elizabeth
"It's Up to Me" .... Fodorski
"The Fight Song" (Reprise) .... Fodorski and Company
"It's Fun to Think" .... The Company

(Closed May 26, 1962)

I CAN GET IT FOR YOU WHOLESALE

(81 performances)
(Continued)

Musical based on the novel by Jerome Weidman; book by Mr. Weidman; music and lyrics by Harold Rome. Produced by David Merrick at the Sam S. Shubert Theatre, March 22, 1962.

Miss Marmelstein .... Barbra Streisand
Maurice Pulvermacher .... Jack Kruschen
Meyer Bushkin .... Ken LeRoy
Harry Bogen .... Elliott Gould
Tootsie Maltz .... James Hickman
Ruthie Rivkin .... Marilyn Cooper
Mrs. Bogen .... Lillian Roth

Martha Mills .... Sheree North
Mario .... William Reilly
Mitzi .... Barbara Monte
Eddie .... Edward Verso
Blanche Bushkin .... Bambi Linn
Teddy Asch .... Harold Lang
Buggo .... Kelly Brown
Miss Springer .... Pat Turner
Velma .... Francine Bond
Lenny .... William Sumner
Norman .... Stanley Simmonds
Manette .... Luba Lisa
Gail .... Wilma Curley
Rosaline .... Marion Fels
Noodle .... Jack Murray
Sam .... Don Grilley
Moxie .... Ed Collins
Sheldon Bushkin .... Steve Curry
Edith .... Margaret Gathright

Time: the 1930's. Place: New York's garment district and the Bronx.

Staged by Arthur Laurents; settings and lighting by Will Steven Armstrong; costumes by Theoni V. Aldredge; musical staging by Herbert Ross; musical direction and vocal arrangements by Lehman Engel; orchestrations by Sid Ramin; dance and incidental music arranged by Peter Howard; production stage manager, Richard Blofson; stage manager, May Muth; press, Harvey B. Sabinson. The activities of a hell in New York's garment industry.

ACT I

"Well Man" .... Miss Marmelstein and Mr. Pulvermacher
"The Way Things Are" .... Harry
"When Gemini Meets Capricorn" .... Ruthie and Harry
"Momma, Momma" .... Harry and Mrs. Bogen
"The Sound of Money" .... Harry, Martha, Mitzi, Mario, Eddie
"Family Way" .... Mrs. Bogen, Harry, Ruthie, Teddy, Blanche, Meyer
"Too Soon" .... Mrs. Bogen
"Who Knows?" .... Ruthie
"Have I Told You Lately?" .... Blanche and Meyer
"Ballad of the Garment Trade" .... Miss Marmelstein, Ruthie, Blanche, Harry, Teddy, Meyer and Company

ACT II

"A Gift Today" .... Sheldon, Harry, Mrs. Bogen, Blanche, Meyer, Ruthie
Dance .... Blanche, Meyer and Sheldon
"Miss Marmelstein" .... Miss Marmelstein
"The Sound of Money" (Reprise) .... Harry
"A Funny Thing Happened" .... Ruthie and Harry
"What's in It for Me?" .... Teddy and Martha
"What Are They Doing to Us Now?" .... Miss Marmelstein, Buggo, Tootsie, Manette, Gail, Springer and Creditors
"Eat a Little Something" .... Mrs. Bogen and Harry
Epilogue .... The Company

GREAT DAY IN THE MORNING

(13 performances)

Play by Alice Cannon. Produced by the Theatre of Michigan Company, Inc., Theodore Mann and George C. Scott at Henry Miller's Theatre, March 28, 1962.

Phoebe Flaherty .... Colleen Dewhurst
Sis McAnany .... Peggy Burke
Joe McAnany .... J. D. Cannon
Alice McAnany .... Frances Sternhagen
Richie McAnany .... Jeff Herrod
Tricky Hennessey .... Thomas Carlin
Mrs. Grace .... Eulabelle Moore
Dutchy .... Elisabeth Fraser
Father Finney .... Gene Roche
Schultz .... Lou Frizzell
Brennan Farrell .... Clifton James
Owen Brady .... David Canary
First Policeman .... James Mishler
Second Policeman .... Michael Bradford

Time: May, 1928. Place: Phoebe Flaherty's home in St. Louis, Missouri.

Staged by José Quintero; setting and lighting by Lester Polakov; costumes by Noel Taylor; production stage manager, Elliot Martin; stage manager, Don Garner; press, James D. Proctor. An Irish Catholic household is ruled by a warm-hearted but violent-tempered relative.

(Closed April 7, 1962)

A THOUSAND CLOWNS

(60 performances)
(Continued)

Play by Herb Gardner. Produced by Fred Coe and Arthur Cantor at the Eugene O'Neill Theatre, April 5, 1962.

Murray Burns .... Jason Robards, Jr.
Nick Burns .... Barry Gordon
Albert Amundson .... William Daniels
Sandra Markowitz .... Sandy Dennis
Arnold Burns .... A. Larry Haines
Leo Herman .... Gene Saks

Time: the present. Place: Murray Burns' apartment and Arnold Burns' office in Manhattan.

Staged by Mr. Coe; settings and lighting by George Jenkins; costumes by Ruth Morley; production stage manager, Porter Van Zandt; stage manager, Tom Porter; press, Gertrude Kirschner, Tony Geiss and Violet Welles.

See page 217.

VENUS AT LARGE

(4 performances)

Play by Henry Denker. Produced by Joel Schenker at the Morosco Theatre, April 12, 1962.

Betty Stone .... Sally Gracie
Sonny Stone .... David Wayne
Jack Carr .... Leon Janney
Olive Ogilvie .... Joyce Jameson
Mick Mandelbaum .... Jack Bittner

Alec Grimes .... William Prince
Russell .... Robert Yuro
J. B. Bannister .... Ernest Truex
Mr. Kronheim .... Boris Tumarin

Time: the present. Place: the living room of a suite in a hotel on Central Park South.

Staged by Rod Amateau; setting and lighting by Donald Oenslager; costumes by Ann Roth; production stage manager, Jean Barrere; stage manager, Arthur Marlowe; press, Harvey B. Sabinson and Lee Solters. Comedy about a movie queen who comes to New York to study at the Actors Studio.

(Closed April 14, 1962)

A FUNNY THING HAPPENED ON THE WAY TO THE FORUM

(23 performances)
(Continued)

Musical based on the plays of Plautus; book by Burt Shevelove and Larry Gelbart; music and lyrics by Stephen Sondheim. Produced by Harold Prince at the Alvin Theatre, May 8, 1962.

Prologus .... Zero Mostel
The Proteans .... Eddie Phillips, George Reeder, David Evans
Senex, a citizen of Rome .... David Burns
Domina, his wife .... Ruth Kobart
Hero, his son .... Brian Davies
Hysterium, slave to Senex and Domina .... Jack Gilford
Lycus, a dealer in courtesans .... John Carradine
Pseudolus, slave to Hero .... Zero Mostel
Tintinabula .... Roberta Keith
Panacea .... Lucienne Bridou
The Geminae .... Lisa James, Judy Alexander
Vibrata .... Myrna White
Gymnasia .... Gloria Kristy
Philia .... Preshy Marker
Erronius, a citizen of Rome .... Raymond Walburn
Miles Gloriosus, a warrior .... Ronald Holgate

Time: 200 B.C. Place: a street in Rome.

Staged by George Abbott; choreography and musical staging by Jack Cole; settings and costumes by Tony Walton; lighting by Jean Rosenthal; musical direction by Hal Hastings; orchestrations by Irwin Kostal and Sid Ramin; dance music arranged by Hal Schaefer; production stage manager, Ruth Mitchell; stage manager, James Bronson; press, Sol Jacobson, Lewis Harmon and Mary Bryant. Farce about young love in which assorted comic characters inhabit the stage, each trying to outwit the other.

ACT I

"Comedy Tonight" .... Prologus, the Proteans and Company
"Love, I Hear" .... Hero
"Free" .... Pseudolus, Hero
"The House of Marcus Lycus" .... Lycus, Pseudolus and Courtesans
"Lovely" .... Hero, Philia
"Pretty Little Picture" .... Pseudolus, Hero, Philia
"Everybody Ought to Have a Maid" .... Senex, Pseudolus, Hysterium, Lycus
"I'm Calm" .... Hysterium
"Impossible" .... Senex, Hero
"Bring Me My Bride" .... Miles, Pseudolus, Courtesans and Protean

ACT II

"That Dirty Old Man" .... Domina
"That'll Show Him" .... Philia
"Lovely" (Reprise) .... Pseudolus, Hysterium
Funeral Sequence and Dance .... Pseudolus, Miles, Courtesans and Proteans
"Comedy Tonight" (Reprise) .... The Company

THE ROYAL DRAMATIC THEATRE OF SWEDEN

(8 performances)

Repertory of three plays: "The Father" (May 14, 16, 19, 1962, 3 performances), "Long Day's Journey into Night" (May 15 & 17, 1962, 2 performances), "Miss Julie" (May 16, 18, 19, 1962, 3 performances). Produced by the Seattle World's Fair performing arts division, in association with Roger L. Stevens, at the Cort Theatre, May 14, 1962.

THE FATHER

Tragedy by August Strindberg

The Cavalry Captain .... Lars Hanson
Laura, his wife .... Irma Christenson
Bertha, his daughter .... Catrin Westerlund
Doctor Östermork .... Bengt Ekerot
The Pastor, Laura's brother .... Hans Straat
The Wet Nurse .... Elsa Carlsson
Nojd, a soldier .... Jan-Erik Lindqvist
An Orderly .... George J. Nils

Staged by Bengt Ekerot; setting by Sven Fahlstedt.

LONG DAY'S JOURNEY INTO NIGHT

Play by Eugene O'Neill

James Tyrone .... Georg Rydeberg
Mary Cavan Tyrone, his wife .... Inga Tidblad
James Tyrone, Jr., their elder son .... Ulf Palme
Edmund Tyrone, their younger son .... Jarl Kulle
Cathleen .... Catrin Westerlund

Staged by Mr. Ekerot; setting by Georg Magnusson; costumes by Gunnar Gelbort.

MISS JULIE

Naturalistic Tragedy by August Strindberg

Miss Julie .... Inga Tidblad
Jean .... Ulf Palme
Kristin, the cook .... Irma Christenson

Staged by Alf Sjoberg; setting by Yngve Larson; costumes by Mr. Gelbort; press, Samuel Lurie. The three revivals were presented in Swedish.

(Closed May 19, 1962)

BRAVO GIOVANNI

(9 performances)
(Continued)

Musical adapted from the novel "The Crime of Giovanni Venturi" by Howard Shaw; book by A. J. Russell; music by Milton Schafer; lyrics by Ronny Graham. Produced by Philip Rose at the Broadhurst Theatre, May 19, 1962.

Giovanni Venturi .... Cesare Siepi
Signor Bellardi .... George S. Irving
Uriti Waiters .... Rico Froehlich, Joe McGrath, Ed Dumont, Barney Johnston
Amedeo .... David Opatoshu
Furniture Dealer .... Harry Davis
Nino .... Al Sambogna
Gino .... Thatcher Clarke
Dino .... Buzz Miller
Miranda .... Michele Lee
Moscolito .... Arnold Soboloff
Carlo .... Al Lanti
Signora Pandolfi .... Maria Karnilova
Musicians .... Gene Varrone, Nino Banome, Rico Froehlich
Night Club Manager .... Buzz Miller
Professor Panfredoni .... Harry Davis
Troubadour .... Gene Varrone
Celestina .... Lu Leonard
Head Chef .... Buzz Miller
Pizza Maker .... Gene Varrone
Salad Chef .... Gene Gavin
Bakers .... Nino Banome, Larry Fuller
Soup Cook .... Thatcher Clarke
Helpers .... Alan Peterson, Alvin Beam, Al Sambogna
Signora Elli .... Penny Gaston
La Contessa .... Lainie Kazan
Signor Brancusi .... John Taliaferro
Professor Musa .... Rico Froehlich
Brigadiere .... Gene Varrone
Policeman .... Barney Johnston

Singers: Jyll Alexander, Norma Donaldson, Penny Gaston, Marcia Gilford, Maria Graziano, Lainie Kazan, Betty Kent, Rita Metzger, Ed Dumont, Tom Head, Barney Johnston, Ronald Knight, Joe McGrath, Richard Park, John Taliaferro.

Dancers: Ann Barry, Ellen Halpin, Shellie Farrell, Michele Franchi, Herad Gruhn, Baayork Lee, Barbara Richman, Nikki Sowinski, Nino Banome, Alvin Beam, Thatcher Clarke, Larry Fuller, Gene Gavin, Alan Peterson, Al Sambogna, Claude Thompson.

Time: the present. Place: Rome.

Directed by Stanley Prager; settings and lighting by Robert Randolph; costumes by Ed Wittstein; choreography by Carol Haney; assistant choreographer, Buzz Miller; musical direction, continuity, vocal arrangements, Anton Coppola; arrangements and orchestrations, Robert Ginzler; dance music arranged and orchestrated by Luther Henderson; production stage manager, Samuel Liff; stage managers, Gene Perlowin, Mike Abel; press, James D. Proctor. About the competition between the proprietor of a small café and the owner of a larger and newer restaurant.

ACT I

"Rome" .... Giovanni
"Uriti" .... Bellardi and Ensemble
"Breachy's Law" .... Giovanni and Amedeo
"I'm All I've Got" .... Miranda
"The Argument" .... Giovanni and Bellardi

"Signora Pandolfi" ......Amedeo, Pandolfi, Manager and Musicians
"The Kangaroo" ....Pandolfi, Manager, Waiters, Musicians and Kitchen Help
"If I Were the Man" ....Giovanni
"Steady, Steady" ....Miranda
"We Won't Discuss It" ....Giovanni and Amedeo
"Ah, Camminare" ....Troubadour, Giovanni and Company

ACT II

"Breachy's Law" (Reprise) ....Giovanni, Amedeo, Pandolfi and Miranda
"Uriti Kitchen" ....Bellardi, Moscolito, Carlo, Head Chef, Pizza Maker, Salad Chef, Bakers, Soup Cook and Helpers
"Virtue Arrivederci" ....Bellardi
"Bravo, Giovanni" ....Giovanni, Bellardi and Singing Ensemble
"One Little World Apart" ....Miranda
"Connubiality" ....Pandolfi and Amedeo
"Miranda" ....Giovanni

CAN-CAN

(16 performances)

Musical with book by Abe Burrows; music and lyrics by Cole Porter. Revived by the New York City Center Light Opera Company (Jean Dalrymple, Director) at the New York City Center, May 16, 1962.

Bailiff ....Phil Roth
Registrar ....Peter Saul
Policemen ....George Del Monte, Darrell Sandeen
Judge Paul Barriere ....Warner Schreiner
Court President ....Charles Reynolds
Judge Aristide Forestier ....George Gaynes
Claudine ....Mara Lynn
Gabrielle ....Maggie Worth
Marie ....Lillian D'Honau
Celestine ....Marilyn D'Honau
Hilaire Jussac ....Ferdinand Hilt
Boris Adzinidzinadze ....Gabriel Dell
Hercule ....Iggie Wolfington
Theophile ....Bob Dishy
Etienne ....Jack Fletcher
Waiter ....Michael Cavallaro
La Mome Pistache ....Genevieve
Second Waiter ....Darrell Sandeen
Café Waiter ....Phil Roth
Nun ....Nora Bristow
Model ....Betty Linton
Mimi ....Dorothy D'Honau
Customers ....Nora Bristow, Darrell Sandeen
Doctor ....Charles Reynolds
Second ....Darrell Sandeen
Rainbow ....Victor Duntiere
Prosecutor ....Jack Davison

Dancers: Joseph Ahumada, Marilyn Charles, Sterling Clark, Victor Duntiere, Gloria Danyl, Dorothy D'Honau, Lillian D'Honau, Marilyn D'Honau, Don Emmons, Natasha Grishin, Janan Hart, Douglas Hinshaw, Robert Holloway, Betty Linton, Sally Lou Lee, David Lober, Jami Landi, Mary Jane Moncrieff, Louise Quick, Peter Saul, Fabian Stuart, Alice Shanahan.

Staged by Gus Schirmer, Jr.; scenery and lighting adaptations of the originals by Joe Mielziner; original designs by Helen Pond; costumes by Stanley Simmons; choreography by Ellen Ray; musical director, James Leon; production stage manager, Herman Shapiro; stage manager, Bert Wood; press, Lillian Libman. CAN-CAN was first produced by Cy Feuer and Ernest H. Martin at the Shubert Theatre, May 7, 1953, for 892 performances.

(Closed May 27, 1962)

BRIGADOON

(2 performances)
(Continued)

Musical with book and lyrics by Alan Jay Lerner; music by Frederick Loewe. Revived by the New York City Center Light Opera Company (Jean Dalrymple, Director) at the New York City Center, May 30, 1962.

Tommy Albright .... Peter Palmer
Jeff Douglas .... Farley Granger
Sandy Dean .... Kenny Adams
Meg Brockie .... Ann Fraser
Archie Beaton .... Moultrie Patten
Harry Beaton .... Edward Villella
Andrew MacLaren .... Alexander Clark
Fiona MacLaren .... Sally Ann Howes
Jean MacLaren .... Jenny Workman
Angus McGuffie .... Walter Blocher
Charlie Dalrymple .... Harry Snow
Maggie Anderson .... Gemze de Lappe
Sword Dancers .... Richard Rutherford, James Clouser, James McArdle, David Shields, Frank Andre
Mr. Lundie .... John C. Becher
Bagpiper .... Maurice Eisenstadt
Frank .... Felice Orlandi
Jane Ashton .... Susan Fellows

Singers: Faith Daltry, Beverly G. Evans, Susan Fellows, Helen Guile, Marilyn Mason, Hanna Owen, Betty Jane Schwering, Kelli Scott, Lynn Wendell, Kenny Adams, John Aman, Ken Ayers, Donald E. Becker, Jerry Crawford, Harris W. Davis, Marvin Goodis, Robert Lenn, George T. McWhorter, John Sarkis.

Dancers: Barbara Beck, Lynn Broadbent, Mickey Gunnerson, Michele D. Hardy, Rosalie Kurowska, Lucia Lambert, Loi Leabo, Anna-Marie, Jane Meserve, Esther Villavicencio, Frank André, Robert Bishop, James Clouser, Ben Gillespie, Art Hutchinson, Vernon Lusby, Jim McArdle, Charles B. McCraw, Richard Rutherford, David Shields.

Staged by John Fearnley; dances and musical numbers staged by Agnes de Mille; assistant choreographer, James Jamieson; settings by Oliver Smith; costumes by Stanley Simmons, art director, Watson Barratt; musical director, Julius Rudel; production stage manager, Chet O'Brien; stage manager, Kermit Kegley; press, Lillian Libman. BRIGADOON was first produced by Cheryl Crawford at the Ziegfeld Theatre, March 13, 1947, for 581 performances.

ACT I

"Once in the Highlands" .... Chorus
"Brigadoon" .... Chorus
"Down on MacConnachy Square" ...... Sandy, Meg and Townsfolk
"Waitin' for My Dearie" .... Fiona and Girls
"I'll Go Home with Bonnie Jean" .... Charlie and Townsfolk
Dance .... Maggie, Harry, the Fishmongers and Dancers
"The Heather on the Hill" .... Fiona and Tommy

"The Love of My Life" .... Meg
"Jeannie's Packin' Up" .... Girls
"Come to Me, Bend to Me" .... Charlie
Dance .... Jean and Dancers
"Almost Like Being in Love" .... Tommy and Fiona
"The Wedding Dance" .... Jean, Charlie and Dancers
"Sword Dance" .... Harry, Sword Dancers and Dancers

ACT II

"The Chase" .... Men of Brigadoon
"There But for You Go I" .... Tommy
"My Mother's Weddin' Day" .... Meg and Townsfolk
Funeral Dance .... Maggie
"From This Day On" .... Tommy and Fiona
Finale .... Townsfolk

PLAYS PRODUCED OFF BROADWAY

June 1, 1961—May 31, 1962
(Plays marked with asterisk were still running on June 1, 1962)

NOONTIDE (70 perfs.)—By Howard Hart, based on "Partage de Midi" by Paul Claudel. Producers Mary Jordan, Sam Silverberg. Theatre Marquee, June 1, 1961.

Mesa ....Michael Wager
Yse ....Tani Seitz
De Ciz ....George Morgan
Almaric ....Martin B. Rudy

A boat in the Indian Ocean, Hong Kong and an abandoned Confucian Temple about 1900. Director Paul E. Davis; designer Peter Harvey; lighting Walter S. Russell; stage manager Earl Dossey; press Ben Kornzweig, Karl Bernstein. Four travellers to China all realize their appropriate destinies there.

RED EYE OF LOVE (169 perfs.)—By Arnold Weinstein. Producers Sam Cohn, John Wulp, in association with Julia Miles. Living Theatre, June 12, 1961.

Wilmer ....George Latchford
O. O. Martinas ....Michael Vale
Selma Chargesse ....Jane Romano
First Policeman, a music lover ....Al Mancini
Second Policeman, a people hater ....Jim Gormley
Cab Driver ....Barry Primus
Vendor ....Jerry DeLuise
Frances ....K. C. Townsend
Waitress ....Julia Miles
Young Bez ....Gregory Deutsch
Scrublady ....Sarah Braveman
Night Watchman ....Robb Grace
Tough ....Barry Primus
Big Bez ....Benjamin Hayeem
Uncle Sam ....Jerry DeLuise
First Soldier ....John Weston
Second Soldier ....Robb Grace
Third Soldier ....Jim Tiroff
Enemy Soldier ....Benjamin Hayeem
A Boy ....Gregory Deutsch
His Mother ....Sarah Braveman
High Hat Robber ....Martha Shaw
Victim ....Robert World

Director and designer Mr. Wulp; costumes Willa Kim; lighting Nicola Cernovich; incidental score William Bolcom; stage manager C. B. Grey; press James Spicer. Comic history of clash between idealism and materialism in America over the past thirty years.

A FIG LEAF IN HER BONNET (23 perfs.)—By Jesse Torn. Producers Marilyn Thorson, Carlo F. Salmaggi, Robert Horen, Serge Lentz. Gramercy Arts Theatre, June 14, 1961.

Director Basil Langton. With Henderson Forsythe and Claudia Morgan. Based on the relationship between George Bernard Shaw and Mrs. Patrick Campbell concerning the 1914 production of "Pygmalion."

PARADISE ISLAND (75 perfs.)—Hawaiian musical fantasy with book, music and lyrics by Carmen Lombardo and John Jacob

Loeb. Producer Guy Lombardo. Jones Beach Marine Theatre, June 22, 1961.

Director Francis Swann; settings George Jenkins; lighting Peggy Clark; choreography June Taylor. With Elaine Malbin, Arthur Treacher, William Gaxton and Guy Lombardo and His Royal Canadians. Musical numbers: ACT I, "A Happy Hakilau," "Once Upon a Time," "Coconut Wireless," "My World and Your World," "The Menehume," "Hokunani," "Luau Chant," "What Could Be More Romantic," "Paradise Island." ACT II, "The Invasion," "It's a Great Day for Hawaii," "I'll Just Pretend," "Never Any Time to Play," "Beyond the Clouds," "Ceremonial Chant," "Ceremonial March," "Now the Time Has Come."

DOUBLE BILL (5 perfs.)—Two one-act plays: WEST OF THE MOON by Robert Heide and THE BLOOD BUGLE by Harry Tierney, Jr. Producer New Playwrights Theatre. New Playwrights Theatre, June 28, 1961.

Director Lee Paton. With Paul Giovanni, Joe Ponazecki, James Cahill, Jerry Pagane and William Severs. The first play has two beatniks discussing their theories on world problems, and the second concerns a retired general's plot to overthrow the president of some unspecified country.

SUSAN SLEPT HERE (16 perfs.)—By Steve Fisher and Alex Gottlieb. Producers Barbara Griner, Eleanor Horn. Forty-first Street Theatre, July 11, 1961.

Director Matt Cimber. With Alan Dale and Joy Harmon. From the movie about a Hollywood writer who takes a juvenile delinquent under his wing and ends up marrying her. This play, along with two-week revivals of THE VOICE OF THE TURTLE with Mindy Carson, THE LITTLE HUT with Denise Darcel, THE TENDER TRAP with Jean Shepherd and THE MOON IS BLUE with Donald Cook (his last New York appearance), was given summer stock treatment in a season lasting from June 27 through September 3.

THE STUDENT PRINCE (13 perfs.)—Revival of 1924-25 Sigmund Romberg-Dorothy Donnelly musical. Producers Greenwich Players, Stella Holt, David Lipsky. Greenwich Mews Theatre, July 13, 1961.

Director Dorothy Raedler. With the American Savoyards.

THE PIRATES OF PENZANCE (55 perfs.)—Revival of the 1880 Gilbert and Sullivan operetta, as interpreted by Tyrone Guthrie. Producer Theatre, Inc. (T. Edward Hambleton, Norris Houghton). Phoenix Theatre, September 6, 1961.

Director Tyrone Guthrie, Norman Campbell; settings and costumes Brian Jackson; dances Douglas Campbell; musical director Louis Applebaum. With Eric House, Marion Studholme, Andrew Downie, Howell Glynne and the Stratford Ontario Festival Company.

THE LIVING THEATRE—Repertory of three plays. Producer The Living Theatre at the Living Theatre. After a summer of touring abroad, the Living Theatre began its season of repertory with THE CONNECTION on September 12, 1961.

THE CONNECTION (120 perfs.)—By Jack Gelber. Director Judith Malina; designer Julian Beck; lighting Nicola Cernovich. Premiered July 15, 1959. (See *The Best Plays of 1959-1960.*)

MANY LOVES (19 perfs.)—By William Carlos Williams. Director and designer Mr. Beck; lighting Mr. Cernovich. Premiered January 13, 1959. A revised version of the play opened May 15, 1961, and opened this season on October 31, 1961.

IN THE JUNGLE OF CITIES (80 perfs.)—By Bertolt Brecht, translated by Gerhard Nellhaus. Director Miss Malina; designer Mr. Beck; lighting Mr. Cernovich; music Teiji Ito. Premiered December 20, 1960 and reopened November 2, 1961. (See *The Best Plays of 1960-1961.*) THE APPLE by Jack Gelber was placed in repertory with the above on December 7, 1961. Note: total performances, if regarded as continuous: THE CONNECTION 602 (continued), IN THE JUNGLE OF CITIES 110 (continued), MANY LOVES (unavailable).

DOUBLE BILL (32 perfs.)—Return engagement of two one-act plays: KRAPP'S LAST TAPE by Samuel Beckett and THE ZOO STORY by Edward Albee. Originally presented January 14, 1960 for 582 performances, this revival commenced its run September 12, 1961 at the East End Theatre.

Donald Davis, the original Krapp, returned to play that role, which Herbert Berghof had taken over last season. In THE ZOO STORY Ben Piazza replaced Mark Richman, who had followed George Maharis as Jerry, and William Daniels recreated the role of Peter.

COCKEYED KITE (7 perfs.)—By Joseph Caldwell. Producers William Nichols, Van Varner. Actors Playhouse, September 13, 1961.

Director Neil McKenzie. With Jerry Pagano, Audra Lindley, Alfred Hinckley, Gaye Ellen Huston, Peggy Pope and Barbara Winchester. The troubles of a teen-age boy with a heart condition.

I WANT YOU (4 perfs.)—Musical with book by Stefan Kanfer and Jess J. Korman; music and lyrics by Mr. Kanfer, Mr. Korman and Joseph Grayhon. Producers Theodore J. Flicker, Sam W. Gelfman, Mr. Crayhon, in association with David W. Carter. Maidman Playhouse, September 14, 1961.

Director Mr. Flicker. With Joshua Shelley, Barbara Quaney and Al Mancini. Satire about an opportunistic publisher of patriotic songs during World War I. Musical numbers: ACT I, "My Daddy Was Right," "I Want You," "This Is a Dollar Bill," "Perfect Man," "The Farewells," "Remarkable," "That's What the Public Wants," "Ain't It Funny," "So Long, Yesterday," "You Devil You." ACT II, "Loyal American," "The Street," "Hong Kong Gong," "Perfect Man" (Reprise), "Take Every Opportunity," "You Devil You" (Reprise), Finale.

HAPPY DAYS (28 perfs.)—By Samuel Beckett. Producer Theatre 1962 (Clinton Wilder, Richard Barr). Cherry Lane Theatre, September 17, 1961.

Winnie ....Ruth White Willie ....John C. Becher

Director Alan Schneider; designer William Ritman; production stage manager, Kenneth Geist; stage manager, Helen Page Camp; press, Howard Atlee. Optimism and the struggle for survival vs. pessimism and defeat. This was played in repertory with Edward Albee's THE AMERICAN DREAM and THE DEATH OF BESSIE SMITH (see *Best Plays 1960-1961*), and was subsequently presented by the same performers as a reading at the 92nd Street Y.M.H.A. and out of town.

ONE WAY PENDULUM (40 perfs.)—By N. F. Simpson. Producer Caroline Swann. East Seventy-fourth Street Theatre, September 18, 1961.

Kirby Groomkirby	Dino Narrizano	Stan Honeyblock	John Milligan
Robert Barnes	James Kenny	Judge	Carey Nairnes
Mabel Groomkirby	Betty Leighton	Policeman	Elliott Landon
Sylvia Groomkirby	Audree Rae	Clerk of the Court	Joel Fabiani
Aunt Mildred	Margaretta Warwick	Usher	Charles Gerald
Myra Gantry	Anna Russell	Prosecuting Counsel	Paxton Whitehead
Arthur Groomkirby	Gerald Hiken	Defending Counsel	Noel Davis

Action takes place in the Groomkirby's living room.
Director Douglas Seale; designer Peter Harvey; lighting Walter Russell; stage manager, Edward Payson Call; press, Frank Goodman, Ben Washer, Leo Stern. Farce about an off-beat British family and their strange hobbies.

GHOSTS (216 perfs.)—By Henrik Ibsen, adapted by Carmel Ross from the translation by R. Farquharson Sharpe. Producer David Ross. Fourth Street Theatre, September 21, 1961.

Regina Engstrand	Carrie Nye	Manders	Staats Cotsworth
Engstrand	John McQuade	Mrs. Alving	Leueen MacGrath
Oswald Alving	Joseph Marino		

Director Mr. Ross; costumes Theoni V. Aldredge; settings and lighting Charles Bailey; production stage manager, John O'Neill; stage manager Richard Block; press, Howard Atlee. The play, written in 1881, had its American premiere in 1894 and has been revived many times since. (See *Index to the Best Plays Series, 1899-1950.*)

MISALLIANCE (156 perfs.)—By George Bernard Shaw. Producers Stuart Duncan, Philip Minor. Sheridan Square Playhouse, September 25, 1961.

Bentley Summerhays	George Reinholt	Lord Summerhays	Emery Battis
Johnny Tarleton	Edward Grover	Mr. Tarleton	Donald Moffat
Hypatia Tarleton	Fran Sternhagen	Percival	Wayne Tippit
Mrs. Tarleton	Frances Ingalls	Lina	Lidia Prochnicka
Gunner	James Greene		

The Surrey home of the Tarleton's on a Saturday afternoon.
Director Mr. Minor; setting Edward Burbridge; costumes Greta Richards; lighting Thomas Skelton; stage manager Frank Schmitt; press Marian Graham. Shaw's 1910 comedy about parents and children had its American premiere in 1917, and was revived in 1953 for 146 performances.

THE OPENING OF A WINDOW (24 perfs.)—By Gene Radano. Producers Jerome Guardino, Bram Appel. Theatre Marquee, September 25, 1961.

Director Fran Malis. With Philip Sterling and Olympia Dukakis. An Italian family living in a New York slum tries to overcome the evils of poverty.

A coffee break at a rehearsal of "Ghosts": David Ross (director), Kay Doubleday (who was replaced by Carrie Nye), Warren Finnerty (who was replaced by Jo Marino), Staats Cotsworth and Carmen Mathews (who was replaced by Leueen MacGrath).

THE THRACIAN HORSES (7 perfs.)—By Maurice Valency. Producers Chandler Warren, William S. Boal, in association with the Cliff Dwellers. Orpheum Theatre, September 27, 1961.

Alcestis	Nancy Wickwire	Crito	Thomas Barbour
Myrtilla	Margaret Kenline	Pheres	Nat Burns
Rhodanthe	Beverly Whitcomb	Critias	David Cort
Melita	Shelley Post	Philodorus	Ed English
Watchman	Don Pomes	Heracles	Louis Zorich
Cratylus	Thomas Ruisinger	Death	Algis Mantis
Second Watchman	George Guidall	The Scavenger	Danny Meehan
Admetus	Nicolas Coster	Acastus	Adam Kilgour
Zoilus	Konrad Matthaei	Guard	Algis Mantas
Zeus	Danny Meehan		

The palace of Admetus, King of Pherae.
Director Malcolm Black; setting Peter Harvey; costumes Ray Diffin; lighting Walter Russell; music Arnold Black; stage manager Mark Furness; press Arthur Cantor, Tony Geiss. Comedy, based loosely on the Alcestis legend, about a wife who would rather be immortal and famous than alive and obscure.

4TH AVENUE NORTH (2 perfs.)—Revue with music, lyrics and sketches by George Allan, Michael Batterberry, Shippen Geer, Murray Grand, Cy Walter and others. Producers Michael Betterberry, Shippen Geer. Madison Avenue Playhouse, September 27, 1961.

Director Michael Batterberry. With Clint Anderson, Bob Carey and Gerrianne Raphael. Musical numbers and sketches: ACT I, "Fourth Avenue North," Sunrise Semester, "Love at an Auction," "White Russian New Year," "Jenny," Doorman, "Let's Have a Party," Martin's Coming Up, "Mr. Corbett," T-Party, Thank God for the Civil War, "March," "So Long as He Loves You," "Musac," "Lonely Man," The Medium, Park Avenue Rapid Transit. ACT II, "Happy House," "Hold Me," "Lennox Hill Laundramat," "Beauty Treatment," A Cleaner N.Y., "Not So Easy," To the Dentist, "Christmas Trees," "Troubador," "Let's Not Go Away This Summer," Long Time No See, Open Air Market, The Director, "Institute for Psychodrama," Finale.

HI, PAISANO! (3 perfs.)—Musical with book by Ernest Chambers; music by Robert Holton; lyrics by June Carroll. Producer Aaron Gardner. York Playhouse, September 30, 1961.

Director Vassili Lambrinos. With David Canary and Marie Santell. How a young Italian immigrant manages to remain in the United States. Musical numbers: ACT I, "What Is Your Name?," "Cubes and Abstracts," "Dino Repetti," "Office Under the Sky," "Hi, Paisano," Ballet, "Time We Talked," "Dino's in Love," "Faith," "Cubes and Abstracts" (Reprise), "Sounds of Silence," "Girl He Adores," "It Happens Every Day," "Born in America," "Teresa," "Carousel." ACT II, "Reason to Marry," "Dozen Husbands," "Born in America" (Reprise), "Over Forty," "Time We Talked" (Reprise), "Table Tango," "I Know What He's Up To," "Let Me Drown," Finale.

THE SAP OF LIFE (49 perfs.)—Musical with book and lyrics by Richard Maltby, Jr.; music by David Shire; in collaboration with William Francisco. Producer Quartet Productions. One Sheridan Square, October 2, 1961.

Andrew	Kenneth Nelson	Ruthanne, the neighbor's girl	Patricia Bruder
Horatio	Jerry Dodge	Sally Ann, another neighbor's girl	Lee Powell
Oscar, their father	Jack Bittner		
Jessie, their mother	Dina Paisner		
Dot, the old aunt	Lilian Fields		

Time: the present. Place: home and the city.
Director Mr. Francisco; settings and costumes John Conklin; lighting Peter Hunt; orchestrations and arrangements David Shire, Julian Stein; musical director Mr. Stein; stage manager A. Berney Jones, Jr.; press Howard Atlee. An elder son is sent out into the world by his parents so that he may become a man. Musical numbers: ACT I, "Saturday Morning," "Farewell, Family," "Charmed Life," "Fill Up Your Life with Sunshine," "Good Morning," "Watching the Big Parade Go By," "The Love of Your Life." ACT II, "A Hero's Love," "Children Have It Easy," "She Loves Me Not," "Mind Over Matter," "Time and Time Again," Finale.

BETWEEN WHISKY AND VODKA (8 perfs.)—German language revue with sketches by Kay and Lore Lorentz and Eckard Hacgfeld; music by Werner Krause, Emile Schuchardt and Rolf

Liebermann. Producers Felix Gerstman, Gert von Gontard, in association with the Deutsches Theatre of New York. Barbizon-Plaza, October 3, 1961.

THE WINGS OF THE DOVE (3 perfs.)—World premiere of an opera based on the novel by Henry James, with libretto by Ethan Ayer; music by Douglas Moore. Producer New York City Center of Music and Drama. The New York City Center, October 12, 1961.

Kate Croy .... Regina Sarfaty
Homer Croy, her father ..... Paul Ukena
Aunt Maud Lowder, her aunt .... Martha Lipton
Miles Dunster .... John Reardon
Milly Theale .... Dorothy Coulter
Susan Stringham, her companion .... Mary Lesawyer
Lord Mark .... Norman Kelley
Steffans, a servant .... Richard Fredricks
Lecturer .... Maurice Stern
Guiliano .... Fredric Milstein
Players in "Janus Ballet":
Janus ... Gerald Arpino, Paul Sutherland
Goddess of Spring .... Francoise Martinet
Her Attendants ...... Rita Bradley, Mary Ellen Jackson
Goddess of Winter .... Brunilda Ruiz
Her Attendants ...... Suzanne Hammons, Marie Paquet

Warriors: James DeBolt, James Howell, Nels Jorgenson, Lawrence Rhodes, John Wilson.

Time: 1902. Place: London and Venice.

Director Christopher West; conductor Julius Rudel; settings Donald Oenslager; costumes Patton Campbell; choreography Robert Joffrey; chorus master William Jonson.

ACT I

"There Was a Day" .... Mr. Croy
"Kate, Would You Mind if We Were Poor?" .... Kate and Dunster
"I Can Bite Your Head Off Any Day" .... Aunt Maud
"Dove Song" .... Milly
"Susan and I Missed You" .... Milly and Mark

ACT II

"Everything Is Likely Looking" .... Milly
"Although I Came from Boston" .... Susan
"You Shall Have Money" .... Kate and Dunster
* "Minstrel's Song" .... Narrator
"I Have the One You See" .... Milly and Dunster

ACT III

"Constanza Lepolelli Was the Daughter" .... Milly
"Kate, Kate, What Have We Done" .... Dunster
"To Write This Letter" .... Kate
"Can You Forgive Me?" .... Kate and Aunt Maud

* "Minstrel's Song" was not included in the original production and appears only in the revised version of the opera published by G. Schirmer, Inc.

THE CAVE DWELLERS (6 perfs.)—By William Saroyan. Producers Stella Holt, Elizabeth Roberts, Maurice Schadad, in association with Arthur Loeb. Greenwich Mews Theatre, October 16, 1961.

Director Michael Lindsay-Hogg. With Geraldine Fitzgerald. About a former stage star and the people who inhabit her backstage world. Originally presented on Broadway October 17, 1957 for 97 performances.

DIFF'RENT (88 perfs.)—By Eugene O'Neill. Producers Torquay Company, Ruth Kramer. Mermaid Theatre, October 17, 1961.

Director Paul Shyre. With Marian Seldes, Michael Higgins and Robert Drivas. Tragedy of a young woman who rejects her ship captain fiance because she feels he's been unfaithful to her. After 30 years of celibacy she throws herself at a young boy and the captain hangs himself. THE LONG VOYAGE HOME was added as a companion piece on December 4, 1961 and played 32 performances. (See *Index to the Best Plays Series 1899-1950* for previous productions of these two plays.)

ANOTHER EVENING WITH HARRY STOONES (1 perf.)—Revue with sketches, music and lyrics by Jeff Harris. Producer Stenod Productions. Gramercy Arts Theatre, October 21, 1961.

Staged by G. Adam Jordan. With Diana Sands, Barbra Streisand, Sheila Copelan, Kenny Adams, Ben Keller and Dom De Luise. Satire on the "Evening with . . ." type of show.

BEI MIR BIST DU SCHOEN (88 perfs.)—Yiddish-American musical with book by Louis Freiman; music by Sholom Secunda; lyrics by Jacob Jacobs. Producer Mr. Jacobs. Phyllis Anderson Theatre, October 21, 1961.

Director Leo Fuchs. With Mr. Fuchs and Mr. Jacobs. The hero's break with Jewish tradition and his romance with two women, who in the end turn out to be long lost mother and daughter.

TWO BY SAROYAN (98 perfs.)—Two one-act plays by William Saroyan: TALKING TO YOU and ACROSS THE BOARD ON TOMORROW MORNING. Producers Shelley Gordon, Barry Gordon. East End Theatre, October 22, 1961.

Director Arthur Storch. With Milt Kamen, Nicholas Colasanto, Cal Bellini and James Broderick. The first play laments the fate of the good man in a wicked world, and the second burlesques the world of class distinction and prejudices. (See *Index to the Best Plays Series, 1899-1950* for previous productions.)

THE CRUCIBLE (3 perfs.)—World premiere of an opera based on the play by Arthur Miller, with libretto by Bernard Stambler; music by Robert Ward. Producer New York City Center of Music and Drama. New York City Center, October 26, 1961.

Betty Parris	Joyce Ebert	Rev. John Hale	Norman Treigle
Rev. Samuel Parris	Norman Kelley	Elizabeth Proctor	Frances Bible
Tituba	Debria Brown	Mary Warren	Joy Clements
Abigail Williams	Patricia Brooks	Ezekiel Cheever	Harry Theyard
Ann Putnam	Mary Lesawyer	Judge Danforth	Ken Neate
Thomas Putnam	Paul Ukena	Sarah Good	Joan Kelm
Rebecca Nurse	Eunice Alberts	Ruth Putnam	Lorna Ceniceros
Francis Nurse	Spiro Malas	Susanna Walcott	Helen Guile
Giles Corey	Maurice Stern	Mercy Lewis	Nancy Roy
John Proctor	Chester Ludgin	Martha Sheldon	Elizabeth Schwering
Bridget Booth	Beverly Evans		

Time: 1692. Place: Salem, Massachusetts.
Director Allen Fletcher; conductor Emmerson Buckley; settings Paul Sylbert; costumes Ruth Morley.

O MARRY ME (21 perfs.)—Musical based on Goldsmith's "She Stoops to Conquer," with book and lyrics by Lola Pergament; music by Robert Kessler. Producer Lily Turner. Gate Theatre, October 27, 1961.

Tony Lumpkin ....James Harwood	Dick Muggins, a servant ...Frank Echols
Squire Hardcastle ....Joe Silver	Kate Hardcastle ....Chevi Colton
Mrs. Hardcastle ....Muriel Greenspon	Constance Neville ....Elly Stone
Little Aminidab, a servant ...Ken Golden	Stingo, tavern keeper ....Paul Bain
Diggory, a servant ....Maurice Edwards	Bett Bouncer, barmaid ...Judith Burkette
Roger, a servant .....Christopher Marsh	Young Marlow .....Ted Van Griethuysen
Pimple, a housemaid ....Caroline Rausch	George Hastings ....Leonard Drum
Bridget, the cook ....Sylvia O'Brien	Sir Charles Marlow ....Frank Echols

Director Michael Howard; settings and lighting Herbert Senn and Helen Pond; costumes Sonia Lowenstein; orchestrations Sam Morgenstern; musical director Lowell Farr; stage manager Albert Schoemann; press Bernard Simon, Leo Stern.

ACT I

"I Love Everything That's Old" ....Squire Hardcastle
"Time and Tide" ....Squire and Mrs. Hardcastle
"The Kind of Man" ....Kate
"The Kind of Man" (Reprise) ....Kate
"Ale House Song" ....Tony, Stingo and Ensemble
"Proper Due" ....Tony
"Be a Lover" ....Marlow and Hastings
"Perish the Baubles" ....Constance and Hastings
"The Meeting" ....Kate and Marlow
"Fashions" ....Mrs. Hardcastle and Hastings
"Fashions" (Reprise) ....Mrs. Hardcastle and Tony
"Say Yes, Look No" ....Kate, Constance, Mrs. Hardcastle, Pimple and Bridget

ACT II

"Let's All Be Exactly and Precisely What We Are" ....Ensemble
"The Braggart Song" ....Marlow and Kate
"O Marry Me!" ....Kate
"Betrayed" ....Mrs. Hardcastle, Constance, Hastings, Marlow and Tony
"O Marry Me!" (Reprise) ....Kate
"Motherly Love" ....Mrs. Hardcastle and Tony
"A Child's Worst Friend Is His Mother" ....Squire Hardcastle
Finale ....Entire Company

GO SHOW ME A DRAGON (3 perfs.)—By Gene Feldman. Producer Hanneford Productions, in association with Jerry Feldman. Midway Theatre, October 27, 1961.

Director John Ben Tarver. With Philip Lawrence and Sharlene Stevens. What happens to a beatnik colony's inhabitants when a famous but alcoholic poet takes up residence there.

THREE ONE-ACT PLAYS (16 perfs.)—Off-Bowery Theatre, October 29, 1961.

THE DISCONTENT OF A RUSSIAN PRINCE by Diane Di Prima. Director Jerry Benjamin. With Fred Herko, Penny Ross. A burlesque fairy tale.

PILLOW by Michael McClure. Director Mr. Benjamin. With Ron Faber, Louis Waldon, Jeanne Thomas. Verse drama about love and hate among some elegant beatniks.

DANTE by Le Roi Jones, from "The Systems of Dante's Hell." With Louis Waldon, Ron Faber, Alan Marlowe, Karl Schenzer. A modern parallel of The False Comforters theme.

CLANDESTINE ON THE MORNING LINE (24 perfs.)—By Josh Greenfeld. Producers John T. Weems, Robert Buccolo, in association with Ted White. Actors Playhouse, October 30, 1961.

Director Allen Davis. With Rosetta LeNoire and James Earl Jones. An optimistic mother believes in both the stars and the people she tries to help.

THE BUSKERS (6 perfs.)—By Kenneth Jupp. Producers Lois Bianchi, Amnon Kabatchnik. Cricket Theatre, October 30, 1961.

Director Mr. Kabatchnik. With Grayson Hall and Wallace Engelhardt. A group of itinerant entertainers (buskers) spend ten years searching for one of their group.

GO FIGHT CITY HALL (77 perfs.)—Yiddish-American musical, with book by Harry Kalmanowich; music by Murray Rumshinsky; lyrics by Bella Mysell. Producers Irving Jacobson, Julius Adler. Mayfair Theatre, November 2, 1961.

Director Menachem Rubin. With Mr. Jacobson, Mr. Rubin, Mae Schoenfeld, Bruce Adler and Henrietta Jacobson. Plot involves a widow, her two children, her suitor and various friends.

* TIME, GENTLEMEN PLEASE (330 perfs.)—English musical revue. Producers John Krimsky and the Players Theatre of London. Strollers Theatre-Club, November 4, 1961.

Fred Stone (Chairman), Joan Sterndale Bennett, Margaret Burton, Sheila Bernette, Tony Bateman, Archie Harradine, Kyra Vayne, Jean Rayner, Geoffrey Webb, Jerry Terheyden.

Director Don Gammell; director in New York Mr. Stone; choreography Tony Bateman; settings Thea Neu; costumes Reginald Woolley; lighting Victor Gabriel Junquera; stage manager, Jack Ryland; press Phillip Bloom. A new program of songs was substituted for the original on January 16, 1962. Musical numbers: ACT I, "Jolly Good Luck to the Girl Who Loves a Sailor," "Daddy Wouldn't Buy Me a Bow-Wow," "The Polka and the Choir Boy," "Just Like the Ivy I'll Cling to You," "Jane, Jane from Maiden Lane," "The Girl I Kissed on the Stair." ACT II, "Gay Bohemia," "Marble Arch to Leicester Square," "Hold Your Hand Out, Naughty Boy!," "The Bells," "At the Seaside." ACT III, "Who Were You with Last Night?," "Little Yellow Bird," "Miss Julia, Whose Behavior Was Very Peculiar!," "The Honeysuckle and the Bee," "O Se Sapeste from La Fauciulla del West," "The Shooting of Dan McGrew," Chairman's Remarks and Finale.

SHARON'S GRAVE (6 perfs.)—By John B. Keane. Producer the Irish Players, in association with Cassie Meer. Maidman Playhouse, November 8, 1961.

Director Sonia Moore. With Helena Carroll, Dermot McNamara, Byron Russell and Grania O'Malley. An Irish girl's struggle to protect her home and younger brother against a cruel environment.

ALL IN LOVE (141 perfs.)—Musical based on Sheridan's "The Rivals," with book and lyrics by Bruce Geller; music by Jacques Urbont. Producers Mr. Urbont, J. Terry Brown, Jr., Stella Holt, in association with George Peters, Herbert Steinmann. Martinique Theatre, November 10, 1961.

Pages	Sean Gillespie, Bonita Belle	Lucius O'Trigger	Michael Davis
Lucy	Christina Gillespie	Sir Percival Crumble	Fidel Romann
Mrs. Malaprop	Mimi Randolph	Sir William Holdfast	Robert Quint
Sir Anthony Absolute	Lee Cass	Sir Roger Backstep	Roy Hausen
Lydia Languish	Gaylea Byrne	Sir Thomas Standpat	John Dennison
Jack Absolute	David Atkinson	Lady Garter	Lorraine Bergstrom
Bag	Charles Kimbrough	Lady Climber	Elizabeth Burgess
Bob Acres	Dom De Luise	Lady Barter	Wanda Cooke

Lady Slattern-Lounger ..Mary Jane Wilson

Director Tom Brennan; settings and costumes Charles Lisanby; lighting Jules Fisher; musical staging Jack Beaber; musical direction and vocal arrangements Mr. Urbont; dance arrangements Anne Sternberg; orchestrations Jonathan Tunick; stage manager Robert Moss; press David Lipsky.

ACT I

"To Bath Derry-O" .... Bag and Gentry
"Poor" .... Lydia and Jack
"What Can It Be" .... Lucy and Gentry
"Odds" .... Bob Acres and Jack
"I Love a Fool" .... Jack
"A More Than Ordinary Glorious Vocabulary" .... Mrs. Malaprop
"Women Simple" .... Sir Anthony
"The Lady Was Made to Be Loved" .... Sir Anthony and Jack
"The Good Old Ways" .... Grenadiers
"Honour" .... O'Trigger
"The Good Old Ways" (Reprise) .... Sir Anthony and Grenadiers

ACT II

"I Found Him" and "Day Dreams" .... Lucy and Servants
"Don't Ask Me" .... Jack and Lydia
"Why Wives" .... O'Trigger, Bag and Grenadiers
"I Love a Fool" (Reprise) .... Lydia
"Quickly" .... Mrs. Malaprop, Lydia, Lucy and Bag
"All in Love" .... Jack and the Company
Finale .... Sir Anthony and the Company

THE AUTOMOBILE GRAVEYARD (8 perfs.)—By Fernando Arrabal, translated by Richard Howard. Producer Gian Sciandra. Forty-first Street Theatre, November 13, 1961.

Director Herbert Machiz. With Gabe Dell, Leila Martin and Estelle Parsons. Avant garde play about some goings on in an old junk yard.

BELLA (6 perfs.)—Musical with book by Tom O'Malley and Lance Barklie; music by Jane Douglas; lyrics by Mr. O'Malley. Producers Mr. Barklie, Ned Hendrickson. Gramercy Arts Theatre, November 16, 1961.

Director Richard C. Shank. With Dodo Denney, Will B. Able and Gloria LeRoy. Satire on the whodunit type of mystery story. Musical numbers: ACT I, "On the Seashore by the Sea," "It Isn't the Same," "All About Evelyn," "Could Be," "Time," "The Seven Seas," "Hand in Hand," "Love Doesn't Grow on Trees," "I'm Happy," "My Card," "Kiss Me." ACT II, "Madame from Paree," "Big, Big," "Could Be" (Reprise), "Take a Chance," "Way Down in 'Lil' Old Texas," "For Love or Money," Finale.

'TOINETTE (31 perfs.)—Musical based on Moliere's "La Malade Imaginaire," with book by J. I. Rodale; music and lyrics by Deed Meyer. Producer Bickerstaff Productions. Theatre Marquee, November 20, 1961.

Director Curt Conway. With Logan Ramsey and Ellie Wood. Musical numbers: ACT I, "Rags," "Bonjour," "Come on Outside and Get Some Air," "Why Shouldn't I?," "A Father Speaks," "A Lullaby," "Honest Honore," "Someone to Count On," "Un, Dieux, Trois," "Fly Away," " 'Toinette." ACT II, "Madly in Love with You Am I," "Someone to Count On" (Reprise), "Beat, Little Pulse," "Even a Doctor Can Make a Mistake," "Dr. Iatro," "Small Apartment," "Small Apartment" (Reprise), "Recitative," "You're the Most Impossible Person," Finale.

DOUBLE BILL (48 perfs.)—Two one-act plays. Producer Theatre, Inc. (T. Edward Hambleton, Norris Houghton). Phoenix Theatre, November 21, 1961.

ANDROCLES AND THE LION (48 perfs.)—By George Bernard Shaw. Director Tom Gruenewald; settings and costumes by Peter Wingate. With John Heffernan, Dana Elcar, Nicholas Kepros, Alison Howard, Frederic Warriner and Ted Graeber.
THE POLICEMAN (23 perfs.)—By Slawomir Mrozek, translated by Leonides D-Ossetynski. Director Mr. D-Ossetynski. With Lionel Stander, Jack Gilford, Marcie Hubert, Leon Janney and Robert Pastene. Satire on a totalitarian state where the police are forced to create a rebel to justify their existence. This play was replaced December 12 by Shaw's DARK LADY OF THE SONNETS, which played 24 performances.

DOUBLE BILL (6 perfs.)—Two one-act plays by John Mortimer: WHAT SHALL WE TELL CAROLINE? and THE DOCK BRIEF. Producer Rose Lynch. Midway Theatre, November 21, 1961.

Director Steve Chernak. With Anthony Deardon, Margot Welch, Joseph Booley and Mary Cooper. The first play deals with an apparently mute girl, her parents and her mother's lover, and the second examines an elderly barrister's defense of a murderer.

RED ROSES FOR ME (176 perfs.)—By Sean O'Casey. Producers Stella Holt, Beverly Landau, in association with J. Terry Brown, Jr., Milton Reverby. Greenwich Mews Theatre, November 27, 1961.

Director Adrian Hall; settings Robert Soule. With Martin Green, Ted van Griethuysen, Kipp Currie and Margaret Lenert. This play was first produced on Broadway December 28, 1955 for 29 performances.

THIS WAY TO THE TOMB (6 perfs.)—By Ronald Duncan, with incidental music by Benjamin Britten. Presented by the Program in Religious Drama at the Union Theological Seminary, November 30, 1961.

Director E. Martin Browne; with James Malcolm, Hunter Tillman, Judith Sykes. Two parts: MASQUE tells in richly patterned verse the story of a saint's search for God, and ANTI-MASQUE satarizes the religiosity of our own day.

SHADOW OF HEROES (20 perfs.)—By Robert Ardrey. Producers Warner Le Roy, Paul Libin, Bunker Jenkins. York Playhouse, December 5, 1961.

Author .... Muni Seroff
Gestapo Men ... Thomas Gaines, Douglas Easley
Julia Rajk .... Salome Jens
Laszlo Rajk .... Bernard Grant
Janos Kadar .... Sam Gray
Viktor .... Abe Vigoda
Comrades .. Ron Rosenthal, Brinton Turkle
Captain Szabo .... Edgar Daniels
Women Prisoners .. Tracey Phelps, Jane Chaback, Edythe Byrnes, Dimitra Steris
Office Worker .... Michael Cetta
Office Guard .... Thomas Gaines
Matyas Rakosi .... Rudolf Weiss
Erno Gero .... George Gaynes
Beater .... Douglas Easley
Poet .... Algis Mantas
Survivors .... Brinton Turkle, Norman Heidinger
Russian Soldiers .... Mike Valen, Allan Sferios
Secretary .... Ron Rosenthal
Mother .... Lillian Kaufman
Doctor .... Brinton Turkle
Gabor Peter .... Louis Zorich

Mihaly Farkus .... Abe Vigoda
Vladimir Markas ...... Akila Couloumbis
Mrs. Kovacs .... Frieda Altman
Laszlo Rajk, Jr. .... Robby Reed
Sandor Horvath .... Thomas de Bien
Committee Chairman ..... Brinton Turkle
Student .... Thomas Gaines
Young Woman .... Tracey Phelps
Mikoyan .... Peter Boyle
Hegedus .... Michael Cetta
General Janza .... Edgar Daniels
Friends of Rajk .... Ron Rosenthal, Thomas Gaines, Lillian Kaufman, Brinton Turkle
General Maleter .... Mark Duffy
General Suslov .... I. W. Klein
Imre Nagy .... Louis Zorich
Andropov .... George Nestor

Others: Dean Delk, Nick Murray, Bob Spivak.
Director Mr. Le Roy; settings Kim Swados; lighting Jane Reisman; costumes Deidre Cartier; press Karl Bernstein, Ben Kornzweig.

See page 150.

SING MUSE! (39 perfs.)—Musical with book and lyrics by Erich Segal; music by Joseph Raposo. Producer Robert D. Feldstein. Van Dam Theatre, December 6, 1961.

Director Bill Penn; settings Boyd Dumrose. With Karen Morrow, Paul Michael, Bob Spencer and Ralph Stantly. About Helen of Troy. Musical numbers: ACT I, "Helen Quit Your Yellin'," "I Am a Travelling Poet," "O Pallas Athene," "Your Name May Be Paris," "Out to Launch," "Sing Muse!," "You're in Love," "The Wrath of Achilles," "No Champagne," "The Wrath of Achilles" (Reprise), "Please Let Me Read." ACT II, "Business Is Bad," "In Our Little Salon," "Fame!," "Your Name May Be Paris" (Reprise), "We'll Find a Way," "The Way," Finale.

THE APPLE (64 perfs.)—By Jack Gelber. Producer The Living Theatre. The Living Theatre, December 7, 1961.

Director Judith Malina; setting Julian Beck; lighting Nicola Cernovich; stage manager, Charles Weatherford. With Julian Beck, Marilyn Chris, John A. Coe, James Earl Jones, Fred Miller, Marion Jim and Henry Proach. A zany comedy with fantastic overtones about a group of actors who simultaneously play themselves, their professional presumptions, and various characters they invent for a series of rather morbid scenes.

BLACK NATIVITY (57 perfs.)—Christmas song-play by Langston Hughes. Producers Michael R. Santangelo, Barbara Griner, in association with Eric Franck. Forty-first Street Theatre, December 11, 1961.

Director Vinnette Carroll. With Marion Williams and the Stars of Faith, Professor Alex Bradford and Singers, Clive Thompson, Cleo Quitman, Carl Ford and Howard Sanders. Musical numbers: ACT I, THE CHILD IS BORN; "Joy to the World," "My Way Is Cloudy," "No Room at the Inn," "Most Done Travelling," "Oh, Jerusalem, in the Morning," "Poor Little Jesus," "What You Gonna Name Your Baby?", "Wasn't That a Mighty Day!," "Christ Was Born," "Go Tell It on the Mountain," "Rise Up, Shepherd, and Follow!," "What Month Was Jesus Borned In?," "Sweet Little Jesus Boy," "Oh, Come All Ye Faithful," "If Anybody Asked You Who I Am?," "Children, Go Where I Send Thee." ACT II, THE WORD IS SPREAD; "Meetin' Here Tonight," "Holy Ghost, Don't Leave Me," "We Shall Be Changed," "The Blood Saved Me," "Leak in the Building," "Nobody Like the Lord," "His Will Be Done," "Said I Wasn't Gonna Tell Nobody," "Get Away Jordan," "Packin' Up," "God Be With You."

* THE HOSTAGE (196 perfs.)—By Brendan Behan. Producers Norma Frances, Robert Margulies, Bell Productions. One Sheridan Square, December 12, 1961.

Pat, the caretaker of a lodging house ....Alan Nunn
Meg Dillon ....Paddy Croft
Monsewer ....Norman Roland
Old Ropeen ....Kathleen Roland
Colette ....Marge Burnett
Princess Grace, an American prize-fighter ...Rae Saunders
Rio Rita ....James Cahill
Mr. Mulleady ....Gavin Payne
Miss Gilchrist, a social worker ....Patricia Ripley
Leslie, a British soldier ...Geoff Garland
Teresa, a country girl ....Jane McArthur
I.R.A. Officer ....William Bassett
Volunteer ....Vince O'Connor
Russian sailor ....Richard Sabol
Bill, the pianist ....Bill Johnson

Director Perry Bruskin; designer Karl Hueglin; original costumes Margaret Bury; stage manager Kenneth Costigan; press Abner D. Klipstein, Lorella Val-Mery. This play was produced on Broadway September 20, 1960 for 127 performances.

SIGNS ALONG THE CYNIC ROUTE (93 perfs.)—Revue with sketches by Will Holt and Dolly Jonah; music and lyrics by Mr. Holt. Producer Precarious Productions. Actors Playhouse, December 14, 1961.

Director Walt Witcover. With Will Holt, Dolly Jonah and Robert Barend. Musical numbers and sketches: ACT I, "Signs," Welcome, Second Glances, Bertha, Modern Housing, "I Know You," News Item, "Carnival," Marriage Counsel, "The Social Director's Song," The Rise and Fall of the City of Movieville. ACT II, "Four More Shopping Days," "Weekend," Princeton Pastorale, Summer Stock, "The Blonde's Song," Discussion, "Tin Can Incantation," Croquet, "Kulturny," Seconds, "Till the Birds Sing," "Last."

ALL KINDS OF GIANTS (16 perfs.)—Musical with book and lyrics by Tom Whedon; music by Sam Pottle. Producer Noel Weiss. Cricket Theatre, December 18, 1961.

Director Peter Conlow. With Claiborne Cary, Richard Morse, Bill Hinnant and Tom Rummler. Fairy tale about a commoner who seeks to marry a princess, despite the opposition of her father. Musical numbers: ACT I, "State of the Kingdom," "My Prince," "Paint Me a Rainbow," "Logic!," "If I Were Only Someone." ACT II, "To Be a King," "Suddenly Stop and Think," "My Star," "All Kinds of Giants," "Friends." ACT III, "Here Are We," "Be Yourself," "Be Myself," "Duel," Finale.

POPPA IS HOME (3 perfs.)—By Monroe Schneider. Producer Quaker Productions. Gate Theatre, December 19, 1961.

Director Robert T. Seymour. With Ester Benson, Philip Fox, Theo Goetz and Max Gulack. The relationships between the parents and children of a large family.

NOT WHILE I'M EATING (2 perfs.)—Revue with sketches and lyrics by Arthur Sherman; music by Arthur Siegel. Producer David Silberman, Jr. Madison Avenue Playhouse, December 19, 1961.

Director Warren Enters. With Hal Buckley, Wisa D'Orso, Buzz Halliday, Judd Jones and Irene Perri.

THE TICKET-OF-LEAVE MAN (31 perfs.)—By Tom Taylor. Producers John M. Grissmer, William F. DeSeta. Midway Theatre, December 22, 1961.

Director Robert Moore. With Philip Bosco, Mary Harrigan, James Forster, Joseph Plummer and William Cottrell. Melodrama about a detective looking for the man who killed his partner; it was first produced in 1863.

MADAME APHRODITE (13 perfs.)—Musical with book by Tad Mosel; music and lyrics by Jerry Herman. Producers Howard Barker, Cynthia Baer, Robert Chambers. Orpheum Theatre, December 29, 1961.

Director Robert Turoff; settings David Ballou; costumes Patricia Zipprodt. With Nancy Andrews, Jack Drummond, Cherry Davis, and Rod Colbin. About a peddler of beauty creams and the people she fools. Musical numbers: ACT I, "I Don't Mind," "Sales Reproach," "Beat the World," "Miss Euclid Avenue," "Beautiful," "You I Like," ". . . And a Drop of Lavender," "The Girls Who Sit and Wait," "Beat the World" (Reprise). ACT II, "You I Like" (Reprise), "Afferdytie," "There Comes a Time," "Miss Euclid Avenue" (Reprise), "Only Love," "Take a Good Look Around," "Beautiful" (Reprise).

TWO AT LES DEUX—Two one-act plays. Producer Morton Lewis. Les Deux Megots, December 31, 1961.

IN GLASS HOUSES by Jerome A. Kass. Director Mr. Lewis. With Joan Perry, Don Vezdic, Marion Meade. A 14-year-old Dead End girl is seduced by a 16-year-old idealist, who then becomes frightened and deserts her.

A TWENTIETH CENTURY GUY by Ellen Green. Director Mr. Lewis. With Mr. Lewis. A young jazz musician in a monologue shows the audience his reactions to his wife's having left him and, in the end, to her return.

FORTUNA (5 perfs.)—Musical adapted from a drama by Eduardo de Filippo and Armando Curcio; book and lyrics by Arnold Weinstein; music by Francis Thorne. Producers John Wulp, Sam Cohn, in association with Julia Miles. Maidman Playhouse, January 3, 1962.

Director Glen Tetley. With Gabriel Dell, Jane Connell, Ted Beniades and Pat Birch. An impoverished Italian receives news of a huge inheritance, whose provisions he has just violated. Musical numbers: ACT I, "A Deal," "Someone Such as Me," "Checking the Facts," "Call Him Papa," "In My Heart," "So What? Why Not!," "The Ice House Fire," "O Stomach of Mine, We Eat!," "Police!" ACT II, "Angelica," "Speak in Silence," "Premeditated Luck," "Speech," "What a Lovely Dream," "Million Goes to Million," "Premeditated Luck" (Reprise).

* BRECHT ON BRECHT (170 perfs.)—Stage reading, arranged and translated by George Tabori. Producers the Greater New York Chapter of ANTA and Cheryl Crawford. Theatre de Lys, January 3, 1962.

Director Gene Frankel; designer Wolfgang Roth; stage manager Don Gilliland; press Howard Atlee. With Dane Clark, Anne Jackson, Lotte Lenya, Viveca Lindfors, George Voskovec and Michael Wager. Program: PART I, LIFE; The Lion (L. Lenya), Pine Trees (G. Voskovec), On Lighting (M. Wager), The Solution (D. Clark), The Mask of Evil (A. Jackson), The Dog (L. Lenya), Maria (V. Lindfors), Advice to Actors (A. Jackson), Letter to Some New York Actors (M. Wager), On Critics (G. Voskovec), "The Solomon Song" (L. Lenya; music Kurt Weill; words Marc Blitzstein), Of Poor B.B. (G. Voskovec; translated by Eric Bentley), Spring 1938 (D. Clark), Written on the Wall (Ensemble), Questions from a Worker (D. Clark), Ballad of Marie Farrar (A. Jackson; translated by H. R. Hays), The Jews (George Voskovec), "Song of a German Mother" (L. Lenya; music Hanns Eisler; words E. Bentley), The Flood (M. Wager), Changing Wheels (L. Lenya), Finland (V. Lindfors), Bad Times (M. Wager), Extracts from "Conversations in Exile" (D. Clark, G. Voskovec), Landscapes of Exile (A. Jackson; translated by H. R. Hays), "Pirate Jenny" (L. Lenya; music Kurt Weill; words Marc Blitzstein), Hollywood Elegies (V. Lindfors, A. Jackson, M. Wager, D. Clark), Burning of the Books (L. Lenya), Some Stories About Herr K. (G. Voskovec, D. Clark, V. Lindfors), Last Song (L. Lenya). PART

II, THEATRE; On Casting (A. Jackson), Song from "Mother Courage" (L. Lenya; music Paul Dessau), The Playwright's Song (D. Clark), From "The Good Woman of Setzuan" (A. Jackson; translated by E. Bentley), From "The Life of Galileo" (G. Voskovec, M. Wager, A. Jackson; translated by Charles Laughton), From "St. Joan of the Stockyards" (L. Lenya; translated by Frank Jones), The Old Hat (D. Clark), The Jewish Wife (V. Lindfors, G. Voskovec; translated by E. Bentley), Envoi (D. Clark).

WHO'LL SAVE THE PLOWBOY? (56 perfs.)—By Frank D. Gilroy. Producer Theatre, Inc. (T. Edward Hambleton, Norris Houghton). Phoenix Theatre, January 9, 1962.

Albert Cobb ....Gerald O'Loughlin
Helen Cobb ....Rebecca Darke
Larry Doyle ....William Smithers
The Man ....Tom Sawyer
Mrs. Doyle ....Dorothy Peterson
The Doctor ....Burton Mallory
The Boy ....Patrick O'Shaughnessy

Time: the present. Place: New York.

Director Daniel Petrie; settings and costumes Norris Houghton; lighting John Robertson; stage manager, Bigelow Green; press Ben Kornzweig, Karl Bernstein. A young man visits the home of a man whose life he saved during the war, and finds that his act, which is costing him his own life, has preserved his friend only for a wretched existence.

SEACOAST OF BOHEMIA (258 perfs.)—Revue with scenes and dialogue created by the company. Producers Bernard Sahlins, Howard Alk, Paul Sills. Square East, January 10, 1962.

Directors Paul Sills, Alan Arkin; music William Mathieu; settings Larry Klein; lighting Gary and Timmy Harris. With the Second City Company: Howard Alk, Alan Arkin, Severn Darden, Andrew Duncan, Barbara Harris, Lynda Segal and Eugene Troobnick. This was a different revue by the same company that performed in FROM THE SECOND CITY on Broadway earlier in the season. Musical numbers and sketches: ACT I, Nightclub Interview, Candid Camera, Vend-A-Buddy, Colonel Clevis in West Berlin, "The Question Song," Met's Vets, Abduction from the Ladder. ACT II, Happy Birthday, Clothes Make the Man, No, George, Don't, Khrushchev-Kennedy Interview, Pagan Place, "The Girls in Their Summer Dresses."

* PLAYS FOR BLEECKER STREET (162 perfs.)—Three one-act plays by Thornton Wilder. Producers Theodore Mann, José Quintero. Circle in the Square, January 11, 1962.

INFANCY

(From the series "The Seven Ages of Man," No. I)

Patrolman Avanzino ....Jack Dodson
Miss Milly Wilchick ....Mary Doyle
Tommy ....MacIntyre Dixon
Mrs. Boker ....Charlotte Jones
Moe ....Richard Libertini

Conversations between a mother and a nursemaid and their charges.

CHILDHOOD

(From the series "The Seven Ages of Man," No. II)

Dodie ....Debbie Scott
Caroline ....Susan Towers
Billee ....Philip Visco
Mother ....Betty Miller
Father ....Dana Elcar

Fantasy involving the play-acting of three small children who pretend to attend their parents' funeral.

SOMEONE FROM ASSISI

(From the series "The Seven Deadly Sins," No. IV, Lust)

Pica ....Sandra MacDonald
Mona Lucrezia ....Betty Miller
Mother Clara ....Dolores Dorn
Father Francis ....Lee Richardson

Anne Jackson, Michael Wager, Viveca Lindfors, George Voskovec and Dane Clark listen to Lotte Lenya recite in "Brecht on Brecht." Mr. Brecht studies the group from above.

Study of the former relationship between a poor crazy woman and St. Francis.
Director Mr. Quintero; settings and lighting Peter Harvey; costumes Keith Cuerden; stage manager, Byron Ringland; press James D. Proctor.

MOON ON A RAINBOW SHAWL (105 perfs.)—By Errol John. Producers Kermit Bloomgarden, Harry Joe Brown, Jr. East Eleventh Street Theatre, January 15, 1962.

Ephraim	James Earl Jones	Sailor	Michael Barton
Ketch	Robert Hill II	Sophia Adams	Vinnette Carroll
Esther	Kelly Marie Berry	Old Mack	Melvin Stewart
Mavis	Cicely Tyson	Rosa	Ellen Holly

Fisherwoman ....Gertrude Jannette
Policeman ....Ronald Mack
Prince ....Bill Gunn
Charlie Adams ....Robert Earl Jones
Soldier ....Peter Owens
Janette ....Carolyn Strictland
A Boy ....Wayne Grice
Taxi Driver ....Warren Berry

Time: a year or so after V-J Day. Place: Port-of-Spain.
Director George Roy Hill; settings Lloyd Burlingame; lighting Jules Fisher; costumes Charles Gelatt; sound Gigi Cascio; stage manager, David Eliscu; press Max Eisen. Against a background of life in Trinidad, the hero hangs on to his dreams of a better life.

A STAGE AFFAIR (8 perfs.)—By Paul Crabtree. Producer Barry C. Tuttle. Cherry Lane Theatre, January 16, 1962.

Director Mr. Crabtree. With Tom Pedi, Carleton Carpenter, Louise King, Maryann Gudzin and Richard Higgs. Under the title of "A Story for a Sunday Evening," this play appeared on Broadway November 17, 1950 for 11 performances.

THE CANTILEVERED TERRACE (39 perfs.)—By William Archibald. Producers Geoffrey Jones, Albert Penn, in association with Morton Zolotow. Forty-first Street Theatre, January 17, 1962.

Frederick Perpetua ....Colgate Salsbury
Lawrence Juniper ....John Harkins
Sophia Perpetua ....Marcie Hubert
Mr. Perpetua ....Don McHenry
Mrs. Perpetua ....Mildred Dunnock
Angela ....Fran Bennett

Time: the present. Place: a terrace overlooking the sea.
Director Mr. Archibald; setting, lighting and costumes Paul Morrison; stage manager, Sherman Wayne; press Howard Atlee. About a rich and aristocratic American family, whose elder members have become unnecessary if graceful left-overs in a democratic and materialistic age, and whose younger members are lost, over-protected adults facing the unsentimental and logical realities of their position.

THE BANKER'S DAUGHTER (68 perfs.)—Musical based on Boucicault's "Streets of New York," with book and lyrics by Edward Eliscu; music by Sol Kaplan. Producers Claire Nichtern, Paul Libin. Jan Hus House, January 21, 1962.

Captain Fairweather ....Tony Kraber
Mrs. Charlotte Fairweather ....Karen Morley
Nursemaid ....Karen Duke
Jonas Puffy ....Tom Noel
Gideon Bloodgood ....Lloyd Gough
Oliver Badger ....Phil Leeds
Financial Investors ...Kermit Herd, Cliff Wayne, Frank Groseclose, Fred Patrick, Kathryn Humphreys, Evelyn Kingsley
Lucy Fairweather ....Joelle Jons
John Taylor ....Cliff Wayne
Alida Bloodgood ....Helena Scott
Mark Livingston ....David Daniels
Edwards ....Frank Groseclose
Police Officer ....Fred Patrick
Policeman ....Tony Kraber
Florist ....Kermit Herd
Valet ....Cliff Wayne
Lady's Maid ....Kathryn Humphreys
Rowe Schuyler ....Fred Patrick
Lily ....Evelyn Kingsley
Sophie ....Kathryn Humphreys
Parlor Maid ....Evelyn Kingsley

Time: 1837-1857. Place: around New York City.
Director David Brooks; sets Kim Swados; costumes Peter Joseph; lighting Jules Fisher; musical director Arthur Lief; musical arrangements Mr. Kaplan; stage manager, Heinz Neumann; press Karl Bernstein, Ben Kornzweig. Musical numbers: ACT I, "One More Day," "Gentlemen's Understanding," "Such a Beautiful World," "Genteel," "In a Brownstone Mansion," "Such a Beautiful World" (Reprise), "Both Ends Against the Middle," "The Sun Rises," "Father's Daughter," "Say No More," "Father's Daughter" (Reprise). ACT II, "Unexpectedly," "More Than One More Day," "In Time," "In Time" (Reprise), "Nero, Caesar, Napoleon," "Head in the Stars," "Sleep, O Sleep," "A Carriage for Alida," "It's So Heartwarming."

MY BEGINNING (70 perfs.)—By Brendan Larnen, O.P. Producer the Blackfriars' Guild. Blackfriars' Theatre, January 23, 1962.

With Nonie Stewart, John Fisher, Vicki Blankenship, Patricia Mertens, A. J. Embie, Robert Milton. The last four months in the life of Mary of Scotland and her execution at the block.

THE CREDITORS (46 perfs.)—By August Strindberg, adapted by Paul Shyre. Producers the Torquay Company, in association with Ruth Kaner, Walter Juda. Mermaid Theatre, January 25, 1962.

Adolf ....James Ray Gustav ....Donald Davis
Tekla ....Rae Allen

Time: 1885. Place: a Swedish resort hotel.
Director Mr. Shyre; setting David Johnston; lighting Jules Fisher; costumes Joe Davies; music Robert Rines; stage manager John Benson; press Max Eisen. A man deliberately wrecks the lives of his former wife and her weak second husband.

THE LOVERS IN THE METRO (19 perfs.)—Three one-act plays by Jean Tardieu, translated by George Wellwarth. Producers Ann Giudici, Paul Krassner, in association with Actors Repertory Theatre. Van Dam Theatre, January 30, 1962.

THE INFORMATION BUREAU

The Official ....John M. Kimbro The Man ....Willy Switkes

Director Harry Basch. A timid little man hopes that an official will tell him how to run his life.

THE KEYHOLE

The Woman ....Judy Granite The Man ....John LaGioia

Director Lionel Shepard. The ecstasy of a voyeur watching a beautiful girl undress, through a keyhole, is ridiculed.

THE LOVERS IN THE METRO

First Gentleman, Lay Reader, Old Man, Interpreter, Newspaper Reader ....John M. Kimbro
Second Gentleman, Lame Man, Religious Reader, Plumber ....John LaGioia
He ....John Dark
She ....Rosemarie Forno
Hurrying Lady, Co-ed, Young Girl, Foreigner, Movie Star ....Judy Granite
Affected Man, Student, Old Man, Man ....Willy Switkes
Affected Woman, Aunt, Foreigner, Offended Flirt ....Connie Kelly

Director Ann Giudici; assistant Harry Basch; settings Jarvin Parks; lighting Barry Hoffman. Passersby comment on the love making of a boy and girl in a Paris subway station.

THE MERCHANT OF VENICE (37 perfs.)—By William Shakespeare. Producer Gateway Productions. Gate Theatre, February 2, 1962.

Director Boris Tumarin; settings Helen Pond, Herbert Senn. With Mr. Tumarin, Carol Gustafson, Douglas Watson, Joel Stuart and Kathryn Loder.

THE JACKHAMMER (2 perfs.)—By Val Coleman. Producers F. E. S. (Plays) Ltd., Nancy W. Green. Theatre Marquee, February 5, 1962.

Director Fred Sadoff. With Ben Hays, Richard Shepard, James Karen and Jared Reed. Six characters are locked together in a room for thirty-six hours.

FLY BLACKBIRD (127 perfs.)—Musical with book, music and lyrics by C. Jackson and James Hatch. Producer Helen Jacobson. Mayfair Theatre, February 5, 1962.

William Piper	Avon Long
Police Officer Jonsen	Elwood Smith
Members of the Lodge	Paul Reid Roman, Gilbert Price, Jack Crowder, Jim Bailey, William Sugihara
Carl	Robert Guillaume
Josie	Mary Louise
Susie	Thelma Oliver
Gladys	Chele Abel
Camille	Micki Grant
George	William Sugihara
Paul	Paul Reid Roman
Lou	Jim Bailey
Gail	Gail Ziferstein
Palmer	Jack Crowder
Roger	Gilbert Price
Big Betty	Glory Van Scott
Mr. Crocker	Michael Kermoyan
Police Matron Jonsen	Helen Blount

Time: the present. Place: somewhere down South.

Director Jerome Eskow; settings Robert Soule; costumes Robby Campbell; lighting Jules Fisher; musical director Gershon Kingsley; choreography Talley Beatty; production stage manager Bob Borod; stage manager William Sugihara; press Howard Atlee, Jane Randall, David Rothenberg. Conflict between a group of Negroes who want immediate equality and those who are for a wait-and-see policy. Musical numbers: ACT I, "Everything Comes to Those Who Wait," "Now," "Big Betty's Song," "I'm Sick of the Whole Damn Problem," "Who's the Fool?," "Right Way," "Couldn't We," "The Housing Cha-Cha," "Natchitoches, Louisiana," "Fly Blackbird," "The Gong Song," "Rivers to the South." ACT II, "Lilac Tree," "Twilight Zone," "The Love Elixir," "Mister Boy," "Old White Tom," "Natchitoches, Louisiana" (Reprise), "Who's the Fool?" (Reprise), "Wake Up."

THE BOOK OF JOB (12 perfs.)—By Orlin Corey, adapted from the "Book of Job." Producers the Drama Committee of Christ Church Methodist and Day Tuttle. Christ Church Methodist, February 9, 1962.

Director Mr. Corey; designer Irene Corey; lighting Jules Fisher. With Warren Hammack, Joseph Boley, Bram Nossen, Robert Shy and Hal Hackett. This play has given over 300 performances during the past four years, toured England and was seen at the Brussels World's Fair.

AN EVENING OF BRECHT (1 perf.)—By Bertolt Brecht. Brooklyn College's George Gershwin Theatre, February 10, 1962.

PART I: POEMS AND SONGS OF BRECHT, played, sung and recited by Eric Bentley.

PART II: THE EXCEPTION AND THE RULE, translated by Eric Bentley. Directors Isaiah Sheffer, Carlo Mazzone; music Stefan Wolpe; settings Paul Gorrin, Dan Snyder; costumes Lisa Lyman. With David Kennedy, Stuart Michaels, Gahan Hanmer, Gail Baugher. A merchant mistakes his collie's offering him a drink from his canteen as an attack, and he kills him. He is absolved of murder by the court, which decides that the rule is that a laborer must want to attack his employer and that the merchant could not be expected to know that this was an exception.

THEATRE OF THE ABSURD (55 perfs.)—Repertory of nine plays. Producer Theatre 1962 (Richard Barr, Clinton Wilder). Cherry Lane Theatre, February 11, 1962.

ENDGAME by Samuel Beckett. Director Alan Schneider; with Ben Piazza, Vincent Gardenia, John C. Becher and Sudie Bond. (Produced Off Broadway in 1957-58.)

BERTHA by Kenneth Koch. Director Nicola Cernovich; music Virgil Thompson.

Old Man	John C. Becher	Counselor	M. J. Grimaldi
Bertha	Sudie Bond	Noble	Vincent Romeo
Young Man	Vincent Romeo	Girl	Alice Drummond
Second Barbarian	Mylo Quam	Barbarian Chief	Tony Musante

GALLOWS HUMOR by Jack Richardson. Director George L. Sherman; with Wyman Pendleton, Vincent Gardenia, Alice Drummond and Arthur Anderson. (Produced Off Broadway April 16, 1961 for 40 performances.)

THE SANDBOX by Edward Albee. Director Mr. Albee; with Jane Hoffman, John C. Becher, Herman Price, Vincent Romeo and Sudie Bond. (Produced Off Broadway 1959-1960.)

DEATHWATCH by Jean Genet. Director Donald Davis; with Mylo Quam, Ben Piazza, Vincent Romeo and M. J. Grimaldi. (Produced Off Broadway in 1958-1959.)

PICNIC ON THE BATTLEFIELD by Fernando Arrabal. Director Gene Feist; with John C. Becher, Jane Hoffman, Vincent Romeo and Mylo Quam. (Produced Off Broadway in 1959-1960.)

THE AMERICAN DREAM by Edward Albee. Director Alan Schneider; with Jane Hoffman, John C. Becher, Sudie Bond, Alice Drummond and Ben Piazza. (Produced Off Broadway January 24, 1961 for 370 performances.)

THE ZOO STORY by Edward Albee. Director Richard Barr; with Ben Piazza and Arthur Anderson. (Produced Off Broadway January 14, 1960 for 582 performances, and had a brief revival earlier this season.)

THE KILLER by Eugene Ionesco. Director Richard Barr; with Vincent Gardenia, Sudie Bond, Vincent Romeo, Arthur Anderson, Jane Hoffman and John C. Becher. (Produced Off Broadway March 22, 1960 for 16 performances.)

THE GOLDEN APPLE (112 perfs.)—Musical with book by John LaTouche; music by Jerome Moross. Producer Dorothy Olim, Gerald Krone. York Playhouse, February 12, 1962.

Director Robert Turoff. With Jane Connell, Roberta MacDonald, Julia Ross, Michael Dominico and Jan McArt. Produced on Broadway March 11, 1954 for 125 performances. (See *The Best Plays of 1953-54.*)

DUMBBELL PEOPLE IN A BARBELL WORLD (13 perfs.)—By Dan Blue. Producers Kenneth J. Stein, Maxwell Silverman. Cricket Theatre, February 14, 1962.

Director George Mallonee. With Jan Miner, Teresa Hughes and Ann Laurence. In three separate playlets we are shown apparent misfits who are really people of dignity and worth.

A CHEKHOV SKETCHBOOK (94 perfs.)—Three one-act plays adapted for the stage by Luba Kadison and Helen Waren from three stories by Anton Chekhov. Producers Stanley and Helen Waren. Gramercy Arts Theatre, February 15, 1962.

THE VAGRANT

A Vagrant	Joseph Buloff	Ptach	Frank C. Borgman
Nikander	David Ford		

The way in which a man keeps up his courage while being led off to exile in Siberia.

THE WITCH

Siveli	Joseph Buloff	Raisa	Sylvia Miles
Postman	David Ford		

Study of a young woman's snowbound loneliness with her aged husband.

THE MUSIC SHOP

Ivan	Joseph Buloff	Shopkeeper	Frank C. Borgman

Comedy of a henpecked and forgetful husband, sent to buy a piece of sheet music. Director Mr. Waren; settings, lighting and costumes Tom Jewett; stage manager, Peter M. Forward; press David Lipsky, Richard Falk.

JULIUS CAESAR (10 perfs.)—By William Shakespeare. Producer the New York Shakespeare Festival, sponsored by the New York City Board of Education. Heckscher Theatre, February 19, 1962.

Director Joseph Papp; settings Thea Neu; costumes Eldon Elder; lighting Martin Aronstein; music David Amram. With Leonard Hicks, Richard Roat, Gerald E. McGonagill, Jerome Raphel, Charles Durning and Garnett Smith. Performed for New York City High School students.

THIS SIDE OF PARADISE (87 perfs.)—By Sydney Sloane, adapted from F. Scott Fitzgerald's novel. Producers Jess Osuna, Alice Scudder. Sheridan Square Playhouse, February 21, 1962.

Amory	Paul Roebling	Mrs. Connage	Carol Risser
Beatrice	Jane Lowry	Rosalind	Sydney Sloane
He	Moss Cohen	Dawson Ryder	George Vlachos
She	Julie Arenal	Mr. Barlow	Alex Szogyi
Alec	Joseph Jacobs	Garvin	E. J. Poggi
Jesse	Robert McHaffey	Ferrensby	Robert Snively
Tom	Donald Hotton	Jill	Ginette Martin
Isabelle	Alice Borsuk	Miss Wayne	Chiquita Colomby
Monsignor Darcy	Jess Osuna	Tully	Jeremy Stevens
Cecelia	Carole Ann Lewis	Detective	Robert Zampino

Director Herbert Berghof; designer Charles Evans; lighting Jules Fisher; costumes Ann Roth; choreography J. C. McCord; production stage manager Mr. Osuna; stage manager Jeremy Stevens; press Max Eisen, Warren Pincus.

* OH DAD, POOR DAD, MAMMA'S HUNG YOU IN THE CLOSET AND I'M FEELIN' SO SAD (107 perfs.)—By Arthur Kopit. Producers Theatre, Inc. (T. Edward Hambleton, Norris Houghton), in association with Roger L. Stevens. Phoenix Theatre, February 26, 1962.

Madame Rosepettle	Jo Van Fleet	Rosalie	Barbara Harris
Jonathan	Austin Pendleton	Commodore Roseabove	Sandor Szabo
Head Bellboy	Tony Lo Bianco		

Bellboys: Jaime Sanchez, David Faulkner, Ernesto Gonzalez, Louis Waldon, Anthony Ponzini, Barry Primus.

Time: the present. Place: a hotel suite in Port Royal, a city somewhere in the Caribbean.

Director Jerome Robbins; setting William and Jean Eckart; costumes Patricia Zipprodt; lighting Thomas Skelton; music Robert Prince; production stage manager, Thomas Stone; stage manager Andrew Mihok; press Ben Kornzweig, Karl Bernstein.

See page 202.

DON CARLOS (26 perfs.)—By Friedrich Schiller. Producer New Repertory Theatre. Masque Theatre, February 27, 1962.

Director Patricia Newhall. With Joan Cunningham, Konrad Matthaei, Sy Travers and Ann Fielding. The rivalry between King Philip II of Spain and his son. It was last seen here in 1906 with Richard Mansfield. A revival of THE STORM by Alexander N. Ostrovsky joined the above in repertory March 30, 1962 for 10 performances, and was directed by John Hancock, with Jonathan Frid and Stuart Geddes.

3 x 3 (4 perfs.)—Three one-act plays. Producers Sam Cohn, John Wulp, in association with Julia Miles. Maidman Playhouse, March 1, 1962.

THE TWENTY-FIVE CENT WHITE CAP by Arnold Weinstein. Director Arthur Storch; designer John Wulp; lighting Charles Levy; music William Bolcom. With MacIntyre Dixon, Richard Libertini, Robert Foley. A man regrets having sold his favorite cap.

GEORGE WASHINGTON CROSSING THE DELAWARE by Kenneth Koch. Director Mr. Storch; designer Alex Katz; lighting Mr. Levy; music selected by Joan O'Brien. With Richard Libertini, MacIntyre Dixon, Robert Anzell, Philip J. Roth, Dermot McNamara, Carol Wolveridge, Susan Reiselt. Parody about Washington's defeat of Cornwallis in the American Revolution.

NOT ENOUGH ROPE by Elaine May. Director William Rickey; designer Mr. Wulp; lighting Mr. Levy. With Jane Romano, William Hickey and Sylvia Burnell. A lonely girl decides to hang herself and then changes her mind.

* THIS WAS BURLESQUE (110 perfs.)—Revue with material by Joe Dimona. Producers Mike Iannucci, Milton Warner. Casino East, March 1, 1962.

With Ann Corio, Steve Mills and Conny Ryan. Burlesque in the old tradition.

BLACK MONDAY (16 perfs.)—By Reginald Rose. Producer William Hunt. Van Dam Theatre, March 6, 1962.

Director Mr. Hunt. With Nancy Coleman, Billie Allen, Daniel Jackson, Robert Blackburn and Yaphet Kotto. The struggle for school integration in a Southern town. The play was previously done on television and in summer stock.

DUESSELDORF SCHAUSPIELHAUS (14 perfs.)—Program of two plays: NATHAN THE WISE by Gotthold Ephraim Lessing and BEFORE SUNDOWN by Gerhart Hauptmann. Producers Gert von Gontard, Felix G. Gerstman, in association with the Deutsches Theatre, Inc. Fashion Institute of Technology, March 6, 1962.

PERFORMER	NATHAN THE WISE	BEFORE SUNDOWN
Evelyn Balser	Recha	Ottilie Klamroth
Eva Boettcher	Sittah	Paula Clausen
Ernst Deutsch	Nathan	Geheimrat Clausen
Ingrid Ernest		Inken Peters
Peter Esser		Professor Geiger
Otto Griess		Hanefeldt, Justizrat
Wolfgang Jarnach		Dr. Wuttke
Arthur Jaschke		Stadtverordnetenvorsteher
Wolfgang Lukschy	Sultan Saladin	Erich Klamroth
Max Mairich	Klosterbruder	
Karl-Heinz Martell	Junger Tempelherr	Egmont Clausen
Gerda Maurus	Daja	Frau Peters
Arthur Mentz	Patriarch von Jerusalem	Ebisch, Gaertner
Heinrich Ortmayr		Winter, Diener
Otto Rouvel	Derwisch	Dr. Steynitz
Ingeborg Weirich		Bettina Clausen
Hermann Weisse		Pastor Immoos
Hans Wypraechtiger		Wolfgang Clausen

DEAR LIAR (40 perfs.)—"Comedy of Letters," adapted for the stage by Jerome Kilty from the correspondence of Mrs. Patrick Campbell and Bernard Shaw. Producer Frank Gero. Theatre Marquee, March 17, 1962.

Director Mr. Kilty; designer Robert Fletcher. With Mr. Kilty and Cavada Humphrey. This play was produced on Broadway March 17, 1960 for 52 performances.

APA REPERTORY (38 perfs.)—Three plays: THE SCHOOL FOR SCANDAL by Richard B. Sheridan (March 17, 16 perfs.): THE SEAGULL by Anton Chekhov, translated by Alex Szogyi (March 21, 11 perfs.); THE TAVERN by George M. Cohan (April 3, 11 perfs.). Producer the Association of Producing Artists. Folksbiene Playhouse.

Director Ellis Rabb; designer Lloyd Burlingame; composer and musical director Conrad Susa; production stage manager Geoffry Brown; press Howard Atlee, Jane Randall.

PERFORMER	THE SCHOOL FOR SCANDAL	THE SEAGULL	THE TAVERN
Tucker Ashworth	Crabtree		Zach
Clayton Corzatte	Charles	Konstantine	
Ellen Geer	Maria		Sally
George Grizzard	Joseph		Vagabond
Rosemary Harris	Lady Teazle	Nina	Virginia
David Hooks	Sir Oliver	Dorn	Freeman
Gerry Jedd		Masha	Violet
Page Johnson	Snake	Medvedenko	Willum
William Larsen	Rowley	Shamrayeff	Sheriff
Nicholas Martin	Backbite		Stevens
Nancy Marchand	Lady Sneerwell	Arkadina	
Earl Montgomery		Sorin	Lamson
Joanna Roos	Mrs. Candour	Paulina	Mrs. Lamson
Paul Sparer		Trigorin	Tom Allen

Others: George Barry, Robert Bernard, Claude Harz, Yafa Lerner, Charlotte Moore.

THE FRENCH WAY (1 perf.)—Three one-act plays by Rene de Obaldia, adapted by Gertrude Corey: "The Deceased," "The Grand Vizier" and "Edward and Agrippina." Producer Juniper Productions. East End Theatre, March 20, 1962.

Director Will Hare. With Gertrude Corey, Leo Lucker and Leigh Wharton.

PILGRIM'S PROGRESS (8 perfs.)—Musical drama by Edwin Greenburg. Producer Normen Taurog. Gate Theatre, March 20, 1962.

Director Ted Vermont. With Michael Davis, Delmar Roos and Francis Bernard. In an English dungeon, John Bunyan writes about his fellow prisoners and man's search for God.

ELECTRA (7 perfs.)—By Euripides, translated by Gilbert Murray. Producer The Shakespearwrights. Players Theatre, March 21, 1962.

Director Philip Lawrence. With Laura Stuart, Byrne Piven, Peter Hale, Lorraine Serabian and Dimitra Steris.

NATHAN THE WISE (14 perfs.)—By Gotthold Ephraim Lessing, adapted by Sydney Walker and Roy Franklyn. Producer Roy Franklyn Productions. Seventy-eighth Street Theatre, March 22, 1962.

Director Mr. Franklyn. With George Ebeling and Rick Tobin. First performed in Germany in the 1780's, the play has to do with man's nobility and courage.

MUMMERS AND MEN (6 perfs.)—By David Lifson. Producer the Village Repertory Company. Provincetown Playhouse, March 26, 1962.

Director Herbert Ratner. With Marie Jordan, Graham Velsey and Don Wallace. Murder mystery involving a summer stock company.

THE LONG AND THE SHORT AND THE TALL (22 perfs.)—By Willis Hall. Producer Jack Greenwald. Maidman Playhouse, March 29, 1962.

Cpl. Johnstone, E.	W. B. Brydon	Pvt. Bamforth, C.	James Douglas
Sgt. Mitchem, R.	Jeremy Wilkin	Pvt. Evans, T. E.	James Beggs
L./Cpl. MacLeish, A. J.	Jay Shannon	Pvt. Smith, P.	Claude Rae
Pvt. Whitaker, S.	Neville Granger	Jap Soldier	Toru Nagai

Time: 1942. Place: Malayan Jungle.

Director Murray Davis; setting Bob deMora; stage manager John Stuart Marwick; press Reginald Denenholz. A seven-man patrol captures a Jap soldier and each man wants to either kill or save this enemy for their own specific reason.

ROMEO AND JULIET (7 perfs.)—By William Shakespeare. Producer White Feather Productions. Midway Theatre, April 2, 1962.

Director Hubert Rolling. With Richard Novello, Robert Morea, Naomi Riseman and Howard Green.

MAN OUT LOUD, GIRL QUIET (16 perfs.)—By William Herman. Producers A. N. Jimsohn, Anthea Productions, Inc. Cricket Theatre, April 3, 1962.

Director Paul E. Richards; designer David Johnston. With Alan Arkin, Gabriel Dell and Barbara Burris. A young college graduate tries to escape life's problems by hiding out in a loft. THE SPANISH ARMADA, also by Mr. Herman, was performed as a curtain-raiser and dealt with a man's seduction of his best friend's wife.

EYES UPON THE CROSS (6 perfs.)—By Don A. Mueller. Presented by the Program in Religious Drama at the Union Theological Seminary, April 3, 1962.

Director William Guilford. With Larry Stell, Jean Webster, Hunter Tillman. Cycle of eight contemporary plays on Lenten themes which bridges the past and present through the timeless feelings of those who were witnesses to the drama of Passion Week.

HALF-PAST WEDNESDAY (2 perfs.)—Musical with book by Anna Marie Barlow; music by Robert Colby; lyrics by Mr. Colby and Nita Jonas. Producers Hal Raywin, Jerome Rudolph. Orpheum Theatre, April 6, 1962.

Director Mr. Raywin; settings Lloyd Burlingame; costumes Robert Fletcher; lighting Jules Fisher; choreography Gene Bayliss. With Dom De Luise, Sean Garrison, David Winters, Audre Johnston and Charles Welch. Musical version of "Rumplestiltskin." Musical numbers: ACT I, "Give 'Em a Lollipop And . . . ," "I've Got a Goose," "What's the Fun of Being King," "You're the Sweet Beginning," "Who? Where? What?," "Spinning Song," "Jumpin' Jehosephat," "If You Did It Once," "How Lovely, How Lovely," "Spinning Song" (Reprise). ACT II, "Ladies in Waiting," "You're the Sweet Beginning" (Reprise), "Grandfathers," "To-Whit—To Whoo," "What's the Name of What's-His-Name?," "If-If-If-If," "Companionship," "We Know a Secret."

ENTERTAIN A GHOST (8 perfs.)—By Louis Peterson. Producers Ira Cirker, in association with Ruth Wilk Notkins. Actors Playhouse, April 9, 1962.

Curt	Stuart Damon	Clarence	Alfred Hinckley
Naomi	Lenore Dekoven	Chet	Allan Miller
Miss Chisholm	Lesley Woods	Joel	Chet Leaming
Pam	Carol Rossen	Ham	Don Lamb
Marshall	Hal DeWindt	Telephone Man	Paul Barby
Jo	Loretta Leversee	Bob	Herb Davis
Tony	Anthony Bardusk		

Time: shortly after World War II.
Director Mr. Cirker; designer Robin Wagner; stage manager Don Lamb; press Betty Lee Hunt. A play within a play, with the plot of both being the marital difficulties between the author and his star, who are also husband and wife.

* ROSMERSHOLM (58 perfs.)—By Henrik Ibsen, translated by Carmel Ross. Producer David Ross. Fourth Street Theatre, April 11, 1962.

Rebecca West	Nancy Wickwire	Johannes Rosmer	Donald Woods
Mrs. Helseth	Joan Croydon	Ulric Brendel	Bramwell Fletcher
Professor Kroll	Patrick Waddington	Peter Mortensgaard	Barnard Hughes

Director Mr. Ross; setting Charles Bailey; costumes Theoni V. Aldredge; stage manager, Eugene Stuckmann; press David Lipsky. The play had its American premiere in 1904 and has been revived a few times since. (See *Index to the Best Plays Series, 1899-1950.*)

KING OF THE WHOLE DAMN WORLD (43 perfs.)—Musical with book by George Panetta; music and lyrics by Robert Larimer. Producer Norman Forman. Jan Hus Playhouse, April 14, 1962.

Iggie	Alan Howard	Mrs. Babbson	Bobbi Lange
Socrates	Jerry Brent	Mrs. McKinney	Kathy Crawford
Joey	Jackie Perkuhn	Mrs. Romani	Floria Mari
Sarge	Brendan Fay	Jimmy Potts	Sheldon Golomb
Maloney	Joseph Macaulay	Neighbor	Esther Hollis
Hippo	Tom Pedi	Interne	Henry Sutton
Hannah Klein	Francine Beers	Ambulance Driver	Bob Shane
Enrico Romani	Boris Aplon	Willie	Charlotte Whaley
Bleecker Street Women	Kathy Crawford, Lois Grandi	Nurse Phelps	Lois Grandi
DeWolfe	David C. Jones	Nurse Duffy	Bobbi Lange
Leo	Kenneth McMillan	Dr. Thorndyke	David C. Jones
Bleecker Street Men	Joseph Liberatore, Merlin Bruce, Mell Johnson, Bob Shane	Surgical Nurse	Esther Hollis
		Dr. Jamison	Merlin Bruce
		Surgeon	Mell Johnson
		Surgeon's Nurse	Kathy Crawford

Time: 1940. Place: Greenwich Village.

Director Jack Ragotzy; settings Jack Cornwell; costumes Rachel Mehr; lighting William Rittman; choreographer Zachary Solov; musical director Dobbs Franks; musical arrangements and ballet music Gershon Kingsley; stage manager Henry Sutton; press David Lipsky. Based on Mr. Panetta's play COMIC STRIP (produced Off Broadway in 1958), plot has to do with a cop and the people on his beat. Musical numbers: ACT I, "What to Do?," "Grasshop Song," "Poor Little Boy," "The Night Gondolfo Got Married," "King of the World," "Who's Perfect?," "Little Dog Blue," "March You Off in Style," "The Riddle of You." ACT II, "How Do They Ever Grow Up?," "What's a Momma For?," "Iggie's Nightmare," "Don't Tear Up the Horse Slips," "Who's Perfect for You?," "Far Rockaway," "There's Gotta Be a Villain," "King of the World" (Reprise).

BRING ME A WARM BODY (16 perfs.)—By Robert Dale Martin. Producers Frank C. Romanski, Jr., Merton Y. Koplin, in association with Herman B. Sarno, Theodore H. McNabb. Martinique Theatre, April 16, 1962.

Director Eric Daniell. With Don Galloway, Rosalyn Newport, Barbara Davis, Robert Bowers and Eugene R. Wood. Study of a dynamic and successful film director who tortures a young actor into giving a vivid performance. (Song, "Say After Me," by Robert Dale Martin.)

WITCHES' SABBATH (14 perfs.)—By Harry Granick. Producer Jay Broad. Madison Avenue Playhouse, April 19, 1962.

Director Mr. Broad. With Ray Poole, Salem Ludwig, Abe Vigoda, Daniel Ades and Michael Del Medico. The Inquisition in 14th century France and the hero's fight for justice.

ALCESTIS COMES BACK (8 perfs.)—By Arthur Marya Swinarski, adapted by Anthony Patric Smith. Producer Leonidas-D-Ossetynski. Mermaid Theatre, April 23, 1962.

Director Mr. D-Ossetynski. With Lidia Prochnicka, Edgar Daniels, Byrne Piven, Cynthia Belgrave and Carl Esser. Cynical version of the Alcestis legend. AT SEA by Slawomir Mrozek was also on the bill, and concerned three men on a raft, one of whom had to be eaten if the others were to survive.

A PAIR OF PAIRS (16 perfs.)—DEUCES WILD by Holly Beye opened April 24, 1962 and CHARLATANS by Claude Fredericks opened April 26, 1962. Producers The Artists' Theatre, in association with Alfred T. Manacher. Van Dam Theatre.

Director Herbert Machiz; designer Robert Soule. With Conrad Bain, Larry Bryggman, Elizabeth Burke, Michael Higgins, Irma Hurley, Gaby Rodgers and Sylvia Stone. The two plays appearing under the title of DEUCES WILD were THUS and IT'S ALL YOURS, and the two plays appearing under the title of CHARLATANS were ON CIRCE'S ISLAND and A SUMMER GHOST.

THE DIFFICULT WOMAN (3 perfs.)—Musical based on a play by Conrado Nale Roxlo, translated and adapted by Ruth C. Gillespie and Malcolm Stuart Boylan; music by Dick Frietas; lyrics by Morty Neff and George Mysels; additional material and dialogue by Maurice Alevy. Producers Nikardi Productions, Donald C. Fetzko. Barbizon-Plaza, April 25, 1962.

Director Mr. Alevy. With Odetta McEwen, Jack Russell and Warren Robertson. About a woman who marries a condemned prisoner to irritate the man who has been trying to make her his mistress. Musical numbers: ACT I, "Grandioso," "Ulterior Motive," "Siesta," "One in My Position," "The Hangman's Plea," "Ungrateful," "El Cuando" Minuet, "Poor Isabel," "What a Life," "Bull Blood and Brandy," "Patience and Gentleness," Dream Ballet. ACT II, "Tormented," "Taking Inventory," "I Won't Take No for an Answer," "This Is the Day," "Throw the House Out the Window," "Ulterior Motive" (Reprise), "Patience and Gentleness" (Reprise).

SOLO (1 perf.)—Program of six scenes by Sylvia Leigh and Mark Justin. Producer Franklin Klein. East End Theatre, April 26, 1962.

Director and designer Mr. Justin. With Sylvia Leigh and Jeanne Sisco. Miss Leigh portrayed six characters ranging from an escaped lunatic to a neurotic pianist.

DOUBLE BILL (6 perfs.)—Two one-act plays by Bunker Jenkins: COME OUT, CARLO! and IN THE PENAL COLONY, adapted from a short story by Franz Kafka. Producers Herbert Duncan, in association with the Zimet Brothers. Forty-first Street Theatre, May 3, 1962.

Director Norman Rose. With Claude Gersene, Ruth Manning and Robert Readick. The first play concerns a family whose members are more interested in themselves than in each other. The second is about a modern torturing machine that finally claims as its victim one of its creators.

HOP, SIGNOR (8 perfs.)—By Michael de Ghelderode. Producer Lynn Michaels. St. Marks Playhouse, May 7, 1962.

With Jane White and Jerome Guardino. A bitter and mystical play, set in 16th Century Flanders, about a hunchbacked nobleman who is ignominiously killed by a mob when he tries to defend his honor.

IF FIVE YEARS PASS (22 perfs.)—By Federico Garcia Lorca. Producers Joel W. Schenker, Stage 73 Company. Stage 73, May 10, 1962.

Director Valerie Bettis. With Dino Narrizano, Tamzen Allen, Thomas Barbour, Sharon Laughlin and Victoria Thompson. Poetic fantasy about love and death.

* ANYTHING GOES (19 perfs.)—Musical with book by Guy Bolton, P. G. Wodehouse, Howard Lindsay and Russel Crouse; music and lyrics by Cole Porter. Producers Jane Friedlander, Michael Parver, Gene Andrewski. Orpheum Theatre, May 15, 1962.

Elisha J. Whitney	Warren Wade	Ching	Jeff Siggins
Steward	Robert Fitch	Ling	Martin J. Cassidy
Hope Harcourt	Barbara Lang	Reno Sweeney	Eileen Rodgers
Sir Evelyn Oakleigh	Kenneth Mars	Angels: Purity	Diane McAfee
Mrs. Wadsworth T. Harcourt	Mildred Chandler	Chastity	Sally Ann Carlson
		Charity	Tobie Lynn
Reporter	Jim Franklin	Virtue	Chee Davis
Photographer	Jim Jarrett	Billy Crocker	Hal Linden
First Girl Passenger	Bonnie Walker	Purser	D. Bruce Rabbino
Second Girl Passenger	Kay Norman	Bonnie	Margery Gray
Third Girl Passenger	Rawley Bates	Moon	Mickey Deems
Bishop	Neal Patrick	Captain	Neal Patrick

Time: the 1930's. Place: aboard the S.S. *American.*

Director Lawrence Kasha; musical numbers and dances staged by Ronald Field; setting and lighting Don Jensen; costumes Bill Hargate; musical conductor Ted Simons; stage manager, Morgan James; press, Howard Atlee. ANYTHING GOES was first produced on Broadway by Vinton Freedley at the Alvin Theatre, November 21, 1934, for 420 performances. (In the following list of musical numbers those in italics were not in the original production.) Musical numbers: ACT I, "Opening," "You're the Top," "Bon Voyage," *"It's Delovely," "Heaven Hop," "Friendship,"* "I Get a Kick Out of You," "Anything Goes." ACT II, "Public Enemy Number One," *"Let's Step Out," "Let's Misbehave,"* "Blow, Gabriel, Blow," "All Through the Night," "Be Like the Bluebird," *"Take Me Back to Manhattan,"* Finale.

* DOUBLE BILL (4 perfs.)—Two one-act plays. Producers Paul Libin, Round Table Review, in association with Madeline Lee. Martinique Theatre, May 28, 1962.

THE BARROOM MONKS by Joseph Carroll. Director Phoebe Brand, designer Peter Wexler; costumes Ann Roth; music Irma Jurist. With Michael Kane, Sarah Cunningham, Clayton Corzatte, Frank Hamilton, Neil Fitzgerald. A barroom tale of a drunken priest and a newly widowed woman who offers herself to him.

A PORTRAIT OF THE ARTIST AS A YOUNG MAN by Frederic Ewen, Phoebe Brand and John Randolph, adapted from the novel by James Joyce. Director Miss Brand; designer Mr. Wexler; costumes Miss Roth; music Miss Jurist. With Robert Brown, Michael Kane, Sarah Cunningham, Neil Fitzgerald, Clayton Corzatte.

* ALARUMS AND EXCURSIONS (6 perfs.)—Revue with scenes and dialogue created by the company. Producers Bernard Sahlins, Howard Alk, Paul Sills. Square East, May 29, 1962.

Director Alan Myerson; music William Mathieu; settings Larry Klein; lighting Ronald Colby. With the Second City Company: Howard Alk, Alan Arkin, John Brent, Andrew Duncan, Patricia Englund, Anthony Holland, Lynda Segal and Eugene Troobnick. Musical numbers and sketches: ACT I, "Everybody's in the Know But Me," Technical Assistants in Vietnam, The Commercial, The Drawing Room, The Pretzel Peddler, Do It Yourself Playwriting, Die Konzert, The Adventures of Businessman. ACT II, A Group Improvisation, BBC-TV Presents, "Dink" Smith's Teen Age Band Party, A Grecian Urn, Wigs, Springtime at Vassar, Kennedy-Khrushchev Interview, Joey's Song.

* THE CATS' PAJAMAS (1 perf.)—Revue with material by the company. Producer P.G.J. Productions. Sheridan Square Playhouse, May 31, 1962.

Director Herb Sufrin, musical directors Arthur Siegel, Monte Aubrey; settings James A. Taylor; lighting Gigi Cascio. With The Stewed Prunes (Richard Libertini and MacIntyre Dixon) and Sylvia Lord. Sketches: Cyril Suitcase, Monsier Toad, Mr. Fisby, Dual Pianists, Presentation, Parade, The Cats' Pajamas, Blues, Ties, The Tenor, Puppets and People. Musical numbers (by Miss Lord): "Do It Again," "Makin' Whoopee," "Home on the Range," "Love Is a Good Thing for You."

ANTA MATINEE THEATRE SERIES—The Greater New York Chapter of ANTA's Matinee Theatre Series, under the direction of Lucille Lortel, presented four afternoon programs at the Theatre de Lys, New York City.

BRECHT ON BRECHT: HIS LIFE AND ART (2)—Arranged and translated by George Tabori. Nov. 14, 1961 (afternoon) and Nov. 20, 1961 (evening). Director Gene Frankel; with George Gaynes, Dolly Haas, Anne Jackson, Lotte Lenya, Viveca Lindfors, George Voskovec, Michael Wager, Eli Wallach. This production was done later at the Theatre de Lys on a regular run basis and is listed elsewhere as a regular Off Broadway production.

CAYENNE PEPPER and THE GRAND VIZIR (1)—By Rene de Obaldia, English adaptation by Howard Hart. Dec. 12, 1961. Director Robert Cordier; with Jerome Raphel, Barry Primus, Stephen Hart, Lucielle Gould. Two one-act plays: the first is comprised of dialogue between two prisoners in a French penal colony, and the second is an improvisation dealing with a *menage a trois*.

IN THE FIRST PLACE (1)—By William Packard. Feb. 20, 1962. Director Richard Banter; with Monroe Arnold, Edward Chiaro, Charlotte Jones, P. L. Pfeiffer, Delos V. Smith, Lane Smith, Nick Smith, Arnold Soboloff. The insanity of the inmates of an asylum is compared with the "sanity" of the staff and the outside world.

OBJECTIVE CASE (1)—One-act play by Lewis J. Carlino. Performed at ANTA's Fourth Annual Assembly, Hotel New Yorker, Mar. 4, 1962. Director Luther James; with Alan Bergmann, Carol Teitel. An expressionistic investigation of modern society's intellectualization and cerebration of love, to the point where it cannot be communicated without hate and chaos.

SWEET OF YOU TO SAY SO (1)—One-act play by Page Johnson. Apr. 10, 1962. Director Mr. Johnson; with Paula Bauersmith, Alice Drummond. Two southern women spend their time gossiping on a back porch. This play was on a double bill with SQUIRREL, a one-act play by Jack Dunphy, which was directed by Richard Barr and starred David Hooks, Vincent Romeo, Alice Drummond. A vignette of city life set in a park during lunch hour.

AMERICAN SAVOYARDS—The following revivals, produced and directed by Dorothy Raedler, were presented by the American Savoyards.

THE MIKADO (5)—Operetta with libretto and lyrics by W. S. Gilbert; music by Arthur Sullivan. Greenwich Mews Theatre, June 1, 1961. With Raymond Allen, Mary Ann Staffa, L. D. Clements, Sally Birckhead. The following Gilbert and Sullivan operettas were also presented for five performances each, with the above performers: H.M.S. PINAFORE (June 8, 1961), THE GRAND DUKE (June 15, 1961), PRINCESS IDA (June 22, 1961), H.M.S. PINAFORE (June 29, 1961).

THE MERRY WIDOW (12)—Music by Franz Lehar. Jan Hus House, Oct. 26, 1961. With Mary Ann Staffa, Thomas S. Vasiloff, Donna Curtis, James Mitchell, Raymond Allen, Clifton Steere.

UTOPIA, LIMITED (12)—By W. S. Gilbert and Arthur Sullivan. Jan Hus House, Nov. 9, 1961. With Raymond Allen, Mary Ann Staffa, L. D. Clements, Sally Birckhead.

THE VAGABOND KING (12)—Book and lyrics by Justin Huntley McCarthy; music by Rudolf Friml. Jan Hus House, Nov. 23, 1961. With Thomas S. Vasiloff, Mary Ann Staffa, Bonnie Glasgow, Raymond Allen.

THE GONDOLIERS (6)—By W. S. Gilbert and Arthur Sullivan. Jan Hus House, Dec. 7, 1961. With Raymond Allen, Sally Birckhead, Mary Ann Staffa, John Bridson, L. D. Clements, Allan Abrahamson, Donna Curtis, Joyce Miko.

THE STUDENT PRINCE (14)—Book and lyrics by Dorothy Donnelly; music by Sigmund Romberg. Jan Hus House, Dec. 21, 1961. With L. D. Clements, Mary Ann Staffa, William Duval, Raymond Allen.

EQUITY LIBRARY THEATRE—The following revivals were produced by the Equity Library Theatre at the Master Theatre, New York City.

THE CORN IS GREEN (10)—By Emlyn Williams. Sep. 30, 1961. Director Frederick Rolf; with Blanche Yurka, Bruce Glover, Margaret de Priest.

LOVE'S OLD SWEET SONG (10)—By William Saroyan. Oct. 21, 1961. Director Mesrop Kesdekian; with Mary Ann Lowe, William Martel, Tony Lo Bianco.

GODS OF THE LIGHTNING (10)—By Maxwell Anderson, G. H. Hickerson. Nov. 4, 1961. Director Davey Marlin-Jones; with Gil Rogers, Harry White, Clifford Pellow, Ann Whiteside.

TRELAWNY OF THE "WELLS" (9)—By Sir Arthur Wing Pinero. Nov. 25, 1961. Director Raphael Kelly; with Jeanette Williams, Keith Herrington, King Wehrle.

THE STORY OF MARY SURRATT (9)—By John Patrick. Dec. 9, 1961. Director Herbert Nielsen; with Jay Barney, Kate Wilkinson, Julie Sommars.

THE DISENCHANTED (9)—By Budd Schulberg, Harvey Breit. Jan. 6, 1962. Director Vinnette Carroll; with Ion Berger, Monica May, Darrell Stewart.

THE MERRY WIVES OF WINDSOR (9)—By William Shakespeare. Feb. 3, 1962. Director Edward Payson Call; with Richard Graham, Naomi Riseman, Martha Miller.

PAINT YOUR WAGON (9)—Musical with book and lyrics by Alan Jay Lerner; music by Frederick Loewe. Feb. 24, 1962. Director Alex Palermo; with Robert Penn, Paula Wayne, Seth Riggs.

J. B. (9)—By Archibald MacLeish. Mar. 17, 1962. Director Victor Gabriel Junquera; with Gaylord Mason, Chase Crosley, John Cazale, Edward Grover.

CHARLEY'S AUNT (9)—By Brandon Thomas. Apr. 7, 1962. Director James Dyas; with Bob Randall; Joseph Masiell, Steven Shaw.

SEVENTEEN (9)—Musical based on the Booth Tarkington novel; book by Sally Benson; music by Walter Kent; lyrics by Kim Gannon. May 5, 1962. Director Dania Krupska; with Lorrie Bentley, George Anderson, Laurence Watson.

PLAYS THAT CLOSED OUT OF TOWN

June 1, 1961—May 31, 1962

A SHORT HAPPY LIFE

(37 performances)

Play by A. E. Hotchner, based on the works of Ernest Hemingway. Produced by A. E. Hotchner, in association with Jerome Brody, at the Moore Theatre (Seattle), September 12, 1961.

Harry Davis .... Rod Steiger
Helen Davis .... Nan Martin
Old Lady .... Judith Lowry
Nick .... Keir Dullea
Marjorie .... Salome Jens
Red .... Harvey Lembeck
Teo .... Nat Horne

Others: Joe McWherter, Al Sambogna, Robert Levenson, Frederick Noad, Seldon Powell.

Staged by Frank Corsaro; settings and lighting by Jo Mielziner; costumes by Theoni V. Aldredge; choreography by Matt Mattox; music by Bernardo Segall; production stage manager, Henri Caubisens; stage manager, Kenneth Costigan; press, Harvey B. Sabinson. An injured big game hunter lies dying on Mt. Kilimanjaro and relives the important episodes of his past life.

(Closed Los Angeles, October 21, 1961)

HIGH FIDELITY

(4 performances)

Play by Arthur Carter. Produced by Lynn Loesser, in association with Sy Kasoff, at the Walnut Theatre (Philadelphia), September 14, 1961.

Max Freed .... Leon Belasco
Tilly Freed .... Vicki Cummings
Hip Blake .... Billy King
Alice Blake .... Dody Heath
Ginny .... Julie Wilson
Ozzie Blake .... John Newton
Freddie Jones .... John Varnum
Mr. Hilton .... Gin-Gin Spelvin

Place: the living room of the Blake home in New Jersey. Time: the present.

Staged by Jack Ragotzy; setting by David Ballou; costumes by J. Michael Travis; production stage manager, Ross Bowman; stage manager, Arnold Margolin; press, Ben Kornzweig and Karl Bernstein. A young producer's home life and career are threatened by the star-director of his show.

(Closed September 16, 1961)

KICKS & CO.

(4 performances)

Musical with book, music and lyrics by Oscar Brown, Jr.; in collaboration with Robert B. Nemiroff. Produced by Burt Charles D'Lugoff and Mr. Nemiroff at the Arie Crown Theatre (Chicago), October 11, 1961.

Mr. Kicks .... Burgess Meredith
Robber .... Herman Howell
Policeman .... Ross Lashbrook
Teenagers .... Jack Eddleman, Jan Goldin, Mabel Robinson, Mark Taylor, Barbara Wallach, Dudley Williams
Honeymoon Couple .... Carol Arthur, Gino Conforti
Other Woman .... Louanna Gardner
Other Man .... Darrell J. Askey
Will Wenchin .... William Dwyer
Laurie Lee .... Lynne Forrester
Dorothy .... Miriam Burton
June Young .... Vi Velasco
Eggy .... Bernard Johnson
White Coed .... Nancy Ray Noel
Lillian .... Zabethe Wilde
Larry .... Paul Reid Roman
Barbara .... Caryl Paige
Virginia .... Ella Thompson
Milt .... Gus Solomons, Jr.
Ernest Black .... Lonnie Sattin
Waitress .... Carol Arthur
Traveller .... Gino Conforti
Customers .... Jan Goldin, Ross Lashbrook, Barbara Wallach
Troopers .... Jack Eddleman, Mark Taylor
J. D.'s .... Barbara Creed, Darrell J. Askey
Silky Satin .... Al Freeman, Jr.
Hazel Sharpe .... Nichelle Nichols
Coeds .... Lavinia Hamilton, Leu Comacho, Jacqueline Walcott
The Blonde .... Nancy Ray Noel

Ensemble: Betty Anders, Carol Arthur, Darrell J. Askey, Miriam Burton, Leu Comacho, Gino Conforti, Barbara Creed, Chuck Daniel, Jack Eddleman, Mercedes Ellington, Louanna Gardner, Jan Goldin, Herman Howell, Bernard Johnson, Tommy Johnson, Ross Lashbrook, Carmen Morales, Nancy Ray Noel, Thelma Oliver, Caryl Paige, Rod Perry, Harold Pierson, Gilbert Price, Pearl Reynolds, Mabel Robinson, Jaime Rogers, Paul Reid Roman, Gus Solomons, Jr., Kathleen Stanford, Mark Taylor, Kent Thomas, Ella Thompson, Jacqueline Walcott, Barbara Wallach, Zabethe Wilde, Dudley Williams, Joseph Williams.

Time: the present. Place: on and around the campus of Freedman University, Chicago.

Staged by Lorraine Hansberry; choreography by Donald McKayle and Walter Nicks; settings and lighting by Jack Blackman; costumes by Edith Lutyens Bel Geddes; musical direction and vocal arrangements by Jack Lee; arrangements, orchestrations, additional music by Alonzo Levister; dance music and additional arrangements by Dorothea Freitag; production stage manager, Marvin Kline; stage manager, Nathan Caldwell, Jr.; press, Dorothy Ross. The Devil (Mr. Kicks) attempts to stir up trouble at a Negro University. This musical had been auditioned on Dave Garroway's early morning show because of Mr. Garroway's enthusiasm for its young author-composer.

ACT I

"Prologue" .... Kicks and Company
"Mr. Kicks" .... Kicks
"What's in It for Me?" .... Laurie Lee
"Lucky Guy" .... Will Wenchin
"Hooray for Friday" .... June and Students
"While I Am Still Young" .... June, Barbara, Lillian, Virginia
"Opportunity, Please Knock" .... Ernest
"Turn the Other Cheek" .... Kicks and Company
"Hazel's Hips" .... Silky, Hazel and Male Students
"I'll Get You Killed" .... Hazel Sharpe

ACT II

"The Comb Is Hot" .... Virginia, Lillian, Barbara
"Beautiful Girl" .... Ernest and Students
"Like a Newborn Child" .... Hazel, June, Ernest
"Virtue Is Its Own Reward" .... Kicks, Silky, Virginia, Barbara, Lillian, Eggy, Milt, Larry
"Most Folks Are Dopes" .... Kicks

ACT III

"Call of the City" .... Kicks, Will, Blonde, Laurie Lee, Hazel, Silky, June, Ernest and Company
"World Full of Grey" .... Ernest
"Hazel's Ballet" .... Kicks, Hazel and Company
"While I Am Still Young" (Reprise) .... June
Finale .... Kicks and Entire Company

(Closed October 14, 1961)

NINE O'CLOCK REVUE

(40 performances)

Revue starring Lena Horne. Produced by Alexander H. Cohen, in association with André Goulston, at the O'Keefe Centre (Toronto), October 16, 1961.

Lena Horne
The Delta Rhythm Boys
Augie & Margo
Don Adams

Staged and lighted by Ralph Alswang; musical direction by Lennie Hayton; stage manager, Joseph Brownstone; press, Charles Washburn. Glorified night club act, with Miss Horne singing songs from "Jamaica" and those of such composers as Arlen, Ellington, Porter, Styne and Rodgers and Hammerstein. It made an extensive cross-country tour.

(Closed New Haven, November 18, 1961)

THE UMBRELLA

(9 performances)

Play by Bertrand Castelli, in collaboration with Jack Raphael Guss. Produced by Ketti Frings, in association with Robert Evans, at the New Locust Theatre (Philadelphia), January 20, 1962.

Cornelius V. Stolts ....Arthur O'Connell
Sister Bonaventure ....Geraldine Page
Pfc. Wango ....Anthony Franciosa

Time: a tomorrow which we hope will never come. Place: a man-made oasis . . . somewhere.

Staged by Gene Frankel; setting by Rouben Ter-Arutunian; costumes by Theoni V. Aldredge; lighting by John Harvey; ensemble movement by Daniel Nagrin; sound by Robert W. Stringer; stage manager, Gene Perlowin; press, Merle Debuskey and Seymour Krawitz. An examination of the self-deceptions being practiced by the last three people on earth: a former prostitute who passes herself off as a nun, a petty thief who plays the big tycoon, and a GI who, though emasculated, poses as a Don Juan and war hero.

(Closed January 27, 1962)

WE TAKE THE TOWN

(30 performances)

Musical adapted from the screenplay "Viva Villa!"; book by Felice Bauer and Matt Dubey; music by Harold Karr; lyrics by Mr. Dubey. Produced by Stuart Ostrow at the Shubert Theatre (New Haven), February 19, 1962.

Fierro ....Mike Kellin
Tomas ....Eddie Roll
Pedro ....H. F. Green
Mayor ....Leon B. Stevens
Don Miguel ....Eugene Wood
Judge ....David Gold
Pancho Villa ....Robert Preston
Don Felipe del Castillo ....Lester Rawlins
Rudolfo Pascal ....Mark Lenard
Johnny Sykes ....John Cullum
Rosita Morales ....Carmen Alvarez
Emilio Chavito ....Joe Ross
Children ....Pia Zadora, Jolina Warren, Tommy Pitegoff, Ernesto Agosto
Francisco Madero ....Romney Brent
Teresa del Castillo ....Kathleen Widdoes

Dorados, peons, aristocrats, townspeople: Kip Andrews, John Aristides, Loyce Baker, Margery Beddow, Connie Burnett, Johanna Carothers, Mona Elson, David Gold, Lee Hooper, Nathan Horne, Woody Hurst, Violetta Landek, Herb Mazzini, Jane Ann Meserve, Caroline Parks, Claire Richard, Jaime Rogers, Noel Schwartz, Larry Shadur, Robert Sharp, Gerald Teijlo, Harry Theyard, Ken Urmston, Terry Violino, John Wheeler, Eugene Wood, Arline Woods.

Place: Mexico. Time: early 20th Century.

Staged by Alex Segal; choreography by Donald Saddler; settings by Peter Larkin; costumes by Motley; lighting by Tharon Musser; musical and vocal direction by Colin Romoff; orchestrations by Robert Russell Bennett and Hershy Kay; dance music arranged by Mordecai Sheinkman; production stage manager, Terence Little; stage manager, Arthur Rubin; press, Harvey B. Sabinson. The career of Pancho Villa: soldier, bandit and president.

ACT I

"Viva Villa!" ....The Dorados and Pancho Villa
"Silverware" ....Fierro, Tomas, Pedro
"I Marry You" ....Pancho Villa
"I Don't Know How to Talk to a Lady" ....Pancho Villa
"How Does the Wine Taste?" ....Teresa
"Good Old Porfirio Diaz" ....The Dorados

"Please Don't Despise Me" .... Fierro
"Pleadle-Eadle" .... Fierro and Tomas
"I've Got a Girl" .... Johnny Sykes
"We Take the Town" .... Pancho Villa, Johnny, the Dorados
"Mr. Madero and Pancho" .... Pancho Villa and Madero
"Good Old Porfirio Diaz" (Reprise) .... The People of Juarez

ACT II

"When?" .... Pancho Villa and Rosita
"Ode to a Friend" .... Johnny
"Beautiful People" .... Teresa and Aristocrats of Mexico City
"Little Man" .... Pancho Villa
"The Only Girl" .... Pancho Villa

(Closed Philadelphia, March 17, 1962)

INFIDEL CAESAR

(4 performances)

Play by Gene Wesson. Produced by Ray Shaw, in association with J. and M. Mitchell, Bernard A. Lang and Peter Petrallo, at the Music Box Theatre, April 27, 1962.

Flavius .... Charles Gerald
Carpenter .... Frank Ferrer
Marullus .... Alan Ansara
Cobbler .... Steve Vincent
Cesar .... Michael Ansara
Calpurnia .... Marta Perez
Antonio .... Gene Wesson
Soothsayer .... Albert Popwell
Cassios .... John Cullum
Casca .... Mark Margolis
Metellos Cimber .... Armand Alzamora
Cinna .... James Earl Jones
Octavios .... Shelby Taylor
Lepidos .... Frank Ferrer
Antonio's Servant .... Agustin Mayor
Brutos .... John Ireland
Lucios .... Rafael Campos
Portia .... Maria Brenes
Ligarios .... Ramon Novarro
Soldiers .... Vic Campos, Dan Fern, Guy Grasso, Robert Earl Jones, Joseph Roman
Dancer .... Ann Johnson
Diplomat .... Charles Gerald
Cinna, the poet .... Manuel Suarez
Aide Officer .... Charles Rappaport

Citizens: Jo Ann Brier, Martha Coatsworth, Akila Couloumbis, Joyce Jurnovoy, Lucky Largo, Vic Ramos, Jose Rabelo, Barbara Saturnine, John Varnum, Milton J. Williams.

Time: today. Place: a Caribbean island.

Staged by Mr. Wesson; designed by Burr Smidt; music composed and arranged by Paul Davis; stage manager, Don Doherty; press Dorothy Ross. This was an adaptation of Shakespeare's "Julius Caesar," but with the setting moved to the Caribbean. The production never played out of town, but gave four preview performances in New York, closing after the fourth.

(Closed April 30, 1962)

THE SHAKESPEARE FESTIVALS

IT is a well-kept secret that the current epidemic of Shakespeare Festivalitis first struck America twenty-seven years ago on the West Coast. True the festivals there began as amateur productions, but there has been a recent trend toward professionalizing them with the happy result that the three plays presented at the Old Globe Theatre in San Diego's Balboa Park constituted the best of the 1961 summer's Shakespeare seances. Jacqueline Brookes's gauchely charming Viola in William Ball's fresh staging of *Twelfth Night;* Morris Carnovsky's greatest of all modern Shylocks which he reproduced for grateful West Coast audiences; and Douglas Watson's urgent and hard-working *Richard III* which featured the most successful wooing of Anne scene within recent memory; these were the highlights of a brilliant achievement by an excellent young company in an intimate theatre.

At Ashland, Oregon, where the Festival operates on a semi-professional basis with recent drama school graduates and acting teachers who wish to keep their hand in, the season was the most interesting in many years. One might quarrel with Richard D. Risso's volatile and unromantic conception of Hamlet, which turned the prince into an almost menacing little figure, but Monte Markham's Horatio was ideal as he transformed the character from the usual actor waiting to say "Goodnight" to *our* healthy representative in a hopelessly decayed court.

Way back east at Stratford, Connecticut, a *Macbeth* starring Pat Hingle was not only vocally inadequate, but dull and strangely unexciting for one of our most dynamic actors. An *As You Like It* which set out to spoof itself became unbearably cute. And a *Troilus and Cressida,* which made an interesting attempt to heighten the play's meaning by giving it an American Civil War setting, eventually jarred us too much with its anachronisms and reduced the play's size to something smaller than Shakespearean size.

Stratford, Ontario, also pushed *Coriolanus* forward from ancient Rome to the period immediately following the French Revolution. This shifted the emphasis from the legend of a super-hero with one tragic flaw, and gave us instead a more modern story about the loss of values in a society recently changed from aristocracy to democracy. Paul Scofield portrayed a gentle Coriolanus who somehow just barely pulled himself up to meeting the demands of nobility. It was interesting but didn't quite work, particularly when the final duel was fought with pistols. The Canadian *Henry VIII* was a sunny over-all production that failed to generate much of the melodramatic suspense inherent in the play. Michael Langham and Tanya Moiseiwitsch combined to mount a pure sugar crystal production of *Love's Labour's Lost* that was visually delightful despite the overly artificial quality of its performance.

In a temporary theatre set up in Central Park's Wollman Rink, the New York Shakespeare Festival presented three plays with self-assurance. *Much Ado About Nothing,* staged in Goya-style costumes, took much too long to get going, but when it did created great fun. Moreover it wisely kept reminding us that this was a comedy designed for the sole purpose of showing us the ridiculous yet human follies that go with being in love. The other two productions were less fortunate. A somewhat too blatantly comic *A Midsummer Night's Dream* pleased the crowd and demonstrated with John Call's Puck that this character can be much more effective when played as a scheming little man of this world, but the verse and the magic evaporated. The final production, *Richard II,* valiantly tackled a difficult play, but nevertheless demonstrated that this open-air company was probably better at comedy and at action than it was at verse or tragic contemplation.

England's Stratford-upon-Avon season featured Vanessa Redgrave in an *As You Like It* so popular that it was taken to London as part of the repertory program at the Aldwych, and Christopher Plummer in a stirring *Richard III.* Somewhat less successful were productions of *Romeo and Juliet* and *Much Ado About Nothing.* And the special season's end presentation of *Othello,* from which so much was expected, proved disappointing when the combination of director-designer Franco Zeffirelli and actors Sir John Gielgud (Othello) and Ian Bannen (Iago) mixed poorly with each other. Mr. Bannen also played *Hamlet* during the season.

The following pages list the productions given by the five most established Shakespeare Festivals in North America. There are additional Shakespeare Festivals of widely ranging quality and duration at Boulder, Colorado, Banff, Alberta, Altadena, California, Ross, California, Washington, D. C., Atlanta, Georgia, Lakewood, Ohio, and Yellow Springs, Ohio. And in March of 1962 the Pittsburgh Playhouse brought Milton Katselas in as guest director to stage a controversial *Macbeth* starring Robert Loggia and Salome Gens.

CANADIAN SHAKESPEAREAN FESTIVAL

(107 performances)

Repertory of three plays by William Shakespeare. "Coriolanus" (June 19, 1961; 32 perfs.): staged by Michael Langham; designed by Tanya Moiseiwitsch; music by Louis Applebaum. "Henry VIII" (June 20, 1961; 42 perfs.): staged by George McCowan; designed by Brian Jackson; music by Mr. Applebaum. "Love's Labour's Lost" (June 21, 1961; 33 perfs.): staged by Mr. Langham; designed by Miss Moiseiwitsch; music by John Cook. Presented by the Stratford Shakespearean Festival at the Festival Theatre, Stratford, Ontario, Canada.

PERFORMER	"CORIOLANUS"	"HENRY VIII"	"LOVE'S LABOUR'S LOST"
Mary Anderson	Citizen	Lady-in-waiting	Maria
Claude Bede	Senator	Bishop	Gardener
Bernard Behrens	Sicinius	Guildford	
Mervyn Blake		Griffith	Dull
Zoe Caldwell			Rosaline
Douglas Campbell	Menenius	Henry	
Eric Christmas		Lord Chamberlain	Costard
Leo Ciceri		Norfolk	Ferdinand
John Colicos	Tullus Aufidius		Berowne
Jack Creley	Nicanor	Buckingham	Holofernes
Peter Donat		Surrey	Longaville
Maureen Fitzgerald	Gentlewoman	Old Lady	
Pat Galloway	Valeria	Anne Boleyn	
Robin Gammell	Officer	Surveyor	
Bruno Gerussi	Brutus	Cranmer	
Robert Goodier	Cominius	Lord Sands	
Lewis Gordon	Servant	Purse Bearer	Attendant
Max Helpmann	Citizen	Gardiner	
Edward Holmes	Conspirator	Lord Abergavenny	Officer
Alvin Kozlik	Servant	Bishop	Footman
Gary Krawford	Herald	Bearer	Dumain
Michael Learned	Virgilia		Katharine
Peter Needham	Officer	Lovell	
William Needles		Campeius	Nathaniel
Louis Negin	Servant	Capucius	
Joy Parker			Princess
James Peddie	Citizen	Cromwell	
Douglas Rain		Wolsey	Boyet
Kate Reid		Queen Katharine	Jaquenetta
Paul Scofield	Coriolanus		Don Armado
Murray Scott			Moth
Eleanor Stuart	Volumnia		
John Vernon	Titus Lartius	Suffolk	

Soldiers, citizens, lords, ladies, attendants, peasants and others: Guy Belanger, Christine Bennett, Ingi Bergmann, Douglas Chamberlain, Dinah Christie, Marcia Clare, Michael Davidson, Miranda Davies, Fred Euringer, Garrick Hagon, Adrienne Harris, Barry Lord, John MacKay, Hedley Mattingly, Tommy Murray, Nelson Phillips, Tony Robinow, Joseph Rutten, Louis Turenne.

THE CANVAS BARRICADE (6 perfs.)—By Donald Lamont Jack. Staged by George McCowan; settings and costumes by Mark Negin; lighting by Len Smith; music by Harry Freedman. Presented by the Stratford Shakespearean Festival at the Festival Theatre, August 7, 1961.

With Peter Donat, Kate Reid, Maureen Fitzgerald, Jack Creeley; Amelia Hall, Eleanor Stuart, Christine Bennett, Douglas Rain, Zoe Caldwell and Eric Christmas. Satirical comedy about the modern art racket.

(Closed September 23, 1961)

AMERICAN SHAKESPEAREAN FESTIVAL

(112 performances)

Repertory of three plays by William Shakespeare. "As You Like It" (June 6, 1961; 45 perfs.): staged by Word Baker; lighting by Tharon Musser; music and songs by David Amram. "Macbeth" (June 8, 1961; 44 perfs.): staged by Jack Landau; lighting by Mr. Musser; music by Mr. Amram. "Troilus and Cressida" (July 18, 1961; 23 perfs.): staged by Mr. Landau; lighting by Charles Elson; music by Herman Chessid. For the entire festival: settings by Robert O'Hearn; costumes by Motley. Presented by the American Shakespearean Festival at the Festival Theatre, Stratford, Connecticut.

PERFORMER	"AS YOU LIKE IT"	"MACBETH"	"TROILUS AND CRESSIDA"
Thayer David			Ajax
Donald Davis	Jacques	Duncan	Achilles
Guil Dudley	Second Lord	Sergeant	Paris
Theodore Eliopoulos			Antenor
Bill Fletcher	Charles	Caithness	Deiphobus
Will Geer	Banished Duke	Siward	Priam
Sam Greene	Amiens	Murderer	Calchas
Donald Harron	Orlando	Banquo	Thersites
Patrick Hines	Frederick	Ross	Agamemnon
Pat Hingle		Macbeth	Hector
Kim Hunter	Rosalind	Weird Woman	Helen
Carla Huston	Phebe	Weird Woman	
Lois Kibbee	Lady	Gentlewoman	Hecuba
William Larsen	Laughing Lord	Mentieth	Nestor
Kathryn Loder	Audrey	Weird Woman	Andromache
Alan Marlowe	Silvius	Angus	Helenus
Julian Miller	William	Servant	Alexander
Carrie Nye	Celia	Lady Macduff	Cressida
Billy Partello		Macduff's Son	
Alek Primrose	Adam	Doctor	Menelaus
Mylo Quam	Dennis	Fleance	
James Ray	Oliver	Malcolm	Diomedes
Colgate Salsbury	First Lord	Seyton	Patroclus
George Sampson	Jacques de Boys	Young Siward	Servant
Hiram Sherman	Touchstone	Porter	Pandarus
Paul Sparer	Corin	Lennox	Ulysses
Jessica Tandy		Lady Macbeth	Cassandra
Ted van Griethuysen	M. Le Beau	Donalbain	Troilus
Richard Waring	Oliver Mar-Text	Macduff	Aeneas

Lords, ladies, soldiers, attendants and others: John Bazarini, Alan Becker, Rick Branda, James Conway, Jacqueline Coslow, David Coxwell, William Curtis, Michela Eisen, Hugh Faegin, Jack Gardner, Clifford Landis, Albert Malafront, James McMahon, Gail Metcalf, Richard Miller, Peter J. Nevard, Garth Pillsbury, Conrad Pomereau, Joseph Prete, James Puzinsky, Stephen Scherban, Deane Selmier, Douglas Sherman, Robert Smith, Noel Thomas, Joe Vakarela, Valerie von Volz, Louis Waldon, Allan Willig.

(Closed September 10, 1961)

NEW YORK SHAKESPEAREAN FESTIVAL

(46 performances)

Program of three plays by William Shakespeare. "Much Ado About Nothing" (July 5, 1961; 16 perfs.): staged by Joseph Papp; costumes by Theoni V. Aldredge; lighting by John Robertson; dances by Matt Mattox. "A Midsummer Night's Dream" (August 1, 1961; 18 perfs.): staged by Joel J. Friedman; costumes by Miss Aldredge; lighting by Mr. Robertson; dances by Mr. Mattox. "Richard II" (August 28, 1961; 12 perfs.): staged by Gladys Vaughan; costumes by Lewis Brown; lighting by Martin Aronstein. For the entire festival: settings by Eldon Elder; music by David Amram. Presented by Joseph Papp at the Wollman Memorial Skating Rink, Central Park, New York.

PERFORMER	"MUCH ADO ABOUT NOTHING"	"A MIDSUMMER NIGHT'S DREAM"	"RICHARD II"
John Call	Dogberry	Puck	
J. D. Cannon	Benedick		Bolingbroke
Jonathan Farwell		Demetrius	
Anne Fielding		Hermia	
Margaret Hall		Helena	
Ben Hayes	Claudio		Richard II
Bette Henritze	Margaret		Duchess of York
James E. Jones		Oberon	Lord Marshall; Gardener's Assistant
R. A. Jordan		Lysander	Aumerle
Philip Kenneally	Borachio	Theseus	Bushy
Ric Lavin	Conrade		Fitzwater
Barbara Lester	Ursula		Duchess of Glouster
Lex Luce	Antonio		Bishop of Carlisle
Gerald E. McGonagill	Don Juan		Mowbray; Sir Pierce
Nan Martin	Beatrice		
Anne Pearson	Hero		
Donald Plumley	Sergeant		Keeper
Albert Quinton	Leonato	Bottom	Duke of York
Philip Sterling	Don Pedro		Northumberland
Jerry Terheyden	Friar Francis	Philostrate	
Abe Vigoda			John of Gaunt
Kathleen Widdoes		Titania	Queen to Richard

Others: Jack Adams, Daniel Ades, Michael Baseleon, Burney Bell, Art Berwick, Lawrence Blassingame, Charles Bolender, Walton Butterfield, Lew Ciulla, Johanna Carothers, Hope Clarke, Kenneth Creel, Grenville Cuyler, John Dorman, William Duell, Anne Draper, Bruce Edwards, Lloyd Edwards, Frank Farmer, Cornelius Frizell, Richard Graham, Chris Grenko, Don Gunderson, Betty Hader, William Herndon, Leonard Hicks, Jean Hilzinger, Ralph Hoffmann, Bruce C. Howard, Herman D. Howell, Walter Julio, Sheila Kortlucke, Sherman Lloyd, Tony McGrath, Jan Mickens, Peg

Murray, Rosemarie Nardone, Jackie Perkuhn, Roger O. Serbagi, Bob Schwartz, John W. Smith, Deborah Steinberg, Paul Stiller, Ray Stubbs, Basil Thompson, Philip Visco, Clyde Wadlow, Don Wesley, Harry White, Karl E. Williams, Wayne Wilson.

(Closed September 9, 1961)

NATIONAL SHAKESPEAREAN FESTIVAL

(84 performances)

Repertory of three plays by William Shakespeare. "Twelfth Night" (June 27, 1961; 31 perfs.): staged by William Ball. "The Merchant of Venice" (July 5, 1961; 31 perfs.): staged by Allen Fletcher. "King Richard III" (July 26, 1961; 22 perfs.): staged by Mr. Fletcher. For the entire festival: settings and costumes by Peggy Kellner; music by Conrad Susa. Presented by the San Diego National Shakespearean Festival at the Old Globe Theatre, San Diego, California.

PERFORMER	"TWELFTH NIGHT"	"MERCHANT OF VENICE"	"RICHARD III"
Elizabeth Bork	Lady	Jessica	
Jacqueline Brookes	Viola	Portia	Elizabeth
Morris Carnovsky	Malvolio	Shylock	King Edward IV
Ludi Claire	Olivia	Nerissa	Lady Anne
Clayton Corzatte	Feste	Gratiano	Duke of Clarence
Philip Hanson	Andrew Aguecheck	Prince of Arragon	Duke of Buckingham
Charles Herrick		Lancelot Gobbo	Richard Ratcliffe
Taldo Kenyon	Valentine	Lorenzo	Lord Hastings
Christopher Knight	Sebastian	Bassanio	Henry
James Maloney	Sir Toby Belch	Duke of Venice	Thomas Stanley
Anthony Ristoff	Priest	Gobbo	William Gatesby
Joanna Roos	Maria		Margaret
David Varnay	Officer	Prince of Morocco	James Blunt
Douglas Watson	Orsino	Antonio	Richard

Lords, ladies, soldiers, servants and others: Ann Abernathy, Vincent Andres, Joe Angarola, Ed Boverie, Steve Brown, Stephen Carnovsky, Nils Engberg, Ken Frankel, Harry Frazier, Janice Fuller, David Gallagher, Martin Garrish, John Herring, John Higgins, Barry Kraft, Kevin Madden, Minerva Marquis, David Miles, Robert Peterson, Jim Prendergast, Joel Riggs, Dennis Robertson, Robert Sherman, Gregory Smith, William Starr, William Van Vechten, Adrienne Webb, Susan Webb, Leonard Wisniew.

(Closed September 10, 1961)

OREGON SHAKESPEAREAN FESTIVAL

(42 performances)

Program of four plays by William Shakespeare and one play by Ben Jonson. Presented by the Oregon Shakespearean Festival Association at Ashland, Oregon, June 24, 1961.

A MIDSUMMER NIGHT'S DREAM

(10 performances)

Staged by B. Iden Payne. With Rod Alexander, Robert Palmer, Linda Marshall, William Kinsolving, Graham Woodruff, Eugene Peyroux, Mary Jane Hales and Shirley Patton.

HAMLET

(10 performances)

Staged by Robert B. Loper. With Richard D. Risso, Peter D. MacLean, Michael Fuchs, Monte Markham, Elise Hunt and Molly Riley.

ALL'S WELL THAT ENDS WELL

(10 performances)

Staged by Charles G. Taylor. With Elizabeth Huddle, John Hales, Rod Alexander, Gerard Larsen, Molly Riley and Nagle Jackson.

KING HENRY IV, PART I

(9 performances)

Staged by Richard D. Risso. With Angus Bowmer, Eugene Peyroux, Monte Markham, Rod Alexander, Christopher Newton, Graham Woodruff and Peter D. MacLean.

THE ALCHEMIST

(3 performances)

Staged by Edward S. Brubaker. With Gerard Larson, Nagle Jackson, Elizabeth Huddle and Hugh Evans.

(Closed September 10, 1961)

A SELECTED LIST OF PLAYS FIRST PRODUCED OUTSIDE NEW YORK CITY

By George Freedley

The following list is comprised of plays which premiered around the United States from June 1, 1961 through May 31, 1962.

ANATOL. See page 41.

THE ANVIL by Julia Davis. Jefferson County Court House, Charlestown, W. Va., Aug. 5, 1961. The trial of John Brown.

BANNERS OF STEEL by Barry Stavis. Univ. of Southern Illinois, May 18, 1962. Drama about John Brown, his Harper's Ferry Raid and his death.

THE BASHFUL GENIUS by Harold Callen. UCLA, Dec. 2, 1961. The first two years of George Bernard Shaw's married life.

THE BEAUTY PART by S. J. Perelman. Bucks County Playhouse, New Hope, Pa., Sep. 18, 1961. Satire on the idea that everyone in America today must express himself artistically.

BIG DEAL by Paul Sills, based on "The Beggar's Opera" by John Gay; music by William Mathieu; lyrics by David Shepherd. Playwrights' Theatre, Chicago, Ill., Aug. 16, 1961. Satire on Chicago politics.

BROUSILLE AND THE JUST by Gratien Gelinas, trans. by Kenneth Johnstone and Joffre Dechene. International Theatre, Vancouver, B.C., Aug. 5, 1961. A French Canadian family hounds to his death a simple "little man," rather than let him give the evidence that will lead to the conviction of their no-good brother for murder.

BRISIUS AND THE SERGEANT by Richard Schechner. Tulane University, Apr. 26, 1962. A kaleidoscopic satire on militarism over the centuries.

THE BURNING OF THE LEPERS. See pages 39 and 45.

THE CANNIBAL CAT by Jackson Burgess. Sausalito Little Theatre, Sausalito, Calif., Mar. 17, 1962. The shaking off of cultural influences.

CHICKEN SOUP WITH BARLEY by Arnold Wesker. Dobama Theatre, Cleveland, Ohio, May 17, 1962. Portrait of hereditary weakness in a family of London East End Jews.

THE CHILD BUYER by Paul Shyre, adapted from John Hersey's novel. UCLA, Apr. 27, 1962. Study of the psychological relationship between an adult, his need of a child, and the corruption of human values.

CONVERSATION AT MIDNIGHT by Edna St. Vincent Millay. Coronet Theatre, Los Angeles, Calif., Nov. 7, 1961. At midnight—when it is neither evening nor morning—seven men argue about the profundities and trivia of life.

THE CROSSING. See page 43.

DRUMS IN THE NIGHT by Bertolt Brecht. State University of Education, Albany, N. Y., Aug. 2, 1961. A German soldier returns home at the end of World War I and joins the Communist uprising in Berlin. Finally recognizing idealism as "phoney" and "self" as the prime obligation, he sends his converts to the revolution off to the fray while he retreats to the bed of his former girl friend.

FOUR MEN by Andre Davis. Pittsburgh Playhouse, Pittsburgh, Pa., Sep. 26, 1961. Four young men of widely differing political persuasions combine to assassinate the British Prime Minister.

FRIEDMAN & SON. See page 45.

GARDEN SPOT, USA. See page 43.

THE GREAT RAGE OF PHILIP HOTZ by Max Frisch, trans. by James L. Rosenberg. Univ. of Rochester, May 1, 1962. A wife's infidelity causes her husband to join the French Foreign Legion.

HERE COMES SANTA CLAUS by Joel Oliansky. Yale University, May, 1962. Concerns a harrassed man with a radio program, a wife who is a mental case, and a father trying to relive a glamorous stage past.

HERE TODAY—GONE TOMORROW by Mel Shapiro. Playhouse in the Park, Cincinnati, Ohio, Mar. 28, 1962. Comic fantasy about some illusory modern aristocrats whose dream life is shattered by three conformist and realist spies.

HIGH TIME ALONG THE WABASH by William Saroyan. Purdue University, Dec. 1, 1961. Trilogy about race relations in Indiana.

HONEY IN THE ROCK by Kermit Hunter. Grandveiw State Park, Beckley, W. Va., June 27, 1961. Historical outdoor "symphonic drama" about the admission of the state of West Virginia into the Union in 1862.

IMPEACHMENT by Jack Lezebnick. Stephens College, Columbia, Mo., Jan. 25, 1962. Senator Thaddeus Stevens vs. President Andrew Johnson.

IMPROMPTU by Tad Mosel. Adelphi College, Garden City, N. Y., Nov., 1961. Four actors find themselves in a situation where they must examine the delicate balance between truth and illusion in their lives on stage and off.

THE INTERPRETER by Eric Rudd. Bucks County Playhouse, June 26, 1961. Concerns a summit conference between the President of the United States and the Premier of Russia in 1970. The central character is the chief interpreter of the United Nations, and the play deals with his efforts to save the conference and the world by deliberately misinterpreting.

THE LAST DAYS OF LINCOLN by Mark Van Doren. Florida State University, Oct. 11, 1961. Literally the last days—April, 1865.

LET THE DOGS BARK. See page 43.

MEN, WOMEN AND ANGELS by Herman Briffault and Alex Szoggi, based on "Sodom and Gomorrah" by Jean Giraudoux. Queen Elizabeth Theatre, Vancouver, B. C., Aug. 14, 1961.

NAKED TO MINE ENEMIES. See page 44.

NATURAL AFFECTION by William Inge. Sombrero Playhouse, Phoenix, Ariz., Feb. 6, 1962. A young and neglected boy feels an unnatural affection for his mother.

ORESTES POISED by Bernard Beckerman. Hoffstra College, Hempstead, N. Y., May 11, 1962. Through the narration of Pylades, the play probes the dilemma facing Orestes as to whether or not he should kill his mother, Clytemnestra.

THE PORTABLE YENBERRY by Marc Connelly. Purdue University, May 24, 1962. A comedy about parapsychology.

PUNTILA by Bertolt Brecht, revised translation by Gerhard Nellhaus. Carnegie Tech, May 23, 1962. A comic exploration of the relationship between a Finnish land-owner and his hired man Matti.

PUT IT IN WRITING, sketches by Bud McCreery, Bill Dana, Jay Thompson, David Panich, Robert Kessler; music by Charles Strouse, Jerry Bock, Mr. Kessler. Royal Poinciana Playhouse, Palm Beach, Fla., Feb. 19, 1962. Musical revue.

SERJEANT MUSGRAVE'S DANCE. See page 45.

SIMON by Ben Hecht, adapted from the play "Die Gesichte Ber Simon Marchand" by Bertolt Brecht and Leon Feuchtwanger. Playhouse, Cleveland, Ohio, Jan. 31, 1962. A young French girl dreams that she is Joan of Arc and incites her Nazi-occupied town against its captors.

TURN ON THE NIGHT by Jerome Lawrence and Robert E. Lee. John B. Kelly Playhouse, Philadelphia, Pa., Aug. 7, 1961. Actors, playwrights, theatrical customs may come and go, but the theatre is everlasting.

VIOLETTES by Georges Schehadé, trans. by Mother Adele Fiske and Leon Katz; music by Joseph Kosma. Manhattanville College of the Sacred Heart, Purchase, N. Y., Mar. 30, 1962.

OTHER PLAYS: ABE LINCOLN OF PIGEON CREEK by William E. Wilson; Univ. of Indiana. THE ACROBATS by Barry Fleming; White Barn Theatre, Westport, Conn. THE AFTERMATH by John Crilley; Pioneer Playhouse, Danville, Ky. AND ALL MEN KILL by Albert Brenner; Pioneer Playhouse. AND WHEN IT RAINS by Ernest A. Charles; El Lobero Theatre, Santa Barbara, Calif. THE ANIMAL FAIR by George Selden; Pioneer Playhouse. BARABBAS by Michel de Ghelderode, trans. by Hugh Dickinson; Playhouse, Woodstock, N. Y. BETWEEN SEASONS by Malcolm Welles; Berkshire Playhouse, Stockbridge, Mass. BLUE CHIPS by Manuel Seff; Pioneer Playhouse. BOUND FOR KENTUCKY by Kermit Hunter; Memorial Auditorium, Louisville, Ky. THE BROMLEY TOUCH by Kay Arthur; Pioneer Playhouse. BUILD ME A BRIDGE by Mary Drayton; Playhouse, Cleveland, Ohio. THE CALM; see page 41. CECILE by Jean Anouilh, trans. by Luce and Arthur Klein; Olney Theatre, Olney, Md. CHRYSANTHEMUM, musical with book and lyrics by Neville Phillips, Robin Chancellor; music by Robert Stewart; Royal Poinciana Playhouse. COME UP AND SEE MY CASSEROLE by Frank M. Mosier; Playwright's Showcase, New Orleans, La. CONFLICT by Chaunce Skilling, music by Robert Skilling; Starlight Theatre, Pawling, N. Y. THE CORAL by Georg Kaiser, trans. by Winifred Katzin; Tulane University. DANCIN' by John Reese; Stage Society Theatre, Los Angeles, Calif. THE DEADLY by David Swift; Valley Playhouse, Los Angeles, Calif. DEVILS AND ANGELS; see page 42. DING DONG BELL by Gurney Campbell and Daphne Athas; Country Playhouse, Westport, Conn. THE DRY DOLPHIN by William Werbung; Pioneer Playhouse. The EAGLE AND THE ROCK by Frank M. Mosier; Playwright's Showcase. ENTER SOLLY GOLD by Bernard Kops; Troubador Cafe, Los Angeles, Calif. FACE OF A STRANGER by Pauline K. Schmookler; Univ. of Arkansas. FLIGHT by Wallace

Dace; Univ. of Arkansas. THE FLORESTAN DIMENSION; see page 42. FROM SWERVE OF SHORE TO BEND OF BAY; see page 41. FUTURE PERFECT by Whitfield Cook; Cape Playhouse, Dennis, Mass. GANGWAY, musical by Marc Ross, Kathryn Offill; music by Miss Offill; lyrics by Marylou P. Dunn; Community Playhouse, Long Beach, Calif. THE GIFT by Kenneth Dewey; Mission Neighborhood Playhouse, San Francisco, Calif. GOLEM by Stephen Lackner; Des Moines Community Theatre, Des Moines, Iowa. GREENSLEEVES' MAGIC by Marian Jonson; Los Angeles State College, Calif. GUIDEBOOK TO BIGAMY by Vernon Weddle; Okoboji Summer Theatre, Spirit Lake, Iowa. HARDLY A KIND WORD ABOUT ANYBODY, revue with sketches and lyrics by Budd Frena; music by Leon Peber; Coronet Theatre. AN HEIR OF VIRTUE by Alex Gaby; Community Playhouse, Rochester, N. Y. HOCUS POCUS by Mel Dinelli, Stephen Joseph, adapted from their play "Abracadabra"; Royal Poinciana Playhouse. IN A BACKWARD COUNTRY by Evan Jones; White Barn Theatre. THE INKWELL by Harold J. Kennedy; Drury Lane Theatre, Chicago, Ill. JACQUES AND JILL, musical by Robert Dow; Centre Stage, Toronto, Ontario. THE JAR; see page 41. JOURNEY TO THE DAY by Roger Hirson; Country Playhouse, Westport, Conn. THE JULES FEIFFER SHOW; see page 41. LETTER TO CORINTH I by Virginia Scott; State Univ. of Iowa, Iowa City, Iowa. THE LIMBO KID by Robert Downing; Little Theatre, Raleigh, N. C. LOOK AHEAD, musical with book and lyrics by Lou Peterson; music by Morris Surdin; Canadian Theatre Centre, Winnipeg, Canada. LORNA; see page 42. LOVE AMONG THE PLATYPI by Richard F. Stockton, Peggy Plympton; Bucks County Playhouse. LOVE CAN ALSO DIE by Chris Blake; Univ. of Arkansas. THE MAD MUSICIAN; see page 42. MAIDENS' VOWS by Alexander Fredo, trans. by Arthur P. Coleman, Marion M. Coleman; Highland Park Town Hall; Dallas, Texas. A MAN ABOUT THE HOUSE by Joseph Julian; Bucks County Playhouse. MAN BETTER MAN by Errol Hill; Yale University. MAN OF THE HOUSE by Robert A. Blair; Univ. of Arkansas. MR. FLANNERY'S OCEAN by Lewis J. Carlino; White Barn Theatre. MR. GILBERT, MR. SULLIVAN AND MR. GREEN by Frank Wilson; John B. Kelly Playhouse. MOVE BACK THE STARS by Robert G. Armstrong; Cecilwood Theatre, Fishkill, N. Y. MUCH ADO, musical version of "Much Ado About Nothing"; St. Mary's College, Notre Dame, Ind. NA'AHAMO by Jean Charlot; Rugen Theatre, Honolulu, Hawaii. O GENTLE TROUT by Perry Stieglitz; Pioneer Playhouse. ONLY THE GOOD by Clyde Ware; Hollywood Center Theatre, Los Angeles, Calif. PIECE AND PRECISE by Lewis J. Carlino; White Barn Theatre. PLAIN BETSY, musical by Marion Weaver, William Brooker; music and lyrics by Miss Weaver; Gretna Playhouse, Mt. Gretna, Pa. POE REVISITED by Robert Minford; arranged from the stories and poems of E. A. Poe; Vallison Vantage Theatre, Los Angeles, Calif. POINT OF VIEW, revue with sketches by Charles Martin; lyrics by Paul Francis Webster, Ray Gilbert; music by Hal Borne; Vine St. Theatre, Los Angeles, Calif. THE PORTABLE TIGER; see page 41. PORTRAIT by Ving Engeron; Playwright's Showcase. PROLOGUE TO FREEDOM by Elizabeth B. Dooley; Parris Island, Beaufort, S. C. THE PURIST AGONY by Harry Tierney, Jr.; White Barn Theatre. A RESOUNDING TINKLE by N. F. Simpson; Univ. of Indiana. THE SAN JOSE MISSION STORY by Ethel W. Harris, Dorothy Cinclair; San Antonio, Texas. SEXTETTE by Mae West; Edgewater Beach Hotel Theatre, Chicago, Ill. THE SHIFTING HEART by Richard Begnon; Crest Theatre, Toronto, Ontario. SIMON SAYS GET MARRIED by Bernard Slade; Crest Theatre. A SINGLE MOUNTAIN by Albert C. Smelko; Ohio University. SISTER WAS A SPORT by John J. Wolf; Civic Auditorium, Kalamazoo, Mich. A SONG FOR SMALL VOICES by David M. Jones; Mountain Theatre, Braddock Heights, Md. THE SPARTA FOX by Andrew C. Bidwell; Pioneer Playhouse. SPITE FENCE by Kenneth Keskinen; George School, Pa. STEP-IN-THE-HOLLOW by Donagh MacDonagh; State University of Education, Albany, N. Y. A STRIPED SACK OF PENNY CANDY by Max Hodge; Starlight Theatre. THE SWEET OLD THING by William H. Crain, Jr.; Univ. of Texas. THE TABLE by Jack Dunphy; White Barn Theatre. TENDER LOVING CARE by Elena Miramova; Coconut Grove Playhouse, Miami, Fla. THE THEATRE OF ROBERT FROST; see page 41. THE TIGER KITTENS bv Albert J. Zuckerman; Pioneer Playhouse. TIME OUT FOR LOVE by Ramon Delgado; Lyman School Auditorium, Longwood, Fla. THE TREE WITCH; see page 41. TRIP NO FURTHER by Monroe Stern; Pioneer Playhouse. THREE WORDS IN NO TIME by Lyon Phelps; Provincetown Playhouse, Provincetown, Mass. TOP OF THE LIST, musical by Bill Dana, Ronny Graham; music by Bud McCreery; Mansions Theatre, Warrensburg, N. Y. THE TRESPASSERS by Ralph Arzoomanian; State University of Iowa. THE TRUTH BOMB by Dan Stein; Univ. of Arkansas. TWO QUEENS OF LOVE AND BEAUTY by Bill Hoffman; Bucks County Playhouse. THE TYPIST by Murray Schisgal; White Barn Theatre. UP FROM EVEREST by George Hitchcock; San Francisco Conservatory of Music, Calif. THE VIRGIN KING by Elizabeth Kaeburn; Los Angeles, Calif. THE YELLOW LOVES; see page 41. YESTERDAY'S TOMORROW by Gerald Stanford; Vallison Vantage Theatre.

FACTS AND FIGURES

STATISTICAL SUMMARY

(Last Season Plays Which Ended Runs After June 1, 1961)

ON BROADWAY

Plays	*Opening Date*	*Number Perform-ances*	*Closing Date*
A Call on Kuprin	May 25, 1961	12	June 3, 1961
Wildcat	Dec. 16, 1960	171	June 3, 1961
Big Fish, Little Fish	Mar. 15, 1961	101	June 10, 1961
Hamlet	Mar. 16, 1961	102	June 11, 1961
The Devil's Advocate	Mar. 9, 1961	116	June 17, 1961
The Happiest Girl in the World	Apr. 3, 1961	96	June 24, 1961
Pal Joey	May 31, 1961	31	June 25, 1961
An Evening with Nichols and May	Oct. 8, 1960	306	July 1, 1961
The Miracle Worker	Oct. 19, 1959	700	July 1, 1961
The Best Man	Mar. 31, 1960	520	July 8, 1961
Donnybrook!	May 18, 1961	68	July 15, 1961
Rhinoceros	Jan. 9, 1961	240	Aug. 5, 1961
A Taste of Honey	Oct. 4, 1960	376	Sept. 9, 1961
All the Way Home	Nov. 30, 1960	333	Sept. 16, 1961
Bye Bye Birdie	Apr. 14, 1960	607	Oct. 7, 1961
Fiorello!	Nov. 23, 1959	795	Oct. 28, 1961
A Far Country	Apr. 4, 1961	271	Nov. 25, 1961
Irma La Douce	Sept. 29, 1960	524	Dec. 31, 1961
Do Re Mi	Dec. 26, 1960	400	Jan. 13, 1962
The Unsinkable Molly Brown	Nov. 3, 1960	532	Feb. 10, 1962

OFF BROADWAY

Plays	Opening Date	Number Performances	Closing Date
Stewed Prunes	Nov. 14, 1960	295	June 8, 1961
Hedda Gabler	Nov. 9, 1960	340	Sept. 3, 1961
Under Milk Wood	Mar. 29, 1961	202	Oct. 22, 1961
The Threepenny Opera	Sept. 20, 1955	2,611 *	Dec. 17, 1961
The Balcony	Mar. 3, 1960	672	Dec. 31, 1961
The American Dream	Jan. 24, 1961	370	Jan. 7, 1962
The Death of Bessie Smith	Mar. 1, 1961	328	Jan. 7, 1962

* Not including the 96 performances registered by the same production between its original opening Mar. 10, 1954 and its closing May 30, 1954.

LONG RUNS ON BROADWAY

To June 1, 1962

(Plays marked with asterisk were still playing June 1, 1962)

Plays	Number Performances	Plays	Number Performances
Life with Father	3,224	Carousel	890
Tobacco Road	3,182	Hats Off to Ice	889
* My Fair Lady	2,574	Fanny	888
Abie's Irish Rose	2,327	Follow the Girls	882
Oklahoma!	2,212	The Bat	867
Harvey	1,775	My Sister Eileen	865
South Pacific	1,694	White Cargo	864
Born Yesterday	1,642	Song of Norway	860
The Voice of the Turtle	1,557	A Streetcar Named Desire	855
Arsenic and Old Lace	1,444	Comedy in Music	849
Hellzapoppin	1,404	You Can't Take It with You	837
The Music Man	1,375	La Plume de Ma Tante	835
Angel Street	1,295	Three Men on a Horse	835
Lightnin'	1,291	Inherit the Wind	806
The King and I	1,246	No Time for Sergeants	796
Guys and Dolls	1,200	Fiorello!	795
Mister Roberts	1,157	Where's Charlie?	792
Annie Get Your Gun	1,147	The Ladder	789
The Seven Year Itch	1,141	State of the Union	765
Pins and Needles	1,108	The First Year	760
Kiss Me, Kate	1,070	Two for the Seesaw	750
Pajama Game	1,063	Death of a Salesman	742
The Teahouse of the August Moon	1,027	Sons o' Fun	742
Damn Yankees	1,019	Gentlemen Prefer Blondes	740
* The Sound of Music	1,009	The Man Who Came to Dinner	739
Anna Lucasta	957	Call Me Mister	734
Kiss and Tell	957	West Side Story	732
The Moon Is Blue	924	High Button Shoes	727
Bells Are Ringing	924	Finian's Rainbow	725
Can-Can	892		

Plays	*Number Performances*
Claudia	722
The Gold Diggers	720
The Diary of Anne Frank	717
I Remember Mama	714
Tea and Sympathy	712
Junior Miss	710
Seventh Heaven	704
Gypsy	702
The Miracle Worker	700
Cat on a Hot Tin Roof	694
Li'l Abner	693
Peg o' My Heart	692
The Children's Hour	691
Dead End	687
The Lion and the Mouse	686
Dear Ruth	683
East Is West	680
The Most Happy Fella	676
The Doughgirls	671
Irene	670
Boy Meets Girl	669
Blithe Spirit	657
The Women	657
A Trip to Chinatown	657
Bloomer Girl	654
The Fifth Season	654
Rain	648
Witness for the Prosecution	645
Call Me Madam	644
Janie	642
The Green Pastures	640
Auntie Mame	639
The Fourposter	632
The Tenth Man	623
* Camelot	622
Is Zat So?	618
Anniversary Waltz	615
The Happy Time	614
Separate Rooms	613
Affairs of State	610
Star and Garter	609
The Student Prince	608
Bye Bye Birdie	607
Broadway	603
Adonis	603
Street Scene	601
Kiki	600
Flower Drum Song	600
Wish You Were Here	598
A Society Circus	596
Blossom Time	592
The Two Mrs. Carrolls	585
Kismet	583
Detective Story	581
Brigadoon	581
Brother Rat	577
Show Boat	572
The Show-Off	571
Sally	570
One Touch of Venus	567
Happy Birthday	564
Look Homeward, Angel	564
The Glass Menagerie	561
Wonderful Town	559
Rose Marie	557
Strictly Dishonorable	557
A Majority of One	556
Toys in the Attic	556
Sunrise at Campobello	556
Jamaica	555
Ziegfeld Follies	553
Floradora	553
Dial "M" for Murder	552
Good News	551

VARIETY'S TABULATION OF FINANCIAL HITS AND FLOPS

HITS

An Evening with Yves Montand
How to Succeed in Business Without Really Trying
A Man for All Seasons
The Night of the Iguana
A Shot in the Dark
Take Her, She's Mine
Write Me a Murder

STATUS NOT YET DETERMINED

Bravo Giovanni
A Funny Thing Happened on the Way to the Forum
I Can Get It for You Wholesale
Milk and Honey
No Strings
Subways Are for Sleeping
A Thousand Clowns

FAILURES

All American
The Aspern Papers
The Billy Barnes People
Blood, Sweat and Stanley Poole
The Captains and the Kings
The Caretaker
The Complaisant Lover
A Cook for Mr. General
Daughter of Silence
Do You Know the Milky Way?
The Egg
Everybody Loves Opal
A Family Affair
First Love
From the Second City
The Garden of Sweets
The Gay Life
General Seeger
Giants, Sons of Giants
Gideon
A Gift of Time
Great Day in the Morning
Isle of Children
Kean
Kwamina
Let It Ride
Look: We've Come Through
New Faces of 1962
A Passage to India
Purlie Victorious
Romulus
Ross
Sail Away
Something About a Soldier
Sunday in New York
Venus at Large

MISCELLANEOUS

Brigadoon
Can-Can
Greek Tragedy Theatre
Old Vic Company
Royal Dramatic Theatre of Sweden

CLOSED DURING TRYOUT TOUR

High Fidelity
Kicks and Co.
The Lena Horne Show
A Short Happy Life
The Umbrella
We Take the Town
Infidel Caesar (closed after preview)

Holdovers from the 1960-61 Season, Since Clarified

HITS

Camelot
Carnival
Come Blow Your Horn
A Taste of Honey
The Unsinkable Molly Brown

FAILURES

All the Way Home
Big Fish, Little Fish
The Devil's Advocate
Do Re Mi
Donnybrook
A Far Country
The Happiest Girl in the World
Rhinoceros
Wildcat

DRAMA CRITICS CIRCLE VOTING 1961-1962

The New York Drama Critics Circle voted *The Night of the Iguana* as the Best American Play with 12 votes over *Gideon* (6). As the Best Foreign Play it chose *A Man for All Seasons* (15) over *The Caretaker* (3). And the Best Musical Production award went to *How to Succeed in Business Without Really Trying* (17) over *No Strings* (1). John McCarten and John McClain were not present, but their unofficial choices are listed below in parenthesis.

	AMERICAN	FOREIGN	MUSICAL
Whitney Bolton—Telegraph	Iguana	Seasons	Succeed
John Chapman—News	Iguana	Seasons	Succeed
Ethel Colby—Journal of Commerce	Iguana	Seasons	Succeed
Robert Coleman—Mirror	Gideon	Seasons	Succeed
Richard Cooke—Wall St. Journal	Gideon	Seasons	Succeed
Thomas Dash—Women's Wear Daily	Gideon	Seasons	Succeed
Jack Garver—U.P.	Gideon	Seasons	Succeed
William H. Glover—A.P.	Gideon	Seasons	Succeed
Henry Hewes—Saturday Review	Iguana	Caretaker	Succeed
Walter Kerr—N.Y. Herald Tribune	Iguana	Seasons	Succeed
Theodore Kalem—Time	Iguana	Caretaker	Succeed
Emery Lewis—Cue	Iguana	Seasons	Succeed
John McCarten—New Yorker	(Look: We've Come Through)	(Seasons)	(Succeed)
John McClain—Journal American	(Iguana)	(Seasons)	(Succeed)
Ward Morehouse—Newhouse Papers	Iguana	Seasons	Succeed
Norman Nadel—World Telegram and Sun	Iguana	Seasons	Succeed
Joseph T. Shipley—WEVD	Gideon	Seasons	No Strings
Howard Taubman—N.Y. Times	Iguana	Caretaker	Succeed
Richard Watts—Post	Iguana	Seasons	Succeed
Thomas Wenning—Newsweek	Iguana	Seasons	Succeed

NEW YORK DRAMA CRITICS CIRCLE AWARDS

Listed below are the New York Drama Critics Circle Awards, given each season for (1) Best American Play, (2) Best Foreign Play, (3) Best Musical Production.

1935-36—(1) Winterset
1936-37—(1) High Tor
1937-38—(1) Of Mice and Men, (2) Shadow and Substance
1938-39—(1) No Award, (2) The White Steed
1939-40—(1) The Time of Your Life
1940-41—(1) Watch on the Rhine, (2) The Corn Is Green
1941-42—(1) No Award, (2) Blithe Spirit
1942-43—(1) The Patriots
1943-44—(1) No Award, (2) Jacobowsky and the Colonel
1944-45—(1) The Glass Menagerie
1945-46—(1) No Award, (2) No Award, (3) Carousel
1946-47—(1) All My Sons, (2) No Exit, (3) Brigadoon
1947-48—(1) A Streetcar Named Desire, (2) The Winslow Boy
1948-49—(1) Death of a Salesman, (2) The Madwoman of Chaillot, (3) South Pacific
1949-50—(1) The Member of the Wedding, (2) The Cocktail Party, (3) The Consul
1950-51—(1) Darkness at Noon, (2) The Lady's Not for Burning, (3) Guys and Dolls
1951-52—(1) I Am a Camera, (2) Venus Observed, (3) Pal Joey (Special citation to Don Juan in Hell)
1952-53—(1) Picnic, (2) The Love of Four Colonels, (3) Wonderful Town
1953-54—(1) The Teahouse of the August Moon, (2) Ondine, (3) The Golden Apple
1954-55—(1) Cat on a Hot Tin Roof, (2) Witness for the Prosecution, (3) The Saint of Bleecker Street
1955-56—(1) The Diary of Anne Frank, (2) Tiger at the Gates, (3) My Fair Lady
1956-57—(1) Long Day's Journey into Night, (2) Waltz of the Toreadors, (3) The Most Happy Fella
1957-58—(1) Look Homeward, Angel, (2) Look Back in Anger, (3) The Music Man
1958-59—(1) A Raisin in the Sun, (2) The Visit, (3) La Plume de Ma Tante
1959-60—(1) Toys in the Attic, (2) Five Finger Exercise, (3) Fiorello!
1960-61—(1) All the Way Home, (2) A Taste of Honey, (3) Carnival
1961-62—(1) The Night of the Iguana, (2) A Man for All Seasons, (3) How to Succeed in Business Without Really Trying

PULITZER PRIZE WINNERS

The Pulitzer Prize was awarded to the musical *How to Succeed in Business Without Really Trying,* for which Abe Burrows, Willie Gilbert, and Jack Weinstock wrote the book, and Frank Loesser the music and lyrics.

Pulitzer awards have been—

1917-18—Why Marry?, by Jesse Lynch Williams
1918-19—No award.
1919-20—Beyond the Horizon, by Eugene O'Neill
1920-21—Miss Lulu Bett, by Zona Gale
1921-22—Anna Christie, by Eugene O'Neill
1922-23—Icebound, by Owen Davis
1923-24—Hell-bent for Heaven, by Hatcher Hughes
1924-25—They Knew What They Wanted, by Sidney Howard
1925-26—Craig's Wife, by George Kelly
1926-27—In Abraham's Bosom, by Paul Green
1927-28—Strange Interlude, by Eugene O'Neill
1928-29—Street Scene, by Elmer Rice
1929-30—The Green Pastures, by Marc Connelly
1930-31—Alison's House, by Susan Glaspell
1931-32—Of Thee I Sing, by George S. Kaufman, Morrie Ryskind, Ira and George Gershwin
1932-33—Both Your Houses, by Maxwell Anderson
1933-34—Men in White, by Sidney Kingsley
1934-35—The Old Maid, by Zoë Akins
1935-36—Idiot's Delight, by Robert E. Sherwood
1936-37—You Can't Take It with You, by Moss Hart and George S. Kaufman
1937-38—Our Town, by Thornton Wilder
1938-39—Abe Lincoln in Illinois, by Robert E. Sherwood
1939-40—The Time of Your Life, by William Saroyan
1940-41—There Shall Be No Night, by Robert E. Sherwood
1941-42—No award.
1942-43—The Skin of Our Teeth, by Thornton Wilder
1943-44—No award.
1944-45—Harvey, by Mary Coyle Chase
1945-46—State of the Union, by Howard Lindsay and Russel Crouse
1946-47—No award.
1947-48—A Streetcar Named Desire, by Tennessee Williams
1948-49—Death of a Salesman, by Arthur Miller
1949-50—South Pacific, by Richard Rodgers, Oscar Hammerstein II and Joshua Logan

1950-51—No award.
1951-52—The Shrike, by Joseph Kramm
1952-53—Picnic, by William Inge
1953-54—The Teahouse of the August Moon, by John Patrick
1954-55—Cat on a Hot Tin Roof, by Tennessee Williams
1955-56—The Diary of Anne Frank, by Frances Goodrich and Albert Hackett
1956-57—Long Day's Journey into Night, by Eugene O'Neill
1957-58—Look Homeward, Angel, by Ketti Frings
1958-59—J. B., by Archibald MacLeish
1959-60—Fiorello!, by Jerome Weidman, George Abbott, Sheldon Harnick and Jerry Bock
1960-61—All the Way Home, by Tad Mosel
1961-62—How to Succeed in Business Without Really Trying, by Abe Burrows, Willie Gilbert, Jack Weinstock and Frank Loesser

The season's best performance: Donald Pleasence as Davies in "The Caretaker"

ADDITIONAL PRIZES AND AWARDS 1961-1962

The following pages attempt to list most of the prizes and awards given during the season. However, it is a complicated matter. The *Variety* Drama Critics Poll confines itself to Broadway, while the Obie and the Vernon Rice Awards confine themselves to Off Broadway. The Antoinette Perry (Tony) Award has slightly different categories and covers an April to April season rather than a June to June one, as does the Page One Newspaper Guild Awards and the Clarence Derwent Awards.

In condensing and clarifying the long list as much as possible, we have taken some liberties and blurred some distinctions. For instance, *Variety* gives only one award to the best supporting (other) role in a play or musical, whereas the Tony awards one for each of these categories. We have therefore listed the Straight Play actor or actors who received the most votes in *Variety*, and the Musical actor or actors who received the most votes, which means that while strictly speaking the *Variety* Award for the Best Supporting Actor went only to Charles Nelson Reilly, the listing indicates that it went to Mr. Reilly, and to Walter Matthau and George Rose who tied for second behind Mr. Reilly, but who would have been tied for first, if Mr. Reilly were placed in a separate category.

When there is a tie for an award the two winners are each listed as having won the award.

Some awards fall outside the convenient categories, and these are listed below.

TONY AWARDS. Drama Producer: Robert Whitehead and Roger L. Stevens (A MAN FOR ALL SEASONS). Musical Producer: Cy Feuer and Ernest Martin (HOW TO SUCCEED). Drama Author: Robert Bolt (A MAN FOR ALL SEASONS). Musical Author: Abe Burrows, Jack Weinstock, Willie Gilbert (HOW TO SUCCEED). Musical Conductor: Elliot Lawrence (HOW TO SUCCEED). Stage Technician: Michael Burns (A MAN FOR ALL SEASONS). There were special awards for Brooks Atkinson, Franco Zeffirelli, and Richard Rodgers.

VERNON RICE AWARD. APA Repertory.

OBIE AWARD. Best Foreign Play Off Broadway: HAPPY DAYS. Best Musical Off Broadway: FLY BLACKBIRD. Special Citations to Ellis Rabb for conceiving and maintaining the APA Repertory and to THE HOSTAGE.

LOLA D'ANNUNZIO AWARD. Nancy Wickwire for her continued outstanding contribution to Off Broadway (ROSMERSHOLM, THE THRACIAN HORSES, A CLEARING IN THE WOODS, AS YOU LIKE IT, THE GIRL OF THE GOLDEN WEST, MEASURE FOR MEASURE, UNDER MILK WOOD, THE WAY OF THE WORLD, and other performances.)

KELCEY ALLEN AWARD. Edward F. Kook, Vice-Chairman of the Greater New York Chapter of ANTA's Board of Standards and Planning.

OUTER CIRCLE AWARDS: NO STRINGS, George Abbott, ANYTHING GOES, OH DAD, POOR DAD, George Freedley, National Repertory Theatre.

BARTER THEATRE AWARDS: Abe Burrows.

MALE PERFORMANCES

LEAD IN A PLAY	Paul Scofield as *Sir Thomas More* in A MAN FOR ALL SEASONS (V) (T) (B)	Donald Pleasence as *Davies* in THE CARETAKER (B) (P)
OTHER ROLE IN A PLAY	Walter Matthau as *Benjamin Beaurevers* in A SHOT IN THE DARK (V) (T)	George Rose as *The Common Man* in A MAN FOR ALL SEASONS (V) (B)
LEAD IN A MUSICAL	Robert Morse as *J. Pierrepont Finch* in HOW TO SUCCEED IN BUSINESS WITHOUT REALLY TRYING (V) (T) (B)	Zero Mostel as *Pseudolus* in A FUNNY THING HAPPENED ON THE WAY TO THE FORUM (B)
OTHER MUSICAL ROLE	Charles Nelson Reilly as *Bud Frump* in HOW TO SUCCEED (V) (T) (B)	Rudy Vallee as *J. B. Biggley* in HOW TO SUCCEED (OC)
BROADWAY DEBUT	Peter Fonda as *Pvt. Robert Oglethorpe* in BLOOD, SWEAT AND STANLEY POOLE (V)	Ralph Williams as *Bobby Kraweig* in LOOK: WE'VE COME THROUGH (B)

OTHER OUTSTANDING MALE PERFORMANCES: Fredric March as *The Angel* in GIDEON (B), Philip Bosco as *Hawkshaw* in THE TICKET-OF-LEAVE MAN (B), Geoff Garland as *Leslie* in THE HOSTAGE (R), James Earl Jones as *Ephraim* in MOON ON A RAINBOW SHAWL (O), Gene Wilder as *Dutch Valet* in THE COMPLAISANT LOVER (CD).

VARIETY RUNNERS-UP: Pleasence, Mostel, Williams, Wilder, Alfred Drake (KEAN), Douglas Campbell (GIDEON), Robert Shaw (THE CARETAKER), Sorrell Booke (PURLIE VICTORIOUS), Barry Gordon (A THOUSAND CLOWNS), Cesare Siepi (BRAVO GIOVANNI), Zia Mohyeddin (A PASSAGE TO INDIA), Keith Baxter (A MAN FOR ALL SEASONS), Patrick O'Neal (THE NIGHT OF THE IGUANA), Hugh O'Brian (FIRST LOVE).

OBIE CITATIONS: Garland, Clayton Corzatte (APA Repertory), Gerald O'Loughlin (WHO'LL SAVE THE PLOWBOY?) Paul Roebling (THIS SIDE OF PARADISE).

THEATRE WORLD PROMISING PERSONALITIES: Fonda, Jones, Baxter, John Stride (ROMEO AND JULIET), Robert Redford (SUNDAY IN NEW YORK), Sean Garrison (HALF PAST WEDNESDAY), Don Galloway (BRING ME A WARM BODY).

(B) Selected as an outstanding performance by *Best Plays* editor.
(CD) Winner of the Clarence Derwent Award for best non-featured performance.
(O) Winner of Obie Award for Off Broadway performance.
(R) Winner of Vernon Rice Award for outstanding contribution to Off Broadway.

FEMALE PERFORMANCES

LEAD IN A PLAY	Margaret Leighton as *Hannah Jelkes* in THE NIGHT OF THE IGUANA (V) (T) (B) (P)	Colleen Dewhurst as *Phoebe Flaherty* in GREAT DAY IN THE MORNING (B)
OTHER ROLE IN A PLAY	Sandy Dennis as *Sandra* in A THOUSAND CLOWNS (V)	Patty Duke as *Deirdre Striden* in ISLE OF CHILDREN (B)
LEAD IN A MUSICAL	Diahann Carroll * as *Barbara Woodruff* in NO STRINGS (V) (B)	Sally Ann Howes as *Eve* in KWAMINA (B)
OTHER MUSICAL ROLE	Barbra Streisand as *Miss Marmelstein* in I CAN GET IT FOR YOU WHOLESALE (V)	Phyllis Newman as *Martha Vail* in SUBWAYS ARE FOR SLEEPING (T)
BROADWAY DEBUT	Barbara Harris FROM THE SECOND CITY (V)	Noelle Adam as *Jeanette Valmy* in NO STRINGS (B)

OTHER OUTSTANDING FEMALE PERFORMANCES: Elizabeth Ashley as *Mollie Michaelson* in TAKE HER, SHE'S MINE (T), Barbara Harris as *Rosalie* in OH DAD, POOR DAD (B) (O) (R), Cicely Tyson as *Mavis* in MOON ON A RAINBOW SHAWL (R), Rebecca Darke as *Helen Cobb* in WHO'LL SAVE THE PLOWBOY? (CD).

VARIETY RUNNERS-UP: Dewhurst, Howes, Adam, Ashley, Janet Margolin (DAUGHTER OF SILENCE), Julie Harris (A SHOT IN THE DARK), Wendy Hiller (THE ASPERN PAPERS), Barbara Cook (THE GAY LIFE), Elaine Stritch (SAIL AWAY), Lillian Roth (I CAN GET IT FOR YOU WHOLESALE), Ruby Dee (PURLIE VICTORIOUS), Zohra Lampert (LOOK: WE'VE COME THROUGH), Maria Karnilova (BRAVO GIOVANNI), Bernice Massi (NO STRINGS).

OBIE CITATIONS: Vinnette Carroll (MOON ON A RAINBOW SHAWL), Sudie Bond (THEATRE OF THE ABSURD), Rosemary Harris (APA Repertory), Ruth White (HAPPY DAYS).

THEATRE WORLD PROMISING PERSONALITIES: Barbara Harris, Margolin, Ashley, Dennis, Brenda Vaccaro (EVERYBODY LOVES OPAL), Karen Morrow (SING MUSE).

OUTER CIRCLE AWARD: Margot Moser (MY FAIR LADY).

* Anna Maria Alberghetti received the Tony Award for the best musical performance in CARNIVAL, which opened during the 1960-1961 season.
(P) Page One Award.
(T) Winner of Tony (Antoinette Perry) Award for best performance.
(V) Winner of *Variety* Poll of Drama Critics.
(OC) Winner of Outer Circle Award for outstanding contribution.

BEST DIRECTOR—STRAIGHT PLAY

Donald McWhinnie	Noel Willman	John Wulp
THE CARETAKER (V)	A MAN FOR ALL SEASONS (V) (T)	RED EYE OF LOVE (O)

* Franco Zeffirelli (ROMEO AND JULIET), José Quintero (GREAT DAY IN THE MORNING), Frank Corsaro (THE NIGHT OF THE IGUANA).

BEST DIRECTOR—MUSICAL

Abe Burrows	* Joe Layton
HOW TO SUCCEED (V) (T) (OC)	NO STRINGS

BEST SCENE DESIGNER

David Hays †	Norris Houghton
NO STRINGS (V)	RED EYE OF LOVE (O)

* Motley (A MAN FOR ALL SEASONS), Ben Edwards (PURLIE VICTORIOUS), Franco Zeffirelli (ROMEO AND JULIET), Oliver Smith (THE NIGHT OF THE IGUANA, THE GAY LIFE).

BEST COSTUME DESIGNER

Lucinda Ballard	Donald Brooks and Fred Voelpel
THE GAY LIFE (V) (T)	NO STRINGS (V)

* Robert Fletcher (HOW TO SUCCEED), Ed Wittstein (KEAN), Motley (A MAN FOR ALL SEASONS).

BEST CHOREOGRAPHER

Agnes DeMille	Joe Layton
KWAMINA (T)	NO STRINGS (T)

BEST COMPOSER

Richard Rodgers
NO STRINGS (V) (T)

* Jerry Herman (MILK AND HONEY), Harold Rome (I CAN GET IT FOR YOU WHOLESALE), Frank Loesser (HOW TO SUCCEED).

BEST LYRICIST

Frank Loesser
HOW TO SUCCEED (V)

* Stephen Sondheim (A FUNNY THING HAPPENED), Howard Dietz (THE GAY LIFE), Harold Rome (I CAN GET IT FOR YOU WHOLESALE).

MOST PROMISING PLAYWRIGHT

Herb Gardner	Arthur L. Kopit	Frank D. Gilroy
A THOUSAND CLOWNS (V)	OH DAD, POOR DAD (R)	WHO'LL SAVE THE PLOWBOY? (O)

* Harold Pinter (THE CARETAKER), Ossie Davis (PURLIE VICTORIOUS).

* *Variety* runners-up. † Will Steven Armstrong received the Tony Award for the best scenic designer for CARNIVAL, which opened during the 1960-1961 season.

BOOKS ON THE THEATRE

1961-1962

MAINLY FOR REFERENCE

The Best Plays of 1960-1961. Louis Kronenberger. Dodd, Mead. $6.00.
Digests of Great American Plays. John Lovell, Jr. Crowell. $5.95.
Encyclopaedia of Theatre Music. Richard Lewine and Alfred Simon. Random House. $8.95.
Index to the Best Plays Series, 1949-1960. Dodd, Mead. $3.50.
The London Stage, 1660-1800. (Part III: 1729-1747.) Arthur H. Scouten. Southern Illinois University. Two volume set $50.00.
The Opera Companion. George Martin. Dodd, Mead. $12.50.
Stubs (Twentieth Anniversary Edition). Meyer Schattner. $1.00.
Theatre Language: A Dictionary of Terms in English. Walter F. Bowman and Robert H. Ball. Theatre Arts. $6.95.
Theatre World 1960-1961. Daniel Blum. Chilton. $6.00.
Theatre World Annual (of London). Frances Stephens. Macmillan. $5.50.
Who's Who in the Theatre (Thirteenth Edition). Freda Gaye. Pitman. $20.00.
Who's Where. Show Business. $2.75.

HISTORY AND PICTORIAL

The American Musical Stage Before 1800. Julian Mates. Rutgers. $6.00.
The American Theatre as Seen by Hirschfeld (1926-1961). Drawings by Al Hirschfeld. Braziller. $9.95.
The Best Remaining Seats: The Illustrated Story of the Movie Palace. Ben M. Hall. Clarkson N. Potter. $15.00.
A Picture History of Vaudeville. Bernard Sobel. Citadel. $6.95.
Return Engagement. Norris Houghton. Holt, Rinehart & Winston. $5.00.
Russian Theatre: From the Empire to the Soviets. Marc Slonim. World. $7.50.
The Seven Ages of the Theatre. Richard Southern. Hill & Wang. $5.95.
The Theatre. Helen and Richard Leacroft. Roy. $3.25.
The Theatre of the Bauhaus. Edited by Walter Gropius. Wesleyan University. $7.50.
The Theatre of India. Balwant Gargi. Theatre Arts. $6.95.
The Theatre of Jean-Louis Barrault. Jean-Louis Barrault. Hill & Wang. $5.95.
The Theatres of London. Raymond Mander and Joe Mitchenson. Hill & Wang. $6.00.
Thespis: Myth and Drama in the Ancient Near East. Theodor H. Gaster. Hill & Wang. $6.00.

CRITICAL AND ANALYTIC

James Agate: An Anthology. Edited by Herbert Van Thal. Hill & Wang. $6.00.
The Art of the Theatre. Henri Gheon. Hill & Wang. $1.25.
The Contemporary Theatre. Allan Lewis. Crown. $4.95.
The Decline of Pleasure. Walter Kerr. Simon & Schuster. $5.00.
Elizabethan Drama: Modern Essays in Criticism. Ralph J. Kaufman. Oxford. $2.25.
The Matter with Ireland: Previously Uncollected Writings by Bernard Shaw. Edited by Dan H. Laurence and David H. Greene. Hill & Wang. $5.00.
Platform and Pulpit: Previously Uncollected Speeches of Bernard Shaw. Edited by Dan H. Laurence. Hill & Wang. $5.00.
Romance and Tragedy. Prosser H. Frye. University of Nebraska. $1.25.
The Theatre of the Absurd. Martin Esslin. Doubleday. $1.45.
Twentieth Century French Drama. David I. Grossvogel. Columbia University. $1.95.

BIOGRAPHICAL AND INDIVIDUAL STUDIES

Harold Arlen: Happy with the Blues. Edward Jablonski. Doubleday. $4.95.
Samuel Beckett: A Critical Study. Hugh Kenner. Grove. $5.00.
Bertolt Brecht. Ronald Gray. Grove. $0.95.
Cocteau. Andre Fraigneau. Grove. $1.35.
Famous American Actors and Actresses. Frederick Wagner and Barbara Brady. Dodd, Mead. $3.00.
Feathers from the Green Crow. Sean O'Casey. University of Missouri.
David Garrick, Director. Kalman A. Burnim. University of Pittsburgh. $5.00.
George. Emlyn Williams. Random House. $5.95.
Alec Guiness: An Illustrated Study. Kenneth P. Tynan. Macmillan. $3.75.
Here Comes/There Goes/You Know Who. William Saroyan. Simon & Schuster. $5.95.
Eugene Ionesco. Richard N. Coe. Grove. $0.95.
Kean: The Imaginary Memoirs of an Actor. Julius Berstl. Orion. $5.00.
Arthur Miller. Dennis Welland. Grove. $0.95.
Molly and Me. Gertrude Berg and Cherney Berg. McGraw-Hill. $4.95.
Mrs. Patrick Campbell. Alan Dent. Museum. $5.00.
O'Neill. Arthur and Barbara Gelb. Harper. $12.50.
O'Neill and His Plays: Four Decades of Criticism. Oscar Cargill, N. Bryllion Fagin, and William J. Fisher. $7.50.
Sartre: The Origins of a Style. Fredric Jameson. Yale. $5.00.
The Tempering of Eugene O'Neill. Doris Alexander. Harcourt, Brace & World. $5.95.
Thornton Wilder. Rex Burbank. Twayne. $3.50.
Tennessee Williams. Signi Lenea Falk. Twayne. $7.50.
Tennessee Williams: The Man and His Work. Benjamin Nelson. Ivan Obolensky. $5.00.
Tennessee Williams: Rebellious Puritan. Nancy M. Tischler. Citadel. $5.00.

SHAKESPEARE

As They Liked It. Alfred Harbage. Harper. $1.50.

The Case for Shakespeare's Authorship of the Famous Victories. Seymour M. Pitcher. New York State University. $6.00.

A Casebook on Othello. Leonard F. Dean. Crowell. $2.50.

The Cease of Majesty: Politics in Shakespeare's History Plays. M. M. Reese. St. Martins. $8.00.

Davenant's Macbeth from the Yale Manuscript. Christopher Spencer. Yale. $5.00.

The Facts About Shakespeare. William A. Neilson and Ashley H. Thorndike. Macmillan. $1.95.

Henslowe's Diary. Edited by R. A. Foakes and R. T. Rickert. Cambridge. $11.50.

The Masks of Othello. Marvin Rosenberg. University of California. $5.00.

Narrative and Dramatic Sources of Shakespeare: Volume IV, Later English History Plays. Edited by Geoffrey Bullough. Columbia University. $7.50.

Shakespeare and the Nature of Man. Theodore Spencer. Macmillan. $1.50.

Shakespeare at the Globe, 1599-1609. Bernard Beckerman. Macmillan. $5.95.

Shakespeare Said It. Selected and annotated by William Dodge Lewis. Syracuse University. $6.50.

Shakespeare Survey: An Annual Survey of Shakespearean Study and Production. No. 15. Edited by Allardyce Nicoll. Cambridge. $5.50.

Studies in the Elizabethan Theatre. Edited by Charles T. Prouty. Shoe String. $4.75.

William Shakespeare. Iris Noble. Julian Messner. $2.95.

PLAYS

Most of the successful Broadway plays are published in hard cover editions by Random House ($3.50 each) or, when it involves certain authors, by these writers' exclusive publishers. Other Broadway plays are often printed in paper-bound acting editions published either by Samuel French ($1.25) or by Dramatist's Play Service ($1.10). The following list of published plays is therefore restricted to plays which have not yet been produced on Broadway, classic drama, and collections. The reader is also reminded that many interesting new plays and new translations of foreign plays are published in periodicals such as *The Tulane Drama Review,* Purdue University's *First Stage, Theatre Arts Monthly,* and *The Evergreen Review.*

The American Dream. Edward Albee. Coward-McCann. $2.50.

The Apple. Jack Gelber. Grove. $1.75.

The Beggar's Opera. John Gay. Commentaries by Louis Kronenberger and Max Goberman. Argonaut. $10.00.

Best American Plays, 1918-1958. (Supplementary Volume.) John Gassner. Crown. $5.95.

The Birthday Party and *The Room.* Harold Pinter. Grove. $3.50.

Bertolt Brecht, Seven Plays by. Edited by Eric Bentley. Grove. $8.50.

The Caretaker and *The Dumb Waiter.* Harold Pinter. Grove. $1.75.

Chikamatsu, The Major Plays of. Translated by Donald Keene. Columbia University. $8.50.
The Chinese Wall. Max Frisch; translated by James Rosenberg. Hill & Wang. $4.00.
The Classic Theatre: Volume IV (French). Eric Bentley. Doubleday. $1.45.
The Clouds. Aristophanes; translated by William Arrowsmith. University of Michigan. $4.50.
Cocteau: Five Plays. Jean Cocteau. Hill & Wang. $1.95.
Curtmantle. Christopher Fry. Oxford. $3.50.
Drama: The Major Genres. Robert Hogan and Sven E. Molin. Dodd, Mead. $4.45.
Drama on Stage. Randolph Goodman. Holt, Rinehart & Winston. $4.50.
English One-Act Plays of Today. Edited by Donald FitzJohn. Oxford. $3.00.
Fairy Tales of New York. J. P. Donleavy. Random House. $3.50.
Fings Ain't Wot They Used To Be. Frank Norman. Grove. $1.75.
Four Contemporary American Plays (*The Tenth Man, A Raisin in the Sun, Toys in the Attic, The Andersonville Trial*). Edited by Bennett Cerf. Vintage. $1.45.
Gallows Humor. Jack Richardson. Dutton. $1.15.
The Genius of the French Theatre. Albert Bermel. Mentor. $0.95.
The Ginger Man. J. P. Donleavy. Random House. $3.50.
Happy Days. Samuel Beckett. Grove. $1.45.
The Kitchen. Arnold Wesker. Random House. $3.50.
The Lion in Love. Shelagh Delaney. Grove. $1.75.
Luther. John Osborne. Criterion. $2.95.
Masters of Modern Drama. Edited by Haskell M. Block and Robert G. Shedd. Random House. $12.95.
John Mortimer: The Dock Brief, What Shall We Tell Caroline, and *I Spy.* Grove. $1.95.
Sean O'Casey: Behind the Green Curtains, Figuro in the Night, and *The Moon Shines on Kylenamoe.* St. Martins. $2.95.
John O'Hara, Five Plays by. Random House. $5.00.
One Way Pendulum. N. F. Simpson. Grove. $1.75.
Luigi Pirandello: To Clothe the Naked, The Rules of the Game, and *The Pleasure of Honesty.* Translated by William Murray. Dutton. $4.50.
Racine, Three Plays of. Translated by George Dillon. University of Chicago. $1.95.
Red Eye of Love. Arnold Weinstein. Grove. $1.75.
Satan, Socialites, and *Solly Gold: Three New Plays from England.* Ronald Duncan, Kenneth Jupp, Bernard Kops. Coward-McCann. $4.50.
Serjeant Musgrave's Dance. John Arden. Grove. $1.75.
Bernard Shaw: Complete Plays with Prefaces. Dodd, Mead. 6 Volumes. $7.50 per volume.
Bernard Shaw: The Theatre of. Ten plays chosen and discussed by Alan Downer. Dodd, Mead. 2 Volumes. $2.75 per volume.
Terence, the Comedies of. Edited by Robert Graves. Doubleday. $1.45.
The Tree Witch. Peter Viereck. Scribners. $3.50.
Waiting in the Wings. Noel Coward. Doubleday. $2.95.

The Wakefield Mystery Plays. Edited by Martial Rose. Doubleday. $5.95.
Emlyn Williams, The Collected Plays of. Random House. $4.50.

TECHNICAL

Acting: A Guide. Mary-Averett Seelye. American Association of University Women. $0.60.
Actors Talk About Acting: Fourteen Interviews with Stars of the Theatre. Lewis Funke and John E. Booth. Random House. $6.95.
Bibliography of Speech and Allied Areas: 1950-1960. Dorothy I. Mulgrave. Chilton. $6.50.
The Business of Show Business. Gail Plummer. Harper. $6.75.
The Craft and Context of Translation: A Symposium. William Arrowsmith and Roger Shattuck. University of Texas. $4.75.
Creating a Role. Constantin Stanislavski. Theatre Arts. $4.00.
Masks and Mask Makers. Karl Hunt and Bernice Wells Carlson. Abingdon. $2.75.
The Mime. Jean Dorcy. Robert Speller. $3.95.
Open Stage Check List. Prepared by The Board of Standards and Planning for the Living Theatre. The Greater New York Chapter of ANTA. $2.50.
Stories for Creative Acting. Compiled by C. Robert Kase. Samuel French. $5.00.
Your Career in the Theatre. Bruce Savan. Doubleday. $3.95.

PREVIOUS VOLUMES OF BEST PLAYS

Plays chosen to represent the theatre seasons from 1899 to 1961 are as follows:

1899-1909

BARBARA FRIETCHIE, by Clyde Fitch. Life Publishing Co.

THE CLIMBERS, by Clyde Fitch. Macmillan.

IF I WERE KING, by Justin Huntly McCarthy. Samuel French.

THE DARLING OF THE GODS, by David Belasco. Little, Brown.

THE COUNTY CHAIRMAN, by George Ade. Samuel French.

LEAH KLESCHNA, by C. M. S. McLellan. Samuel French.

THE SQUAW MAN, by Edwin Milton Royle.

THE GREAT DIVIDE, by William Vaughn Moody. Samuel French.

THE WITCHING HOUR, by Augustus Thomas. Samuel French.

THE MAN FROM HOME, by Booth Tarkington and Harry Leon Wilson. Samuel French.

1909-1919

THE EASIEST WAY, by Eugene Walter. G. W. Dillingham and Houghton Mifflin.

MRS. BUMPSTEAD-LEIGH, by Harry James Smith. Samuel French.

DISRAELI, by Louis N. Parker. Dodd, Mead.

ROMANCE, by Edward Sheldon. Macmillan.

SEVEN KEYS TO BALDPATE, by George M. Cohan. Published by Bobbs-Merrill as a novel by Earl Derr Biggers; as a play by Samuel French.

ON TRIAL, by Elmer Reizenstein. Samuel French.

THE UNCHASTENED WOMAN, by Louis Kaufman Anspacher. Harcourt, Brace and Howe.

GOOD GRACIOUS ANNABELLE, by Clare Kummer. Samuel French.

WHY MARRY?, by Jesse Lynch Williams. Scribner.

JOHN FERGUSON, by St. John Ervine. Macmillan.

1919-1920

ABRAHAM LINCOLN, by John Drinkwater. Houghton Mifflin.

CLARENCE, by Booth Tarkington. Samuel French.

BEYOND THE HORIZON, by Eugene G. O'Neill. Boni & Liveright.

DÉCLASSÉE, by Zoë Akins. Liveright, Inc.

THE FAMOUS MRS. FAIR, by James Forbes. Samuel French.

THE JEST, by Sem Benelli. (American adaptation by Edward Sheldon.)

JANE CLEGG, by St. John Ervine. Henry Holt.

MAMMA'S AFFAIR, by Rachel Barton Butler. Samuel French.

WEDDING BELLS, by Salisbury Field. Samuel French.

ADAM AND EVA, by George Middleton and Guy Bolton. Samuel French.

1920-1921

DEBURAU, adapted from the French of Sacha Guitry by H. Granville Barker. Putnam.

THE FIRST YEAR, by Frank Craven. Samuel French.

ENTER MADAME, by Gilda Varesi and Dolly Byrne. Putnam.

THE GREEN GODDESS, by William Archer. Knopf.

LILIOM, by Ferenc Molnar. Boni & Liveright.

MARY ROSE, by James M. Barrie. Scribner.

NICE PEOPLE, by Rachel Crothers. Scribner.

THE BAD MAN, by Porter Emerson Browne. Putnam.

THE EMPEROR JONES, by Eugene G. O'Neill. Boni & Liveright.

THE SKIN GAME, by John Galsworthy. Scribner.

1921-1922

ANNA CHRISTIE, by Eugene G. O'Neill. Boni & Liveright.

A BILL OF DIVORCEMENT, by Clemence Dane. Macmillan.

DULCY, by George S. Kaufman and Marc Connelly. Putnam.

HE WHO GETS SLAPPED, adapted from the Russian of Leonid Andreyev by Gregory Zilboorg. Brentano's.

SIX CYLINDER LOVE, by William Anthony McGuire.

THE HERO, by Gilbert Emery.

THE DOVER ROAD, by Alan Alexander Milne. Samuel French.

AMBUSH, by Arthur Richman.

THE CIRCLE, by William Somerset Maugham.

THE NEST, by Paul Geraldy and Grace George.

1922-1923

RAIN, by John Colton and Clemence Randolph. Liveright, Inc.

LOYALTIES, by John Galsworthy. Scribner.

ICEBOUND, by Owen Davis. Little, Brown.

YOU AND I, by Philip Barry. Brentano's.

THE FOOL, by Channing Pollock. Brentano's.

MERTON OF THE MOVIES, by George Kaufman and Marc Connelly, based on the novel of the same name by Harry Leon Wilson.

WHY NOT? by Jesse Lynch Williams. Walter H. Baker Co.

THE OLD SOAK, by Don Marquis. Doubleday, Page.

R.U.R., by Karel Capek. Translated by Paul Selver. Doubleday, Page.

MARY THE 3D, by Rachel Crothers. Brentano's.

1923-1924

THE SWAN, translated from the Hungarian of Ferenc Molnar by Melville Baker. Boni & Liveright.

OUTWARD BOUND, by Sutton Vane. Boni & Liveright.

THE SHOW-OFF, by George Kelly. Little, Brown.

THE CHANGELINGS, by Lee Wilson Dodd. Dutton.

CHICKEN FEED, by Guy Bolton. Samuel French.

SUN-UP, by Lula Vollmer. Brentano's.

BEGGAR ON HORSEBACK, by George Kaufman and Marc Connelly. Boni & Liveright.

TARNISH, by Gilbert Emery. Brentano's.

THE GOOSE HANGS HIGH, by Lewis Beach. Little, Brown.

HELL-BENT FER HEAVEN, by Hatcher Hughes. Harper.

1924-1925

WHAT PRICE GLORY? by Laurence Stallings and Maxwell Anderson. Harcourt, Brace.

THEY KNEW WHAT THEY WANTED, by Sidney Howard. Doubleday, Page.

DESIRE UNDER THE ELMS, by Eugene G. O'Neill. Boni & Liveright.

THE FIREBRAND, by Edwin Justus Mayer. Boni & Liveright.

DANCING MOTHERS, by Edgar Selwyn and Edmund Goulding.

MRS. PARTRIDGE PRESENTS, by Mary Kennedy and Ruth Hawthorne. Samuel French.

THE FALL GUY, by James Gleason and George Abbott. Samuel French.

THE YOUNGEST, by Philip Barry. Samuel French.

MINICK, by Edna Ferber and George S. Kaufman. Doubleday, Page.

WILD BIRDS, by Dan Totheroh. Doubleday, Page.

1925-1926

CRAIG'S WIFE, by George Kelly. Little, Brown.

THE GREAT GOD BROWN, by Eugene G. O'Neill. Boni & Liveright.

THE GREEN HAT, by Michael Arlen.

THE DYBBUK, by S. Ansky, Henry G. Alsberg-Winifred Katzin translation. Boni & Liveright.

THE ENEMY, by Channing Pollock. Brentano's.

THE LAST OF MRS. CHEYNEY, by Frederick Lonsdale. Samuel French.

BRIDE OF THE LAMB, by William Hurlbut. Boni & Liveright.

THE WISDOM TOOTH, by Marc Connelly. George H. Doran.

THE BUTTER AND EGG MAN, by George Kaufman. Boni & Liveright.

YOUNG WOODLEY, by John van Druten. Simon & Schuster.

1926-1927

BROADWAY, by Philip Dunning and George Abbott. George H. Doran.

SATURDAY'S CHILDREN, by Maxwell Anderson. Longmans, Green.

CHICAGO, by Maurine Watkins. Knopf.

THE CONSTANT WIFE, by William Somerset Maugham. George H. Doran.

THE PLAY'S THE THING, by Ferenc Molnar and P. G. Wodehouse. Brentano's.

THE ROAD TO ROME, by Robert Emmet Sherwood. Scribner.

THE SILVER CORD, by Sidney Howard. Scribner.

THE CRADLE SONG, translated from the Spanish of G. Martinez Sierra by John Garrett Underhill. Dutton.

DAISY MAYME, by George Kelly. Little, Brown.

IN ABRAHAM'S BOSOM, by Paul Green. McBride.

1927-1928

STRANGE INTERLUDE, by Eugene G. O'Neill. Boni & Liveright.

THE ROYAL FAMILY, by Edna Ferber and George Kaufman. Doubleday, Doran.

BURLESQUE, by George Manker Watters and Arthur Hopkins. Doubleday, Doran.

COQUETTE, by George Abbott and Ann Bridgers. Longmans, Green.

BEHOLD THE BRIDEGROOM, by George Kelly. Little, Brown.

PORGY, by DuBose Heyward. Doubleday, Doran.

PARIS BOUND, by Philip Barry. Samuel French.

ESCAPE, by John Galsworthy. Scribner.

THE RACKET, by Bartlett Cormack. Samuel French.

THE PLOUGH AND THE STARS, by Sean O'Casey. Macmillan.

1928-1929

STREET SCENE, by Elmer Rice. Samuel French.

JOURNEY'S END, by R. C. Sherriff. Brentano's.

WINGS OVER EUROPE, by Robert Nichols and Maurice Browne. Covici-Friede.

HOLIDAY, by Philip Barry. Samuel French.

THE FRONT PAGE, by Ben Hecht and Charles MacArthur. Covici-Friede.

LET US BE GAY, by Rachel Crothers. Samuel French.

MACHINAL, by Sophie Treadwell.

LITTLE ACCIDENT, by Floyd Dell and Thomas Mitchell.

GYPSY, by Maxwell Anderson.

THE KINGDOM OF GOD, by G. Martinez Sierra; English version by Helen and Harley Granville-Barker. Dutton.

1929-1930

THE GREEN PASTURES, by Marc Connelly (adapted from "Ol' Man Adam and His Chillun," by Roark Bradford). Farrar & Rinehart.
THE CRIMINAL CODE, by Martin Flavin. Horace Liveright.
BERKELEY SQUARE, by John Balderston.
STRICTLY DISHONORABLE, by Preston Sturges. Horace Liveright.
THE FIRST MRS. FRASER, by St. John Ervine. Macmillan.
THE LAST MILE, by John Wexley. Samuel French.
JUNE MOON, by Ring W. Lardner and George S. Kaufman. Scribner.
MICHAEL AND MARY, by A. A. Milne. Chatto & Windus.
DEATH TAKES A HOLIDAY, by Walter Ferris (adapted from the Italian of Alberto Casella). Samuel French.
REBOUND, by Donald Ogden Stewart. Samuel French.

1930-1931

ELIZABETH THE QUEEN, by Maxwell Anderson. Longmans, Green.
TOMORROW AND TOMORROW, by Philip Barry. Samuel French.
ONCE IN A LIFETIME, by George S. Kaufman and Moss Hart. Farrar & Rinehart.
GREEN GROW THE LILACS, by Lynn Riggs. Samuel French.
AS HUSBANDS GO, by Rachel Crothers. Samuel French.
ALISON'S HOUSE, by Susan Glaspell. Samuel French.
FIVE-STAR FINAL, by Louis Weitzenkorn. Samuel French.
OVERTURE, by William Bolitho. Simon & Schuster.
THE BARRETTS OF WIMPOLE STREET, by Rudolf Besier. Little, Brown.
GRAND HOTEL, adapted from the German of Vicki Baum by W. A. Drake.

1931-1932

OF THEE I SING, by George S. Kaufman and Morrie Ryskind; music and lyrics by George and Ira Gershwin. Knopf.
MOURNING BECOMES ELECTRA, by Eugene G. O'Neill. Horace Liveright.
REUNION IN VIENNA, by Robert Emmet Sherwood. Scribner.
THE HOUSE OF CONNELLY, by Paul Green. Samuel French.
THE ANIMAL KINGDOM, by Philip Barry. Samuel French.
THE LEFT BANK, by Elmer Rice. Samuel French.
ANOTHER LANGUAGE, by Rose Franken. Samuel French.

BRIEF MOMENT, by S. N. Behrman. Farrar & Rinehart.

THE DEVIL PASSES, by Benn W. Levy. Martin Secker.

CYNARA, by H. M. Harwood and R. F. Gore-Browne. Samuel French.

1932-1933

BOTH YOUR HOUSES, by Maxwell Anderson. Samuel French.

DINNER AT EIGHT, by George S. Kaufman and Edna Ferber. Doubleday, Doran.

WHEN LADIES MEET, by Rachel Crothers. Samuel French.

DESIGN FOR LIVING, by Noel Coward. Doubleday, Doran.

BIOGRAPHY, by S. N. Behrman. Farrar & Rinehart.

ALIEN CORN, by Sidney Howard. Scribner.

THE LATE CHRISTOPHER BEAN, adapted from the French of René Fauchois by Sidney Howard. Samuel French.

WE, THE PEOPLE, by Elmer Rice. Coward-McCann.

PIGEONS AND PEOPLE, by George M. Cohan.

ONE SUNDAY AFTERNOON, by James Hagan. Samuel French.

1933-1934

MARY OF SCOTLAND, by Maxwell Anderson. Doubleday, Doran.

MEN IN WHITE, by Sidney Kingsley. Covici-Friede.

DODSWORTH, by Sinclair Lewis and Sidney Howard. Harcourt, Brace.

AH, WILDERNESS, by Eugene O'Neill. Random House.

THEY SHALL NOT DIE, by John Wexley. Knopf.

HER MASTER'S VOICE, by Clare Kummer. Samuel French.

NO MORE LADIES, by A. E. Thomas.

WEDNESDAY'S CHILD, by Leopold Atlas. Samuel French.

THE SHINING HOUR, by Keith Winter. Doubleday, Doran.

THE GREEN BAY TREE, by Mordaunt Shairp. Baker International Play Bureau.

1934-1935

THE CHILDREN'S HOUR, by Lillian Hellman. Knopf.

VALLEY FORGE, by Maxwell Anderson. Anderson House.

THE PETRIFIED FOREST, by Robert Sherwood. Scribner.

THE OLD MAID, by Zoë Akins. Appleton-Century.

ACCENT ON YOUTH, by Samson Raphaelson. Samuel French.

MERRILY WE ROLL ALONG, by George S. Kaufman and Moss Hart. Random House.

AWAKE AND SING, by Clifford Odets. Random House.

THE FARMER TAKES A WIFE, by Frank B. Elser and Marc Connelly.

LOST HORIZONS, by John Hayden.

THE DISTAFF SIDE, by John van Druten. Knopf.

1935-1936

WINTERSET, by Maxwell Anderson. Anderson House.

IDIOT'S DELIGHT, by Robert Emmet Sherwood. Scribner.

END OF SUMMER, by S. N. Behrman. Random House.

FIRST LADY, by Katharine Dayton and George S. Kaufman. Random House.

VICTORIA REGINA, by Laurence Housman. Samuel French.

BOY MEETS GIRL, by Bella and Samuel Spewack. Random House.

DEAD END, by Sidney Kingsley. Random House.

CALL IT A DAY, by Dodie Smith. Samuel French.

ETHAN FROME, by Owen Davis and Donald Davis. Scribner.

PRIDE AND PREJUDICE, by Helen Jerome. Doubleday, Doran.

1936-1937

HIGH TOR, by Maxwell Anderson. Anderson House.

YOU CAN'T TAKE IT WITH YOU, by Moss Hart and George S. Kaufman. Farrar & Rinehart.

JOHNNY JOHNSON, by Paul Green. Samuel French.

DAUGHTERS OF ATREUS, by Robert Turney. Knopf.

STAGE DOOR, by Edna Ferber and George S. Kaufman. Doubleday, Doran.

THE WOMEN, by Clare Boothe. Random House.

ST. HELENA, by R. C. Sherriff and Jeanne de Casalis. Samuel French.

YES, MY DARLING DAUGHTER, by Mark Reed. Samuel French.

EXCURSION, by Victor Wolfson. Random House.

TOVARICH, by Jacques Deval and Robert E. Sherwood. Random House.

1937-1938

OF MICE AND MEN, by John Steinbeck. Covici-Friede.

OUR TOWN, by Thornton Wilder. Coward-McCann.

SHADOW AND SUBSTANCE, by Paul Vincent Carroll. Random House.

ON BORROWED TIME, by Paul Osborn. Knopf.

THE STAR-WAGON, by Maxwell Anderson. Anderson House.

SUSAN AND GOD, by Rachel Crothers. Random House.

PROLOGUE TO GLORY, by E. P. Conkle. Random House.

AMPHITRYON 38, by S. N. Behrman. Random House.

GOLDEN BOY, by Clifford Odets. Random House.

WHAT A LIFE, by Clifford Goldsmith. Dramatists' Play Service.

1938-1939

ABE LINCOLN IN ILLINOIS, by Robert E. Sherwood. Scribner.

THE LITTLE FOXES, by Lillian Hellman. Random House.

ROCKET TO THE MOON, by Clifford Odets. Random House.
THE AMERICAN WAY, by George S. Kaufman and Moss Hart. Random House.
NO TIME FOR COMEDY, by S. N. Behrman. Random House.
THE PHILADELPHIA STORY, by Philip Barry. Coward-McCann.
THE WHITE STEED, by Paul Vincent Carroll. Random House.
HERE COME THE CLOWNS, by Philip Barry. Coward-McCann.
FAMILY PORTRAIT, by Lenore Coffee and William Joyce Cowen. Random House.
KISS THE BOYS GOOD-BYE, by Clare Boothe. Random House.

1939-1940

THERE SHALL BE NO NIGHT, by Robert E. Sherwood. Scribner.
KEY LARGO, by Maxwell Anderson. Anderson House.
THE WORLD WE MAKE, by Sidney Kingsley.
LIFE WITH FATHER, by Howard Lindsay and Russel Crouse. Knopf.
THE MAN WHO CAME TO DINNER, by George S. Kaufman and Moss Hart. Random House.
THE MALE ANIMAL, by James Thurber and Elliott Nugent. Random House, New York, and MacMillan Co., Canada.
THE TIME OF YOUR LIFE, by William Saroyan. Harcourt, Brace.
SKYLARK, by Samson Raphaelson. Random House.
MARGIN FOR ERROR, by Clare Boothe. Random House.
MORNING'S AT SEVEN, by Paul Osborn. Samuel French.

1940-1941

NATIVE SON, by Paul Green and Richard Wright. Harper.
WATCH ON THE RHINE, by Lillian Hellman. Random House.
THE CORN IS GREEN, by Emlyn Williams. Random House.
LADY IN THE DARK, by Moss Hart. Random House.
ARSENIC AND OLD LACE, by Joseph Kesselring. Random House.
MY SISTER EILEEN, by Joseph Fields and Jerome Chodorov. Random House.
FLIGHT TO THE WEST, by Elmer Rice. Coward-McCann.
CLAUDIA, by Rose Franken Meloney. Farrar & Rinehart.
MR. AND MRS. NORTH, by Owen Davis. Samuel French.
GEORGE WASHINGTON SLEPT HERE, by George S. Kaufman and Moss Hart. Random House.

1941-1942

IN TIME TO COME, by Howard Koch. Dramatists' Play Service.
THE MOON IS DOWN, by John Steinbeck. Viking.
BLITHE SPIRIT, by Noel Coward. Doubleday, Doran.
JUNIOR MISS, by Jerome Chodorov and Joseph Fields. Random House.
CANDLE IN THE WIND, by Maxwell Anderson. Anderson House.

LETTERS TO LUCERNE, by Fritz Rotter and Allen Vincent. Samuel French.

JASON, by Samson Raphaelson. Random House.

ANGEL STREET, by Patrick Hamilton. Constable & Co., under the title "Gaslight."

UNCLE HARRY, by Thomas Job. Samuel French.

HOPE FOR A HARVEST, by Sophie Treadwell. Samuel French.

1942-1943

THE PATRIOTS, by Sidney Kingsley. Random House.

THE EVE OF ST. MARK, by Maxwell Anderson. Anderson House.

THE SKIN OF OUR TEETH, by Thornton Wilder. Harper.

WINTER SOLDIERS, by Dan James.

TOMORROW THE WORLD, by James Gow and Arnaud d'Usseau. Scribner.

HARRIET, by Florence Ryerson and Colin Clements. Scribner.

THE DOUGHGIRLS, by Joseph Fields. Random House.

THE DAMASK CHEEK, by John van Druten and Lloyd Morris. Random House.

KISS AND TELL, by F. Hugh Herbert. Coward-McCann.

OKLAHOMA!, by Oscar Hammerstein 2nd and Richard Rodgers. Random House.

1943-1944

WINGED VICTORY, by Moss Hart. Random House.

THE SEARCHING WIND, by Lillian Hellman. Viking.

THE VOICE OF THE TURTLE, by John van Druten. Random House.

DECISION, by Edward Chodorov.

OVER 21, by Ruth Gordon. Random House.

OUTRAGEOUS FORTUNE, by Rose Franken. Samuel French.

JACOBOWSKY AND THE COLONEL, by S. N. Behrman. Random House.

STORM OPERATION, by Maxwell Anderson. Anderson House.

PICK-UP GIRL, by Elsa Shelley.

THE INNOCENT VOYAGE, by Paul Osborn.

1944-1945

A BELL FOR ADANO, by Paul Osborn. Knopf.

I REMEMBER MAMA, by John van Druten. Harcourt, Brace.

THE HASTY HEART, by John Patrick. Random House.

THE GLASS MENAGERIE, by Tennessee Williams. Random House.

HARVEY, by Mary Chase.

THE LATE GEORGE APLEY, by John P. Marquand and George S. Kaufman.

SOLDIER'S WIFE, by Rose Franken. Samuel French.

ANNA LUCASTA, by Philip Yordan. Random House.

FOOLISH NOTION, by Philip Barry.

DEAR RUTH, by Norman Krasna. Random House.

1945-1946

STATE OF THE UNION, by Howard Lindsay and Russel Crouse. Random House.

HOME OF THE BRAVE, by Arthur Laurents. Random House.

DEEP ARE THE ROOTS, by Arnaud d'Usseau and James Gow. Scribner.

THE MAGNIFICENT YANKEE, by Emmet Lavery. Samuel French.

ANTIGONE, by Lewis Galantière (from the French of Jean Anouilh). Random House.

O MISTRESS MINE, by Terence Rattigan. Published and revised by the author.

BORN YESTERDAY, by Garson Kanin. Viking.

DREAM GIRL, by Elmer Rice. Coward-McCann.

THE RUGGED PATH, by Robert E. Sherwood. Scribner.

LUTE SONG, by Will Irwin and Sidney Howard. Published version by Will Irwin and Leopoldine Howard.

1946-1947

ALL MY SONS, by Arthur Miller. Reynal & Hitchcock.

THE ICEMAN COMETH, by Eugene G. O'Neill. Random House.

JOAN OF LORRAINE, by Maxwell Anderson. Published by Maxwell Anderson.

ANOTHER PART OF THE FOREST, by Lillian Hellman. Viking.

YEARS AGO, by Ruth Gordon. Viking.

JOHN LOVES MARY, by Norman Krasna. Copyright by Norman Krasna.

THE FATAL WEAKNESS, by George Kelly. Samuel French.

THE STORY OF MARY SURRATT, by John Patrick. Dramatists' Play Service.

CHRISTOPHER BLAKE, by Moss Hart. Random House.

BRIGADOON, by Alan Jay Lerner and Frederick Loewe. Coward-McCann.

1947-1948

A STREETCAR NAMED DESIRE, by Tennessee Williams. New Directions.

MISTER ROBERTS, by Thomas Heggen and Joshua Logan. Houghton Mifflin.

COMMAND DECISION, by William Wister Haines. Random House.

THE WINSLOW BOY, by Terence Rattigan.

THE HEIRESS, by Ruth and Augustus Goetz.

ALLEGRO, by Richard Rodgers and Oscar Hammerstein 2d. Knopf. Music published by Williamson Music, Inc.

EASTWARD IN EDEN, by Dorothy Gardner. Longmans, Green.

SKIPPER NEXT TO GOD, by Jan de Hartog.

AN INSPECTOR CALLS, by J. B. Priestley.

ME AND MOLLY, by Gertrude Berg.

1948-1949

DEATH OF A SALESMAN, by Arthur Miller. Viking.

ANNE OF THE THOUSAND DAYS, by Maxwell Anderson. Sloane.

THE MADWOMAN OF CHAILLOT, by Maurice Valency, adapted from the French of Jean Giraudoux. Random House.

DETECTIVE STORY, by Sidney Kingsley. Random House.

EDWARD, MY SON, by Robert Morley and Noel Langley. Random House, New York, and Samuel French, London.

LIFE WITH MOTHER, by Howard Lindsay and Russel Crouse. Knopf.

LIGHT UP THE SKY, by Moss Hart. Random House.

THE SILVER WHISTLE, by Robert Edward McEnroe. Dramatists' Play Service.

TWO BLIND MICE, by Samuel Spewack. Dramatists' Play Service.

GOODBYE, MY FANCY, by Fay Kanin. Samuel French.

1949-1950

THE COCKTAIL PARTY, by T. S. Eliot. Harcourt, Brace.

THE MEMBER OF THE WEDDING, by Carson McCullers. Houghton Mifflin.

THE INNOCENTS, by William Archibald. Coward-McCann.

LOST IN THE STARS, by Maxwell Anderson and Kurt Weill. Sloane.

COME BACK, LITTLE SHEBA, by William Inge. Random House.

THE HAPPY TIME, by Samuel Taylor. Random House.

THE WISTERIA TREES, by Joshua Logan. Random House.

I KNOW MY LOVE, by S. N. Behrman. Random House.

THE ENCHANTED, by Maurice Valency, adapted from a play by Jean Giraudoux. Random House.

CLUTTERBUCK, by Benn W. Levy. Dramatists' Play Service.

1950-1951

GUYS AND DOLLS, by Jo Swerling, Abe Burrows and Frank Loesser.

DARKNESS AT NOON, by Sidney Kingsley and Arthur Koestler. Random House.

BILLY BUDD, by Louis O. Coxe and Robert Chapman. Princeton University Press.

THE AUTUMN GARDEN, by Lillian Hellman. Little, Brown & Co.

BELL, BOOK AND CANDLE, by John van Druten. Random House.

THE COUNTRY GIRL, by Clifford Odets. Viking Press.

THE ROSE TATTOO, by Tennessee Williams. New Directions.

SEASON IN THE SUN, by Wolcott Gibbs. Random House.

AFFAIRS OF STATE, by Louis Verneuil.

SECOND THRESHOLD, by Philip Barry. Harper & Bros.

1951-1952

MRS. McTHING, by Mary Coyle Chase.
THE SHRIKE, by Joseph Kramm. Random House.
I AM A CAMERA, by John van Druten. Random House.
THE FOURPOSTER, by Jan de Hartog.
POINT OF NO RETURN, by Paul Osborn. Random House.
BAREFOOT IN ATHENS, by Maxwell Anderson. Sloane.
VENUS OBSERVED, by Christopher Fry. Oxford.
JANE, by S. N. Behrman and Somerset Maugham. Random House.
GIGI, by Anita Loos and Colette. Random House.
REMAINS TO BE SEEN, by Howard Lindsay and Russel Crouse. Random House.

1952-1953

THE TIME OF THE CUCKOO, by Arthur Laurents. Random House.
BERNARDINE, by Mary Coyle Chase.
DIAL "M" FOR MURDER, by Frederick Knott. Random House.
THE CLIMATE OF EDEN, by Moss Hart. Random House.
THE LOVE OF FOUR COLONELS, by Peter Ustinov.
THE CRUCIBLE, by Arthur Miller. Viking.
THE EMPEROR'S CLOTHES, by George Tabori. Samuel French.
PICNIC, by William Inge. Random House.
WONDERFUL TOWN, by Joseph Fields, Jerome Chodorov, Betty Comden and Adolph Green. Random House.
MY 3 ANGELS, by Sam and Bella Spewack.

1953-1954

THE CAINE MUTINY COURT-MARTIAL, by Herman Wouk. Doubleday & Company, Inc.
IN THE SUMMER HOUSE, by Jane Bowles. Random House.
THE CONFIDENTIAL CLERK, by T. S. Eliot. Harcourt, Brace and Company, Inc.
TAKE A GIANT STEP, by Louis Peterson.
THE TEAHOUSE OF THE AUGUST MOON, by John Patrick. G. P. Putnam's Sons.
THE IMMORALIST, by Ruth and Augustus Goetz. Dramatists' Play Service.
TEA AND SYMPATHY, by Robert Anderson. Random House.
THE GIRL ON THE VIA FLAMINIA, by Alfred Hayes.
THE GOLDEN APPLE, by John Latouche and Jerome Moross. Random House.
THE MAGIC AND THE LOSS, by Julian Funt. Samuel French.

1954-1955

THE BOY FRIEND, by Sandy Wilson.

THE LIVING ROOM, by Graham Greene. Viking.

BAD SEED, by Maxwell Anderson. Dodd, Mead.

WITNESS FOR THE PROSECUTION, by Agatha Christie.

THE FLOWERING PEACH, by Clifford Odets.

THE DESPERATE HOURS, by Joseph Hayes. Random House.

THE DARK IS LIGHT ENOUGH, by Christopher Fry. Oxford.

BUS STOP, by William Inge. Random House.

CAT ON A HOT TIN ROOF, by Tennessee Williams. New Directions.

INHERIT THE WIND, by Jerome Lawrence and Robert E. Lee. Random House.

1955-1956

A VIEW FROM THE BRIDGE, by Arthur Miller. Viking.

TIGER AT THE GATES, by Jean Giraudoux, translated by Christopher Fry. Oxford.

THE DIARY OF ANNE FRANK, by Frances Goodrich and Albert Hackett. Random House.

NO TIME FOR SERGEANTS, by Ira Levin. Random House.

THE CHALK GARDEN, by Enid Bagnold. Random House.

THE LARK, by Jean Anouilh, adapted by Lillian Hellman. Random House.

THE MATCHMAKER, by Thornton Wilder. Harper.

THE PONDER HEART, by Joseph Fields and Jerome Chodorov. Random House.

MY FAIR LADY, by Alan Jay Lerner and Frederick Loewe. Coward-McCann.

WAITING FOR GODOT, by Samuel Beckett. Grove.

1956-1957

SEPARATE TABLES, by Terence Rattigan. Random House.

LONG DAY'S JOURNEY INTO NIGHT, by Eugene O'Neill. Yale University Press.

A VERY SPECIAL BABY, by Robert Alan Aurthur. Dramatists Play Service.

CANDIDE, by Lillian Hellman, Richard Wilbur, John Latouche, Dorothy Parker and Leonard Bernstein. Random House.

A CLEARING IN THE WOODS, by Arthur Laurents. Random House.

THE WALTZ OF THE TOREADORS, by Jean Anouilh, translated by Lucienne Hill. Coward-McCann.

THE POTTING SHED, by Graham Greene. Viking.

VISIT TO A SMALL PLANET, by Gore Vidal. Little, Brown.

ORPHEUS DESCENDING, by Tennessee Williams. New Directions.

A MOON FOR THE MISBEGOTTEN, by Eugene O'Neill. Random House.

1957-1958

LOOK BACK IN ANGER, by John Osborne. Criterion Books.
UNDER MILK WOOD, by Dylan Thomas. New Directions.
TIME REMEMBERED, by Jean Anouilh, adapted by Patricia Moyes. Coward-McCann.
THE ROPE DANCERS, by Morton Wishengrad. Crown.
LOOK HOMEWARD, ANGEL, by Ketti Frings. Scribner's.
THE DARK AT THE TOP OF THE STAIRS, by William Inge. Random House.
SUMMER OF THE 17TH DOLL, by Ray Lawler. Random House.
SUNRISE AT CAMPOBELLO, by Dore Schary. Random House.
THE ENTERTAINER, by John Osborne. Criterion Books.
THE VISIT, by Friedrich Duerrenmatt, adapted by Maurice Valency. Random House.

1958-1959

A TOUCH OF THE POET, by Eugene O'Neill. Yale University Press.
THE PLEASURE OF HIS COMPANY, by Samuel Taylor with Cornelia Otis Skinner. Random House.
EPITAPH FOR GEORGE DILLON, by John Osborne and Anthony Creighton. Criterion Books.
THE DISENCHANTED, by Budd Schulberg and Harvey Breit. Random House.
THE COLD WIND AND THE WARM, by S. N. Behrman. Random House.
J. B., by Archibald MacLeish. Houghton Mifflin.
REQUIEM FOR A NUN, by William Faulkner and Ruth Ford. Random House.
SWEET BIRD OF YOUTH, by Tennessee Williams. New Directions.
A RAISIN IN THE SUN, by Lorraine Hansberry. Random House.
KATAKI, by Shimon Wincelberg.

1959-1960

THE TENTH MAN, by Paddy Chayefsky. Random House.
FIVE FINGER EXERCISE, by Peter Shaffer. Harcourt, Brace & Company.
THE ANDERSONVILLE TRIAL, by Saul Levitt. Random House.
THE DEADLY GAME, by Friedrich Duerrenmatt, adapted by James Yaffe. Alfred A. Knopf, Inc.
CALIGULA, by Albert Camus, translated and adapted by Justin O'Brien. Alfred A. Knopf, Inc.
TOYS IN THE ATTIC, by Lillian Hellman. Random House.
THE BEST MAN, by Gore Vidal. Little, Brown & Company.
DUEL OF ANGELS, by Jean Giraudoux, translated and adapted by Christopher Fry. Oxford University Press.
A THURBER CARNIVAL, by James Thurber.
FIORELLO!, by Jerome Weidman and George Abbott. Random House.

1960-1961

THE HOSTAGE, by Brendan Behan. Grove Press.

A TASTE OF HONEY, by Shelagh Delaney. Grove Press.

BECKET, by Jean Anouilh, translated by Lucienne Hill. Coward-McCann.

PERIOD OF ADJUSTMENT, by Tennessee Williams. New Directions.

ALL THE WAY HOME, by Tad Mosel. Ivan Obolensky.

RHINOCEROS, by Eugene Ionesco, translated by Derek Prouse. Grove Press.

MARY, MARY, by Jean Kerr.

THE DEVIL'S ADVOCATE, by Dore Schary. William Morrow.

BIG FISH, LITTLE FISH, by Hugh Wheeler. Random House.

A FAR COUNTRY, by Henry Denker. Random House.

NECROLOGY

June 1, 1961–May 31, 1962

PERFORMERS

Roscoe Ates (67)—Mar. 1, 1962
Roy Atwell (83)—Feb. 6, 1962
James Barton (71)—Feb. 19, 1962
Wally Brown (57)—Nov. 13, 1961
Leo Carrillo (81)—Sept. 10, 1961
Ruth Chatterton (67)—Nov. 24, 1961
Charles D. Coburn (84)—Aug. 30, 1961
Donald Cook (60)—Oct. 1, 1961
Curtis Cooksey (71)—Apr. 19, 1962
Violet Kemble Cooper (?)—Aug. 17, 1961
Marion Davies (64)—Sept. 22, 1961
Ann Davis (68)—Sept. 3, 1961
Paul Dullzell (82)—Dec. 21, 1961
Frank Fay (63)—Sept. 25, 1961
Louisa Fazenda (66)—Apr. 17, 1962
Elsie Ferguson (76)—Nov. 15, 1961
William Ferguson (41)—Sept. 19, 1961
Bijou Fernandez (84)—Nov. 7, 1961
Harry Gribbon (75)—July 28, 1961
Louise Groody (64)—Sept. 16, 1961
Halliwell Hobbes (84)—Feb. 20, 1962
Harold (Chic) Johnson (66)—Feb. 25, 1962
Billy House (71)—Sept. 23, 1961
Joseph Kearns (55)—Feb. 17, 1962
Fred Keating (64)—June 29, 1961
Fritz Kreisler (85)—Jan. 29, 1962
Ernie Kovacs (43)—Jan. 12, 1962
George Lipton (45)—Mar. 9, 1962
Jack Livesey (60)—Oct. 12, 1961
Chico Marx (70)—Oct. 11, 1961
Kenneth MacKenna (63)—Jan. 15, 1962
Lili Marberg (84)—Apr. 7, 1962
Joan McCracken (38)—Nov. 1, 1961
Esther Minciotti (74)—Apr. 15, 1962
Oliver Oliver (90)—Nov. 7, 1961
Muriel Rahn (50)—Aug. 8, 1961
Brian Reece (48)—Apr. 12, 1962
Gail Russell (36)—Aug. 26, 1961
Maud Scheerer (80)—Sept. 12, 1961
Michael Shepley (54)—Sept. 28, 1961
Thomas P. Shirley (62)—Jan. 24, 1962
Vladimir Sokoloff (72)—Feb. 14, 1962
Louis Sorin (67)—Dec. 14, 1961
Eddie South (57)—Apr. 25, 1962
Madge Titheradge (74)—Nov. 13, 1961
Thomas F. Tracey (86)—Aug. 27, 1961
Helen Trenholme (50)—Jan. 30, 1962
Percy Waram (80)—Oct. 5, 1961
Ann Wheaton (65)—Dec. 25, 1961
Edwin Whitner (53)—Jan. 5, 1962
Bransby Williams (91)—Dec. 3, 1961

PLAYWRIGHTS

William Berney (40)—Nov. 23, 1961
Michel de Ghelderode (63)—Apr. 1, 1962
Moss Hart (57)—Dec. 20, 1961
Ernest Hemingway (62)—July 2, 1961
Dorothy Heyward (71)—Nov. 19, 1961
Robinson Jeffers (75)—Jan. 20, 1962
Charles Kenyon (79)—June 27, 1961
Guido Kolbenhayer (83)—Apr. 12, 1962
Arthur Macrae (53)—Feb. 25, 1962
Mazo de la Roche (82)—July 12, 1961
James Thurber (66)—Nov. 2, 1961

DIRECTORS

Guthrie McClintic (68)—Oct. 29, 1961
John C. Wilson (62)—Oct. 29, 1961

COMPOSERS AND LYRICISTS

Jacques Ibert (71)—Feb. 5, 1962
Marguerite Monnot (58)—Oct. 12, 1961

CONDUCTORS

Leo Reisman (64)—Dec. 18, 1961
Bruno Walter (85)—Feb. 17, 1962

PRODUCERS

Felix Brentano (52)—June 23, 1961
Courtney Burr (70)—Oct. 17, 1961
Henry Duffy (71)—Nov. 18, 1961
Marie L. Elkins (71)—Dec. 12, 1961
Leonard W. Joy (65)—Nov. 21, 1961

SCENE DESIGNERS

John Robertson (35)—Mar. 18, 1962
Marcel Vertes (66)—Oct. 31, 1961

OTHERS

Ned Armstrong (55)—July 13, 1961. Theatre publicist.
Anthony V. Cookman (67)—Apr. 29, 1962. Drama Critic (London *Times*)
Michael Curtiz (73)—Apr. 11, 1962. Motion picture director.
Sawyer Falk (62)—Aug. 30, 1961. Head of Syracuse University Drama Dept.
Jerry Giesler (75)—Jan. 1, 1962. Theatrical lawyer.
Anne B. C. Hambleton (24)—Mar. 18, 1962. Educational Dept. of the Phoenix Theatre.
Zoltan Korda (66)—Oct. 13, 1961. Motion picture director.
Murray Korman (59)—Aug. 9, 1961. Photographer.
John H. H. Lyon (84)—Dec. 18, 1961. Shakespeare authority.
Edmond Pauker (74)—May 6, 1962. Playwrights' representative.
Richard Pleasant (52)—July 4, 1961. Theatre publicist.
Ben Ray Redman (65)—Aug. 2, 1961. Literary critic.
Joseph M. Schenck (83)—Oct. 20, 1961. Motion picture producer.
Jack Small (52)—Apr. 27, 1962. Theatre manager.
Lawrence A. Weiner (62)—Nov. 15, 1961. Theatrical advertising executive.

INDICES

INDEX OF AUTHORS AND PLAYWRIGHTS

INDEX OF PLAYS AND CASTS

Bold face page numbers refer to pages on which Cast of Characters may be found.

INDEX OF PRODUCERS, DIRECTORS, DESIGNERS, STAGE MANAGERS, COMPOSERS, LYRICISTS AND CHOREOGRAPHERS